0147331

IVN (Bir)

KU-548-562

This book is due for return on or before the last date shown below.

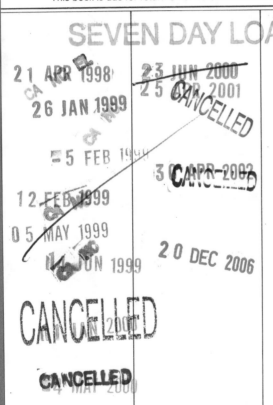

SEVEN DAY LOAN

21 APR 1998

26 JAN 1999

5 FEB 1999

12 FEB 1999

05 MAY 1999

14 JUN 1999

CANCELLED

CANCELLED

23 JUN 2000

25 APR 2001

CANCELLED

30 APR 2002

CANCELLED

20 DEC 2006

Don Gresswell Ltd., London, N.21 Cat. No. 1208

DG 02242/71

LANCASTER

D483
7000

IVN
(Bir)

Innovations in the Psychological Management of Schizophrenia

0471929352

THE WILEY SERIES IN CLINICAL PSYCHOLOGY

Series Editors

Fraser N. Watts
MRC Applied Psychology Unit,
Cambridge, UK

J. Mark G. Williams
Department of Psychology,
University College of North Wales,
Bangor, UK

Severe Learning Disability and Psychological Handicap
John Clements

Cognitive Psychology and Emotional Disorders
J. Mark G. Williams, Fraser N. Watts,
Colin MacLeod and Andrew Mathews

Community Care in Practice
Services for the Continuing Care Client
Edited by Anthony Lavender and Frank Holloway

Attribution Theory in Clinical Psychology
Freidrich Försterling

Panic Disorder
Theory, Research and Therapy
Edited by Roger Baker

Measuring Human Problems
A Practical Guide
Edited by David Peck and C. M. Shapiro

Clinical Child Psychology
Social Learning, Development and Behaviour
Martin Herbert

The Psychological Treatment of Insomnia
Colin A. Espie

The Challenge of Severe Mental Handicap
A Behaviour Analytic Approach
Edited by Bob Remington

Microcomputers and Clinical Psychology
Issues, Applications and Future Developments
Edited by Alastair Ager

Anxiety
Theory, Research and Intervention
in Clinical and Health Psychology
Robert J. Edelmann

Innovations in the Psychological
Management of Schizophrenia
Assessment, Treatment and Services
Edited by Max Birchwood and Nicholas Tarrier

Innovations in the Psychological Management of Schizophrenia

Assessment, Treatment and Services

Edited by

Max Birchwood
All Saints Hospital, Birmingham, UK

Nicholas Tarrier
University of Manchester, UK

JOHN WILEY & SONS
Chichester · New York · Brisbane · Toronto · Singapore

Copyright © 1992 by John Wiley & Sons Ltd,
Baffins Lane, Chichester,
West Sussex PO19 1UD, England

All rights reserved.

No part of this book may be reproduced by any means, or transmitted, or translated into a machine language without the written permission of the publisher.

Other Wiley Editorial Offices

John Wiley & Sons, Inc., 605 Third Avenue,
New York, NY 10158–0012, USA

Jacaranda Wiley Ltd, G.P.O. Box 859, Brisbane,
Queensland 4001, Australia

John Wiley & Sons (Canada) Ltd, 22 Worcester Road,
Rexdale, Ontario M9W 1L1, Canada

John Wiley & Sons (SEA) Pte Ltd, 37 Jalan Pemimpin #05-04,
Block B, Union Industrial Building, Singapore 2057

Library of Congress Cataloging-in-Publication Data

Innovations in the psychological management of schizophrenia : assessment, treatment, and services / edited by Max Birchwood, Nicholas Tarrier.
p. cm. — (The Wiley series in clinical psychology)
Includes bibliographical references and index.
ISBN 0-471-92935-2 (ppc)
1. Schizophrenia—Treatment. I. Birchwood, M. J. II. Tarrier, Nicholas. III. Series.
RC514.I46 1992
616.89'820651—dc20 91–42794
CIP

British Library Cataloguing in Publication Data

A catalogue record for this book is available from the British Library.

ISBN 0-471-92935-2

Typeset in 10/12pt Palatino by Mathematical Composition Setters Ltd, Salisbury, Wiltshire
Printed and bound in Great Britain by Biddles Ltd, Guildford and King's Lynn

Contents

List of Contributors vii

Series Editor's Preface ix

Preface xi

PART 1: ASSESSMENT 1

1 Assessment of Symptoms and Behaviour 3
Philippa Garety

2 Vulnerability Models and Schizophrenia: the Assessment and Prediction of Relapse 21
Keith Clements and Graham Turpin

3 Monitoring Recovery from Acute Psychosis 49
Valerie Drury

PART 2: TREATMENT 77

4 Interventions with Families 79
Christine Barrowclough and Nicholas Tarrier

5 Teaching Social and Coping Skills 103
Jerome V. Vaccaro and Lisa Roberts

6 Early Intervention 115
Max Birchwood, Fiona Macmillan and Jo Smith

7 Management and Modification of Residual Positive Psychotic Symptoms 147
Nicholas Tarrier

8 Management of Long-term Impairments and Challenging Behaviour 171
Lorna Hogg and John Hall

PART 3: SERVICES 205

9 Models of Continuing Care 207
Tony Lavender and Frank Holloway

10 Family Interventions: Service Implications 235
Jo Smith

11 The Balance of Care 253
Matthijs Muijen

12 Service Organisation and Planning 277
Kate Wooff

13 The Psychological Management of Schizophrenia: into the Next Decade 305
Max Birchwood and Nicholas Tarrier

Index 319

List of Contributors

CHRISTINE BARROWCLOUGH	Lecturer in Psychology, School of Psychology, University of New South Wales, Australia
MAX BIRCHWOOD	Consultant Clinical Psychologist, All Saints Hospital, Birmingham and Honorary Senior Lecturer, University of Birmingham, UK.
KEITH CLEMENTS	Lecturer in Psychology, Department of Psychology, Polytechnic South West, Drakes Circus, Plymouth, UK.
VALERIE DRURY	Research Psychologist, Archer Centre, All Saints Hospital, Birmingham, UK.
PHILIPPA GARETY	Senior Lecturer in Psychology, Institute of Psychiatry, London, UK.
JOHN HALL	District Psychologist, Department of Clinical Psychology, Warneford Hospital, Oxford, UK.
LORNA HOGG	Principal Clinical Psychologist, Department of Clinical Psychology, Warneford Hospital, Oxford, UK.
FRANK HOLLOWAY	Consultant Psychiatrist, St Giles Hospital, London, UK.
TONY LAVENDER	Joint Director, Clinical Psychology Training Scheme, David Solomans House, Tunbridge Wells, UK.
FIONA MACMILLAN	Senior Lecturer in Psychiatry, University of Birmingham and Honorary Consultant Psychiatrist, All Saints Hospital, Birmingham, UK.
MATTIJS MUIJEN	Director, Research and Development in Psychiatry, London, UK.
LISA ROBERTS	Staff Research Assistant, UCLA Neuropsychiatric Institute and Hospital, Los Angeles, California, USA.

Jo Smith — Principal Clinical Psychologist, Barnsley Hall Hospital, Bromsgrove, Worcs, UK.

Nicholas Tarrier — Professor of Clinical Psychology, University of Manchester, Manchester, UK.

Graham Turpin — Senior Lecturer and Director, Professional Training Course in Clinical Psychology, University of Sheffield, UK.

Jerome V. Vaccaro — Assistant Professor of Psychiatry, ULLA School of Medicine/Clinical Research Centre for Schizophrenia and Psychiatric Rehabilitation, Los Angeles, California, USA.

Kate Wooff — National Health Service Training Authority, Manchester, UK.

Series Editor's Preface

The Wiley Series in Clinical Psychology seeks to keep readers abreast of topics where significant advances are currently being made. People with long-term, disabling psychological conditions have long represented one of the major challenges to clinical practice. It is very much to be welcomed that recent years have seen real advances in the application of psychological principles to the care and management of people suffering from such conditions. Schizophrenia represents one of the most challenging of these, and is the one on which this volume concentrates.

The editors, themselves established authorities in this field, have drawn together an international group of contributors. Their chapters systematically cover recent advances and current challenges in psychological work in people with schizophrenia. The central part of the book focuses on direct methods of treatment. However, this is preceded by a group of chapters on the relevant methods of clinical assessment, and the book concludes with chapters on the service delivery context in which treatment programmes are necessarily embedded.

The care of people with schizophrenic disorders is always a multidisciplinary enterprise. Though this book is principally concerned with psychological contributions, it will be of interest to the wide range of professions—including psychiatrists, social workers, nurses and other therapists—involved in this challenging and important area of clinical work.

FRASER WATTS
Series Editor

Preface

This book is published at a time that will be seen in years to come as a watershed in the development of services for people with severe mental illness. There are a number of pressures that are converging at the present time causing a realignment of mental-health policy and practice towards this client group.

The gradual closure of our mental hospitals and the pressure on the community to "look after its own", puts a burden on families and carers of the severely mentally ill; but also on services to respond to this burden and to find a means of coordinating the fragmentation of services that has resulted. There has been a change too in our models of understanding the psychoses, particularly schizophrenia. The genuine interaction of biological vulnerability and psychological, psychosocial and cultural influences is increasingly understood; these models have driven a number of innovations in treatment and management which are of proven or promising efficacy. There is also the growing consumer voice of both carer and sufferer which is beginning to influence the nature, style and delivery of care. Mental-health professionals are becoming increasingly sensitive to these pressures and we are aware of a growing demand for practical skills and new models of service provision for work with this disadvantaged and often difficult client group.

Innovations in the Psychological Management of Schizophrenia is a practical text for mental-health professionals wishing to develop and enhance their skills in these new treatment and intervention approaches which include: family interventions and network support; early warning systems to anticipate and control relapse; strategies to control distressing symptoms such as hallucinations and delusions; methods of managing challenging behaviour, motivational and emotional deficits; and improving skills for daily living. We have invited leading experts who are also practitioners from the UK and USA to contribute chapters which "combine scholarly analysis with a practical, clinical approach to their subject".

We have devoted a considerable part of the book to assessment and conceptualisation and to models of service delivery. The latter we feel is particularly important, for without models of implementation, the inertia of systems and vested interests will, we believe, see the coming era of community care as merely a case of "new bottles for old wine".

MAX BIRCHWOOD AND NICHOLAS TARRIER
November 1991

Part 1

Assessment

Chapter 1

The Assessment of Symptoms and Behaviour

PHILIPPA GARETY

INTRODUCTION

The assessment of psychotic symptoms and associated behaviour can be undertaken for a variety of reasons, which can result in very different methodologies and outcomes. In general, such assessments and the detailed investigation of a psychotic person's mental state, known as "phenomenology", have remained the domain of psychiatry throughout most of the twentieth century, and have accordingly focused on a central medical concern, diagnosis. Psychotic symptoms are deemed of interest for their association with a particular diagnosis, whether schizophrenia, depression or mania, and are assessed for this reason (Persons, 1986). Assessment for this purpose naturally emphasises certain descriptive features of the symptom (e.g. auditory hallucinations *in the third person*) found to be associated with a particular diagnosis, and then is concerned to assess presence/absence, rather than a more fine-grained analysis of the phenomenon (Garety and Wessely, 1992).

There are however other reasons for assessing symptoms, besides diagnosis. These include classification, description, analysis of the structure of the individual symptom, determination of treatment or management and the assessment of change. Different functions will result in different methods. In this chapter, the focus will be on assessments relevant to treatment or management and change.

It is clear that the purpose of an assessment influences its form. It is perhaps less clear, but no less true, that the underlying model of schizophrenia held by the assessor will influence the nature of the assessment of presumed constituent symptoms.

"Schizophrenia" is a controversial construct, which has been much criticised and dissected (e.g. Spaulding and Cole, 1984; Bentall, 1990a).

Innovations in the Psychological Management of Schizophrenia.
Edited by Max Birchwood and Nicholas Tarrier. © 1992 John Wiley & Sons Ltd

The simplest model of schizophrenia is the traditional psychiatric "disease model", in which schizophrenia is thought to be an illness or disease with an as yet unidentified biological cause (Crow, 1984; Cutting, 1985). In the model's crudest form, it is assumed that the condition is unitary, and in all respects entirely discontinuous with normal functioning. Thus the symptoms of the disease are abnormal, and are of interest in that they signal the presence of the illness.

Claridge (1985, 1990) has proposed a dimensional model for schizophrenia, in which certain areas of functioning are conceptualised as on a continuum from normality to dysfunction, this continuum representing a vulnerability dimension. The state of malfunction is arbitrarily defined, so that in its mild form or early stages the definition of the illness is not clear-cut. The cause of the disease is multiple, arising from an interaction between the underlying disposition and a range of developmental, accumulating life-long and short-term triggering factors which combine to push the individual along the continuum beyond the threshold for a recognisable disease. In such a model, symptoms again are seen as indicating the presence of a disease, but here presence/absence is less clearly defined, and differing levels of severity of symptoms are to be expected and are of interest. Indeed assessments of clearly non-pathological function are valuable and may assist in identifying at-risk populations.

Claridge's model is in some respect similar to the stress-vulnerability model of Zubin and Spring (1977) and Nuechterlein and Dawson (1984). Here a distinction is made between *vulnerability* to schizophrenia, a relatively enduring trait, and *episodes* of schizophrenic illness when symptoms occur. These episodes occur when the level of environmental stress reaches a threshold for that individual's level of vulnerability. These researchers emphasise less strongly than Claridge the notion of a continuum of functioning.

Foulds and Bedford (1975) have proposed a hierarchical model in which schizophrenia may be seen not as a separate disease entity but as representing the most severe form of psychological disorder, incorporating classes of illness lower down the hierarchy. Thus to recover from schizophrenia involves moving down the hierarchy, and the extent of recovery is assessed by considering whether the patient has also recovered from, for example, symptoms of delusional disorder, obsessional symptoms and states of anxiety, all examples of classes of illness progressively lower in the hierarchy.

Other researchers express some doubt about the existence of "schizophrenia" as a disease entity, and yet argue that we should continue to study it (Hemsley, 1982; Wing, 1988). A number of researchers including Neale and Oltmanns (1980) and Hemsley (1982) propose that schizophrenia should be viewed as an open scientific construct (rather than a single disease entity) capable of being partially defined via a series of measurement operations. They suggest that we should continue to study various combinations of symptoms, usually known as "schizophrenia", to link these combinations to possible causes or pathologies. For Wing the focus of assessment remains ensuring reliable diagnosis, by means of careful definition of individual symptoms.

Bentall (1990b) has been prominent among a number of psychologists who argue that the concept of schizophrenia should be totally abandoned and replaced with the study of individual symptoms of psychosis. He argues that there is little evidence that schizophrenia constitutes a reliably identifiable and valid syndrome distinct from other forms of madness. Moreover, he asserts that the diagnosis has proved to be a poor predictor of outcome, response to treatment or aetiology. Instead, he proposes, psychopathologists should make particular symptoms the objects of their enquiries. There are a number of advantages to this approach. Firstly, the problems of defining and detecting symptoms will be less great than of defining and detecting clusters of symptoms. Secondly, symptoms can readily be conceptualised dimensionally. Thirdly, abnormal experiences and behaviour can be understood and studied in terms of models of "normal" cognitive psychology such as perception, inference and language. Finally, treatments can be developed for the individual symptoms, which have previously been ignored in favour of treatments for the disease.

Models of schizophrenia which emphasise reliably defining the syndrome tend, as noted above, to focus on assessing the presence or absence of symptoms, and descriptive features found, perhaps with some circularity (such as bizarre delusions for schizophrenia) to be statistically associated with particular diagnoses. In contrast, models which propose a dimensional (and sometimes multi-dimensional) approach, in which a continuum from normal processes to "abnormal" symptoms is conceptualised, favour dimensional methods of assessment, even when employing them within a framework retaining a unifying construct of schizophrenia. The most radical model, in which "schizophrenia" is abandoned and symptoms become the focus of study, also employs the dimensional method, but in addition emphasises further refining methods of assessment of individual symptoms by drawing on the theories and methods of cognitive psychology. Finally, the hierarchical model differs from the others in explicitly recognising that an individual experiencing typical symptoms of psychosis will very probably suffer also from other symptoms such as of anxiety and depression. The presence of such symptoms in psychotic patients is often ignored by clinicians, and suitable treatments are frequently not offered.

METHODS OF ASSESSMENT

The phenomena whose assessment will be described in this chapter are "positive" and "negative" symptoms of psychosis, predisposition to such symptoms, bizarre and challenging behaviours and assessments of anxiety and distress associated with psychotic symptoms.

Positive and negative symptoms

Most authors propose that "positive" symptoms refer to the "productive" symptoms of schizophrenia, which consist of delusions, hallucinations and thought disorder, although bizarre behaviour is sometimes also included (Andreasen, 1982). They are called positive or productive because they are regarded as pathological by their presence, rather than by the absence of some aspect of functioning that characterises negative symptoms, such as flatness of affect, poverty of speech, apathy, inattention and social withdrawal (Cutting, 1985). Some have argued that a division of the symptoms of schizophrenia into positive and negative is inadequate, and that a third category, of cognitive disorganisation, should be added (Liddle, 1987; Bentall, Claridge and Slade, 1989; Mortimer, Lund and McKenna, 1990). Thought disorder is said to fall into this third category, rather than be a "positive" symptom.

The instruments concerned with rating symptoms can be divided into three categories, diagnostic interviews, symptom rating scales and instruments designed to assess specific symptoms, such as delusions or hallucinations.

Diagnostic interviews

Firstly, diagnostic interviews, such as the Present State Examination (PSE) (Wing, Cooper and Sartorius, 1974) and the Schedule for Affective Disorders and Schizophrenia (SADS) (Spitzer and Endicott, 1977) are designed to note the presence or absence of categories of symptoms to determine diagnosis. Both are structured interviews providing a large number of questions intended to elicit evidence of, for example, abnormal beliefs and experiences, in a variety of subjects. While the chief goal is to rate presence/absence, simple ratings of severity and frequency are included for some items.

Symptom rating scales

Symptom rating scales may have two principal purposes. Some, such as the ever popular Brief Psychiatric Rating Scale (BPRS) (Overall and

Gorham, 1962), the Manchester Scale (Krawieka, Goldberg and Vaughan, 1977) and the Comprehensive Psychopathological Rating Scale (CPRS) (Asberg et al., 1978) are designed to assess change in subjects in, for example, treatment trials. Thus detailed analysis of individual symptom change is of less interest than total score change. (The PSE has also been modified recently to be more sensitive to symptom change, see Tress et al., 1987.) The Manchester scale is regarded as particularly suitable for the assessment of change in subjects with chronic schizophrenia, and as well as assessing positive symptoms in some detail, also assesses negative symptoms, and symptoms of depression and anxiety. These scales all provide a rating of symptoms, generally on a severity dimension.

Other scales, such as the Positive and Negative Syndrome Scale for Schizophrenia (PANSS) (Kay, Fiszbein and Opler, 1987) and the Andreasen scales (Andreasen, 1982, 1984) the Scale for the Assessment of Positive Symptoms (SAPS) and the Scale for the Assessment of Negative Symptoms (SANS) are concerned with the validity of the positive/negative symptom distinction. In order to ensure that the symptoms thought to fall into either category are reliably assessed and distinguished, they provide detailed clinical descriptions of each symptom. Thus, in the SANS, Andreasen provides five global symptom groups, alogia, affective flattening, avolition-apathy, anhedonia-asociality and attentional impairment, which are defined and then broken down into 25 observable behavioural components that are rated on a six-point severity scale. Some of these scales, however, although treating symptoms as varying principally along a dimension of severity, sometimes also incorporate into the same dimension other aspects, which may not covary with severity. Thus ratings of conviction, preoccupation and action are combined in the rating of delusions in the SAPS, dimensions which have been shown to be relatively independent (Garety and Hemsley, 1987) and not to covary over time (Brett-Jones, Garety and Hemsley, 1987).

A scale has also been designed by Andreasen (1979) for the assessment of thought disorder, the Scale for the Assessment of Thought, Language and Communication (TLC). Andreasen notes that "thought disorder" is inferred from a patient's disorganised speech, and although the term is often used as if it refers to a single phenomenon, the speech and language behaviours through which it becomes manifest are heterogeneous. Eighteen definitions of thought disorder are provided, including, for example, poverty of speech, pressure of speech, incoherence, neologisms and perseveration. The presence/absence of these features of thought disorder and their severity and frequency are rated on the basis of interview responses.

Specific symptom assessments

Instruments designed to assess specific symptoms are likely to be of greater use in the psychological treatment and management of symptoms of schizophrenia, and in the evaluation of outcome, than the measures described above. Such general symptom scales have not been designed to assess change in only one target symptom, and cannot be validly employed for this purpose. If one of these general symptom scales is used, it is desirable to supplement its use with a more detailed multidimensional analysis and investigation of the subject's symptoms, so that, for example, triggering factors and covariables can also be studied.

The assessments of specific symptoms can be sub-divided into standardised and idiographic assessments; in both cases the majority of measures assess delusions and hallucinations, rather than thought disorder or the negative symptoms, which are in effect not single symptoms but groups of symptoms. It is measures of hallucinations and delusions that will be reported in this section.

(i) Delusions. While most measures of delusions now conceptualise delusions as multi-dimensional, there is no clear agreement about which are the important dimensions. The Personal Ideation Inventory (Rattenbury et al., 1984) is a semi-structured interview for assessing "major dimensions" of delusional thinking. There are 71 items which assess various aspects of the content of a delusion, including its relation to pre-morbid concerns and the extent of a patient's conviction, commitment and perspective with respect to her/his central delusion. Conviction refers to how certain the patient is about the reality or accuracy of his or her consensually deviant ideas. Commitment refers to the immediacy of the belief, or how impelling or important it feels to the patient. This measure is based on cognitive signs, preoccupation with and dismissibility of the delusion, and behavioural signs, influence on daily activities. Perspective refers to the patients' view about whether others will regard their ideas as strange or implausible. The interviewer assigns scores to the subject's response, based on predetermined categories. Questions refer both to the present and the time at which the delusion was at its height.

The PII has been used chiefly as a research tool, for example to study the relationship between different dimensions of delusions, the diagnostic specificity of the dimensions, and change in the dimensions over time. It is one of the few detailed assessments of delusions on which data for comparison purposes already exists, although these data are formulated in terms of the three postulated "major" dimensions. Other researchers have posited a greater number of dimensions (Garety and Hemsley, 1987), and suggest that behaviour should not be regarded as falling within a cognitive dimension (Brett-Jones, Garety and Hemsley, 1987), as in the "commitment" dimension of the PII.

The Characteristics of Delusions Rating Scale (Garety and Hemsley, 1987) also takes a dimensional approach to the assessment of delusions, measuring eleven subjective belief characteristics using a visual analogue technique. The characteristics are conviction, preoccupation, interference (identifiable influence on behaviour), resistance, dismissibility, absurdity, worry, unhappiness, reassurance seeking, self-evidentness and pervasiveness. The authors present data on the characteristics of 55 delusions assessed on this scale, but as yet test–retest reliability data are not available. A relatively unusual feature of this scale is the assessment of distress associated with the delusional belief, which was found to be at severe levels in approximately 50% of subjects. This suggests that distress is an important dimension to be considered for the assessment of recovery, in addition to other key dimensions, conviction and preoccupation.

Garety (1985) and Brett-Jones, Garety and Hemsley (1987) devised a method for making assessments of delusional conviction and preoccupation sensitive to small changes when repeated measurements are taken, modifying Shapiro's (1961) Personal Questionnaire technique. This technique is suitable for measuring psychological changes specific to individual psychiatric patients, and uses symptom statements in the patient's own words. The questionnaire aims to provide an ordinal scale of symptom intensity which allows for comparisons within a subject across time, but not between subjects. Garety (1985) and Brett-Jones, Garety and Hemsley (1987) report on the use of the PQ to assess changes in conviction and preoccupation in subjects with whom no intervention was being implemented. Chadwick and Lowe (1990) have since used the technique as an outcome measure in a cognitive behavioural intervention study with delusional beliefs, assessing conviction, preoccupation and also anxiety experienced by the subject while thinking about the delusional belief. They found, in line with other research, that while in some subjects these variables covaried, in others they were unrelated.

Brett-Jones, Garety and Hemsley (1987) report on two further measures which have potential value in interventions with delusions, Reaction to Hypothetical Conviction (RTHC) and Accommodation. Both measures present a model of delusions at odds with the standard psychiatric definition which proposes that delusions are fixed and immutable, unaffected by counter-evidence. Here delusional beliefs are regarded on a continuum with normal beliefs in terms of their responsiveness to disconfirmation. Models drawn from cognitive psychology concerned with belief persistence and change (Hemsley and Garety, 1986) are drawn upon for these measures. RTHC is a method of categorising a subject's potential for accommodating evidence contrary to a (delusional) belief. Subjects are presented with a hypothetical but concrete and plausible piece of evidence contradictory to the belief, and asked how this would affect their belief. Replies are assigned to one of four categories. Accommodation, in contrast, assesses the awareness of the subject of actual occurrences contradictory to the belief, and the effect of these on the belief. Subjects are asked if anything has happened to alter their belief in any way over the past week and replies are assigned to one of five categories. Brett-Jones, Garety and Hemsley (1987) report inter-rater reliabilities, on a sample of 27 interviews, using weighted kappas, of 0.74 ($p < 0.002$) for RTHC and of 0.75 ($p < 0.002$) for accommodation. The usefulness of these measures for interventions with delusions lies in their predictive and monitoring value. Brett-Jones, Garety and Hemsley (1987), in a non-intervention study, found that those subjects who were willing to consider a reduction in conviction in the face of hypothetical contradictory evidence were more likely subsequently to show a complete rejection of their beliefs. Chadwick and Lowe (1990) report similar findings. Of their subjects, the four who were most responsive to hypothetical contradiction were also the most sensitive to the interventions, whereas the two subjects whose conviction scores were affected least by the interventions both flatly denied even the possibility of an instance of disconfirmation. Chadwick and Lowe also found that while no subject reported a single instance of accommodation in the baseline period, after the introduction of cognitive behavioural therapy, subjects reported instances of disconfirmation, suggesting that the measure may be useful for monitoring the effects of an intervention.

(ii) Hallucinations. There are surprisingly few scales of proven reliability and validity which provide detailed information about hallucinations. An interesting, if not entirely standardised, structured interview is described by Aggernaes (1972) to assess seven "reality characteristics" of hallucinations, which serve as criteria for distinguishing between true hallucinations and other related experiences (Slade and Bentall, 1988). These include assessing whether the experience has the quality of perception or of imagination, the quality of existence versus non-existence or of "publicness" versus "privateness". Responses are dichotomous (with an additional "doubtful" category) rather than dimensional. Aggernaes and his colleagues report studies with 41 hallucinating schizophrenics, 29 LSD drug abusers and of "normal" experiences of 15 non-psychotic patients (see also Slade and Bentall, (1988) for details). The interview appears to have more immediate value as a research tool for the detailed investigation of hallucinations than as an instrument to assess response to an intervention.

In a study of the perceptual characteristics of hallucinations, Alpert and Silvers (1970) report eight questions from an interview they devised. These concern frequency, localisation of source, change in frequency with arousal, isolation or light and verbal/non-verbal content. Only yes/no classifications are given. The responses of 45 schizophrenics and 18 patients with alcoholic hallucinosis are reported.

Of possibly more immediate relevance for the clinician attempting to intervene with hallucinations is Slade's (1972) Auditory Hallucinations Record Form. Its purpose is to identify the factors which precipitate the experience of hallucinations in an individual patient. The patient records on the form, at predetermined times, the presence/absence of "voices", their intensity, a series of subjectively assessed environmental variables (e.g. noise, people, activity), mood state, and 15 semantic differential scales to assess the "quality" of the "voices". The patient is asked to complete the form three times a day for a period of a few weeks. The data from the environmental and the mood variables are then contrasted for the occasions on which the voices are present/absent.

A recent paper (Hustig and Hafner, 1990) reports a very similar method of assessing auditory hallucinations, using three times a day self report forms. Dimensions of hallucinatory experience are assessed on visual analogue scales, and include the loudness, clarity, distress, and distractibility of the "voices". Mood is also self-rated. The authors report the test–retest reliability of the measures as adequate.

A number of individual treatment studies have reported measures of aspects of hallucinations (see Slade and Bentall, 1988, for a comprehensive list of references), which include measures of frequency, intensity, duration, clarity, volume and intrusiveness. Most of the measures are represented as dimensional, rather than dichotomous.

Measures of predisposition to symptoms

Chapman and Chapman (1980, 1988) have been foremost among researchers interested in the continuity between psychotic symptoms and normal experience. They have devised scales to assess non-clinical levels of aberrant beliefs (the Magical Ideation Scale, Eckblad and Chapman, 1983) and anomalous experience (the Perceptual Aberration Scale, Chapman, Chapman and Raulin, 1978) in order to identify psychosis prone subjects. As an extension of this work, they devised the Scales for Rating Psychotic and Psychotic-like Experiences as Continua (1980). These are a series of scales based on a modification of parts of the Schedule for Affective Disorders and Schizophrenia (SADS-L) (Spitzer and Endicott, 1977). The scales assess psychotic-like experiences as continua, ranging from normal through "aberrant" to extremely deviant. Each category of experience is scored from 1 to 11, based on judgements of increasing deviancy.

The symptom categories and their attenuated forms considered are transmission of thoughts, passivity experiences, auditory hallucinations, thought withdrawal, delusions and visual hallucinations. Using these scales to interview subjects on two separate occasions 25 months apart, three subjects developed clinical levels of psychosis in the interim. Chapman and Chapman (1988) found that the earlier aberrant beliefs of their subjects seemed to be continuous with the later full-fledged delusions both in content and in degree of deviancy.

The Launay–Slade Hallucination Scale (Launay and Slade, 1981) is a 12-item questionnaire designed to measure hallucinatory predisposition in normals. It includes both pathological items and items representing sub-clinical forms of hallucinatory experience, such as vivid thoughts and daydreams. Subsequent studies have reported acceptable reliability (Bentall and Slade, 1985) and validity (Young et al., 1987).

Assessment of bizarre and challenging behaviours

The association between symptoms of psychosis and behaviour is undoubtedly a complex one, and no simple inference can be made, for example, from the presence of a delusional belief to particular behaviours. Indeed in the case of delusions, it is suggested by many that the extent to which they direct actions is extremely variable (e.g. Mullen, 1979; Taylor, 1982). Nonetheless violence and other difficult behaviours do occur in psychotic patients.

The links between schizophrenia and violent behaviour in particular have been examined intensively. Investigators have studied the behaviour of psychiatric inpatients, violent behaviour in the period leading up to psychiatric admission, and aggression in samples of psychotic patients in prison and the community (Buchanon and Wessely, 1990). This research has been impaired by a lack of agreed measures and definitions of violence. Apparently conflicting findings abound. Nevertheless, there is evidence that the risk of violence in schizophrenia is only slightly higher than in other patient groups or the general population (Sharrock and Taylor, 1992).

It is clear, however, that in certain cases a patient's violent behaviour is related to psychosis (Volavka and Krakowski, 1989). Taylor (1985) reports that of 121 psychotic men in remand for committing a criminal offence, 20% were "directly driven" to offend by their psychotic symptoms and a further 26% were probably so driven. In a review of the literature, Buchanon and Wessely (1990) found that, of the symptoms of psychosis, it is delusions which have been most consistently linked to violent behaviour, and recommend that further studies should attempt to specify those aspects of delusions which are most commonly associated with violence.

While Taylor (1985) attempted to assess the relationship between mental state and criminal behaviour, by asking the man why he had committed the offence, most assessments of bizarre and challenging behaviour simply measure the target behaviour, and make no assumptions about any causal link with specific symptoms.

Baker and Hall (1984), in a scale for assessing the functioning of long term psychiatric patients, provide a "Deviant Behaviour" sub scale. Based on care staff observations over the past week, frequency ratings are made of the occurrence of seven anti-social behaviours including violence, verbal abusiveness, sexually offensive or disinhibited behaviour and talking or laughing to oneself. The scale is reliable and there are extensive long stay patient norms; however the assessment provides only frequency measures, and no measures of, for example, severity.

Wykes and Sturt (1986) assess a number of challenging and bizarre behaviours in their Social Behaviour Schedule, designed for long term psychiatric patients. These include "attention seeking" behaviour, suicidal and self-harming behaviour, acting out of bizarre ideas, posturing and mannerisms and destructive behaviour. The scale also incorporates an assessment of anxiety, tension and depression. The items are assessed by interviewing an informant about the subject's behaviour over the past month, and ratings are made on the basis of frequency or severity.

Adams, Meloy and Moritz (1990) report a study of violent behaviour in imprisoned schizophrenics. They describe a method for scaling the severity of anti-social acts, which was applied to reports of the violent episodes which had occurred before the subjects came to prison. They also devised a Violent Behaviour Rating Scale, of good inter-rater reliability, which was used to rate nurses' notes.

There are a number of other rating scales of violent behaviour, which are described in detail by Sharrock and Taylor (1992). These include the Overt Aggression Scale (Yudofsky et al., 1986), the Staff Observation Aggression Scale (Palmstierna and Wistedt, 1987) and the Scale for the Assessment of Aggressive and Agitated Behaviours (Brizer et al., 1987).

In a major comparative treatment study of institutionalised psychiatric patients, Paul and Lentz (1977) carried out a number of assessments of patient behaviour. "Intolerable", "bizarre" and "troublesome" behaviours were recorded when they occurred on forms requiring details of their nature, setting characteristics and consequences. Frequency of "troublesome" behaviours was also assessed as part of a ward rating scale, the Inpatient Scale of Minimal Functioning. (For full details of these extensive assessments, see Paul and Lentz (1977), Chapter 11, "Methods of Assessing Patient Behaviour".)

For their assessments, Paul and Lentz have essentially systematised good clinical practice, routinely undertaken by psychologists working in learning difficulties and with children, but perhaps rarer in work with psychotic adults. Target behaviours are specified, and baseline data collected using one of a variety of sampling schedules, such as continuous recording, or momentary time-sampling (Hersen and Bellack, 1981). Wallace (1981) provides an extensive, if now somewhat out-dated, review of methods of behavioural observation in psychotic subjects.

Practical applications of the assessments

In this section, the examples of the two people, who experienced distressing psychotic symptoms, are presented, together with the assessments which were employed clinically to assist in the formulation and monitoring of intervention strategies. (The names and personal details have been altered to preserve confidentiality.)

Anny Brown is a 30-year-old woman, convinced that her accommodation emits a powerful offensive odour. This smell impregnates her hair and clothing and can only (if at all) be eradicated by repeated and exhaustive washing. She lives alone and avoids social contact. She believes that people at her work (she is a waitress) comment on her smell and that her supervisor is victimising her to force her to resign. Anny has moved house numerous times in the three years since the problem began, but each time, mysteriously, the flat or room smells. Anny offers many ingenious explanations for this repeated misfortune, and for the failure of plumbers and surveyors to detect and to locate the cause of the smell. Recourse to lawyers having also failed, Anny became despairing, and took an overdose which was nearly fatal. In this way, she was admitted to the psychiatric hospital.

In hospital, Anny was at first relieved to discover that her room and the ward did not smell. After a few days, however, the smell reappeared, and Anny plugged up the drainage holes in her washbasin. She contacted the hospital works department and demanded an inspection. She refused all medication.

Anny was interviewed and gave a full account of the history of the problem. She reported that it started shortly after the ending of a brief and violent marriage, when Anny bought and moved into a flat. She appeared to be suspicious, hostile and critical of all the hospital staff. She did, however, value the opportunity to talk about the smell in detail, and was enthusiastic about undertaking detailed assessments. She completed the Characteristics of Delusions Rating Scale, and was found to score highly on the three dimensions of conviction, preoccupation and distress (worry). Personal questionnaires specifically designed to assess these three dimensions, were drawn up and administered at each subsequent interview. At the first interview, Anny showed no willingness to re-evaluate her belief as assessed by Reaction to Hypothetical Conviction and she resisted all alternative explanations of the problem.

After some weeks, in which Anny became increasingly distressed by the smell, and avoidant of social contact, (when interviewed she sat at the far end of the room beside an open window), she was persuaded to try some medication, on the grounds that it might reduce her distress. She was assured that the regular interviews would continue, to monitor progress. Within a few days the conviction about the smell showed some reduction. Anny became more sociable and less distressed. The PQ measures then showed a total reduction in conviction, but more gradual, and less complete reductions in worry and preoccupation. Anny also complained of unpleasant medication side-effects. She was discharged and offered outpatient appointments. The detailed evaluations and discussion of Anny's beliefs continued; soon, against advice, she discontinued her medication. The belief that there was a smell in Anny's lodgings reappeared, and she moved house. Over the months, and with the addition of other individually devised measures, for shorter periods, such as self-ratings of anxiety in different settings, a collaborative approach to assessing Anny's mental state was developed, which involved setting up hypotheses. Novel situations and social contact were identified as particularly relevant to the onset of the belief about smells, and it was shown that the medication was a consistent help in reducing the conviction and associated distress. Possible reasons for Anny's social difficulties and her poor self-esteem were explored. Discussions also considered how, at times of high anxiety, Anny was more likely to misinterpret ambiguous stimuli (such as mumbled speech) as hostile. Anny is now managing to stay in her current accommodation, and the strength of her belief that it smells fluctuates. The therapy is continuing.

The second person to be described is Tom. He is 27-years-old, and suffered from a major psychotic breakdown at the age of twenty, while at university. After three admissions to hospital within five years, his symptoms stabilised, and shortly before he was first seen he had returned to university (some 60 miles away) to study English Literature. He had asked to see a psychologist because he was becoming increasingly troubled by his "voices", and was fearful that he would have to drop out of college for a second time.

At the first interview, Tom revealed that he believed that he suffered from schizophrenia, an illness with a strong genetic component. The "voices" he experienced were symptoms of the illness, and were, he thought, his own thoughts deviantly experienced as alien, because of some miswiring in the brain. They were frightening only in that they might presage a return of the full illness; however, at the least, they were always distracting and interfered with his work. Tom also had another, more disturbing, symptom. This was "the eyes behind the eyes" experience: he would start to feel as if there were someone else's eyes behind his own eyes, looking out through his. If this feeling took hold, it would start to feel that the devil was inside him, influencing him. He could normally stop this happening by telling himself, as soon as the "eyes" experience started, that he was suffering from one of the symptoms of his illness, which caused some miswiring in the brain, resulting in strange experiences. He knew that other people experienced the same thing, and that he was helped by his medication.

Tom was asked to complete the Auditory Hallucinations Record Form (Slade, 1972) for two weeks. He also monitored the "eyes" experience, on the same basis. On the second interview, Tom returned with the data. It was clear that both experiences were more likely to occur when groups of other people were present: in lectures, seminars, the pub and at church. They did not occur at all when Tom was alone, and rarely when he was with a few friends. He also rated himself as more anxious in those settings where the symptoms occurred. These findings were very revealing to Tom, who had only been dimly aware of the factors associated with the symptom onset. Possible reasons for these findings were explored. Tom described being anxious about people knowing he was schizophrenic, (he had told none of his fellow students), and reported thinking that people could tell when he was hallucinating. His evidence for this was discussed and he agreed that there was no evidential basis for this belief. It was suggested that the sounds of other people speaking in some way facilitated the experience of voices. The role of anxiety in triggering the experiences was also discussed. In order to reduce the overall frequency of these experiences, in the run up to exams, Tom decided to stop attending any lectures, but to continue with seminars, which were, he thought, more important. Some standard anxiety management techniques were also implemented. After a few weeks, the frequency of distressing experiences had reduced, and Tom felt more in control of the symptoms. He reported that his ability to study had improved, and he asked to be referred to a local psychologist for longer term work.

CONCLUSIONS

Recent years have witnessed a change in our understanding of schizophrenia, and a growing interest in assessing the individual symptoms of psychosis. Cognitive models of thinking processes and perception are influencing the nature of assessments of delusions and hallucinations, which many investigators now view as aspects of functioning not qualitatively different from normal processes but continuous with them. The multi-dimensional nature of symptoms is also increasingly recognised, although some instruments continue to assess only severity or frequency, which have been shown to be independent. Scales for assessing groups of symptoms, to assist in diagnosis or to measure global change, in general have good reliability, but may be less useful than the specific symptom assessments for planning and monitoring psychological interventions. Such general scales are less sensitive to small changes, and tend not to provide clinically important information on aspects of the symptoms, such as triggering events, covariables or associated distress. Finally, studies of the association between symptoms of psychosis and behaviour also are shifting. While previously researchers investigated links between diagnosis, or sub-types of schizophrenia, with violence, this research strategy is now less popular. Recent work emphasises linking not only specific symptoms with behaviour, but also attempting to identify key dimensions of individual symptoms; a strategy which in turn requires the further development of more sophisticated assessments of symptoms.

REFERENCES

Adams, J.J., Meloy, J.R. and Moritz, M.S. (1990) Neuropsychological deficits and violent behaviour in incarcerated schizophrenics. *Journal of Nervous and Mental Disease*, **178**, 253–6.

Aggernaes, A. (1972) The experienced reality of hallucinations and other psychological phenomena: an empirical analysis. *Acta Psychiatrica Scandinavica*, **48**, 220–39.

Alpert, M. and Silvers, K.N. (1970) Perceptual characteristics distinguishing auditory hallucinations in schizophrenics and acute alcoholic psychoses. *American Journal of Psychiatry*, **127**, 298–302.

Andreasen, N.C. (1979) Thought, language and communication disorders. *Archives of General Psychiatry*, **36**, 1315–21.

Andreasen, N.C. (1982) Negative symptoms in schizophrenia: definition and reliability. *Archives of General Psychiatry*, **36**, 1325–30.

Andreasen, N. (1984) *Scale for the Assessment of Positive Symptoms* (SAPS). Dept. of Psychiatry, IOWA.

Asberg, M., Montgomery, S., Perris, C., Schalling, D. and Sedvall, G. (1978) The comprehensive psychopathological rating scale. *Acta Psychiatrica Scandinavica Supplement*, **271**, 5–27.

Baker, R. and Hall, T.N. (1984) *The Rehabilitation Evaluation Hall and Baker (REHAB)*. Vine Publishing, Aberdeen.

Bentall, R.P. (Ed.) (1990a) *Reconstructing Schizophrenia*, Routledge, London and New York.

Bentall, R.P. (1990b) The syndromes and symptoms of psychosis or why you can't play 'twenty questions' with the concept of schizophrenia and hope to win. In: R. P. Bentall (ed.), *Reconstructing Schizophrenia*, Ch. 2, Routledge, London and New York.

Bentall, R.P. and Slade, P.D. (1985) Reliability of a measure of disposition towards hallucination. *Personality and Individual Differences*, **6**, 527–9.

Bentall, R.P., Claridge, G.S. and Slade, P.D. (1989) The multi-dimensional nature of schizotypal traits: a factor analytic study with normal subjects. *British Journal of Clinical Psychology*, **28**, 363–75.
Brett-Jones, J., Garety, P.A. and Hemsley, D.R. (1987) Measuring delusional experiences: a method and its application. *British Journal of Clinical Psychology*, **26**, 257–65.
Brizer, D.A., Convit, A., Krakowski, M. and Volavka, J. (1987) A rating scale of reporting violence on psychiatric wards. *Hospital and Community Psychiatry*, **38**, 769–70.
Buchanon, A. and Wessely, S. (1990) Schizophrenia: delusions and violence. Personal communication.
Chadwick, P. and Lowe, C. (1990). The measurement and modification of delusional beliefs. *Journal of Consulting and Clinical Psychology*, **58**, 225–32.
Chapman, L.J. and Chapman, J.P. (1980) Scales for rating psychotic and psychotic like experiences as continua. *Schizophrenia Bulletin*, **6**, 476–89.
Chapman, L.J. and Chapman J.P. (1988) The genesis of delusions. In T.F. Oltmanns and B.A. Maher (eds), *Delusional Beliefs*, John Wiley, New York.
Chapman, L.J., Chapman, J.P. and Raulin, M.L. (1978) Body image aberration in schizophrenia. *Journal of Abnormal Psychology*, **87**, 399–407.
Claridge, G.S. (1985) *Origins of Mental Illness*, Blackwell, Oxford.
Claridge, G.S. (1990) Can a disease model of schizophrenia survive? In R.P. Bentall (eds), *Reconstructing Schizophrenia*. Routledge, London and New York.
Crow, T.J. (1984) A re-evaluation of the viral hypothesis: is psychosis the result of retroviral integration at a site close to the cerebral dominance gene? *British Journal of Psychiatry*, **145**, 243–53.
Cutting, J. (1985) *The Psychology of Schizophrenia*. Churchill Livingstone, Edinburgh.
Eckblad, M. and Chapman, L.J. (1983) Magical ideation as an indicator of schizotypy. *Journal of Consulting and Clinical Psychology*, **51**, 215–25.
Foulds, G.A. and Bedford, A. (1975), Hierarchy of classes of personal illness. *Psychological Medicine*, **5**, 181–92.
Garety, P.A. (1985) Delusions: problems in definition and measurement. *British Journal of Medical Psychology*, **58**, 25–34.
Garety, P.A. and Hemsley, D.R. (1987) Characteristics of delusional experience. *European Archives of Psychiatry and Neurological Science*, **236**, 294–8.
Garety, P.A. and Wessely, S. (1992). The assessment of positive symptoms. In: T.R.E. Barnes and H. Nelson (eds), *Assessment Procedures for the Psychoses: a Practical Handbook*, Clinical Neuroscience, London.
Hemsley, D.R. (1982) Cognitive impairment in schizophrenia. In: A. Burton (ed.), *The Pathology and Psychology of Cognition*, Methuen, London.
Hemsley, D.R. and Garety, P.A. (1986) The formation and maintenance of delusions: a Bayesian analysis. *British Journal of Psychiatry*, **149**, 51–6.
Hersen, M. and Bellack, A.S. (1981) *Behavioral Assessment*, 2nd edn, Pergamon, New York.
Hustig, H.H. and Hafner, R.J. (1990) Persistent auditory hallucinations and their relationship to delusions and mood. *Journal of Nervous and Mental Disease*, **178**, 264–7.
Kay, S., Fiszbein, A. and Opler, L. (1987) The positive and negative syndrome scale for schizophrenia (PANSS). *Schizophrenia Bulletin*, **13**, 261–75.
Krawiecka, M., Goldberg, D. and Vaughan, M. (1977) A standardized psychiatric assessment scale for rating chronic psychiatric patients. *Acta Psychiatrica Scandinavica*, **55**, 299–308.

Launay, G. and Slade, P.D. (1981) The measurement of hallucinatory predisposition in male and female prisoners. *Personality and Individual Differences*, **2**, 221–34.
Liddle, P.F. (1987) The symptoms of chronic schizophrenia: a re-examination of the positive negative dichotomy. *British Journal of Psychiatry*, **151**, 145–51.
Mortimer, A.M., Lund, C.E. and McKenna, P.T. (1990) The positive : negative dichotomy in schizophrenia. *British Journal of Psychiatry*, **157**, 41–9.
Mullen, P. (1979) Phenomenology of disordered mental function. In P. Hill, R. Murray and G. Thorley (eds), *Essentials of Postgraduate Psychiatry*, Academic Press, London.
Neale, J. and Oltmanns, T. (1980) *Schizophrenia*, John Wiley, New York.
Nuechterlein, K.H. and Dawson, M.E. (1984) A heuristic vulnerability–stress model of schizophrenic episodes. *Schizophrenia Bulletin*, **10**, 300–12.
Overall, J.E. and Gorham, D.R. (1962) The Brief Psychiatric Rating Scale. *Psychological Reprints*, **10**, 799–812.
Palmstierna, T. and Wistedt, B. (1987) Staff Observation and Agression Scale (SOAS): presentation and evaluation. *Acta Psychiatrica Scandinavica*, **76**, 657–63.
Paul, G.L. and Lentz, R.J. (1977) *Psychosocial Treatment of Chronic Mental Patients*, Harvard University Press, Cambridge, Mass. and London, England.
Persons, J.B. (1986) The advantages of studying psychological phenomena rather than psychiatric diagnoses. *American Psychologist*, **41**, 1252–60.
Rattenbury, F.R., Harrow, M., Stoll, F.J. and Kettering, R.L. (1984) The Personal Ideation Inventory: an interview for assessing major dimensions of delusional thinking, Microfiche Publications, New York.
Slade, P.D. (1972) The effects of systematic desensitization on auditory hallucinations. *Behaviour Research and Therapy*, **10**, 85–91.
Slade, P.D. and Bentall, R.P. (1988) *Sensory Deception: a Scientific Analysis of Hallucination*, Croom Helm, London.
Shapiro, M.B. (1961) A method of assessing changes specific to the individual psychiatric patient. *British Journal of Medical Psychology*, **34**, 151–5.
Sharrock, R. and Taylor, P.J. (1992) Agression and the potential for violence. In: T.E. Barnes and H. Nelson (eds.), *Assessment Procedures for the Psychoses*, Clinical Neuroscience, London.
Spaulding, W.D. and Cole, J.K. (eds) (1984) *Theories of Schizophrenia and Psychosis*, Nebraska Symposium on Motivation 1983, University of Nebraska Press, Lincoln.
Spitzer, R.L. and Endicott, J. (1977) *Schedule for Affective Disorders and Schizophrenia – Lifetime Version (SADS-L)*, New York State Psychiatric Institute, New York.
Taylor, P. (1982) Schizophrenia and violence. In: J. Gunn and D.P. Farrington (eds), *Abnormal Offenders, Delinquency and the Criminal Justice System*, John Wiley, Chichester.
Taylor, P.J. (1985) Motives for offending among violent and psychotic men. *British Journal of Psychiatry*, **147**, 491–8.
Tress, K.H., Bellenis, C., Brownlow, J.M., Livingston, G. and Leff, J.P. (1987) The Present State Examination Change Rating Scale. *British Journal of Psychiatry*, **150**, 201–7.
Volavka, J. and Kralowski, M. (1989) Schizophrenia and violence. *Psychological Medicine*, **19**, 559–62.
Wallace, C.J. (1981) Assessment of psychotic behavior. In: M. Hersen and A.S. Bellack (eds), *Behavioral Assessment*, 2nd edn, Pergamon, New York. Chapter 10, pp. 328–88.
Wing, J.K. (1988) Abandoning what? *British Journal of Clinical Psychology*, **27**, 325–8.

Wing, J.K., Cooper, J.E. and Sartorius, N. (1974) *The Measurement and Classification of Psychiatric Symptoms*. Cambridge University Press.

Wykes, T. and Sturt, E. (1986) The Social Behaviour Schedule. *British Journal of Psychiatry*, **148**, 1–11.

Young, H.F., Bentall, R.P., Slade, P.D. and Dewey, M.E. (1987) The role of brief instructions and suggestibility in the elicitation of auditory and visual hallucinations in normal and psychiatric subjects. *Journal of Nervous and Mental Disease*, **175**, 41–8.

Yudofsky, S.C., Silver, J.M., Jackson, W., Endicott, J. and Williams, D. (1986) The Overt Aggressive Scale for the objective rating of verbal and physical aggression. *American Journal of Psychiatry*, **143**, 35–9.

Zubin, J. and Spring, B. (1977) Vulnerability—a new view of schizophrenia. *Journal of Abnormal Psychology*, **86**, 103–26.

HAROLD BRIDGES LIBRARY
S. MARTIN'S COLLEGE
LANCASTER

Chapter 2

Vulnerability Models and Schizophrenia: the Assessment and Prediction of Relapse

KEITH CLEMENTS AND GRAHAM TURPIN

INTRODUCTION

The practice of psychological assessment and treatment is usually dictated by the clinician's theoretical understanding of the presenting problem. An essential bridge between assessment and intervention is the formulation of the problem in psychological terms. Clinicians, irrespective of their therapeutic orientation, will analyse and interpret clinical observations within particular theoretical or therapeutic frameworks and arrive at a working formulation of the problem. The main question to be addressed in this chapter is whether there exists a relevant theoretical construction for the formulation of psychological problems experienced by people diagnosed as suffering from "schizophrenia". It will be argued that the lack of agreement concerning theoretical explanations of schizophrenia has hindered the potential application of psychological knowledge and treatments in this area. Indeed, as recently as 1986, Bellack dubbed schizophrenia as "behaviour therapy's forgotten child". Without an adequate framework for psychological formulation, psychologists will remain within the confines of the orphanage. Moreover, given the multidisciplinary nature of services offered to people diagnosed schizophrenic, it is essential that models are developed by psychologists which are accessible to other disciplines. We believe that vulnerability models, the focus of this chapter, have the flexibility to accommodate a range of professional orientations and to provide clinically-meaningful formulations which will direct and assist the development of innovative psychological treatments.

Before discussing vulnerability models, it is first necessary to briefly review traditional aetiological accounts of schizophrenia. Despite the

Innovations in the Psychological Management of Schizophrenia.
Edited by Max Birchwood and Nicholas Tarrier. © 1992 John Wiley & Sons Ltd

recognised existence of the social disabilities and handicaps experienced by many people diagnosed as schizophrenic, the scientific status of the concept of schizophrenia has remained an enigma within psychiatry (Neale and Oltmanns, 1980). Doubts concerning the reliability and validity of schizophrenia as a diagnostic entity have continued to be expressed, especially by researchers from behavioural or psychological backgrounds (e.g. Boyle, 1990). Moreover, controversy still surrounds the identification of aetiological mechanisms which might explain the heterogeneous collection of symptoms and mental states which characterise the condition (Bentall, Jackson and Pilgrim, 1988). On the one hand, biologically-orientated researchers have revealed an accumulation of evidence which is said to indicate specific genetic, anatomical and biochemical substrates, on the other hand, some psychologists have argued in particular for the development of individual theories which might account for the presence of specific symptoms such as hallucinations and delusions, which render an overall theoretical account of the aetiology of schizophrenia redundant (Persons, 1986; Bentall, Jackson and Pilgrim, 1988). The purpose of this chapter is not to judge these opposing positions but to identify an alternative perspective which might provide the bemused clinician with a set of heuristic explanations in order to understand the complexities of the schizophrenic experience.

Traditional aetiological approaches have tended to be unifactorial, stressing either intrapersonal factors (e.g. biological pathogens, psychodynamic processes) or interpersonal factors (e.g. developmental and familial experiences). Indeed, the debate between various different theoretical positions has tended to be polarised by the nature–nurture controversy surrounding the proposed inheritance of schizophrenic disorders (Gottesman and Shields, 1982). Several important developments, however, have taken place over the last three decades which will hopefully lead to a satisfactory resolution of these opposing views. The first concerns the need to account for the development of the risk for schizophrenia within the overall population as opposed to aetiological accounts which solely seek to explain the expression of symptoms in patient groups. Meehl (1962 but also see 1989) first drew attention to the distinction between expressed psychiatric morbidity and various underlying dispositional or risk factors termed schizotaxia and schizotypy. The second development concerns advances in the assessment of schizophrenic phenomenology and the improved reliability and validity of diagnostic and nosological formulations of schizophrenic disorders (see Chapter 3). The third development is in the recognition of multifactorial models which seek to account for the interaction of biological, social and psychological factors in determining both physical and mental health problems. Many authors have critically dismissed the adequacy of unifactorial explanations (e.g. Engel,

1977; Tarrier, 1979; Ohman, 1981a), and instead have espoused biopsychosocial models (Van Praag, 1981; but also see Armstrong, 1987). These models have already been discussed at length elsewhere in relation to schizophrenia (Turpin and Lader, 1986; Turpin, Tarrier and Sturgeon, 1988; Tarrier and Turpin, in press). Finally, greater attention has been paid to the episodic nature of some schizophrenic disorders and the distinction between formative factors which determine initial population risk for the disorder and precipitant factors which may trigger an individual episode of the disorder (Spring and Coons, 1982; Turpin and Lader, 1986). These developments are exemplified by the formulation of vulnerability models such as Zubin and Spring's (1977) classic paper. They will now be discussed in the next section together with a critical examination of research generated by the vulnerability concept.

VULNERABILITY MODELS

In addition to providing an overall framework for understanding schizophrenia, vulnerability models offer the clinician several specific advantages compared to other unifactorial aetiological accounts. Indeed, it is common for recently derived psychological interventions within schizophrenia to identify vulnerability models as a basic rationale for the development of particular treatment approaches (e.g. Hogarty et al., 1986; Tarrier and Barrowclough, 1990). As has already been stressed, they provide a multifactorial account of the processes determining risk and relapse within schizophrenia and, thereby, accommodate a range of aetiological factors and treatment options extending from psychosocial interventions through to medication. The breadth of this approach ensures that the model is accessible both to diverse professions and to lay audiences including relatives, carers, people who experience schizophrenia and the public at large. The specific emphasis upon a stress–vulnerability interaction also promotes the face validity of this model for lay audiences and provides a common model which can be shared between therapist and client, thereby, engendering a working therapeutic relationship and enhancing the education of clients about schizophrenia and its consequences. From a clinician's perspective, it identifies factors which might account for individual relapses and the processes underlying an exacerbation of schizophrenic pathology. It also helps to identify relevant interventions and coping strategies by which relapse can either be ameliorated or, if possible, prevented. For the clinical researcher, vulnerability models provide a backdrop upon which specific theories of schizophrenic processes can be incorporated and synthesised with other mini theories and aetiological accounts. The purpose of this section, therefore, is to provide an overview of vulnerability models and to describe the search for vulnerability markers. The final sections of this chapter will comprise a critique and discussion of the implications of these models for clinical practice.

Description of models

A number of vulnerability models exist: the best known being that proposed by Zubin and Spring (1977). This model shares a number of features with other vulnerability models of schizophrenia and is illustrated in Figure 2.1. First, it is a multifactorial model and attempts to integrate several different aetiological accounts (i.e. ecological, behavioural and biological) within an overall framework, Second, it views schizophrenia as being an episodic disorder. In contrast to Kraepelin's (1919) portrayal of schizophrenia as a continuing disease process leading almost inevitably to a chronic disorder, the vulnerability model takes a more optimistic view of the outcome of schizophrenic episodes. Zubin and colleagues have reviewed the evidence concerning chronicity and argue that the majority of those experiencing a schizophrenic episode return to normal functioning in between episodes (Zubin, Magaziner and Steinhauer, 1983). Long-term impairment is attributed to excessively prolonged episodes, frequent acute episodes, or to poor premorbid functioning which may be exacerbated by the social consequences of the episode. Third, episodes of schizophrenia

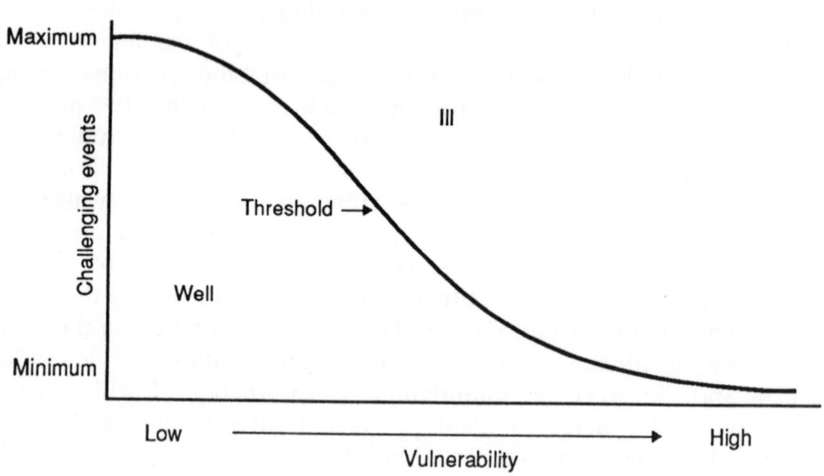

Figure 2.1 Zubin and Spring's model of the interaction between vulnerability and stressful events in triggering an episode of schizophrenia. (Reproduced by permission from Zubin and Spring (1977). Copyright American Psychological Association.)

are triggered, according to the model, by challenging events which primarily refer to forms of environmental stress. Such stressors might include social stress such as high levels of expressed emotion or stressful life events (Brown and Birley, 1968; Leff et al., 1983). If these stressors exceed a threshold, determined by the individual's level of vulnerability, then an episode may be triggered. Vulnerability, according to Zubin and Spring (1977), may be both inherited and environmentally acquired. The inclusion of environmental factors such as birth complications, early experience, peer interactions, etc. differs from earlier diathesis-stress models which tended to emphasise only genetic vulnerability (e.g. Meehl, 1962). Finally, the original model proposed by Zubin and Spring also stressed the importance of a vulnerable individual's capacity to adapt to future episodes of schizophrenia, and to learn from the experience of previous episodes. This was framed within a model of coping, assimilation and adaptation.

Another very influential model has been developed by Nuechterlein and Dawson (1984a), and recently updated by Nuechterlein (1987). This model is displayed in Figure 2.2. It was based upon extensive reviews of the literature concerning the relationships between schizophrenia and both information processing and psychophysiology (Dawson and Nuechterlein, 1984; Nuechterlein and Dawson, 1984b). It represents a significant extension of the original Zubin and Spring model due to its focus upon psychological processes which might underlie the stress–vulnerability interaction. The model suggests four vulnerability characteristics, all of which are expressed in psychological terms and are potentially measurable. These factors interact with socio-environmental stressors to produce an intermediate psychological state which precedes the onset of the clinical disorder and might form the basis of a prodromal state. The symptoms and social disabilities associated with schizophrenia develop from the operation of a positive feed forward loop. It should be noted that the proposed model is not an exhaustive specification of all the factors which are involved in the aetiology of schizophrenia. Rather, it is intended to be an heuristic model to guide research, and concentrates on those factors which influence the course of the disorder. The model also suggests several factors which might influence interventions by identifying vulnerable individuals, predicting the onset of relapse and possibly ameliorating the effects of social stressors. The implications of vulnerability models for clinical practice will be discussed later in greater detail.

Vulnerability research

The emergence of vulnerability models has made a timely contribution to the literature regarding the conceptual status of schizophrenia. However,

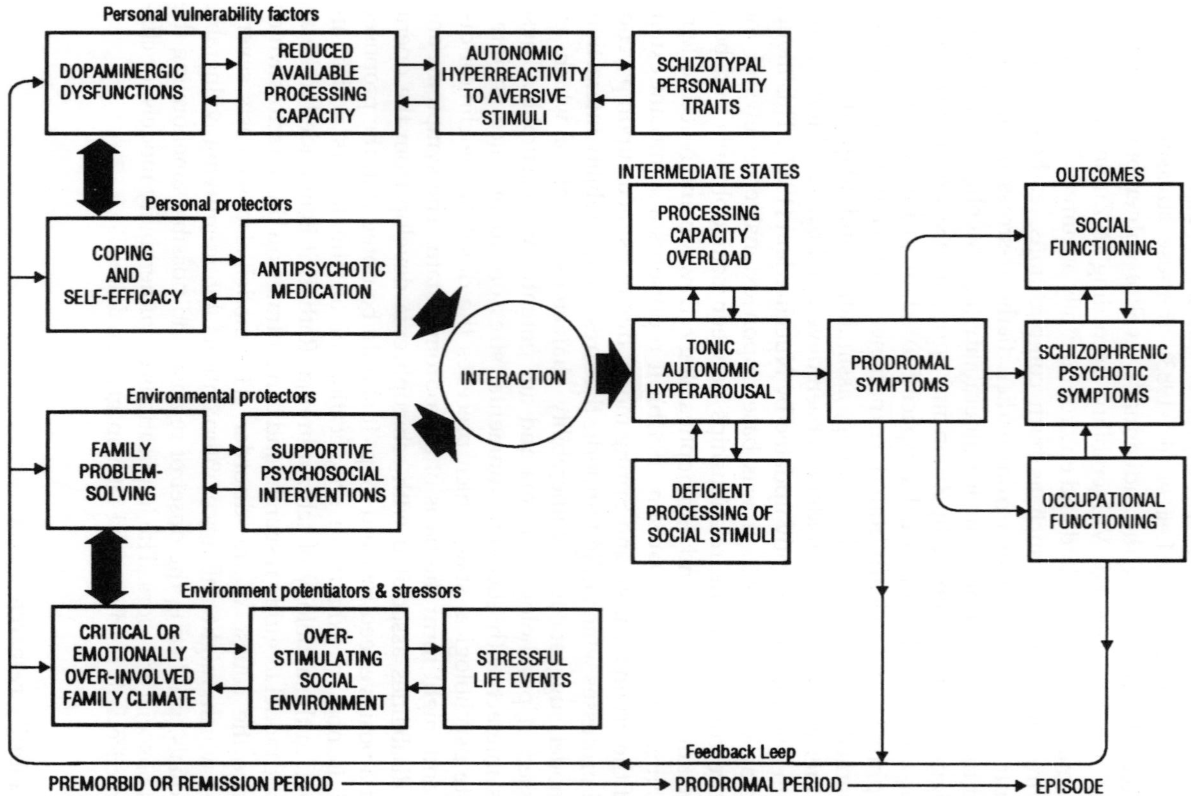

Figure 2.2 Nuechterlein's "Heuristic conceptual framework for possible factors in the development of schizophrenic episodes". (Reproduced by permission from Nuechterlein (1987). Copyright Springer-Verlag.)

these models should also have potential for directing empirical research into the origins of schizophrenic episodes. The purpose of this section, therefore, is to examine the implications of vulnerability models for clinical research and to appraise how these models might be empirically tested.

Perhaps the two most important aspects of vulnerability models which have influenced research in this area are the notion of vulnerability markers and the emphasis upon adopting a longitudinal perspective to study individual episodes of schizophrenia. These approaches should be contrasted with the traditional group diagnostic approach which has sought differences between different diagnostic groups by adopting cross-sectional research designs (Turpin, 1989). If, as vulnerability models suggest, schizophrenia results from a long-standing predisposition, it should be possible to identify those individuals who possess such a diathesis and are at risk of developing schizophrenia. Measures which uniquely indicate the presence of increased risk are termed vulnerability markers. Because vulnerability models stress the involvement of social, psychological and biological processes in the development of a disorder, a variety of markers may need to be studied.

Iacono and Ficken (1989) identify three broad classes of marker. First, there are vulnerability markers, which are observable characteristics which tend to be associated with the risk for a particular disorder. Such characteristics might be associated with an inherited vulnerability or with vulnerability acquired through environmental influences. As vulnerability is assumed to be either stable or incremental over time, vulnerability markers ought, therefore, to show trait properties; being present prior to the onset of the disorder and persisting into remission.

The second type of marker is a subtype of vulnerability marker and indicates the presence of the genetic predisposition underlying a given disorder. Because the search for genetic markers has been of considerable importance in the history of research into psychosis (Baron, 1986), they will be considered separately. Like general vulnerability markers, genetic markers should be present prior to the onset of a disorder and should persist into remission. Genetic markers should also be present in some of the relatives of affected individuals. Because not all individuals who possess the genetic diathesis will become ill, genetic markers may be preferable to the use of diagnoses in studying the inheritance of disorders.

Finally, episode markers indicate the presence of the actual disorder. These should show state properties, being present only during acute episodes of the condition and normalising on remission. Episode markers might be of use in predicting the onset of symptoms, and in separating acute symptomatology from residual deficits.

Putative markers need to meet two criteria. First, they should be sensitive, being able to identify most of the target group. The observed sensitivity might be limited by problems of misdiagnosis and heterogeneity within a diagnostic category. Second, markers should also be specific, being rare in the normal population and able to discriminate between different diagnostic categories. Genetic markers would be expected to be present in the normal population, as not all vulnerable individuals go on to become ill. Consequently a proportion of any non-psychiatric control group would be expected to possess the genetic predisposition. Further different types of vulnerability marker have been suggested by Zubin and Steinhauer (1981), Nuechterlein and Dawson (1984a) and Nuechterlein (1987).

A number of research strategies have been employed in order to identify vulnerability markers and to test individual models. The starting point is usually the observation of a difference between a group of schizophrenic patients and one or more control groups which have been included to rule out the effects of hospitalisation and other confounding factors. However, the presence of a marker within acutely ill patients is insufficient evidence to identify the type of the marker. Both episode and vulnerability markers are present during acute episodes, the distinguishing characteristic is the presence of group differences both during remission and prior to the development of a disorder. One approach, therefore, using a cross-sectional design, is to compare currently ill patients with remitted patients to determine whether a given characteristic persists into remission. An alternative to this cross-sectional approach is to follow patients through from first onset into remission and hence, to distinguish between trait and state characteristics. It may also be possible to study individuals who are at risk of relapse in order to assess changes which precede the recurrence of a schizophrenic episode. This might reveal markers which are predictive of future relapse. Indeed, there is considerable interest in detecting early signs of schizophrenia (e.g. Birchwood et al., 1989) which may include episode markers such as the intermediate states proposed by Nuechterlein and Dawson (1984a). Since these markers would be manifested prior to the appearance of truly diagnostic symptoms, only a prospective approach could be employed. It is possible that some variables may have both state and trait properties. Hence, existing state differences become more prominent with the onset of relapse.

Vulnerability markers may also be present prior to the first episode of schizophrenia. The usual approach used to identify vulnerability markers in asymptomatic individuals is termed the high-risk strategy (e.g. see Watt et al., 1984). The life-time risk of schizophrenia is around 1% (Gottesman and Shields, 1982), thus to obtain a group of ten subjects who would go on to develop schizophrenia a study would need to sample 1000 individuals. High-risk studies attempt to overcome this problem by selecting subjects who are at a higher than normal risk of developing schizophrenia. The usual strategy is to study the children of schizophrenics, who are reported to show a 10–15% life-time risk for schizophrenia (Gottesman and Shields, 1982). A number of such studies have been carried out and have been reviewed elsewhere (reviews of the major studies can be found in Watt et al., 1984, and in an issue of *Schizophrenia Bulletin* edited by Goldstein and Tuma, 1987).

Although the genetic high-risk approach may overcome many of the practical problems involved in studying the developmental course of schizophrenia, it is not without its limitations (see Mednick, 1978; Lewine, Watt and Grub, 1984). Accordingly, a number of alternative high-risk strategies have been developed which do not use a genetic criterion but have sought other indices of risk. For example, a number of researchers (e.g. Simons, 1981; Asarnow, Nuechterlein and Marder, 1983) have selected subjects using psychometric measures (e.g. schizotypy) thought to predict the later development of schizophrenia. Another alternative to genetic high-risk research is the biological risk approach (Siever and Coursey, 1985). This uses biological vulnerability markers, identified using other research strategies, to select putative high risk groups. Cognitive or other measures identified as vulnerability markers could be used in a similar way. Studies which adopt these alternative definitions of risk provide an important means of examining the validity of the putative vulnerability marker selected. Asymptomatic subjects selected on the basis of a valid vulnerability marker would be expected to show other characteristics associated with vulnerability. However, such studies have yet to make a sizeable contribution to high-risk research. At present there is no direct evidence that such measures can, in fact, identify subjects at high-risk for schizophrenia (but see Chapman and Chapman, 1987), or that such measures identify vulnerability traits as distinct from borderline or early psychosis.

VULNERABILITY MARKERS

The purpose of this section is to illustrate the type of markers which are associated with vulnerability models. It is not meant as an exhaustive account, and where appropriate, reference will be made to specific reviews. Many of the measures discussed will have originated directly from clinical research and will seldom be represented in contemporary approaches to clinical assessment. This lack of direct clinical application reflects the emergent status of vulnerability models and the limited opportunity, so far, for them to make an impact on clinical practice. However, it will be argued later in this chapter that vulnerability models may have an important future role in the assessment and management of individual cases of schizophrenia. Accordingly, some of the research measures discussed in this section might conceivably be adapted and applied to routine clinical assessment in the future.

The section is organised loosely around different types of marker: genetic, structural, psychophysiological and cognitive. It should be stressed that this classification is somewhat arbitrary, and that the range of markers is of necessity limited.

Genetic markers

The study of biological markers for schizophrenia has been dominated by the search for genetic indicators (e.g. Baron, 1986). Historically, this research has sought biological variables which covary with genetic vulnerability. Such a relationship might occur due to a causal association between a particular marker and an underlying vulnerability factor. Alternatively, such measures may be linkage markers, with no causal relationship to the vulnerability factor. Linkage markers are associated with an inherited characteristic solely because the gene determining the marker lies on the same chromosome as the target gene, and the two genes are sufficiently close together to be inherited together with a higher than chance frequency. Linkage markers may contribute to the identification of genetic mechanisms but are not directly informative regarding the processes leading from vulnerability to disorder.

Most research has concentrated on finding markers said to directly reflect the presumed causal mechanisms underlying vulnerability. An example of this approach concerns platelet or plasma monoamine oxidase (MAO) activity (e.g. Wyatt, Potkin and Murphy, 1979). These biochemical indices have been studied as possible markers of a disturbance in central aminergic activity, sai⅞ to be associated with schizophrenia (see reviews by Belmaker (1984) and Siever and Coursey (1985)). Early studies provided strong support for an association between lowered platelet MAO activity and schizophrenia. Furthermore, MAO levels are known to show genetic control. However, more recent evidence indicates that early reports were overly optimistic. Several factors cast doubt on the status of MAO activity as a marker for schizophrenia. Firstly, the prevalence of the gene producing lowered MAO levels is too high to make MAO activity a plausible marker for a disorder as rare as schizophrenia (Rice et al., 1984). Secondly, lowered MAO activity has been found to be associated with other attributes such as "alcoholism" (Belmaker, Bracha and Ebstein, 1980) and sensation seeking (Murphy et al., 1977). Finally, although several studies have used MAO levels to select putative high-risk groups from normal populations (e.g. Coursey, Buchsbaum and Murphy, 1979), unequivocal results have not been obtained. While subjects showing lowered MAO activity appear to show increased levels of disturbance, there does not appear to be any specific link between low MAO activity and schizophrenic or schizotypal characteristics.

It seems that lowered MAO activity is a biological marker for a more general vulnerability factor, influencing the experience of a wide range of disorders. It is only to be expected that such markers should emerge. While primary interest lies in obtaining markers for the specific vulnerability to schizophrenia, such risk factors do not operate alone. Inevitably such risk factors interact with other characteristics which may also be under genetic control and have been termed "contributing factors" as opposed to primary aetiological factors (Reider and Gershon, 1978). Lowered platelet MAO activity appears to be a marker for just such a factor. Other biochemical measures have been suggested as possible markers for schizophrenia but at present there is insufficient evidence to substantiate these claims (Baron, 1986).

Recent advances in molecular genetics have generated a renewed interest in linkage markers and stimulated a fresh controversy surrounding the inheritance of schizophrenia. These techniques allow more direct examination of the genetics of vulnerability (e.g. Baron and Rainer, 1988; Mullan and Murray, 1989) and offer the promise of location and, ultimately, identification of the actual genes associated with vulnerability. Such identification would provide the first step in understanding the mechanism by which the gene leads to vulnerability and eventual onset of schizophrenia. If, as seems likely, there are several different mechanisms of transmission of schizophrenia (O'Rourke et al., 1982), genetic markers may provide a clearer picture of the diagnostic heterogeneity within the disorder.

Studies indicate that some familial forms of schizophrenia may share a common genetic locus located at chromosome 5 (Bassett et al., 1988; Sherrington et al., 1988). Although other studies have failed to find such linkage (e.g. Kennedy et al., 1988). While one gene capable of producing vulnerability may have been located, it is clear that not all cases of schizophrenia are due to this gene. Even within the selected samples used for these studies not all pedigrees show this particular form of linkage, and the type of inheritance found is inadequate to explain the observed pattern of inheritance more commonly observed.

Structural markers

Early research using pneumoencephalography indicated that schizophrenia was associated with structural changes in the brain, the most notable being cerebral atrophy. This finding has been replicated and extended by the advent of Computerised Axial Tomography (CAT), which allows direct imaging of structures in the brain (Weinberger, Wagner and Wyatt, 1983). Enlargement of the lateral ventricles has been the most consistent finding, although some studies report enlargement of the third ventricle and atrophy of the cortex and cerebellum. There is some evidence to indicate that ventricular enlargement is associated with negative symptomatology and with poor premorbid adjustment (e.g. Williams et al., 1985).

Whether these CAT abnormalities can be regarded as vulnerability markers is uncertain. Reveley, Reveley and Murray, (1984) report that larger ventricles were found in people diagnosed schizophrenic without a family history. They imply that ventricular enlargement is indicative of exposure to environmental factors leading to psychosis, and so is less likely to be associated with strong genetic predisposition. Other studies, in contrast, have found greater ventricular enlargement in cases of familial schizophrenia (e.g. Kaiya et al., 1989). Studies which have examined normal siblings or monozygotic twin pairs discordant for schizophrenia found that schizophrenic subjects had larger ventricles than their non-schizophrenic siblings, implying that ventricular enlargement might be a correlate of schizophrenia itself, rather than a predisposition to schizophrenia (Reveley et al., 1982; DeLisi et al., 1986).

No studies to date have investigated the possibility of changes in cerebral structure in high-risk groups. Such studies are desirable, as the high-risk approach provides a possible means of disentangling genetic vulnerability, acquired vulnerability and the effects of schizophrenia itself. Differences in cerebral structure between schizophrenic and control subjects may also be confounded by the treatments given to individuals with schizophrenia. Long-term treatment with neuroleptic medication might conceivably lead to changes in neurological function.

Other approaches to assessing possible structural abnormalities to the brain have included neurological signs, neuropsychological testing, performance measures of brain lateralisation and other forms of brain imaging (e.g. see Gruzelier, 1986; Nasrallah and Weinberger, 1986). Much of this research has been directed to elucidating different schizophrenic subtypes. In particular, Crow's proposal concerning the possible existence of two syndromes of schizophrenia (Type I and II), and their relationship to positive and negative symptoms of schizophrenia has been most influential (Crow, 1985). The relevance of these studies to vulnerability models is that they might suggest that a series of individual markers may exist either for separate schizophrenic syndromes or possibly contributing to a continuum of psychosis-proneness.

Psychophysiologial markers

Another major group of biological markers include psychophysiological measures such as electrodermal activity (i.e. skin conductance), evoked potentials and eye movement abnormalities. For recent reviews of this area see Zahn (1986), Dawson, Nuechterlein and Adams (1989) and Steinhauer, Gruzelier and Zubin (in press). Although these measures have been investigated as potential genetic markers, they have also been employed in their own right as indicators of psychological processes such as attention or arousal (Turpin, Tarrier and Sturgeon, 1988; Tarrier and Turpin, in press; Turpin and Clements, in press). Three putative markers appear promising. These are electrodermal orienting, smooth pursuit eye movement abnormalities and evoked potential abnormalities.

Several excellent reviews of orienting research in schizophrenia exist (Ohman, 1981b; Dawson and Nuechterlein, 1984; Bernstein, 1987). The usual finding is that around 40% of schizophrenic subjects do not produce electrodermal orienting responses to non-signal tones. In contrast the rate of non-responding in normal populations is around 10%. There is also evidence that non-responding persists into remission (Iacono, 1982). Furthermore, non-responding has been said to correlate with schizophrenic symptomatology; patients who are non-responders showing a more withdrawn, negative pattern of symptoms (e.g. Straube, 1979; Alm et al., 1984). Non-responding has also been reported to be predictive of poor long-term social functioning (Ohman et al., 1989), although short-term symptom data show worse prognosis for hyper-responsive schizophrenics (Frith et al., 1979; Zahn, Carpenter and McGlashan, 1981). This distinction between short and long-term prognosis may reflect the differing symptom profiles of hyper- and hypo-responsive individuals.

While non-responding is also common in depressed subjects, there are differences in the nature of the deficit between these two disorders. In schizophrenia non-responding appears to reflect an attentional deficit in orienting, since other autonomic measures also appear hyporesponsive. In depression, in contrast, non-responding is limited to the electrodermal system and appears to represent a specific physiological deficit (Bernstein et al., 1988).

High-risk research has generally failed to reveal increased non-responding in children at genetic risk for schizophrenia. Rather such children are usually found to show signs of heightened electrodermal activity (e.g. Mednick and Schulsinger, 1974; Prentky, Salzman and Klein, 1981). A recent study does, however, indicate that non-responding may have prognostic significance in a genetic high-risk sample (Cannon and Mednick, 1988). Elevated rates of non-responding have also been reported in groups selected using psychometric measures believed to identify groups at risk for psychosis (Simons, 1981). It has been claimed that electrodermal non-responding may be associated with process or poor premorbid schizophrenia (Alm et al., 1984). Moreover, since this group might be expected to show low reproductive rates, it may be under-represented in studies examining the offspring of schizophrenics.

Non-responding does not seem to be a general vulnerability marker for schizophrenia since it is only present in less than half of the schizophrenic population and appears to be unrelated to genetic risk for schizophrenia. Where non-responding may have significance is as a prognostic indicator. Ohman et al. (1989) report that non-responding predicts poor social outcome. However, electrodemal measures may also reflect other types of markers relevant to the vulnerability model. For example, electrodermal level and response frequency have been claimed to be associated with various psychosocial triggers such as expressed emotion and life events (Turpin, Tarrier and Sturgeon, 1988; Tarrier and Turpin, in press; Turpin and Clements, in press). Similarly, these measures might precede the onset of future relapse (Dawson, 1990). These data imply that a second electrodermal risk group of hyperresponders might be identified who also demonstrate a poor prognosis but differ in many respects to the previously identified non-responder group (Tarrier and Turpin, in press).

The second major psychophysiological variable to be reviewed concerns smooth pursuit eye-movements. In an extensive review of psychophysiological approaches, Zahn (1986) concluded that smooth-pursuit eye movement (SPEM) abnormalities were the best candidate for a genetic marker, showing acceptable specificity and sensitivity for schizophrenia. Other recent reviews have reached similarly favourable conclusions (e.g. Siever and Coursey, 1985; Dawson, Nuechterlein and Adams, 1989). Abnormalities in eye tracking (usually of a pendulum or similar sinusoidal target) have been consistently reported to occur in 50–85% of schizophrenic samples, as opposed to less than 10% of the normal population (e.g. Holzman, Proctor and Hughes, 1973). Similar dysfunctions have been found in around 40–50% of the close relatives of schizophrenics (e.g. Holzman et al., 1974). Abnormalities are not confined to those relatives displaying schizophrenic symptomatology (Holzman et al., 1977; Holzman et al., 1980). One study demonstrates that abnormalities are present in high risk teenagers (Mather, 1985). Thus there is considerable evidence to indicate that SPEM abnormalities may be associated with the genetic risk factor for schizophrenia.

It has also been reported that subjects selected on the basis of their eye tracking performance show "schizotypal" characteristics (Siever et al., 1984). Unlike MAO activity, there is evidence to indicate that SPEM abnormalities are specifically associated with schizophrenic symptomatology. It should, however, be stated that SPEM abnormalities have also been reported to occur in patients with bipolar affective disorder (Lipton et al., 1983), although this association is probably secondary to the effects of treatment with lithium carbonate (Iacono et al., 1982).

Finally, recent attention has focused on the use of evoked potentials derived from the electroencephalogram (EEG). Event Related Potentials (ERPs) are obtained by averaging the EEG obtained following repeated presentations of a stimulus. This allows the response to the stimulus to be separated from background "noise" (e.g. see Coles, Gratton and Fabiani, 1990). The measure which has received most attention is the P300, which refers to a positive peak appearing 300 msec or more after stimulus onset. It is considered by some researchers to be similar to the orienting response since it is said to reflect central processing and to be sensitive to psychological variables such as motivation, stimulus novelty and significance (see Donchin et al., 1986).

A consistent finding is that schizophrenic subjects show a reduced P300 amplitude, particularly when auditory stimuli are used. There is evidence to indicate that P300 amplitude to auditory targets is stable over time, showing the trait characteristics necessary for a vulnerability marker (Duncan et al., 1987). Surprisingly, this study found that *visual* P300 amplitude was normalised on remission implying that it ought to be considered as an episode marker. Another study also reports reduced P300 amplitude in remitted schizophrenics (Barrett, McCallum and Pocock 1986). These findings are however in need of replication.

It is unclear at present whether reduced P300 amplitude is associated with the genetic risk for schizophrenia. One study reports P300 attenuation in the siblings of schizophrenics (Saitoh et al., 1984). Another group of workers report no abnormalities in children with schizophrenic parents, despite promising results from a preliminary analysis of their data (Friedman, Vaughn and Erlenmeyer-Kimling 1982; Friedman, Erlenmeyer-Kimling and Vaughn, 1985). P300 attenuation has been found in putative high-risk subjects selected using psychometric measures (Simons, 1982; Miller, 1986).

Abnormalities in event-related potentials are usually interpreted in terms of problems in information processing and the attentional deficits thought to underlie schizophrenia. Recent research favours the view that the reduced P300 represents a deficit in late, controlled processing rather than early, automatic processing (e.g. Pfefferbaum et al., 1989).

Cognitive markers

Schizophrenia is thought to result from an abnormality in cognitive functioning, although different theorists disagree as to the nature and/or location of the abnormality. A wide range of proposed vulnerability markers have been suggested, including the psychophysiological measures of attention, discussed above, and a variety of cognitive tasks from experimental psychology such as reaction time and vigilance (see Nuechterlein and Dawson, 1984b). The most commonly used test is the Continuous Performance Test (CPT) developed by Rosvold et al. (1956). This task is a visual vigilance task measuring sustained visual attention. The forced-choice Span of Apprehension Task (SAT) has also been used to investigate the efficiency of selective attention. This task requires selecting an item which appears in a tachistoscopically presented display.

Many schizophrenic individuals have been found to show impaired performance on such tasks (Nuechterlein and Dawson, 1984b), even during remission (Wohlberg and Kornetsky, 1973; Asarnow and MacCrimmon, 1981). This would imply that deficits in attentional performance are not episode markers. Furthermore similar impairments have also been reported in the relatives of schizophrenics (Asarnow, et al., 1977; Cornblatt and Erlenmeyer-Kimling, 1985). Deficits in attention appear to be associated with the genetic risk for schizophrenia. Within high-risk groups poor attentional performance has been found to be predictive of disturbance. Cornblatt and Erlenmeyer-Kimling (1985) report that scores on a composite index of attentional performance are predictive of later behavioural disturbance for the children of schizophrenic parents, but not for the children of other psychiatric patients or controls. Individuals selected on the basis of poor attentional performance have also been found to show elevated scores on a number of measures of schizotypy (Asarnow, Nuechterlein and Marder, 1983), implying that the risk identified may be specific to schizophrenia.

However not all people with schizophrenia perform badly on the CPT, and recent attention has focused on correlates of CPT performance. Nuechterlein et al. (1986) report that poor performance is a correlate of negative symptoms. Similar associations with negative symptoms have been reported for the psychophysiological measures of attention described above.

In addition to the CPT and SAT, investigators have also employed other cognitive measures as possible predictors of schizophrenic outcome. Reaction time, in particular, has enjoyed extensive study (e.g. Zahn and Carpenter, 1978). Recent research is also focusing upon experimental measures of latent inhibition which has also been proposed as a specific deficit (Baruch, Hemsley and Gray, 1988).

Measures of attentional performance appear, at present, to be promising candidates for vulnerability markers. Furthermore, these measures may be broken down into a number of well-defined components, with the potential for precise specification of the deficit associated with schizophrenic vulnerability. Such an analysis would be informative with regard to the aetiology of schizophrenia and might also facilitate understanding of the way in which schizophrenic vulnerability interacts with everyday functioning and experience. Knowledge of the sort of environmental stressors which are likely to exacerbate already poor performance, as well as the strategies that might be used to circumvent such deficits, would have considerable implications for the management of schizophrenia.

The status of vulnerability models

The purposes of this section were to introduce the concept of vulnerability models, describe the research strategies which they have generated, and to briefly review a range of putative vulnerability markers. The question remains as to whether the findings produced by vulnerability research support or disconfirm the proposed models. To date insufficient evidence exists to adequately test such models. Moreover, vulnerability models have been proposed as heuristic frameworks with which to organise schizophrenia research findings, rather than strictly specified theories amenable to scientific testing. Indeed, it could be argued that the lack of precise theoretical specification of vulnerability models, together, with their reliance upon multi-factorial explanations, renders them inappropriate to empirical test and hence, falsifiability. Nevertheless, certain key principles associated with vulnerability models, such as the episodic nature of schizophrenia, the importance of longitudinal research, and the presence of different marker types, have made a useful contribution to our understanding of schizophrenia. A variety of putative markers, particularly psychophysiological and cognitive variables, have been identified which may provide individual estimates of vulnerability. These markers are distinctive since they frequently demonstrate trait characteristics which are independent of the presence of symptoms, may precede or outlast specific schizophrenic episodes, and in some cases, may demonstrate familial aggregation. Future research needs to be conducted in order to extend and replicate these findings.

If reliable vulnerability and episode markers can be established, questions regarding the validity of vulnerability models can then be subjected to empirical scrutiny. For example, Nuechterlein and Dawson's (1984a) model might be assessed by identifying a series of mini theories which attempt to specify the nature of the processes underlying the stress–vulnerability interaction. Parts of this model have already been subjected to provisional examination. Within the model, social stressors such as expressed emotion and life-events are said to lead to states of elevated autonomic arousal in vulnerable individuals. Several studies have now sought to demonstrate a relationship between these variables (see Turpin, Tarrier and Sturgeon, 1988; Tarrier and Turpin, in press). Furthermore, it is suggested that occurrence of hyperarousal may be sufficient to trigger a future episode of schizophrenia. Provisional data by Dawson (1990) suggests that elevated electrodermal activity may actually precede schizophrenic episodes in some individuals.

Although studies such as those described above cannot be considered to be critical tests of the vulnerability concept, they do suggest a direction for future research. Various cohorts of individuals with different levels of vulnerability need to be studied prospectively at various stages of the natural history of the disorder. In doing so, the relationship between putative vulnerability markers and proposed psychosocial stressors can be assessed and compared to the proposed processes outlined by the model.

IMPLICATIONS OF VULNERABILITY MODELS FOR ASSESSMENT AND INTERVENTION

We have already stressed, at the beginning of this chapter that we consider vulnerability models to be still in their infancy and accordingly they have had only a limited impact directly on clinical practice, although such models have had considerable influence on clinical research. However, within this final section we would like to *speculate* upon the possible implications of these models for clinical practice and the development of psychological innovations in the management and provision of services for people with schizophrenia. We will approach this task in two ways: firstly to consider the general impact of vulnerability models upon psychological interventions and, secondly, to examine specific implications of identifying and applying vulnerability markers.

General implications

At a conceptual level vulnerability models have already made an important contribution to current research into interventions with people who experience schizophrenia. Within the last 20 years treatments for schizophrenia have moved steadily away from unimodal pharmacotherapy to multimodal approaches applying a range of interventions which span biological, psychological and social foundations. Vulnerability models offer a unique opportunity of uniting these various approaches within a unifying set of common principles. Indeed, proponents of various psychosocial approaches to treatment frequently espouse vulnerability models as an underlying rationale for the development of particular treatment programmes (e.g. Hogarty et al., 1986; Tarrier and Barrowclough, 1990). It is common to link components of psychosocial rehabilitation programmes directly to specific elements of vulnerability models (i.e. Falloon and Liberman, 1983). Moreover, vulnerability models may themselves suggest theoretically relevant innovative treatment approaches, as yet untried within clinical practice. We would like to argue that just as contemporary conditioning or information processing models can be used as a basis for evolving therapeutic methods for the cognitive–behavioural treatment of anxiety or affective disorders, vulnerability models should yield the same theoretical underpinnings to psychological intervention within schizophrenia. Already, vulnerability models are beginning to incorporate the effects of potential interventions on the stress/vulnerability interaction, the model presented by Nuechterlein (1987) includes personal and environmental protectors, which reduce the sensitivity of vulnerable individuals to environmental stress. These include neuroleptic medication and psychosocial interventions.

There are three possible targets for intervention which derive from vulnerability models. The first is at the level of primary prevention and concerns the possibility of influencing an individual's predisposition or vulnerability for schizophrenia. If the factors which determine vulnerability (both biological and environmental) can be established, together with reliable methods of assessing vulnerability, several important intervention strategies can be identified. First, at the general level, attempts to ameliorate the impact of vulnerability factors, particularly those that are acquired, may be sought, resulting in a preventative approach. Currently our knowledge of such factors is so scant that methods of prevention are non-existent. However, speculative environmental causes such as birth complications, viral agents, family interactions, etc. might suggest future interventions across a range of health, social and political policy arenas. Preventative approaches may be most useful if people who were at high risk for schizophrenia could be identified. This might be achieved if reliable vulnerability markers were identified. However, several serious problems exist with this approach. It is unlikely that any single marker will be sufficiently sensitive or specific to achieve acceptable levels of discrimination or prediction. One solution might be the boot-strap approach whereby a collection of markers are adopted which collectively yield more acceptable levels of accuracy (Golden, Golob and Watt, 1983). More important, however, are the social and political consequences of developing any screening programme for a condition which has potentially serious detrimental social and health consequences. Currently, the pioneering attempts to offer realistic genetic counselling to the relatives of people with schizophrenia, and those affected individuals contemplating parenthood, is indicative of this approach (Reveley, 1985). At present, ethical considerations render the use of vulnerability markers in a screening programme unacceptable.

A second reason for directly altering vulnerability is for those individuals who have already experienced an episode of schizophrenia. If vulnerability could be reversed, a truly curative approach to schizophrenia would have been achieved. We would like to speculate that none of the current, or even future treatment approaches, will achieve this *Holy Grail*.

A second target for intervention concerns the nature of the psychosocial triggering factors. The incidence of episodes of schizophrenia might be reduced if these factors were ameliorated, even in the presence of continuing levels of vulnerability. Current psychosocial interventions (e.g. Tarrier and Barrowclough, 1990) directed at reducing the level of expressed emotion within the client's immediate environment are examples of such an approach. Clearly interventions directed at other social factors such as ineffectual social supports, impoverished social contacts, the psychosocial consequences of poverty and unemployment might also be considered within this context.

The third target for general intervention is the nature of the stress–vulnerability interaction itself, and the psychological processes which mediate its effects. Neuroleptic medication may be incorporated into vulnerability models as a moderating factor which determines the sensitivity of individuals with a particular level of vulnerability to a particular stressor (see Leff et al., 1983). Other protective factors might also be identified (see Nuechterlein, 1987). Indeed, based upon the Nuechterlein and Dawson model there may be a series of coping strategies which might reduce the negative consequences of the so-called "intermediate states". These might include stress-management strategies, conflict resolution skills, social survival skills, etc. (e.g. Falloon, McGill and Boyd, 1984). Specific psychological interventions to ameliorate certain psychotic symptoms might also be addressed at this level (Persons, 1986).

Finally, there exists the possibility that factors associated with resistance to relapse may be identified within vulnerability research. These factors might include the suggested positive influences of effective coping skills, social supports, employment, etc. upon outcome in schizophrenia. The identification of these "invulnerability" factors should be an urgent priority for research.

Clinical utility of vulnerability markers

We have already described above how vulnerability markers might be employed in order to identify high risk individuals. However, we consider this proposal presently unacceptable on both scientific and ethical grounds.

Nevertheless, vulnerability markers may have an important clinical role in the prediction of relapse for those individuals already identified as being at high risk by virtue of having already experienced a schizophrenic episode. Two particular kinds of marker are relevant.

First, episode markers which subtly reflect the onset of the underlying psychotic process might be used prospectively to identify the future occurrence of an episode. This is synonymous with the "early signs approach" (Birchwood et al., 1989; see Chapter 8) which utilises either behavioural observation or self report of prodromal symptoms. Psychophysiological or cognitive episode markers might also yield such information. Several research studies have suggested that measures such as electrodermal activity or reaction time might predict future schizophrenic episodes. If these measures were collected on a regular basis, it might provide both clients and professionals a means of identifying incipient relapse and the introduction of an early intervention approach. Such interventions could be either pharmacological or psychosocial.

Second, specific vulnerability markers might be identified which yield prognostic information concerning outcome and response to treatment. It has already been suggested that certain psychophysiological variables such as electrodermal non-responding might indicate a sub-group of people with schizophrenia who have poor social outcomes and poor treatment response to neuroleptic medication. If these individuals could be identified early on following their first schizophrenic episode, appropriate intensive interventions might be developed and implemented. More importantly, ineffective and potentially deleterious interventions could be disregarded.

CONCLUSION

The main purpose of this chapter has been to describe the advent of vulnerability models within the area of schizophrenia and to examine the implications of adopting such an approach. Although the orientation of the chapter has been largely directed at clinical research, we would like to argue strongly that this approach has important implications for the practitioner. Vulnerability models provide a uniquely multidisciplinary perspective on schizophrenia which should facilitate communication between different practitioners. This ought to lead to more effective treatment outcomes due to the adoption of a range of different interventions derived from the model. Schizophrenia is far too complex a phenomenon to be reduced to the application of unimodal theories and treatments. The combined effects of pharmacological, psychological and social interventions need to be carefully examined and evaluated. Moreover, vulnerability models may also provide the means and an appropriate research framework for such evaluations to take place. The identification of putative vulnerability and episode markers may also assist the targeting of interventions in order to more effectively manage episodes of schizophrenia and, of greater therapeutic importance, prevent their occurrence.

REFERENCES

Alm, T., Lindstrom, L., Ost, L.G. and Ohman, A. (1984) Electrodermal non-responding in schizophrenia: relationships to attentional, clinical, biochemical and computed tomographical and genetic factors. *International Journal of Psychophysiology*, **1**, 195–208.

Armstrong, D. (1987) Theoretical tensions in biopsychosocial medicine. *Social Science and Medicine*, **25**, 1213–18.

Asarnow, R.F. and MacCrimmon, D.J. (1981) Span of apprehension deficits during postpsychotic stages of schizophrenia. *Archives of General Psychiatry*, **38**, 1006–11.

Asarnow, R.F., Steffy, R.A., MacCrimmon, D.J. and Cleghorn, J.M. (1977) An attentional assessment of foster children at risk for schizophrenia. *Journal of Abnormal Psychology*, **86**, 267–75.

Asarnow, R.F., Nuechterlein, K.H. and Marder, S.R. (1983) Span of apprehension performance, neuropsychological functioning, and indices of psychosis proneness. *Journal of Nervous and Mental Disease*, **171**, 662–9.

Baron, M. (1986) Genetics of schizophrenia II: vulnerability traits and gene markers. *Biological Psychiatry*, **21**, 1189–211.

Baron, K. and Rainer, J.D. (1988) Molecular genetics and human disease: implications for modern psychiatric research and practice. *British Journal of Psychiatry*, **152**, 741–53.

Barrett, K., McCallum, W.V. and Pocock, P.V. (1986) Brain indicators of altered attention and information processing in schizophrenic patients. *British Journal of Psychiatry*, **148**, 414–20.

Baruch, I., Hemsley, D.R. and Gray, J.A. (1988) Differential performance of acute and chronic schizophrenics on a latent inhibition task. *Journal of Nervous and Mental Disease*, **176**, 598–606.

Bassett, A.S., McGillivray, B.C., Jones, B. and Pantza, J.T. (1988) Partial trisomy chromosome 5 cosegregating with schizophrenia. *Lancet*, **1**, 799–801.

Bellack, A.S. (1986) Schizophrenia: behavior therapy's forgotten child. *Behavior Therapy*, **17**, 199–214.

Belmaker, R.H. (1984) The lessons of platelet monoamine oxidase. *Psychological Medicine*, **14**, 249–53.

Belmaker, R.H., Bracha, H.S. and Ebstein, R.P. (1980) Platelet monoamine oxidase in affective illness and alcoholism. *Schizophrenia Bulletin*, **6**, 320–23.

Bentall, R.P., Jackson, H.F. and Pilgrim, D. (1988) Abandoning the concept of "Schizophrenia": Some implications of validity arguments for psychological research into psychotic phenomena. *British Journal of Clinical Psychology*, **27**, 303–24.

Bernstein, A.S., Riedel, J., Grae, F., Seidman, D., Steele, H., Connolly, J. and Lubowsky, J. (1988) Schizophrenia is associated with altered orienting activity; depression with electrodermal (cholinergic?) deficit and normal orienting response. *Journal of Abnormal Psychology*, **91**, 3–12.

Bernstein, A.S. (1987) Orienting response research in schizophrenia: Where we have come from and where we might go. *Schizophrenia Bulletin*, **13**, 623–41.

Birchwood, M., Smith, J., MacMillan, F., Hogg, B., Prasad, R., Harvey, C. and Bering, S. (1989) Predicting relapse in schizophrenia: the development and implementation of an early signs monitoring system using patients and families as observers: a preliminary investigation. *Psychological Medicine*, **19**, 649–56.

Boyle, M. (1990) *Schizophrenia: A Scientific Delusion*. Routledge, London.

Brown, G.W. and Birley, J. (1968) Crises and life changes and the onset of schizophrenia. *Journal of Health and Social Behaviour*, **9**, 203–14.

Cannon, T.D. and Mednick S.A. (1988) Autonomic nervous system antecedents of productive and deficit symptoms in schizophrenia. *Psychophysiology*, **25**, 438–39 (abstract).

Chapman, L.J. and Chapman, J.P. (1987) The search for symptoms predictive of schizophrenia. *Schizophrenia Bulletin*, **13**, 497–503.

Coles, M.G., Gratton, G. and Fabiani, M. (1990) Event-related brain potentials. In: J.T. Cacioppo and L.G. Tassinary (eds), *Principles of Psychophysiology: Physical, Social and Inferential Elements*, pp. 413–55, Cambridge University Press.

Cornblatt, B.A. and Erlenmeyer-Kimling, L. (1985) Global attentional deviance as a marker of risk for schizophrenia: Specificity and predictive validity. *Journal of Abnormal Psychology*, **94**, 470–86.

Coursey, R.D., Buchsbaum, M.S. and Murphy, D.L. (1979) Platelet MAO activity and evoked potentials in the identification of subjects biologically at risk for psychiatric disorders. *British Journal of Psychiatry*, **134**, 372–81.

Crow, T.J. (1985) The two-syndrome concept: origins and current status. *Schizophrenia Bulletin*, **11**, 471–86.

Dawson, M.E. (1990) Psychophysiology at the interface of clinical science, cognitive science and neuroscience. *Psychophysiology*, **27**, 243–55.

Dawson, M.E. and Nuechterlein, K.H. (1984) Psychophysiological dysfunctions in the developmental course of schizophrenic disorders. *Schizophrenia Bulletin*, **10**, 204–32.

Dawson, M.E., Nuechterlein, K.H. and Adams, R.E. (1989) Schizophrenic disorders. In: G. Turpin (ed.) *Handbook of Clinical Psychophysiology*, pp. 393–418, John Wiley, Chichester.

DeLisi, L.E., Goldin, L.R., Hamovit, J.R., Maxwell, E., Kurtz, D. and Gershon, E.S. (1986) A family study of the association of increased ventricular size with schizophrenia. *Archives of General Psychiatry*, **43**, 148–53.

Donchin, E., Kris, D., Bashore, T.R., Coles, M.G.H. and Gratton, G. (1986) Cognitive psychophysiology and human information processing. In: M.G.H. Coles, E. Donchin and S.W. Porges (eds), *Psychophysiology: Systems, Processes and Applications*, pp. 244–67, Guilford Press, New York.

Duncan, C.C., Morihasa, J.M., Fawcett, R.W. and Kirch, D.G. (1987) P300 in schizophrenia: state or trait marker. *Psychopharmacology Bulletin*, **23**, 497–501.

Engel, G.L. (1977) The need for a new medical model: a challenge for biomedicine. *Science*, **196**, 129–36.

Falloon, I.R. and Liberman, R.P. (1983) Interactions between drug and psychosocial therapy in schizophrenia. *Schizophrenia Bulletin*, **9**, 543–54.

Falloon, I.R.H., McGill, C.W. and Boyd J.L. (1984) *Family Care of Schizophrenia*, Guilford Press: New York.

Friedman, D., Erlenmeyer-Kimling, L. and Vaughn, H.G. (1985) Auditory event-related potentials in children at risk for schizophrenia revisited: re-diagnosis of the patient parents and inclusion of the psychiatric control group. *Psychophysiology*, **22**, 590.

Friedman, D., Vaughn, H.G. and Erlenmeyer-Kimling, L. (1982) Cognitive brain potentials in children at risk for schizophrenia: preliminary findings. *Schizophrenia Bulletin*, **8**, 514–31.

Frith, C.D., Stevens, M., Johnstone, E.C. and Crow, T.J. (1979) Skin conductance responsivity during acute episodes of schizophrenia as a predictor of symptomatic improvements. *Psychological Medicine*, **9**, 101–6.

Golden, R.R., Golob, H.F. and Watt, N.F. (1982) Bootstrapping conjectural indicators of vulnerability for schizophrenia: a reply to Faradie's critique of Watt, Grubb and Erlenmeyer-Kimling. *Journal of Consulting and Clinical Psychology*, **51**, 937–9.

Goldstein, M.J. and Tuma, A.H. (eds) (1987) High-risk research. *Schizophrenia Bulletin*, **13**, 369–529.

Gottesman, I.I. and Shields, J. (1982) *Schizophrenia: the Epigentic Puzzle*, Cambridge University Press.

Gruzelier, J. (1986) Theories of lateralised and inter-hemispheric dysfunction in syndromes of schizophrenia. In: G.D. Burrows, T.R. Norman and G. Rubenstein (eds), *Handbook of Studies on Schizophrenia*, part 2, pp. 175–96, Elsevier Science Publishers, Amsterdam.

Hogarty, G.E., Anderson, C.M., Reiss, D.J., Kornblith, S.J., Greenwald, D.P., Jarna, C.D. and Madonia, M.J. (1986) Family psychoeducation, social skills training and maintenance chemotherapy in the aftercare treatment of schizophrenia: I One-year effects of a controlled study on relapse and expressed emotion. *Archives of General Psychiatry*, **43**, 633–42.

Holzman, P.S., Proctor, L.R. and Hughes, D.W. (1973) Eye tracking patterns in schizophrenia. *Science*, **181**, 179–81.

Holzman, P.S., Proctor, L.R., Levy, D.L., Yasillo, N.J., Meltzer, H.Y. and Hurt, S.W. (1974) Eye-tracking dysfunctions in schizophrenic patients and their relatives. *Archives of General Psychiatry*, **31**, 143–51.

Holzman, P.S., Kringlen, E., Levy, D.L., Proctor, L.R., Haberman, S.J. and Yasillo, N.J. (1977) Abnormal pursuit eye-movements in schizophrenia: evidence for a genetic indicator. *Archives of General Psychiatry*, **34**, 802–5.

Holzman, P.S., Kringlen, E., Levy, D.L. and Haberman, S.J. (1980) Deviant eye-tracking in twins discordant for psychosis: a replication. *Archives of General Psychiatry*, **37**, 627–31.

Iacono, W.G. (1982) Bilateral electrodermal habituation-dishabituation and resting EEG in remitted schizophrenics. *Journal of Nervous and Mental Disease*, **170**, 91–101.

Iacono, W.G. and Ficken, J.W. (1989) Research strategies employing psychophysiological measures: identifying and using psychophysiological markers. In: G. Turpin (ed.), *Handbook of Clinical Psychophysiology*, pp. 45–70, John Wiley, Chichester.

Iacono, W.G., Peloquin, W.J., Lumry, A.E., Valentine, R.H. and Tuason, V.B. (1982) Eye tracking in patients with unipolar and bipolar affective disorders in remission. *Journal of Abnormal Psychology*, **91**, 35–44.

Kaiya, H., Uematsu, M., Ofuji, M., Nishida, A., Morikiyo, M. and Adachi, S. (1989) Computerised tomography in schizophrenia: familial versus non-familial forms of illness. *British Journal of Psychiatry*, **155**, 444–50.

Kennedy, J.L., Guiffra, L.A., Moises, H.W., Cavalli-Sforza, L.L., Pakstis, A.J., Kidd, J.R., Castiglione, C.M., Sjogren, B., Wetterberg, L. and Kidd, K.K. (1988)

Evidence against linkage of schizophrenia to markers on chromosome 5 in a northern Swedish pedigree. *Nature*, **336**, 167–70.
Kraepelin, E. (1919) *Dementia Praecox and Paraphrenia*, 1971 ed, trans. R.B. Barclay, Krieger, Huntington, New York.
Leff, J.P., Kuipers, L., Berkowitz, R., Vaughn, C. and Sturgeon, D.A. (1983) Life events, relative's "expressed emotion" and maintenance neuroleptics in schizophrenic relapse. *Psychological Medicine*, **13**, 799–806.
Lewine, R.R.J., Watt, N.F. and Grub, T.J. (1984) High risk for schizophrenia research: sampling bias and its implications. In N.F. Watt, E.J. Anthony, L.C. Wynne and J.E. Rolf (eds), *Children at Risk for Schizophrenia: a Longitudinal Perspective*, pp. 557–64, Cambridge University Press.
Lipton, R.B., Levy, D.L., Holzman, P.S. and Levin, S. (1983) Eye movement dysfunction in psychiatric patients: a review. *Schizophrenia Bulletin*, **9**, 13–32.
Mather, J.A. (1985) Eye movements of teenage children of schizophrenics: a possible inherited marker of susceptibility to the disease. *Journal of Psychiatric Research*, **19**, 523–32.
Mednick, S.A. (1978) Berkson's fallacy and high-risk research. In: L.C. Wynne, R.L. Cromwell and L. Mathysse (eds), *The Nature of Schizophrenia: New Approaches to Research and Treatment*, pp. 442–52, John Wiley: New York.
Mednick, S.A. and Schulsinger, F. (1974) Some premorbid characteristics related to breakdown in children with schizophrenic mothers. In: S.A. Mednick, F. Schulsinger, J. Higgins and B. Bell (eds), *Genetics, Environment and Psychopathology*, North-Holland, Amsterdam.
Meehl, P.E. (1962) Schizotaxia, schizotypy, schizophrenia. *American Psychologist*, **17**, 827–38.
Meehl, P.E. (1989) Schizotaxia revisited. *Archives of General Psychiatry*, **46**, 935–44.
Miller, G.A. (1986) Information processing deficits in anhedonia and perceptual aberration: a psychophysiological analysis. *Biological Psychiatry*, **21**, 100–115.
Mullan, M.J. and Murray, R.M. (1989) The impact of molecular genetics on our understanding of the psychoses. *British Journal of Psychiatry*, **154**, 591–5.
Murphy, D.L., Belmaker, R., Buchsbaum, M.S., Martin, N.F., Ciaranello, R. and Wyatt, R.J. (1977) Biogenic amine-related enzymes and personality variations in normals. *Psychological Medicine*, **7**, 149–57.
Nasrallah, H.A. and Weinberger, D.R. (eds) (1986) *The Neurology of Schizophrenia*, vol. 1, Elsevier Science Publishers, Amsterdam.
Neal, J.M. and Oltmanns, T.F. (1980) *Schizophrenia*, John Wiley, Chichester.
Nuechterlein, K.H. (1987) Vulnerability models for schizophrenia: state of the art. In: H. Hafner, W.F. Gattaz and W. Janarzik (eds) *Search for the Causes of Schizophrenia*, Springer, Berlin, Heidleberg.
Nuechterlein, K.H. and Dawson, M.E. (1984a) A heuristic vulnerability–stress model of schizophrenic episodes. *Schizophrenia Bulletin*, **10**, 300–12.
Nuechterlein, K.H. and Dawson, M.E. (1984b) Information processing and attentional functioning in the developmental course of schizophrenic disorder. *Schizophrenia Bulletin*, **10**, 160–203.
Nuechterlein, K.H., Edell, W.S., Norris, M. and Dawson, M.E. (1986). Attentional vulnerability indicators, thought disorder, and negative symptoms. *Schizophrenia Bulletin*, **12**, 408–46.
Ohman, A. (1981a) The role of experimental psychology in the scientific analysis of psychopathology. *International Journal of Psychology*, **16**, 229–321.
Ohman, A. (1981b) Electrodermal activity and vulnerability to schizophrenia: a review. *Biological Psychology*, **123**, 87–145.

Ohman, A., Ohlund, L.S., Alm, T., Wieselgren, I.M., Ost, L.G. and Lindstrom, L.H. (1989) Electrodermal non-responding, premorbid adjustment and symptomatology as predictors of long-term social functioning in schizophrenics. *Journal of Abnormal Psychology*, **98**, 426–35.

O'Rourke, D.H., Gottesman, I.I., Suarez, B.K. and Reich, T. (1982) Refutation of the general single-locus model for the etiology of schizophrenia. *American Journal of Human Genetics*, **34**, 630–49.

Persons, J.B. (1986) The advantages of studying psychological phenomena rather than psychiatric diagnoses. *American Psychologist*, **41**, 1252–60.

Pfefferbaum, A., Ford, J.M., White, P. and Roth, W.T. (1989) P3 in schizophrenia is affected by stimulus modality, response requirements, medication status and negative symptoms. *Archives of General Psychiatry*, **46**, 1035–44.

Prentky, R.A., Salzman, L.F. and Klein R.H. (1981) Habituation and conditioning of electrodermal response in children at risk. *Schizophrenia Bulletin*, **7**, 281–91.

Reveley, A. (1985) Genetic counselling for schizophrenia. *British Journal of Psychiatry*, **147**, 107–12.

Reveley, A.M., Reveley, M.A. and Murray, R.M. (1984) Cerebral ventricular enlargement in non-genetic schizophrenia: a controlled twin study, *British Journal of Psychiatry*, **144**, 89–93.

Reveley, A.M., Reveley, M.A., Clifford, C.A. and Murphy, R.M. (1982) Cerebral ventricular size in twins discordant for schizophrenia. *Lancet*, **i**, 540–1.

Rice, J., McGuffin, P., Goldin, L.R., Shaskan, E. and Gershon, E.S. (1984) Platelet monoamine oxidase activity: evidence for a single major locus. *American Journal of Human Genetics*, **36**, 36–43.

Reider, R.O. and Gershon, E.S. (1978) Genetic strategies in biological psychiatry. *Archives of General Psychiatry*, **35**, 866–73.

Rosvold, H.E., Mirsky, A., Sarason, I., Bransome, E.D., Jr. and Beck, L.H. (1956) A continuous performance test of brain damage. *Journal of Consulting Psychology*, **20**, 343–50.

Saitoh, O., Niwa, S., Hiramatsu, K., Kameyama, T., Rymar, K. and Itoh, K. (1984) Abnormalities in late positive components of event-related potentials may reflect a genetic predisposition to schizophrenia. *Biological Psychiatry*, **19**, 293–303.

Sherrington, R., Brynjolfsson, J., Petursson, H., Potter, M., Duddleston, K., Barraclough, B., Wasmuth, J., Dobbs, M. and Gurling, H. (1988) Localization of a susceptibility locus for schizophrenia on chromosome 5. *Nature*, **336**, 164–7.

Siever, L.J. and Coursey, R.D. (1985) Biological markers for schizophrenia and the biological high-risk approach. *Journal of Nervous and Mental Disease*, **173**, 4–16.

Siever, L.J., Coursey, R.D., Alterman, I.S., Buchsbaum, M.S. and Murphy, D.L. (1984) Impaired smooth pursuit eye movement: vulnerability marker for schizotypal personality disorder in a normal volunteer population. *American Journal of Psychiatry*, **141**, 1560–6.

Simons, R.F. (1981) Electrodermal and cardiac orienting in psychometrically defined high-risk subjects. *Psychiatry Research*, **4**, 347–56.

Simons, R.F. (1982) Physical anhedonia and future psychopathology: an electrocortical continuity? *Psychophysiology*, **19**, 433–41.

Spring, B. and Coons, H. (1982) Stress as a precursor of schizophrenia. In: R.J.W. Neufeld (ed.) *Psychological Stress and Psychopathology*, pp. 13–54, McGraw-Hill, New York.

Steinhauer, S., Gruzelier, J.H. and Zubin, J. (eds) (in press) *Handbook of Schizophrenia, Volume Five: Neuropsychology, Psychophysiology and Information-Processing*, Elsevier Science Publishers, Amsterdam.

Straube, E.R. (1979) On the meaning of electrodermal non-responding in schizophrenia. *Journal of Nervous and Mental Disease*, **167**, 601–11.

Tarrier, N. (1979) The future of the medical model: a reply to Gruze. *Journal of Nervous and Mental Disease*, **167**, 71–3.

Tarrier, N. and Barrowclough, C. (1990) Family interventions. *Behaviour Modification*, **14**, 408–40.

Tarrier, N. and Turpin, G. (in press) Psychosocial factors, arousal and schizophrenic relapse: a review of the psychophysiological data. *British Journal of Psychiatry*.

Turpin, G. (1989) An overview of clinical psychophysiological techniques: tools or theories? In: G. Turpin (ed.), *Handbook of Clinical Psychophysiology*, pp. 3–44, John Wiley, Chichester.

Turpin, G. and Clements, K. (in press). Psychophysiological contributions to clinical assessment and treatment. In: D. Kavanagh (ed.), *Schizophrenia: an Overview and Practical Handbook*, Chapman and Hall, London.

Turpin, G. and Lader, M. (1986) Life events and mental disorder: biological theories of their mode of action. In: H. Katschnig (ed.), *Life Events and Psychiatric Disorders: Controversial Issues*, pp. 33–62, Cambridge University Press.

Turpin, G., Tarrier, N. and Sturgeon, D. (1988) Social psychophysiology and the study of biopsychosocial models of schizophrenia. In: H.L. Wagner (ed.), *Social Psychophysioloy: Theory and Clinical Applications*, pp. 251–72, John Wiley, Chichester.

Van Praag, H.M. (1981) Sociobiological psychiatry. *Comprehensive Psychiatry*, **22**, 441–7.

Watt, N.F., Anthony, E.J., Wynne, L.C. and Rolf, J.E. (1984) *Children at Risk for Schizophrenia: a Longitudinal Perspective*, Cambridge University Press.

Weinberger, D.R., Wagner, R.L., Wyatt, R.J. (1983) Neuropathological studies of schizophrenia: a selective review. *Schizophrenia Bulletin*, **9**, 183–212.

Williams, A.O., Reveley, M.A., Kolakowska, T., Ardern, M. and Madelbrote, B.M. (1985) Schizophrenia with good and poor outcome: ventricular size and its clinical significance. *British Journal of Psychiatry*, **146**, 239–46.

Wohlberg, G.W. and Kornetsky, C., (1973) Sustained attention in remitted schizophrenics, *Archives of General Psychiatry*, **28**, 533–7.

Wyatt, C.D., Potkin, S.G. and Murphy, D.L. (1979) Platelet monoamine oxidase activity in schizophrenia: a review of the data, *American Journal of Psychiatry*, **136**, 377–85.

Zahn, T.P. (1986) Psychophysiological approaches to psychopathology. In: M.G.H. Coles, E. Donchin and S.W. Porges (eds) *Psychophysiology: Systems, Processes and Applications*, pp. 508–610, Guilford Press, New York.

Zahn T.P. and Carpenter, W.T. Jr. (1978) Effects of short-term outcome and clinical improvement on reaction time in acute schizophrenia. *Journal of Psychiatric Research*, **14**, 59–68.

Zahn, T.P., Carpenter, W.T. and McGlashan, T.H. (1981) Autonomic nervous system activity in acute schizophrenia: II. Relationships to short-term prognosis and clinical state. *Archives of General Psychiatry*, **38**, 260–6.

Zubin, J., Magaziner, J. and Steinhauer, S.R. (1983) The metamorphosis of schizophrenia: from chronicity to vulnerability. *Psychological Medicine*, **13**, 551–71.

Zubin, J. and Spring, B. (1977) Vulnerability: a new view of schizophrenia. *Journal of Abnormal Psychology*, **86**, 260–6.

Zubin, J. and Steinhauer, S. (1981) How to break the logjam in schizophrenia: a look beyond genetics. *Journal of Nervous and Mental Disease*, **169**, 477–92.

Chapter 3

Monitoring Recovery from Acute Psychosis

VALERIE DRURY

INTRODUCTION

Monitoring schizophrenic patients *in remission* in order to detect early signs of relapse may prove a very worthwhile exercise if a florid episode can be forestalled or prevented by early mobilisation of medical and other interventions (see Chapter 6). Monitoring a patient's *recovery* from an acute episode of schizophrenia by mapping the changes in mental state and non-psychotic symptoms (e.g. anxiety, dysphoria), together with gains in insight and disintegration of delusional beliefs may on the face of it look little more than an academic exercise. However, in reality the implications of such an exercise can be many fold. The monitoring process may facilitate the building of rapport between patient and professional with the consequence that the relationship itself may become therapeutic and thus acts as a "safe" environment in which psychological interventions can be introduced and where the patient knows his or her symptoms will be taken seriously. Monitoring could provide the means for measuring efforts to accelerate recovery through psychological intervention and inform the timing and intensity of rehabilitative efforts. Furthermore, monitoring may have medical implications as close observation of non-psychotic symptoms may provide the clinician with supplementary information about the ideal time for medication reduction and discharge.

Detailed, careful monitoring as part of a continuing dialogue between the professional, patient and carers can help to build a "collaborative ethos" in which patient and families regard themselves as partners in the management of schizophrenia (Smith and Birchwood, 1990). Thus participating in a monitoring exercise may be of benefit for patients in its own right in that patients feel they have more "control" over the progression of their illness.

Innovations in the Psychological Management of Schizophrenia.
Edited by Max Birchwood and Nicholas Tarrier. © 1992 John Wiley & Sons Ltd

In this chapter there will be an emphasis on practical strategies used to monitor recovery and a demonstration, by the use of case examples, how the information obtained can be of real clinical benefit.

The literature contains little detailed information on duration of recovery and its relationship with variables such as sex, diagnosis and ethnicity. In a retrospective study by Birchwood et al. (in press) of 169 patients admitted for the first time to psychiatric care with an acute psychotic illness, Asians were found to have a significantly briefer period of in-patient care (7.2 weeks) than whites (9.8 weeks), who in turn had a briefer period of in-patient care than Caribbeans (12.8 weeks). In a prospective study by the Early Signs Research Group (in preparation) of 30 in-patients with a clinical diagnosis of schizophrenia, the mean duration of admission was 17.0 weeks: 19.0 weeks for males and 12.3 weeks for females. Availability of suitable accommodation and good family support networks appeared to be important factors in the earlier discharge of the female patients. Thus length of hospitalisation may be an insensitive instrument for measuring the time taken to recover from an acute psychotic episode. In this chapter I shall review the evidence which suggests that recovery cannot be conceptualised as a smooth, linear progression. Individuals appear to pass through qualitatively different phases, sometimes passing back and forth following a "stormy course" in which "psychological", "psychosocial" and "illness" processes interact—an understanding of which is essential if psychosocial interventions are to be implemented during recovery.

In this first section, stage and dimensional models of recovery will be reviewed together with a proposed model of recovery.

THE PROCESS OF REINTEGRATION

Theoretical models

Few prospective studies have systematically attempted to map the recovery process which follows an acute onset of schizophrenic symptoms. One notable exception is the study by Donlan and Blacker (1973) which suggests that patients pass through four distinct phenomenological stages during reintegration which are qualitatively the same as those passed through in decompensation, but in reverse order (for a more detailed review of stages of decompensation see Chapter 6). Donlan and Blacker carefully monitored 30 consenting out-patients several times per week over a period of eight weeks. During this time the patient's active medication was abruptly withdrawn, replaced by placebo for up to two weeks and then active medication reinstated. The patient was aware that during this time they may be placed on a non-active agent.

Full decompensation "psychic disorganisation and relief from subjective pain" (p. 202) was marked by less distressing auditory hallucinations and the formation of ''compensatory" delusions. In the first stage, there was a withdrawal by the patient into their inner world which prohibited communication. The patient began to feel well but was totally lacking in insight. As reintegration progressed into the next stage subjective distress returned: painful memories and fears of loss of control invaded consciousness. The characteristic affects of this stage were those of panic, horror and fright. The next stage was predominantly marked by a depressive mood associated with loss of appetite, agitation and sleeplessness. The final stage of reintegration before recovery was typified by racing thoughts, anxiety, problems concentrating, feelings of vulnerability, frightening thoughts and dreams and low sexual drive. However, Donlan and Blacker found this progression through the four stages was not inevitable and could be arrested or even reversed if medication was sufficiently below a "therapeutic" dosage.

The limitation of this model, however, for clinical use is that many of the symptoms are explained in terms of psychodynamic theory with the qualitative and quantitative changes taking place in symptomology during the movement from one stage to another not clearly defined. Furthermore, there seems to be considerable overlap between stages.

Other stage theorists (e.g. Kayton, 1973 and Sachar et al., 1970) have also described four phases of reintegration, which although not directly comparable to Donlan and Blacker's stages, do show some resemblances. In Sachar et al. and Donlan and Blacker's models the first two stages of reintegration are concerned with the disintegration of core psychotic symptoms. For instance, Sacher et al. describe how a fixed delusional system in the first stage ("psychotic equilibrium") becomes unstable and fluid in the second stage ("acute psychotic turmoil") with delusions and ideas of reference readily formed but easily discarded. After stage 2 the symptoms described by both Donlan and Blacker and Sachar et al. are predominantly non-psychotic such as depression, anxiety, feelings of vulnerability and low self-esteem. Kayton (1973) devotes just one stage of his model "internal disorganisation" to the resolution of prominent psychotic symptoms but the post psychotic phases are described in more depth and detail than in the other models. For instance, the second stage "post psychotic regression" is marked by disturbed sleep and erratic eating patterns, impaired concentration and comprehension, social withdrawal and depression. The third stage "middle phase of post psychotic regression" is marked by return to normal sleeping and eating patterns with improved concentration and attention to grooming. Social interactions resume but are mainly non-verbal in nature. The fourth stage "termination of post psychotic regression" is marked by the patient taking pleasure in social interactions with a feeling of increased confidence and security. There is a return of ambition but goals are scaled down to realistic levels.

The concept of stages in recovery with the inherent theoretical assumption of boundaries and mutual exclusiveness has been criticised by Carr (1983). Many researchers suggest that the changes in symptomatology are best conceptualised as occurring on several independent dimensions. (Overall, Gorham and Shawver, 1961; Astrachan et al., 1974; Wittenborn, 1977; Dencker et al., 1978). Although these studies were conducted with a wide variety of sample sizes and types (e.g. chronic versus acute schizophrenic patients, those during a florid episode versus those some years into remission) along with different research aims, three groups of symptoms feature fairly consistently: psychoticism (e.g. disorganisation and distortion of thought process possibly with paranoia), retardation (e.g. reduced motor activity and lack of emotion) and dysphoria (e.g. anxiety, agitation and depression).

Carr (1983) has suggested a model whereby recovery can be monitored using five basic dimensions with a patient's position on each dimension not necessarily dependent on his/her position on the other dimensions. These dimensions are as follows:

1. *Psychotic disorganisation* which reflects the "internal disorganisation" described by Kayton (1973, 1975), "acute psychotic turmoil" described by Sachar et al. (1963, 1970) and "panic and horror" described by Donlan and Blacker (1973).
2. *Psychotic restitution* is concerned with the delusional state of the individual reflected in his or her conviction and preoccupation with delusional beliefs as well as the degree of implausibility or level of distortion of consensual reality. The term restitution reflects the individual's attempt to make sense of and adapt to a disturbing primary experience. This reduces anxiety and hence restores a degree of equanimity.
3. *Activation–inhibition* is a bipolar dimension with impulsivity and restlessness at one end versus anergia and withdrawal at the other.
4. *Neurotic restitution* is an attempt by the individual to adapt to dysphoric symptoms by non-psychotic means. A sense of equilibrium is achieved by directing attention away from agitation, low self-esteem, depression, etc towards various obsessions, phobias, compulsions and somatic complaints. (In Donlan and Blacker's study (1973), patients with obsessions and compulsions appeared less depressed.)
5. *Dysphoria* reflects the degree of subjective distress attributable to anxiety and depression. An individual may experience either anxiety and depression alternately or simultaneously. This model would certainly appear to have a great deal more flexibility than stage models whose

> descriptions are not sufficiently comprehensive for clinical use. Also Carr's model is able to incorporate many of the findings of other empirical investigations (Overall, Gorham and Shawver, 1961; Astrachan et al., 1974; Dencker et al., 1978; Pious, 1961; Donlan and Blacker, 1973) and as such has face validity. However, even this model may not do justice to the complexity of changes that occur during recovery. For instance, the disintegration of delusions may be difficult to monitor due to their multi-dimensional character and the "marked de-synchrony and lack of covariance between different aspects of delusional beliefs". (Brett-Jones, Garety and Hemsley, 1987, p. 257).

In describing the changes that occur during recovery, neither stage nor dimensional models alone may be adequate for clinical use. Stage models are likely to be too restrictive and dimensional models cover any eventuality; with patients' positions on one dimension not predicting their position on another. It is suggested that a hybrid between these two models may be more useful—one of overlapping dimensions but with some distinct stages; for instance there may be an initial stage of psychotic disorganisation (with symptoms such as perceptual disturbance, tangentiality, distractibility, incongruity and incoherence of speech) before the other symptom clusters emerge, e.g. Sachar et al. (1963, 1970), Pious (1961). Dysphoric symptoms (particularly anxiety and depression) may be evident almost right through the course of recovery, but with some individuals a final stage may occur where only declining dysphoric symptoms are present, e.g. Donlan and Blacker (1973).

It is hypothesised that the patient's position on each of the dimensions are interdependent (Figure 3.1), for instance, the idea of psychotic restitution or delusion formation as a mastery process over frightening experiences is unlikely to occur until some of the mental chaos has abated. Disintegration of delusions may be related to the cessation of primary experiences such as depersonalisation although there may be a time lag between the two. Neurotic restitution, if it occurs, is likely to happen some time after the symptoms of psychotic disorganisation have subsided. Such a non-psychotic defence mechanism is unlikely to occur in a thought disordered and perceptually or affectively disturbed patient. However, this proposed model of recovery from an acute schizophrenic episode is all speculation with little data at present to support it. Further research involving prospective monitoring of recovering schizophrenic patients is therefore indicated to determine if there is an initial psychotic stage marked by an absence of delusional beliefs and non-psychotic symptoms; a final stage where only non-psychotic symptoms persist; and if the disintegration of delusions relate to changes in other symptom groups.

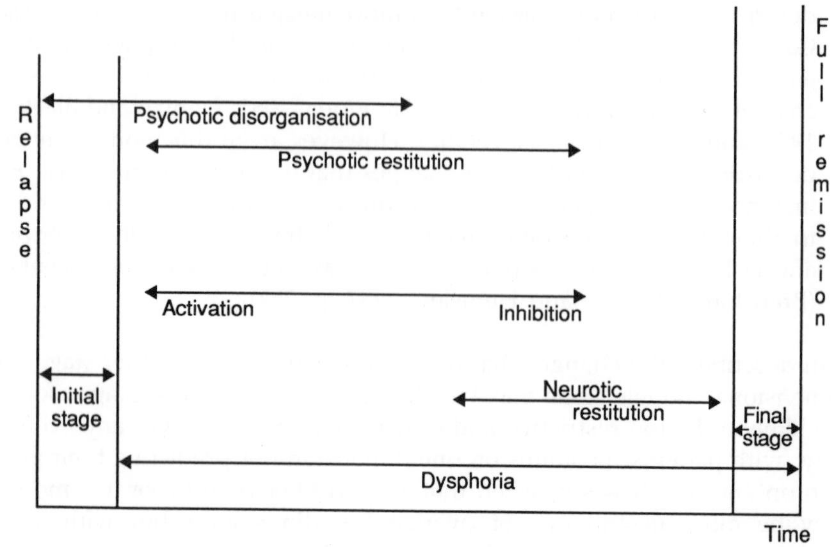

Figure 3.1 A proposed relationship between the five dimensions described by Carr (1983).

Disintegration of delusional beliefs during recovery

Sacks, Carpenter and Strauss (1974) describe three stages in the recovery from delusional thinking. In the *delusional* phase the patient is totally immersed in his or her delusions to the point where what is thought and what is perceived is indivisible. This is followed by the *double awareness* phase where the patient can distance themselves from the delusion and can begin to reality test their beliefs and both accept and reject the beliefs. The patient "increasingly recognises the delusion as a symptom" (Sacks, Carpenter and Strauss, 1974, p. 119). In the final *non-delusional phase* there is an attempt to align the delusional ideas with reality; for instance, one patient who had grandiose delusions, when recovered rationalised that his feeling of great importance when ill was due to the fact that he knew his research data would be written up in textbooks (Sachs, Carpenter and Strauss, 1974). One patient who thought he was telepathic with his sister later rationalised the experience by saying "we are very close, we look alike maybe sometimes we think alike" (Early Signs Research Group, in preparation).

This, however, presents a rather over-simplified view of the changes that occur during the process of recovery from delusions. In a study of nine hospitalised schizophrenic patients, seen weekly soon after admission

(Brett-Jones, Garety and Hemsley, 1987) three key components of recovery from delusions were measured: degree of *conviction* in the belief; *preoccupation* with the belief (that is the amount of time spent thinking about the belief) and the degree to which the belief *interfered* with the everyday life of the individual. In support of the multi-dimensional view, seven of the nine subjects showed fluctuating scores on conviction and preoccupation with decreases in conviction tending to precede decreases in preoccupation. Correlations between conviction and preoccupation and conviction and interference, for the group of patients as a whole, were not significant (although the sample size was small) suggesting that these components are orthogonal dimensions.

Further evidence for the multi-dimensional view of delusions is reported in a study by Chadwick and Lowe (1990). Six clients who held fixed delusional beliefs for two or more years were monitored before, during and after two psychological interventions which consisted of a structured verbal challenge and a reality test. The data for individual clients showed a high degree of desynchrony between conviction, preoccupation and anxiety caused by thinking about the belief as the delusions receded. Many of the patients only sought out confirmatory evidence for their delusional beliefs rather than disconfirmatory objective experiences, which suggested to Brett-Jones, Garety and Hemsley (1987) that there are psychological processes involved in belief maintenance and disintegration which may not be unlike those involved in belief maintenance and decay in normal populations (Maher and Ross, 1984). This suggestion could have considerable significance for the prospects of accelerating recovery from an acute psychotic episode.

Many authors have suggested that some delusions are understandable when seen as an elaboration of, or a way of making sense of, an unusual set of perceptual experiences such as derealisation, depersonalisation and auditory hallucinations. This, however, does not explain *primary* delusions in which for example an individual suddenly becomes convinced that a set of events has special meaning: perhaps it is important to make the distinction between primary and secondary delusions when monitoring recovery. It is possible that patients holding secondary delusions are more likely to show a gradual but fluctuating decline in conviction during recovery as perceptions and beliefs about them are differentiated in the "double awareness" phase while primary delusions may disintegrate more abruptly. Such sudden shifts in conviction of primary delusions may be emotionally rather than cognitively based. In other words, the decline in conviction may not be due to the scrutiny and acknowledgement of objective events which are contrary to the belief but overwhelming *feelings* that the belief is false.

There are yet other delusions which would appear to be logically related and hence to show similar patterns of decline during recovery ("a domino effect"). For instance the secondary delusions "I am dead" (therefore) "I am rotting" (therefore) "I am infectious to children" would all appear to be inextricably linked. Similarly, the three delusions "I have cancer" (because) "I was drenched in Agent Orange" (because) "I fought in the Vietnam war" are obviously connected to one another.

The ability to "relabel delusions as pathological" is seen by David (1990) as an important component of insight. Consequently, as conviction in a delusional belief declines one might expect to see gains in insight.

Non-psychotic symptoms and recovery

Non-psychotic symptoms including anxiety/agitation, depression/withdrawal, disinhibition and early psychotic thinking which herald a relapse of schizophrenia have been successfully monitored using early warning sign measures (Herz Early Signs Questionnaire 1985, Early Signs Scale (ESS), Birchwood, 1989). In a pilot study (Birchwood et al., 1989) carried out with 19 patients and observers over a 9 month period relapse was accurately predicted in 79% of cases using a cut-off point of 30 on their scale. Similar work, as yet unpublished, with recovering patients using this scale suggests that individuals display a mirror image decline in non-psychotic symptoms as recovery proceeds. Certain patients continue to show a decrease in non-psychotic symptoms after remission of positive symptoms which would be in line with those models of recovery that predict non-psychotic symptoms resolve at a later stage than psychotic symptoms: in a study by the Early Signs Research Group (in preparation), 79% of patients who achieved full or partial remission of positive symptoms (hallucinations and delusions) were scoring below the cut-off of 30 at the point of recovery (see Figures 3.2 and 3.3). Of all patients 66% were scoring less than 30 at the point of discharge. This finding would point to the usefulness of a simple cut-off point on the ESS for recovery as well as for relapse.

Insight and recovery

If insight is conceptualised as simply an epiphenomenon of the presence or absence of acute psychopathology then one would assume insight to be low at relapse or just before admission to hospital and complete at recovery or remission of positive symptoms. In a study by McEvoy et al. (1989), however, "... degree of insight was not consistently related to the severity of acute psychopathology—nor did changes in insight during hospitalisation vary consistently with changes in acute psychopathology" (p. 43). It

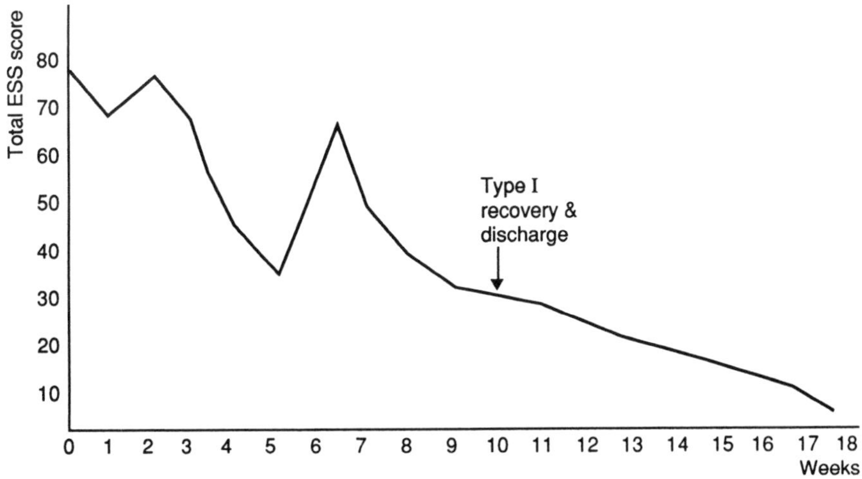

Figure 3.2 Changes in total ESS score during a type I recovery (full remission of positive symptoms).

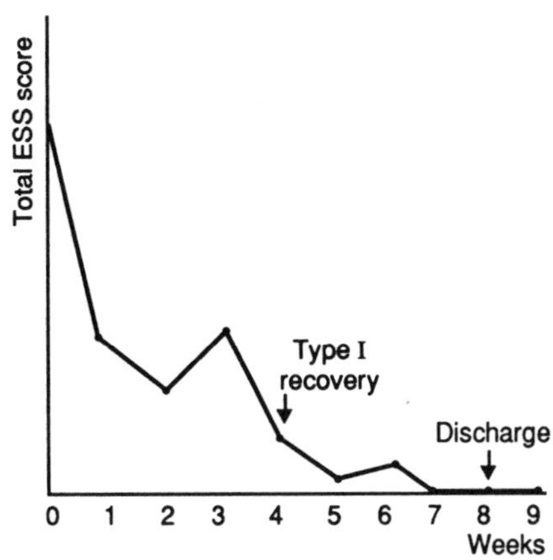

Figure 3.3 Changes in total ESS score during a type I recovery (full remission of positive symptoms).

is possible therefore that insight operates to some degree independently of symptomatology and may, in part, be dependent upon the individual's ability to reflexively examine his or her own experience—the way someone clinically depressed is able to say "I am depressed". In other words insight may require a psychological process. The concept of insight is according to David (1990) "composed of three distinct, overlapping dimensions". These are *treatment compliance, awareness of illness* and *correct relabelling of psychotic* experiences. If so, it is unlikely that in all patients insight will be low at relapse and high at recovery: need for treatment (i.e. to take medication, to be in hospital and to see a doctor) is partly a socially constructed concept and therefore may depend on the patients' attitude to the usefulness of drugs and medical intervention in general. David makes the distinction between "pseudo" and "true" insight. Pseudo insight relates to the regurgitation of psychiatric jargon without real understandings, e.g. "my delusions of grandeur are due to problems with the synapses in my brain". This phenomenon is perhaps only likely to be seen in patients with multiple admissions who have overheard explanations or have taken it on themselves to read psychiatric textbooks. Such utterances taken out of context of the patient's general behaviour and conversation would give a false indication of the level of a patient's insight.

In the study by the Early Signs Research Group (in preparation) insight was not found to be a binary phenomenon (see Figure 3.4), neither did it appear to be an inherent part of symptomatology as in some cases insight lagged behind the cessation of hallucinations and delusions (see Figure 3.4). In 37% of patients correct relabelling of psychotic experiences was either the last thing to be acknowledged or the only aspect never to be acknowledged. It may be that once primary experiences, e.g. auditory hallucinations and perceptual distortions have stopped and the vividness of the experience fades in the memory, it is easier to rationalise the experiences as being "all in the mind" and hence to be part of an "illness". This might also account for the time lag between the disappearance of positive symptoms and the achievement of full insight in some individuals. It

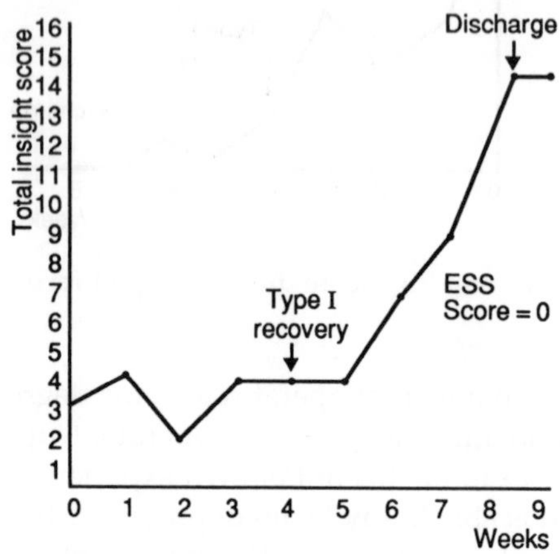

Figure 3.4 Gains in insight during type I recovery (full remission of positive symptoms).

does not explain, however, those patients who despite persistent auditory hallucinations readily accept the voices are "all in their mind", or conversely the patient whose delusions of reference from the TV have stopped many months previously but still holds total conviction they occurred in their past and explains it by saying "I'm not in dire straits anymore; I don't need the newsreader's help so they don't mention my name and give me advice now". Insight could therefore be a separate component of recovery as important as the positive symptoms themselves.

The process of reintegration: conclusions

There are relatively few examples in the literature of prospective studies of recovery from acute psychosis (cf. Donlan and Blacker, 1973; Goldberg, Klerman and Cole, 1967; Bowers and Astrachan, 1967; Pious, 1961; Kayton, 1975; Sachar et al., 1963, 1970). Some of these studies can be criticised for relying too heavily on psychodynamic theory to explain observations and for the limitation of sample size (e.g. Pious used a single case study and Sachar et al. used a sample of four). Some theorists believe discrete stages adequately describe the process of reintegration (Donlan and Blacker, 1973), while others believe the recovery process is best conceptualised as occurring along several independent dimensions (Goldberg, Klerman and Cole, 1965). Although no homogeneous pattern of recovery emerges from these studies, differences in the rate and patterns of decline between symptom groups are often apparent; positive symptoms (e.g. hallucinations, delusions and thought disorder) tend to dominate the clinical picture in the early stages and can show an initial rapid and sharp decline, while negative symptoms (e.g. flattened affect, motor retardation) can either subside equally rapidly or show little change and hence predominate over residual positive symptoms. The decline in non-psychotic symptoms may show a more fluctuating pathway with a final stage of recovery in some individuals where only non-psychotic symptoms persist.

PSYCHOSOCIAL INFLUENCES ON RECOVERY

Ward atmosphere and carers attitudes, i.e. the immediate psychosocial environments in which patients are involved, may play an important role in the recovery process. Kellam et al. (1967) found that wards with a low level of disturbed and aggressive behaviour along with a high degree of social interaction had a marked effect on the decline of paranoid symptoms but had little effect on symptoms of withdrawal. Admission wards with a high level of stress due to disruptive or violent behaviour of some patients could therefore extend rather than promote recovery in those patients where paranoia is a feature of symptomatology.

The concept of "expressed emotion" (EE) is a well established distal measure of interpersonal stress and has been operationalised in terms of the amount of hostility, over-involvement, and number of critical remarks elicited during the course of a factual interview with a carer about the patient (see Chapter 4). Schizophrenia patients with high EE relatives are more likely to relapse in nine months following discharge than those with low EE relatives (Brown, Birley and Wing, 1972).

It may be that those patients from high EE homes with relatives visiting on a regular basis will take longer to recover because of the higher levels of psychological stress they experience. Simpson (1989) considers the possibility that nurses "expressed emotion" may be a variable related to the recovery and outcome of schizophrenic patients.

A favourable convalescent environment defined as providing "a continuing feeling of safety but not hampering individualisation" (Kayton, Beck and Koh, 1976, p. 1271) and a therapeutic relationship defined as a "positive emotional engagement by patient and therapist in the context of help-giving" (Kayton, Beck and Koh, 1976, p. 1271), were both found to be significantly related to "good" outcome in 30 schizophrenic patients (Kayton, Beck and Koh, 1976). Sacks, Carpenter and Strauss (1974) postulate that a therapeutic relationship between researcher and patient may actually aid the recovery process "... he (the patient) is able to give as well as receive. The result is an increase in self-esteem and autonomy that encourages and fosters recovery" (p. 20).

It is suggested a period of convalescence (defined as the task of reintegration back into the community following the disruption of a psychotic episode) may last from a few weeks post discharge up to a full 12 months (Breier and Srauss, 1984). Breier and Strauss (1984) interviewed 20 patients who had been hospitalised for an acute psychotic episode, bi-monthly for one year post discharge. The extent to which social relationships with friends, family and spouse affected their symptoms, self-esteem and overall behaviour was investigated. Patients were asked to describe the most beneficial and most harmful aspects of these relationships. During convalescence, social relationships were seen to fulfil various helpful functions, in particular, ventilation of feelings, material support, help with problem solving, social approval and restoration of a sense of belonging.

During "rebuilding", a phase which follows convalescence and involves reducing reliance upon family and hospital and the cultivation of new friendships: motivation, symptom monitoring and participating as an equal partner in a reciprocal relationship were seen as most important.

The absence of a negative attitude rather than the presence of a very positive attitude towards their illness and the future was found to be associated with good outcome in 30 schizophrenic patients (McGlashan and Carpenter, 1981). Extrapolating from this finding, it may be that interventions to modify a patient's unrealistic positive or negative views about the effect of their illness on the future could have implications for recovery and prognosis. Romanticised positive attitudes of a quick return to normal functioning might prolong recovery if the patient is overwhelmed by depression when expectations are not met. Despairing negative attitudes about the illness might prolong recovery by preventing mobilisation of coping strategies to deal with residual symptoms.

A PROCEDURE FOR MONITORING RECOVERY

The following is a procedure adopted by the Early Signs Research Group at All Saints and Barnsley Hall hospitals in Birmingham, UK and may be a model others wish to consider.

Engagement

Patients should be approached preferably within two weeks of admission or relapse. It is important to stress confidentiality when explaining the purpose of monitoring as the process may be interpreted as further confirmatory evidence for any paranoid delusions that the patient may hold such as "the police are watching me and plotting against me", "the K.G.B. are after me".

A brief verbal explanation of the monitoring exercise should be given before commencement: "We are involved in monitoring the changes that occur in people's feelings and symptoms as they get better from their illness. The results from this exercise may help doctors to decide things like the best time for people to go home and the best time to reduce medication. We would like you to complete three questionnaires each week while in hospital and the same questionnaires every fortnight when you go home for about three months. The forms will be kept in your hospital notes and only those people involved with your care in hospital will have access to them".

There may be a problem with compliance especially as the monitoring involves the same questions repeated weekly. A good therapeutic relationship which has been nurtured between interviewer and patient is, however, likely to offset any tedium created by repetition as shown in a study by the Early Signs Research Group of 30 patients suffering from a relapse or first episode of schizophrenia where none of the patients withdrew their consent while in hospital and only one patient withdrew his consent after a period post discharge.

Frequency and sources of information

Patients complete the phenomenological version of the Early Signs Scale (Birchwood et al., 1989) and an insight scale (Smith and Birchwood, 1991) weekly; in addition the Beliefs and Convictions Scale (Brett Jones, Garety and Hemsley, 1987) is completed weekly with an interviewer. An assessment of the mental state of a patient is made weekly by the interviewer using the Psychiatric Assessment Scale (PAS) (Krawiecka, Goldberg and Vaughn, 1977) and an independent assessment by a clinician is sought on admission, monthly and at discharge. An observer (e.g. a member of the nursing staff, relative or carer) is approached to complete the behavioural (observer) version of the Early Signs Scale. After discharge, for a period of approximately three months, patients and observers are asked to complete the same assessments fortnightly.

The procedure should therefore allow non-psychotic experiences which characterise recovery from an acute schizophrenic episode to be related to changes in psychotic phenomena, levels of insight and strength of delusional conviction.

Standard measures

The Psychiatric Assessment Scale (Krawiecka, Goldberg and Vaughn, 1977)

This scale consists of eight categories of symptoms: depression, anxiety, hallucinations, delusions, flattened incongruous affect, psychomotor retardation, incoherence and irrelevance of speech and poverty of speech. The score for each category ranges from "0" where the item is for all practical purposes absent and "1" (mild) where there is some evidence for the item but it is not considered pathological; through to 2, 3 and 4 where the item is regarded as pathological ranging from moderate to severe. The rater decides on the severity of the item by taking into account the patients' demeanour and behaviour at interview as well as the history the patient gives. The scores for depression and anxiety are then summed together as are those for hallucinations and delusions (positive symptoms) and those for flattened affect and psychomotor retardation (negative symptoms) and those for incoherence and irrelevance of speech and poverty of speech (speech disorder).

The scores for depression and anxiety, positive symptoms, negative symptoms and speech disorder can be graphed separately each week (see Figure 3.5).

Beliefs and convictions (Brett-Jones, Garety and Hemsley, 1987)

Each belief is written down in the patient's own words e.g. "I believe my mother and father are aliens". A maximum of three beliefs are chosen in

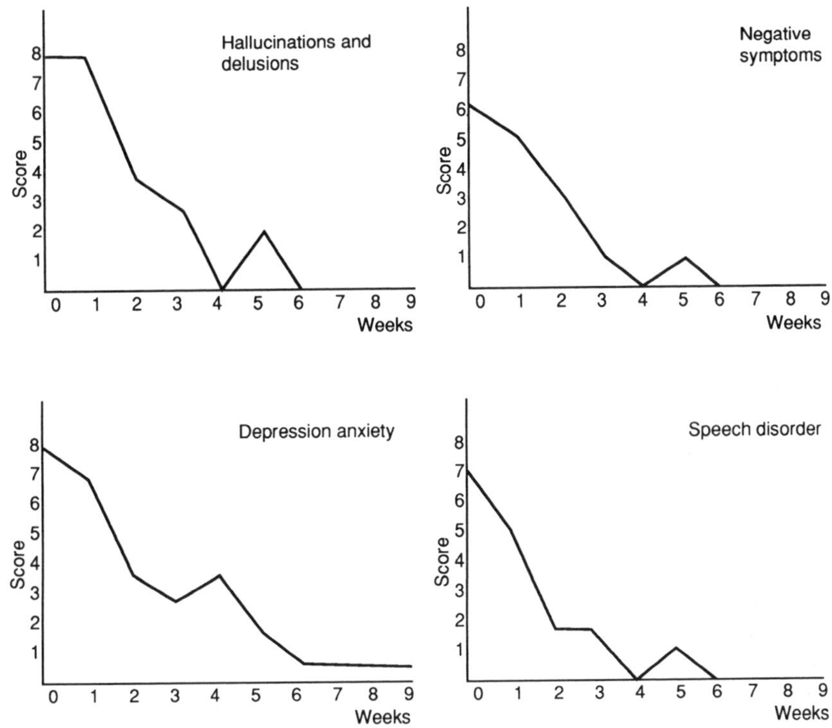

Figure 3.5 Changes in PAS ratings during recovery.

consultation with the patient and these are likely to be those interfering the most with the day-to-day functioning of the individual and/or causing the most anxiety.

Measures of *conviction* and *preoccupation* are elicited in two phases: a construction phase and an administration phase. A measure of *interference* that the belief has on the individual's day-to-day life is made by the interviewer: and a procedure to elicit reaction to hypothetical contradiction is administered.

To determine the level of conviction. In the construction phase, five statements of intensity of conviction are recorded in the patient's own words (with suggestions about intensity from the interviewer if necessary) e.g.:

There is very little chance that ... (statement of belief)
There is a slight chance that ...
I feel fairly sure that/there is a 50–50 chance that ...
I believe strongly that ...
I'm almost positive that ...

These are written on separate pieces of card and are ranked by the patient. In the administration phase, the cards are then presented to the patient separately in random order and the patient must say whether at the time of presentation they are more sure or less sure (about their belief) than the statement on the card.

The score (0–5) is equal to the number of cards to which the patient says his or her level of conviction is greater than that shown on the card.

To determine degree of preoccupation. As with conviction, patients choose five statements in their own words to represent the time they spend thinking about their belief, e.g.:

I hardly ever think about ... (statement of belief)
I think about ... (statement of belief) occasionally
I think about ... (statement of belief) some of the time
I think about ... (statement of belief) most of the time
I think about ... (statement of belief) nearly all the time

These are written on separate pieces of card and are individually presented to the patient in random order. The patient must say whether he or she thinks about his or her belief at the time of presentation more or less of the time than that indicated on the card.

The score (0–5) is equal to the number of cards to which the patients say their degree of preoccupation is greater than that shown on the card.

To determine the degree of interference the belief has on the everyday life of the patient. The rating is made by the interviewer on a 0–3 scale where:

0 is no interference,
1 is minor changes of behaviour are noted, e.g. can only listen to rather than watch TV, has to wear sunglasses indoors (to prevent people 'psyching' him out),
2 is disruption to normal hospital routine, e.g. cannot go to Day Centre, avoids TV room, laundry has to be washed separately from other patients' (as it is believed to be infectious),
3 is severe disruption to normal activities, e.g. cannot leave dormitory, cannot sit in day room when anyone else is present, cannot eat food from the hospital trolley, can only eat food brought in by relatives.

Reaction to hypothetical contradiction. The patient is given a hypothetical but plausible and concrete piece of evidence contradictory to his or her belief and asked how this affects the belief. This part of the scale is used to measure the individual's potential for accommodation of evidence incompatible with their belief as "... it may have some predictive value in picking out

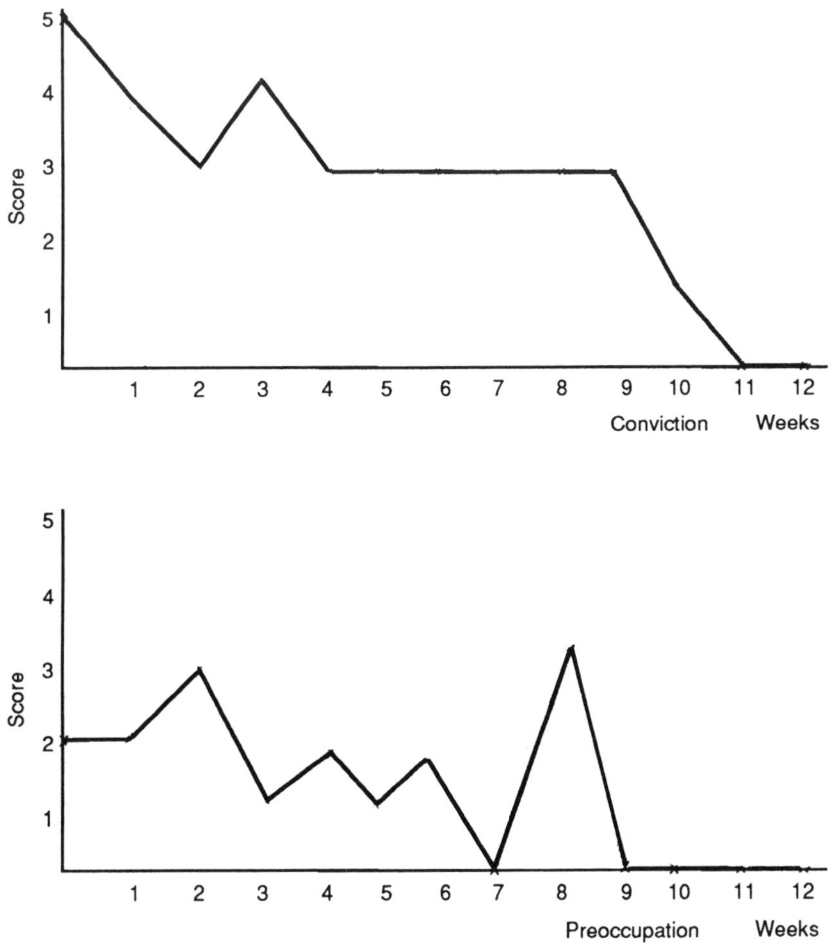

Figure 3.6 Fluctuations in conviction and preoccupation with delusional beliefs during recovery.

those most likely to make a complete recovery" (Brett-Jones, Garety and Hemsley, 1987, p. 264).

Replies are assigned to one of 4 categories:

1. The evidence is ignored or dismissed,
2. the evidence is accommodated into the belief system so that the belief and situation are now compatible, e.g. other people are able to eat the hospital food (which is poisoned) because they take a tablet on the way in,

3. there is a change in conviction but not content of the belief,
4. the belief is dropped.

The scores for preoccupation and conviction can be graphed separately each week (see Figure 3.6).

Insight

The Insight scale is one developed by Birchwood et al. (1992) and consists of eight statements (four negative and four positive) that the patients must either agree with, disagree with or say they are unsure about. The statements can be classified according to four subscales: the need for medication, the need to see a doctor or be in hospital, the acknowledgement of an illness and the relabelling of psychotic experiences.

The requisite agreement or disagreement with a statement scores 2 and a decision of unsure scores 1: the total score out of a maximum of 16 can be graphed weekly (see Figures 3.4 and 3.7). This scale has an advantage over some assessments (e.g. David, 1990) as it is a self-report and not an observer rating; so rendering an objective score rather than a subjective assessment by a rater.

The Early Signs Scale (ESS)

The ESS (Birchwood et al., 1989) is a randomly arranged checklist of 34 items describing feelings and behaviour known to occur in the period prior

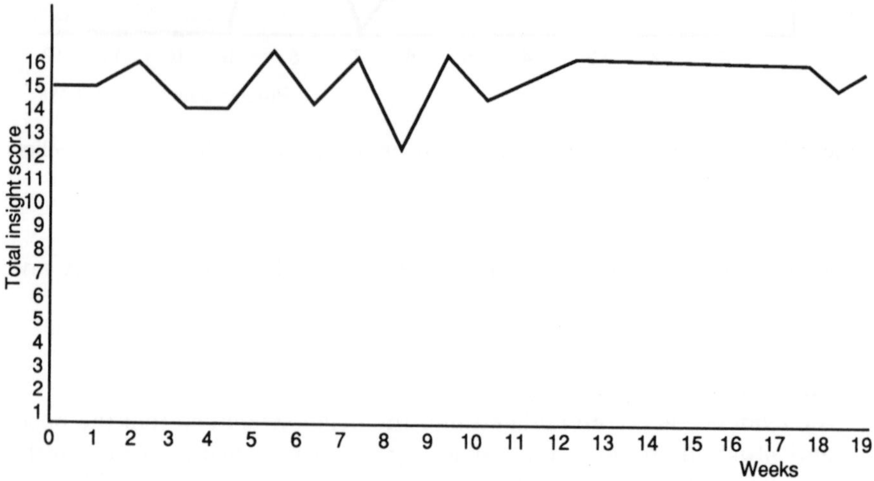

Figure 3.7 Changes in insight during recovery.

to relapse. Two versions of the scale are used: the self-report or phenomenological version and the observer or behavioural version. The items of the scale measure aspects of symptomatology as follows: 6 items represent anxiety, 10 items represent negativity, 7 items represent disinhibition and 11 items represent incipient or early psychosis. Each item is self-rated on a scale of 0–3 where:

0 indicates the item has not occurred and is "not a problem",
1 indicates the item has occurred once a week and is a "little problem",
2 indicates the item has occurred several times a week but not daily and is a "moderate problem",
3 indicates the item has occurred at least once a day and is a "marked problem".

The total score and scores for anxiety, disinhibition, negativity and incipient psychosis are graphed weekly before discharge and fortnightly after discharge.

Conducting the interviews

The interview should proceed as far as possible in a friendly atmosphere of mutual trust and respect with the emphasis on building up a rapport. Often there is a need to be "permission-giving" so individuals feel they can disclose symptoms without it having a detrimental effect on how people will react to them or on their length of stay in hospital. The approach should always be non-confrontational and non-judgemental with the interviewer adopting a reflective, non-directional style especially when discussing delusional beliefs.

It is preferable to complete the questionnaires in the order they have been described so that the ESS self-report does not confound the rater's judgement of the patient's mental state. For instance, the patient may report they have been reasonably cheerful all week, the future doesn't look too bad and their family have been to visit, which is congruous with their facial expression and general demeanour and yet when asked to complete the ESS item "feeling low or depressed" the patient reports this has occurred everyday. Obviously where patients are severely disturbed, aggressive, thought disordered or agitated, completion of the self-report questionnaires may prove difficult or impossible. Until the worst of these symptoms have abated it may only be possible to complete a Psychiatric Assessment Scale and to obtain an observers' version of the ESS.

The Psychiatric Assessment Scale

Some of these ratings are best made using selected questions taken from the Present State Examination (Wing, Cooper and Sartorius, 1974) using modifications of the wording where appropriate. It is important when assessing positive symptoms that, as well as asking relevant global questions pertinent probes are used to "target" known delusions and hallucinations otherwise delusions, ideas of reference, etc may not be elicited: for example, in the case of a young woman who thought that the whole neighbourhood was gossiping about an "affair" with a neighbour's husband it was necessary to ask "how are you getting along with people at the moment ... with your family, friends and neighbours?" before an assessment of her delusional state could be made.

The Beliefs and Convictions Scale

With the emphasis on a low-key, non-confrontational stance, gentle probes are made concerning the belief(s). No more than three beliefs are worked with at any one time and these are likely to be those causing the patient most distress or the ones he or she is most preoccupied with. The following example illustrates the eliciting of a belief that the patient's mother was a member of the KGB and shows the use of hypothetical contradictions.

Eliciting the belief

INTERVIEWER. Is there any particular worry or concern which is troubling you or on your mind a lot at the moment?
PATIENT. Everything is bothering me at the moment.
INTERVIEWER. Has your mother been to see you lately?
PATIENT. Yes, a couple of times this week.
INTERVIEWER. How are you getting along just now?
PATIENT. Dreadful.
INTERVIEWER. Why's that?
PATIENT. My mother is behaving very strangely.
INTERVIEWER. In what way is your mother behaving strangely?
PATIENT. She makes me cross when she goes round talking to the other patients—she's trying to psyche them out.
INTERVIEWER. How are you so sure she's trying to psyche them out?
PATIENT. Because she does it to me *and* she inserts thoughts into my head.
INTERVIEWER. How can she do these things?
PATIENT. Because she's a member of the secret police—she needs information.

Eliciting the evidence

The next stage attempts to elicit further evidence the patient has to support his belief:

INTERVIEWER. What makes you so sure your mother is a member of the secret police?
PATIENT. The things she does.
INTERVIEWER. What things in particular does your mother do which makes you suspect this?
PATIENT. My mother waits in the hospital car park until someone in a certain make of car leaves and then she follows them.
INTERVIEWER. Do you know why your mother does this?
PATIENT. She always drives close to the vehicle in front so she can read and memorise the number plate.
INTERVIEWER. Is there anything else your mother does which makes you suspect she's a member of the secret police?
PATIENT. Yes, she always brings items into the hospital concealed in two Tesco bags so no one can see what she is carrying ... when she leaves there is more in the bags than when she arrived. ... she has an evil glint in her eye and a malevolent smile.

Hypothetical contradiction

This information was met with the following hypothetical contradiction "just supposing an ex-member of the secret police were to tell you that your mother was too old and had inappropriate qualifications for the secret police would this lessen your worry at all?". The patient dismissed this hypothetical contradiction on the grounds that "ex-members wouldn't discuss secret police matters and if you were a member of the secret police you were a member for life". Sometime later when preoccupation but not conviction had decreased, the patient responded to the same hypothetical contradiction by saying his mother was "a lapsed or coerced member of the secret police".

It is important that the hypothetical contradictions are prefixed with statements like ... "just supposing ...", "how would you feel if ...", "some people are under the impression that ...", "some people say ...", so that the person does not feel their belief is under direct "fire" but rather a different point of view is being offered as a possible alternative.

It is also important to differentiate between hypothetical contradictions and verbal challenges. Both may be used in monitoring disintegration of delusional beliefs but only the latter is likely to aid the process of disintegration and therefore have therapeutic value as suggested by Chadwick and Lowe (1990).

To demonstrate the difference between hypothetical contradiction and verbal challenge consider a patient who believed he had AIDS. The belief was partly based on the patient's conviction that there was dirt on the needle the doctor had used to take a blood sample from him shortly after his admission. A hypothetical contradiction would be ..."How would you feel if the same doctor came and saw you and reassured you he used a sterile, clean needle?". A verbal challenge would be "How would you feel knowing that only sterile needles are used in hospital. Needles are supplied to the ward pre-packed in sterile containers and are never re-used. Doctors and nurses are trained in the use of germ-free techniques and would wish to protect themselves. Does having this knowledge affect your belief at all?".

The latter is obviously factual information compared with the former which is simply supposition. Those patients who are willing to consider hypothetical contradictions and change their level of conviction in the light of them, even if only temporarily, are more likely to eventually drop their beliefs (Brett-Jones, Garety and Hemsley, 1987), and is thus a measure of their strength or fragility. It is the experience of the author that when working with floridly ill patients in this way it is preferable to keep the hypothetical contradictions as simple and as plausible as possible, otherwise convoluted ideas and propositions could only add to the mental chaos the patient may already be experiencing.

Early Sign Scale

Low self-report ESS scores may occur when insight is low and denial is occurring. This is to some extent compensated for by having an observer version but recruitment of observers on admission wards may be a problem especially where a key worker system does not operate. Reliability and validity may be compromised where numerous different raters, who do not confer, do not complete the questionnaire in consecutive weeks (for example due to holiday, sickness, etc.); or in cases where patients do not remain on the ward.

MODAL PATTERNS OF RECOVERY

In a study by the Early Signs Research Group (in preparation) of 30 randomly selected in-patients suffering from either a relapse or a first episode of schizophrenia, three distinct categories of recovery were observed: type I was defined as complete remission of positive symptoms:

type II was defined as a partial remission of positive symptoms (a PAS score of $\leqslant 4$ when hallucinations and delusions are summed together): type III was defined as little or no change in ratings of positive symptoms; recovery in type III patients was denoted by a decrease in preoccupation with positive symptoms along with favourable behavioural changes.

Within each of these categories, however, different patterns could be detected. Some individuals (40%) showed a continuing decline in self-report ESS score (i.e. non-psychotic symptoms) after total remission or partial remission of positive symptoms (see Figure 3.2); while in others (20%) the ESS score showed no further decline (see Figure 3.8). Non-psychotic symptoms in this latter group of patients were extremely low by the time positive symptoms totally or partially remitted. It may be that the former group pass through a "convalescent" period in recovery roughly equivalent to the prodrome in relapse where the symptoms are predominantly non-psychotic in nature. This would tie in with Donlan and Blacker's stage theory but the problem is that the phenomenon does not appear to be universal. Carr's proposed dimensional model would allow for this discrepancy. If an individual's position on the psychotic disorganisation, psychotic restitution and dysphoria dimensions is not interdependent then dysphoric symptoms may remit simultaneously or at a later stage than positive symptoms. After full or partial remission of positive symptoms, some individuals (20%) showed an increase in non-psychotic symptoms which coincided with a deterioration in mental state; this resulted in re-hospitalisation of all these individuals, except one who

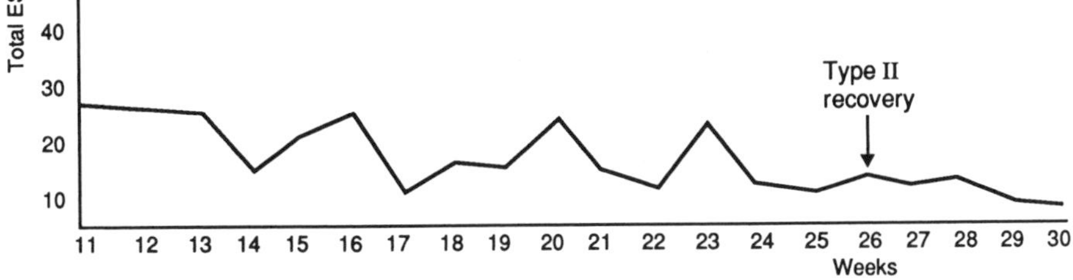

Figure 3.8 Changes in total ESS score during the latter stages of a type II recovery (partial remission of positive symptoms).

underwent "home treatment". In 48% of type I and type II recoveries a total ESS score of below 30 (in three consecutive weeks) for both observer and self-report was a good "rule of thumb" guide to recovery. Of all individuals 20% (predominantly type III recoveries) showed a pattern of fluctuating non-psychotic symptoms with a total ESS score which did not drop below 30; but tended to hover between 30 and 40 once preoccupation with positive symptoms had decreased.

In line with Brett-Jones, Garety and Hemsley (1987) and Chadwick and Lowe (1990) delusional conviction and preoccupation were found to fluctuate independently. Decreases in preoccupation tended to precede decreases in conviction (see Figure 3.6) which is in contrast to the finding of Brett-Jones, Garety and Hemsley (1987) that decreases in conviction preceded decreases in preoccupation. In some cases where delusions remained fixed, preoccupation was the only variable to change. Insight appeared to be inconsistently related to degree of illness as found by McEvoy et al. (1989). Of the 30 patients monitored by the Early Signs Research Group 16 showed a pattern of high insight (score >12) at commencement of monitoring with high insight at discharge; and ten of these 16 patients were seen in the first week after admission (see Figure 3.7). Twelve patients showed a gradual increase in insight during recovery: four of these showed a pattern of low insight (score <6) at commencement of monitoring changing to high insight at discharge; and five patients showed a pattern of low insight at commencement of monitoring and moderate insight at discharge. Two patients showed little change in their low level of insight which was consistent with little change in positive symptoms.

Relabelling of psychotic experiences was the last aspect of insight to show change in over a third of patients; change in other components of insight showed a desynchronous pattern. Fluctuations in insight of first episode patients appeared to be related to "denial" and "coming to terms with the illness". Attitudes of first episode patients towards medication, seeing a doctor and hospitalisation appeared to vacillate much more than patients suffering from a relapse of schizophrenia. Most first episode patients refused to accept their diagnosis and expressed the need to test out the validity of the diagnosis by stopping their medication to see if the illness would return. Patients actively sought out less stigmatising explanations for their symptoms such as stress, abuse of drugs and their upbringing. Taylor and Perkins (1991) suggest denial of the illness may be likened to the denial stage in the ongoing process of grieving after a bereavement whereby disturbing emotions are temporarily refused access to consciousness until more demanding coping strategies such as acceptance can be adopted.

APPLICATIONS AND IMPLICATIONS OF THE MONITORING PROCESS

Timing of medication reduction and discharge

One important application of the monitoring process is that the data generated may be used to assist clinical decisions regarding the timing of medication reduction and discharge. Falling scores on the ESS following the decline of hallucinations and delusions may offer support for a clinical decision to reduce medication. In some individuals whose self-rating ESS score (non-psychotic symptoms) was consistently above 30 during a florid episode; three consecutive weekly total ESS scores below 30 would appear to be a good guide to suitability for discharge providing home circumstances permit. It may be that a low total ESS score (e.g. <10) is a better indicator of true recovery than the cessation of positive symptoms. Of all patients displaying type I and type II recoveries monitored by the Early Signs Research Group (in preparation) 65% were scoring less than ten (self and observer total ESS score) by the completion of monitoring. This score was achieved in most cases one to three months *after* the cessation or stabilisation of positive symptoms. It might be interesting to investigate if those patients whose total ESS score does not drop below 10 after cessation or stabilisation of positive symptoms are more likely to relapse in the first few months post discharge than those patients whose total ESS score does drop below ten. If this were the case it may be that in the former group full recovery has not been achieved so making the individual more vulnerable to stress and other factors. This however awaits further empirical study.

Timing of efforts to accelerate recovery

The monitoring process may indicate when more intensive efforts to accelerate recovery can be employed. When total ESS scores are high (e.g. greater than 50), the emphasis of the relationship should be on the building-up of rapport and trust and the elicitation of core symptoms. As disturbance eases (scores on the ESS in the 30–50 range), other techniques could be employed to speed up the recovery process. These may include attempts to reduce stress, methods to facilitate a search for alternative meanings and explanations of symptoms and experiences and re-engaging the patient in social networks. Indirect and low-key interventions may evolve into more direct and challenging styles as symptoms continue to decline, e.g. offering hypothetical contradictions for delusions may change to verbal challenges; simple one-to-one education may change to discussion with others in a group forum.

Timing of efforts to decrease negative symptoms and increase self-esteem

If efforts are made to "activate" the individual too early this may lead to excessive stimulation and may indeed prolong recovery. The monitoring process could thus give an indication of the best time to engage the individual in group activities and rehabilitation programmes designed to improve confidence, raise self-esteem and decrease negative symptoms.

Fostering long-term engagement of clients with services

Clients who participate in the monitoring process may be more inclined to stay involved with services over the long term as the extra time spent with clients and the process itself is likely to foster the building of rapport and trust. Staff on acute units and in "homecare" models of service provision (see Chapter 11) could find the monitoring process provides them with a useful framework around which to plan care so that they see themselves as having a more positive role.

Throughout this chapter the monitoring of recovery from acute psychosis has been emphasised both as a measurement and therapeutic tool. The community patterns of service provision (Chapter 11) will place greater responsibility upon professional and carer to manage florid illness and it is in this context that the methodology outlined may have particular applications.

Acknowledgement

The Early Signs Research Group would like to thank Research and Development for Psychiatry for their support in funding the study on recovery discussed in this chapter.

REFERENCES

Astrachan, B.M., Brauer, L., Harrow. M. and Schwartz. C. (1974) Symptomatic outcome in schizophrenia. *Archives of General Psychiatry*, **31**, 155–60.
Birchwood, M. (1989) Early Signs Scale (personal communication).

Birchwood, M., Smith, J., Macmillan, F., Hogg, B., Prasad, R., Harvey, C. and Bering, S. (1989) Predicting relapse in schizophrenia: the development and implementation of an early signs monitoring system using patients and families as observers. *Psychological Medicine*, **19**, 649–56.

Birchwood, M., Smith, J., Drury, V., Healy, J. and Slade, M. (1992) The Insight Scale. (Submitted.)

Birchwood, M., Cochrane, R., Macmillan, F., Copestake, S., Kucharska, J. and Cariss, M. (1992) The influence of ethnicity and family structure on relapse in first episode schizophrenia: a comparison of Asian, Caribbean and white patients. *British Journal of Psychiatry* (in press).

Bowers, M.B. Jr. and Astrachan, B.M. (1967) Depression in acute schizophrenic psychosis. *American Journal of Psychiatry*, **123**, 976–9.

Brett-Jones, J., Garety, P. and Hemsley, D. (1987) Measuring delusional experiences: a method and its application. *British Journal of Clinical Psychology*, **26**, 257–65.

Breier, A. and Strauss, J.S. (1984) The role of social relationships in the recovery from psychotic disorders. *American Journal of Psychiatry*, **141**, 949–55.

Brown, G.W., Birley, J.L.T. and Wing, J.K. (1972) The influence of family life on the course of schizophrenia: a replication. *British Journal of Psychiatry*, **121**, 241–58.

Carr, V.J. (1983) Recovery from schizophrenia: a review of patterns of psychosis. *Schizophrenia Bulletin*, **9**, 95–121.

Chadwick, P.D.J. and Lowe, C.F. (1990) The measurement and modification of delusional beliefs. *Journal of Consulting and Clinical Psychology*, **58**, 225–32.

David, A.S. (1990) Insight and psychosis. *British Journal of Psychiatry*, **156**, 798–808.

Dencker, S.J., Frankenberg, K., Lepp, M., Lindberg, D. and Malm, U. (1978) How schizophrenic patients change during 3 years' treatment with depot neuroleptics. *Acta Psychiatrica Scandinavica*, **57**, 115–23.

Donlan, P.T. and Blacker, K.H. (1973) Stages of schizophrenic decompensation and reintegration. *Journal of Nervous and Mental Disease*, **157**, 200–9.

Goldberg, S.C., Klerman, G.L. and Cole, J.O. (1965) Changes in schizophrenic psychopathology and ward behaviour as a function of phenothiazine treatment. *British Journal of Psychiatry*, **111**, 120–33.

Herz, M.I. (1985) Early Signs Questionnaire (personal communication).

Kayton, L. (1973) Good outcome in young adult schizophrenia. *Archives of General Psychiatry*, **29**, 103–10.

Kayton, L. (1975) Clinical features of improved schizophrenics. In: Gunderson, J.G. and Mosher, L.R. (eds), *Psychotherapy of Schizophrenia*, Jason Aronson, New York.

Kayton, L., Beck, J. and Koh, S.D. (1976) Post-psychotic state, convalescent environment and the therapeutic relationship in schizophrenic outcome. *American Journal of Psychiatry*, **133**, 1269–74.

Kellam, S.G., Goldberg, S.C., Schooler, N.R., Berman, A. and Shmelzer, J.L. (1967) Ward atmosphere and outcome of treatment of acute schizophrenia. *Journal of Psychiatric Research*, **5**, 145–63.

Krawiecka, M., Goldberg, D. and Vaughn, M. (1977) Standardised psychiatric assessment scale for chronic psychiatric patients. *Acta Psychiatric Scandinavica*, **36**, 25–31.

Maher, B. and Ross, J.S. (1984) Delusions. In: H.E. Adams and P. Sutker (eds), *Comprehensive Handbook of Psychopathology*, Plenum, New York.

McEvoy, J.P., Apperson, L.J., Applebaun, P.S., Ortlip, P., Brecosky, J., Hammill,

K., Geller, J.L. and Roth, L. (1989) Insight in schizophrenia: its relationship to acute psychopathology. *Journal of Nervous and Mental Disease*, **177**, 43–7.
McGlashan, T.H. and Carpenter, W.T. Jr. (1981) Does attitude towards psychosis relate to outcome? *American Journal of Psychiatry*, **138**, 797–801.
Overall, J.E., Gorham, D.R. and Shawver, J.R. (1961) Basic dimensions of change in the symptomatology of chronic schizophrenics. *Journal of Abnormal and Social Psychology*, **63**, 597–602.
Pious, W.L. (1961) A hypothesis about the nature of schizophrenic behaviour. In: A. Burton (ed.), *Psychotherapy of the Psychoses*, pp. 43–68, Basic Books, New York.
Sachar, E.J., Mason, J.W., Kolmer, H.S. and Artiss, K.L. (1963) Psychoendocrine aspects of acute schizophrenic reactions. *Psychosomatic Medicine*, **25**, 510–37.
Sachar, E.J., Kanter, S.S., Buie, D., Engle, R. and Mehlman, R. (1970) Psychoendocrinology of ego disintegration. *American Journal of Psychiatry*, **125**, 1076–8.
Sacks, M.H., Carpenter, W.T. Jr. and Strauss, J.S. (1974) Recovery from delusions: three phases documented by patients interpretations of research procedures. *Archives of General Psychiatry*, **30**, 117–20.
Simpson, R.B.C. (1989) Expressed emotion and nursing the schizophrenic patient. *Journal of Advanced Nursing*, **14**, 459–66.
Smith, J. and Birchwood, M. (1990) Relatives and patients as partners in the management of schizophrenia. *British Journal of Psychiatry*, **156**, 654–60.
Taylor, K.E. and Perkins, R.E. (1991) Identity and coping with mental illness in long stay psychiatric rehabilitations. *British Journal of Clinical Psychology*, **30**, 73–85.
Wing, J.K., Cooper, J.E. and Sartorius, N. (1974) Measurement and classification of psychiatric symptoms. An instruction manual for the PSE and Catego Program, Cambridge University Press, London.
Wittenborn, J.R. (1977) Stability of symptom ratings for schizophrenic men. *Archives of General Psychiatry*, **34**, 437–40.

Part 2

Treatment

Chapter 4

Interventions with Families

CHRISTINE BARROWCLOUGH AND
NICHOLAS TARRIER

INTRODUCTION

Research programmes designed to assist families in coping with a family member suffering from schizophrenia have generated considerable interest over the last decade. The aims of this chapter are to review the research on these intervention studies and to provide practical guidelines to those who may wish to implement them.

The idea that family environments have a causative role in schizophrenia and the subsequent application of family therapy as a treatment method has a long history (see Falloon, Boyd and McGill, 1984). However, the iatrogenic effects of such family pathology models have now been well documented (Terkelson, 1983; Lefley,1989). In recent years the focus of interest has shifted to the role of family environments in precipitating relapses in vulnerable individuals who have already experienced an episode of schizophrenia: that is, the importance of the domestic environment in the course rather than the aetiology of the illness. If factors in the patient's environment could be identified as contributing to relapse, then in theory, these factors could be modified and relapse prevented. This has been the rationale for family intervention studies.

EARLY INTERVENTIONS STUDIES

Early studies of family interventions were unsuccessful in reducing relapse rates. For example, Hogarty and his colleagues carried out two large scale studies which examined the effects of neuroleptic medication and social case work on relapse (Hogarty et al., 1974a, 1974b, 1979), but neither of these studies reported convincing evidence for the efficacy of the interventions. Similar negative findings were reported by Hudson (1975) and

Innovations in the Psychological Management of Schizophrenia.
Edited by Max Birchwood and Nicholas Tarrier. © 1992 John Wiley & Sons Ltd

Cheek et al. (1971) using operant techniques, although these programmes were somewhat over-simplistic in their conception. The first successful report in favour of family intervention was that by Goldstein et al. (1978) on the use of crisis oriented family therapy. Goldstein and co-workers randomly allocated 104 young first or second episode schizophrenic patients to either moderate or low dose medication and to either psychosocial intervention or standard aftercare. After six weeks there were significant differences in readmission rates for the high dose plus family therapy group (0%) compared to the low dose and standard care (24%). After six months there were still no re-admissions in the high dose and family therapy group. A more recent study comparing family education with family problem solving carried out in a group format found no significant difference in relapses between the two treatments (Ehlert, 1989).

CONTROLLED STUDIES OF FAMILY INTERVENTION BASED ON EE AS A RISK FACTOR

The main impetus for family interventions has been the research on Expressed Emotion (EE). It has been demonstrated in a large number of studies that this index is a remarkably robust predictor of schizophrenic relapse, at least in the short term. Since patients who are discharged into households where a relative is rated high on EE have significantly higher relapse rates, the measure has been viewed not only as a risk factor, but as an explanatory variable in relapse. However, little is known about how EE—essentially a measure of verbal report and tone of voice—translates into a mechanism for relapse in the home environment. From a treatment viewpoint this poses some problems: if the precise nature of stressful interactions in the patient's home cannot be identified, how does one target behaviours for change? In practice, certain assumptions have been made about the kind of problems or deficits associated with high EE families which may contribute to stressful environments: these include misunderstandings about the illness resulting in conflict or unrealistic expectations of the patient; and difficulties with problem solving, communication or coping skills. Interventions have been designed to address these problems, thus reducing EE or ameliorating other sources of stress within the family. These studies are briefly reviewed below, with particular attention directed at outcome measure issues.

Relapse

Most studies have focused on relapse rates as the main outcome measure. The relapse rates achieved by the intervention studies which have targeted high EE families as a high risk group are presented in Table 4.1. Four of these studies demonstrated that family interventions significantly reduced relapse rates when compared to control groups (Falloon et al., 1982; Leff et al., 1982; Hogarty et al., 1986; Tarrier et al., 1988), and a common characteristic of these programmes was the inclusion of both the relative and the patient in the treatment strategies.

Table 4.1 Relapse rates in percentages for high EE households from published Family Intervention studies. Percentages in parentheses represent "treatment takers" only and exclude those who did not complete the intervention programme

Study	Relapse rates (%) 9 or 12 months	24 months
Camberwell Study 1 (Leff et al., 1982, 1985)		
Family intervention	8	20
Routine treatment	50	78
Camberwell Study 2 (Leff et al., 1989, 1990)		
Family therapy	8	33
Relatives groups	17	36
California-USC Study (Falloon et al., 1982, 1985)		
Family intervention	6	17
Individual intervention	44	83
Hamburg Study (Kottgen et al., 1984)		
Group psychodynamic intervention	33	
Control group	43	
Pittsburgh Study (Hogarty et al., 1986, 1987)		
Family intervention	23 (19)	(32)
Social skills training	30 (20)	(42)
Combined FI & SST	9 (0)	(25)
Control group	41	66
Salford Study (Tarrier et al., 1988, 1989)		
Family intervention	12 (5)	33 (24)
Education programme	43	57
Routine treatment	53	60
Sydney Study (Vaughan et al., 1991a)		
Relatives' counselling	41	
Control group	65	

Two studies—the Hamburg (Kottgen et al., 1984) and the Sydney (Vaughan et al., in press (a)) studies—failed to demonstrate a significant reduction in relapse. However, these programmes differed in the nature of their interventions when compared to the four successful ones noted above. The Hamburg study has been criticised on methodological grounds (Vaughn, 1986a); also it was psychoanalytic in orientation, was conducted in a group format, and treated patients and relatives separately. The Sydney study focused solely on the relatives and the research team never saw the patients. A considerable number of patients (58%) were not on medication after discharge, in contrast to the successful studies where medication compliance was good. Furthermore, the research team did not liaise with the team responsible for the patients' clinical management and the intervention itself was relatively short (ten weekly sessions). One other study carried out by Leff and his colleagues (Leff et al., 1989) also focused on the relatives alone, and the results indicated that attending relatives' groups was equivalent to individual family therapy, but the drop-out rate in the relatives' groups was very high and the low subject numbers make the results of this study difficult to interpret. Finally, one study has included a patient-only focused intervention. Hogarty et al. (1986) found that, at least over the first 12 months after discharge, social skills training with the patient alone was equivalent to family management in terms of relapse rates.

Comparisons in the other studies indicate that short educational programmes are ineffective (Tarrier et al., 1988); and that prolonged intervention after the first year prevents relapses proliferating in the second year (Falloon et al., 1985).

From the findings of these studies it is possible to produce a number of guidelines for effective interventions for relapse reduction:

1. Intervention should focus on both relatives and patients in the family unit, but individual intervention with the patient will also be beneficial,
2. Education alone is insufficient, but may be useful as part of a more extensive programme of assistance,
3. Interventions should be maintained over an extended period of time,
4. Interventions should take place in liaison with other aspects of the patient's management, and preferably be integrated with the established mental health services,
5. Intervention should also attempt to maintain medication compliance.

A number of other studies are presently being carried out, although the results from these are not yet available. Of special interest are studies such as the NIMH Collaborative Study and the Munich study which examine the interaction of family management with medication regimes. Why interventions work to reduce relapse is a critical question. All workers in the area have emphasised the importance of stress and stressful home environments but the precise nature of the stressful stimuli in the home have yet to be identified. A series of studies have attempted to examine the effects of the relatives' EE levels on the patients' arousal levels (see Turpin, Tarrier and Sturgeon, 1988; Dawson, Liberman and Mintz, 1989; Tarrier, 1989 for reviews). Although the results of these studies are not completely clear, they suggest that, especially during an acute episode, patients who have been living with a high EE relative have high levels of background tonic arousal and a hyperreactivity to the direct presence of their relative. These psychophysiological studies allow us to produce a tentative explanation of how interventions work. Stressful environments, whether they be in the family home or elsewhere, result in an accumulating increase in the patient's underlying tonic arousal and a hyperreactivity to certain social and environmental stimuli. If this hyperaroused state does not habituate then eventually a threshold is reached and symptoms reappear. This is presumably because high arousal disrupts perceptual processes and information processing capacities. Environments are likely to be stressful when they are complex, unpredictable, ambiguous and emotionally charged, such as living with a critical, hostile or over-involved relative. Interventions will be successful if they decrease the complexity, ambiguity and emotionality and increase the predictability and clarity of the environment. However, it is likely that future research may further refine these hypotheses. There is already some evidence from the literature that criticism and hostility are more predictive of relapse than marked emotional overinvolvement (Hogarty et al., 1986; Vaughan et al., 1991b) and certainly criticism is the more common dimension to score above the high EE threshold in study samples (Vaughn, 1986b). It may be that EE is a binary rather than unitary concept and some aspects of relatives' behaviour included in the high EE classification could present greater stress or problems for patients than other behaviours: for example, coercion may be more stressful than intrusion.

Multiple outcome measures

Although relapse has been the key outcome variable in intervention studies, multiple measures of outcome are more appropriate for assessing the efficacy of work with families (Barrowclough and Tarrier, 1984; Smith and Birchwood, 1990). Some studies have attempted to report other such measures.

Social functioning

Both the California (Falloon, Boyd and McGill, 1984) and Salford (Barrowclough and Tarrier, 1990) studies systematically measured the patient's level of social functioning. Both studies found that patients in the family intervention groups showed significant increases compared to control groups. Leff et al. (1989) reported small but non-significant increases in anecdotal reports on social functioning in patients receiving interventions.

Relatives' burden

There is evidence to suggest that relatives carry a considerable burden in caring for the mentally ill (Creer and Wing, 1974; Fadden, Kuipers and Bebbington, 1987). Controlled trials of community care versus traditional care have not shown a reduction in family burden in the former (Test and Stein, 1980; Reynolds and Hoult, 1984) and there is concern that increasing moves to implement community care and family management will result in extra burden on the family. Falloon and his colleagues (Falloon and Pederson, 1985) have attempted to address this issue. They found decreases in relatives' subjective burden, social and clinical morbidity and increases in family coping behaviour for families receiving family intervention. The authors suggested that these improvements resulted from decreases in positive symptoms and disruptive behaviour in the study patients.

Consumer satisfaction

The acceptability of family interventions by the "consumers" or service recipients is an important but frequently ignored variable. This is important both because it reflects on the quality of the service but also because of a backlash against psychosocial research (e.g. Hatfield, 1987), given that families have at best been implicated in the poor prognosis of patients and at worst blamed for causing schizophrenia. In the Salford study all relatives reported that they were at least "fairly satisfied" with the intervention, and 88% said they were "extremely satisfied". Similarly, 75% indicated that the specific help they had received had been "extremely helpful". This was so even when the relatives did not necessarily feel optimistic about the patients' future recovery.

Economic considerations

Economic factors are becoming increasingly more important in the planning of health services. It is no longer sufficient for the researcher to demonstrate the clinical efficacy of their intervention. The economic viability must also be proven. Of the intervention studies described, two attempted some type of economic analysis. Falloon and his colleagues (Cardin, McGill and Falloon, 1986) undertook a detailed analysis of all direct and indirect costs to the patients, families, health, welfare and community agencies associated with their intervention. A cost-benefit analysis of the twelve month data showed the total costs for family management were 19% less than for individually managed patients (Cardin, McGill and Falloon, 1986). A much less ambitious analysis of the Salford project was undertaken by Tarrier, Lowson and Barrowclough (1991), and only direct costs were analysed. The treatment of patients who received family intervention showed an overall saving of 37% over the high EE control groups, and a saving of 27% on mean per patient costs. In both these studies reducing in-patient days was a big factor in reducing costs.

Working with the families of schizophrenic patients: some practical guidelines

We have emphasised the fact that there are aspects of the relationship between schizophrenic relapse and the behaviour of relatives which are poorly understood. "High EE" relatives are a heterogeneous group, representing a range of problems, coping styles and interaction patterns as well as unique strengths and assets. Thus there are no "cookbook" answers as to the most important targets for behaviour change in relatives, and packages of techniques are premature and inappropriate. Additionally, a cause and effect model of EE and schizophrenic relapse is over simplistic, and it would be unfortunate if therapists adopted such a viewpoint. Illness factors—chronicity and severity of symptoms including behavioural disturbances—may well contribute to the development of problems in families and in difficulties in managing behaviour. Moreover, it is misleading to conceptualise all low EE relatives as calm, effective copers who facilitate rehabilitation and reduce the risk of relapses by creating a stress free domestic atmosphere. Given the severe and pervasive consequences of the illness, one should not assume that any relative of a schizophrenia sufferer is without difficulties; and it has been suggested that a lack of marked criticism or over involvement may sometimes be a function of "burn out" with the distancing of the relative from the patient's problems (Vaughn, in press (b)), or that relapse reduction in low EE homes may be at the cost of reduced social functioning (Birchwood and Smith, 1987). Additionally, it has been suggested that low EE relatives may develop "high EE behaviours" if the patient deteriorates.

These considerations indicate that training in EE assessments is not a necessary prerequisite for working with the families and a "needs led" rather than "EE reduction" approach is more appropriate for clinical practice. Moreover, there should be multiple measures of treatment efficacy and focusing on relapse prevention may obscure the needs of individual families. However, some understanding of the EE measure is helpful in providing a framework for evaluating coping strategies and in pointing to areas of possible need. The Salford intervention study adopted an approach whereby the individual needs of family members were assessed while knowledge about EE informed the therapists' framework for setting priorities for behaviour change. The following guidelines are derived from the study's intervention format.

INITIAL ASSESSMENTS

A comprehensive and detailed assessment of the individual and collective needs of family members is essential to successful intervention with the family. This should be a collaborative exercise whereby the therapists assist the family to express and clarify their difficulties, as well as highlighting their strengths and resources. It is useful to see family members individually for initial assessments so that rapport can be established with individuals and they have the opportunity to assert their own problems, their particular perspective of the situation and any interpersonal difficulties within the family situation. The interactive nature of many problems in the family context is acknowledged, and will be further assessed as the intervention progresses.

The relatives

Six broad assessment themes should be covered during the initial interviewing since these will be critical to the intervention components:

1. Distress in relatives and situations (including thoughts) that trigger distress.
2. Coping strategies used to deal with both positive and negative symptoms, and what effect these have on family members and the patient.
3. The relative's understanding about the illness, the symptoms, medication and so on.
4. The consequences of the illness on the relative, including any restrictions (e.g. to social life, occupation) and financial hardship.
5. The relationship with the patient and the identification of dissatisfactions the relative has about particular aspects of his or her behaviour.
6. Areas of strength: for example an effective coping strategy, social supports, positive relationship with the patient.

The Camberwell Family Interview (CFI) (see Leff and Vaughn, 1985) provides an excellent format for assessing these areas. Since many practitioners may not have access to this instrument some of its important content areas are listed in Table 4.2.

Following the content areas outlined in the table, the interview should establish the chronological history of the patient's illness from the viewpoint of the relative. A time period of the last three months can be used to focus on current problems or symptoms that the relative perceives the patient to be experiencing in the home or community environment. Some details of the nature, frequency and context of such difficulties should be established, the relative's behaviour and feelings in response to the problems, the reactions of other family members, and so on. A more detailed analysis of the behaviours can be made in later stages of the assessment and intervention. The initial interview aims to establish the broad areas of difficulty and to develop rapport with the relative by facilitating them in giving an overview of events and their reactions. Attention should be paid to the assessment of communication problems between family members, and particularly the frequency of expressions of

Table 4.2 Content areas for relative assessment interview

1. *Background information*
Who lives in the household? (their age, sex, relationship to patient, employment) any recent changes in the household composition?
The contact time of the relative and other household members with the patient

2. *Psychiatric history of the patient*
Obtain a chronological account of the history of the illness, beginning "when did you first notice something different about .....'s behaviour"
For all problems or symptoms mentioned ask about onset, severity, context, reactions and effects on the relative and other household members
Note hospital admissions and the reactions of the relative to these

3. *Current problems/ symptoms*
Has the patient experienced problems with sleep/appetite/bodily complaints/under or overactivity/ slowness/ withdrawal/ fears–anxiety/ worry/ depression/self-care/ delusions/hallucinations/odd behaviour/finances/drugs or alcohol?
The nature, severity, frequency of the problems and relatives' reactions and coping responses as well as those of other family members should be ascertained

4. *Relationships between family members*
Irritability/tension or quarrelling from or between members of the household (including the patient) should be assessed

5. *General information about the relative*
Social, occupational activities and interests of the relative; relationship with the patient and other household members; how relationships and activities and interests have been affected by the illness

irritability or the occurrence of disagreements or arguments in the household. It is a good idea to emphasise that irritability and arguing are normal within families and particularly in the context of mental illness, to make relatives feel more at ease with this line of questioning. For example, when discussing the presence of irritability in the patient, the CFI introduces this with: "one of the ways in which this kind of trouble affects people is to make them more snappy, or more likely to fly off the handle at things that would't normally worry them ...". After establishing any irritability of the patient, examples of how this occurs and with which family members should be sought, as well as any examples of arguments or disputes between other family members. The latter might be introduced by suggesting that most people in families disagree or argue from time to time.

The interview may take an hour and a half or longer to complete, since it is often the first time that the relative has been encouraged to talk at length about their experiences. More than one meeting may be necessary for this. It is useful to audiotape the session(s), with the relative's permission, so that its content may be understood and summarised in terms of the relatives's difficulties, strengths and their areas of need (see below).

Other assessments which are useful following from the interview include:

1. A measure of psychological distress in the relative, for example the General Health Questionnaire (GHQ) (Goldberg, 1972) or the Symptom Rating Test (Kellner and Sheffield, 1973).
2. The Family Questionnaire (FQ) (Barrowclough and Tarrier, 1987: Tarrier and Barrowclough, 1987). This is a checklist of patient focused problems. Forty-nine problems are described with one open "other" category to allow for any idiosyncratic difficulties. The relative is requested to indicate, on three 5-point scales, the frequency with which the behaviours occur, the amount of distress the behaviours cause them, and how well they feel able to cope with the difficulty.

Following the interview and the administration of other assessments, it is useful to summarise the relative's situation in terms of their problems, needs and strengths. An example is given in Table 4.3.

Such a constructional approach (Goldiamond, 1974) to difficulties should not be seen as a simple restatement of problems: translating problems into needs shifts the emphasis of the assessment away from family deficits and focuses on directions for positive change. The intervention does not seek to eradicate problems but rather to help formulate and meet the needs of the family using and acknowledging whatever resources they have available. Although problems and needs are categorised in Table 4.3, it is apparent that there is a lot of overlap between categories. For example, sources of distress are also coping difficulties and may arise from lack of

Table 4.3 An example of problems, needs and strengths of a relative (mother) summarised from interview, GHQ and FQ assessments

Problems	Needs
Distress Reports of anxiety with specific situations (e.g. patient drinking excessively and not complying with medication); general worries concerning future of her son; and disagreement with husband about how to react to son's inactivity leading to distress of the mother	Alternative ways of coping with situations that trigger anxiety; further assessment of nature of worries; help with communication and problem solving of difficulties with her husband and son
Coping Strategies Difficulty dealing with the son staying in bed during the day, and how to react to delusional self-talk (as well as situations above)	Problem-solving and advice on coping strategies
Knowledge about illness Feelings of guilt about contributing to the illness cause, belief that delusions are controllable by son, worries that medication is addictive	Information about the illness and its treatment
Restrictions to own life style Little contact with friends due to attending to son's problems and embarrassment about his condition and behaviour; holidays and social life with husband much reduced	To re-establish pleasurable social activities
Dissatisfactions with patient behaviour Annoyed by son's inactivity and lack of attention to personal hygiene	Assistance with helping son to change behaviours, or in coping with the negative symptoms
Strengths Keen to work with family programme, support from husband and daughter, several friends who live locally, positive relationship with son, evidence of successful coping with some problems in past, has maintained and enjoyed a part time job	

understanding about the illness. The function of the summary is to clarify areas of need and to feed these back to the relative; and to indicate the directions of assistance that the intervention might take: success in one aspect of intervention may well facilitate change in another area or meet more than one of the relative's needs.

The patient

If possible, the patient should be interviewed and similar content areas discussed as used with the relatives. In this way, a chronological account of the illness might be obtained from the patient; their report of past and particularly current symptomatology sought and how it has affected or continues to affect everyday activities; details of how the illness has affected his/her life generally; and the nature of any problems in the family or community contexts discussed. In practice, long interviews and detailed questioning of the patient may be impossible, particularly when the patient is acutely ill or actively psychotic. As with the relatives, the aim of the assessment is to identify problems and strengths so that areas of need may be ascertained.

Three broad areas of assessment are important, and it is advisable to use some form of assessment scales to obtain information about them.

1. *Symptomatology*. The Psychiatric Assessment Scale (PAS) (Krawiecka, Goldberg and Vaughan, 1977) is useful for assessing current symptomatology. The reports of other members of the interdisciplinary team should be sought, as well as relatives' assessments and the patient's own report. Past symptomatology may be examined from these reports and careful reading of hospital case notes.
2. *Social functioning*. The Social Assessment Scale (SAS) (Birchwood et al., 1990) is recommended. This may be completed using the relative(s) as informant.
3. *Patient strengths*. This assessment should include the interests of the patient (especially including past interests since often the patient has few current activities or interests); skills and areas of competency; social supports and friends (including positive contacts with agencies such as day care).

The interventions

The interventions may be divided into three components: education about the illness, stress management including coping strategies, and goal setting for patient behaviour change. It should be emphasised that:

1. These components should not be seen as discrete or time limited: for example, giving relatives information about schizophrenia does not end when the education component has been "delivered" to the relatives.
2. The aim of the interventions is to address the needs of the family and accordingly, with each family some components or intervention aspects

will be much more important than others: for example, where relatives are experiencing very high levels of distress and/or where the patient is severely handicapped by unremitting psychotic symptoms, it may be more appropriate to concentrate on helping the relative to manage their distress and to cope with difficult patient behaviours than to set goals aimed at directly changing patient behaviour.
3. Assessment is an integral part of treatment, and each intervention begins with a detailed analysis which takes as a starting point the information collected in the initial assessments with the patient and relatives.
4. At all times, it is important to communicate assessments and interventions with members of the multidisciplinary team who are involved with the patient's treatment.

Education

Beginning the interventions with education about schizophrenia has several useful functions, not least of which is to help "engage" the family members in treatment. Many relatives have been told very little about the illness and most regard access to detailed information about schizophrenia as a need of high priority. The education sessions also serve to present the theoretical framework or rationale in which other work with the family will take place. This rationale emphasises that schizophrenia is a stress-related, biological illness influenced in its course by the social environment: the family members are in no way to blame for having caused the illness, but on the contrary are an important resource in assisting in the patient's recovery.

Assessment prior to giving information

1. In accordance with the collaborative approach to intervention which we have advocated, an understanding of the relatives' beliefs and attitudes about the illness in general and the symptoms of the patient in particular is a necessary precondition to establishing an interactive mode of information presentation rather than delivering a lecture about schizophrenia. If they have not already received much information, it is likely that they will have formulated some ideas of their own, and if they have had some education about the illness they may still have misconceptions and areas of ignorance. Information from the initial interviews will be useful, and it is advisable to collect more detailed information using for example, the Knowledge about Schizophrenia Interview (KASI) (Barrowclough et al., 1987). The KASI aims to assess the relative's

information, beliefs and attitudes about six broad aspects of the illness:
Diagnosis—what kind of problem does the relative think the patient is being treated for?
Symptomatology—does the relative believe the "key" symptoms (such as the relative themself has identified) are part, of the illness or personality related? Is the relative aware of florid symptoms? Do they understand that negative symptoms are features of the illness?
Aetiology—what caused the illness according to the relative?
Medication—is the relative aware of the long term and prophylactic nature of the medication?
Prognosis—does the relative accept the possibility of recurrence and what does he/she think might cause relapse?
Management—what does the relative think he/she should or shouldn't do to assist the patient's recovery?

2. It is also advisable to have a detailed knowledge of the patient's past and present psychopathology: the content of their delusions, nature of hallucinations, behaviours related to these symptoms (e.g. belief that the TV is broadcasting their thoughts is associated with refusal to enter TV room or smashing of TV set), negative symptoms, and variation in symptoms across episodes of acute illness. Is the patient aware of the diagnosis? Do they accept that they have a mental illness? Do they have any objections to disclosing details of their symptoms to their wife, mother, father or other relatives?

A useful format for giving the information component when there is more than one key relative is to assess the relatives' existing level of knowledge in short individual sessions and to present information to them collectively. There are no hard and fast rules as to when and how to include the patient in the sessions: factors such as the age of the patient, their relationship to the relative and their current level of functioning may influence such decisions. A parallel but separate information-giving session for the patient is often useful, with their joint attendance at the end of the relatives' session or at a later session with the rest of the family. In the first instance allowing the relatives to see the therapist without the patient present may be preferable: there are often questions the relative wants to raise which they would feel uncomfortable talking about if the patient were there. For example, will she ever work again? will he ever recover? as well as issues of guilt or embarrassment about the problems. One of the benefits of having the patient attend the later discussion of the illness with the relatives can be their communication of feelings and thoughts experienced during the illness. The relatives only see behavioural correlates of florid symptoms and may be unaware of the thinking and fears behind seemingly impulsive and bizarre behaviours. However not all patients will be able to or will wish to communicate their "experiential" symptoms.

The education component of the intervention may involve two or more initial sessions. The first would consist of a brief assessment followed by presentation and discussion of information paying particular attention to misunderstandings about the illness that the relative holds. Details of aspects of the condition that the relative simply does not know can be given. Discussion should be prompted referring frequently to the relatives' beliefs about the condition (for example, "when we were talking earlier you mentioned that you felt that Peter stayed in bed too much and you wondered whether this was due to his medication or because he was lazy. Another explanation could be the illness itself. Some of the symptoms of the illness are called negative symptoms.These symptoms include difficulty in doing ordinary things, and it is quite common that people want to sleep or to lie around more than usual.") Acceptance of the relative's viewpoint while suggesting alternative explanations is the starting point of changing the relatives' beliefs and engaging them in a more positive approach to the management of patient difficulties. Care should be taken not to overload the relative with too much information or with medical jargon. The aim is to help the relatives acquire information likely to have a beneficial influence on their interactions with the patient rather than to learn academic or technical knowledge.

It is useful to see relatives and patients together for the latter part of the session, and if appropriate the patient is encouraged to describe the thinking which directed his or her actions during periods of acute illness and disturbed behaviour. A short interval between the first education session and follow up is advisable during which time the family is asked to read an information booklet covering the material presented in the session. Relatives occasionally become worried or misunderstand information. An early second appointment provides an opportunity for discussion of such difficulties.

At the second appointment relatives and patient may be seen together, and further discussion prompted. The therapist should actively encourage the relatives to consider any problems they have in assimilating explanations about the illness and its treatment which differ from those previously held. For example, "when we talked earlier, you said that you were worried that your daughter might get addicted to the medication and would be better off without it. What do you think about that now?" A post test of knowledge following this session is useful in assessing areas where further attitude or belief change will be important, since it is unlikely that relatives, particularly those where patients have a long history of illness, will change all their views after a brief educational component.

Stress management and coping responses

This component of the intervention focuses primarily on the needs of the relatives and aims to reduce their levels of reported distress using cognitive behavioural approaches. The decision whether or not to include the patient for all or part of the sessions depends as always on the needs of the family. A flexible approach is the most useful, allowing relatives some time to discuss assessment of stressors without the patient present when the patient may be seen in a parallel session, but bringing the family together to assess situations or to plan change strategies that involve interactions between members.

The component should be introduced with a clear rationale. Some relatives may misguidedly think that they are to blame for the illness or are not coping as well as they might, so care should be taken to not to strengthen these ideas. The rationale might emphasise the following points:

1. Living with a person who suffers from schizophrenia can be very difficult, and most relatives feel stressed and upset, at least some of the time.
2. When the patient returns to live with the family, a lot of the day-to-day help and rehabilitation is carried out by family members. Hence it is important to make sure that they have help in managing their stress and coping with difficult situations if they are to effectively help the patient.
3. Additionally, people who suffer from schizophrenia are unusually sensitive to stress in others, so by feeling more in control oneself, you may indirectly help the patient.

Assessment

As with all cognitive behavioural interventions, a detailed assessment of agreed problems with feedback to the relatives encouraging active participation in finding ways to control and thus reduce stressful situations is the format of the intervention. Hence assessment should be seen as an integral part of treatment. A simple explanation of the tripartite analysis of stress—thoughts, feelings and behaviour—is given, following which relatives are encouraged to give examples of situations which have triggered stress responses in the previous week. Examples from the initial interview or other assessment source may be suggested by the therapist. For example from Table 4.3, the relative would be encouraged to describe thoughts, feelings and behaviours associated with the situations given under "distress" and "coping strategies" headings. The relatives would then be given practice in recording the situations and their responses, and asked to complete individual records of instances which occur during the interval before the next session. These records are then used at subsequent sessions to build up descriptive behavioural analyses of the antecedents and consequences (cognitive, behavioural, physical) of problem situations at home; and the analyses are fed back to the relatives whose collaboration is sought in finding more effective ways of coping with the situations.

Example 1
A mother lives alone with her son, John, a man in his late thirties who has an 18-year history of schizophrenia with unremitting delusions of persecution. John received a monthly depot injection at the local health centre. Each month the day before it was due he would typically announce to his mother that he was going to phone the centre, refuse to have the injection and tell the staff what he thought of them, that is, verbally abuse them and accuse them of plotting against him to make him ill. His mother became extremely distressed and tense, wondering what she would do if he missed the injection and became more ill and was concerned that he would swear at and abuse the centre staff. She felt responsible for John's behaviour: "What will they think of me, letting him phone?" was a predominant thought. She would attempt to reason with John not to phone, an argument would ensue, with John swearing and shouting at his mother. The situation would continue throughout the day, with John threatening to phone and his mother repeatedly attempting to dissuade him. Eventually he would phone and abuse the staff.

Further details of the situation were elicited at interview. "When did you first begin to feel stressed?" The mother reported that she picked up "signs" that John was going to be difficult some time before the problem began, and she would feel physically tense and anticipate difficulties. "What happened when John made the phone call?" It emerged that the staff would usually persuade John to come in for his injection, which he did if not the next day then some days later. Alternative strategies to cope with the situation were explored, including the mother telling John she thought it was important to get his injection, but to phone the centre if he wanted to speak to the staff about it. The consequences of such a strategy were discussed, and the mother's thoughts were challenged, e.g. "the staff will think I'm terrible for letting him speak like that, causing them all that trouble", "If I don't try and persuade him he may not get his medication". The alternative response was role played with the therapist, and work was done helping the mother to calm her anticipatory anxiety with positive self statements when she expected the situation to arise. When the mother felt confident to do so, the strategies were implemented, reviewed and modified, and further difficult situations were then targeted.

Example 2
Andrew was in his mid-twenties, had a three-year history of schizophrenia and lived with his parents. He would frequently leave the bathroom in an untidy state. The father reported that this made him very annoyed. He would think "He's lazy, ill or not, he should be able to hang his clothes up". He would tell his wife who felt that the untidy bathroom was a trivial matter, and since it was she who cleaned the house, did not understand why her husband was annoyed. She felt that her husband was not concerned enough with Andrew's problems and that he did not understand the illness. Andrew's father felt that his wife was "too soft" on the son.

Further analysis of the situation determined that it was usual that the situation was discussed in the mornings when both parents were rushing out to work. It was agreed that they should discuss their attitudes to the son's behaviour more fully at a more appropriate time and reach a consensus agreement. They decided to include Andrew in the discussion about the bathroom, and he agreed to attempt to be tidier, i.e. not leave his clothes and the wet towel on the floor. The therapist discussed the negative symptoms of schizophrenia and the importance of using prompts to initiate behaviours. The use of prompts was rehearsed with the parents in this particular situation, and the assumptions of the father about using prompts were challenged, e.g. "I shouldn't have to remind him to do ordinary things" and of the mother about her husband's behaviour, e.g. "getting annoyed about Andrew and the bathroom means that he doesn't care about his son's real problems".

The approach outlined for intervening to reduce stress in relatives emphasises the following points:

1. A detailed analysis of situations associated with stress is essential, including the interactive nature for other family members. The use of role play may facilitate assessment.
2. It is important to look for predictability in situations. Much stress in relatives is cumulative resulting from difficulties accruing over time. Feelings of irritability, tension or arguments are more understandable and controllable if the pattern of their escalation is highlighted.
3. Patient-focused behaviour may often be the trigger for feelings of stress, but the perceived or actual reactions of other people, especially members of the family, may be the most important factors in increasing and maintaining stress.
4. The use of role play to rehearse alternative strategies is important for their effective implementation. Cognitive factors, for example beliefs about the illness which conflict with proposed strategies or dysfunctional assumptions about the behaviour of others, may interfere with implementation and should be dealt with in the sessions.

Goal setting

One of the principal aims of the intervention is to improve the social functioning of the patient. Using the format of goal planning and seeing the whole family together, the aim is to teach the family a constructional approach to the problems of family members. This entails seeing problems as needs which might be best met through promoting positive behaviour change.

Assessment

The chief assessment tool is a strengths/needs list which is completed about the patient, but which may include the needs of other family members. This tabulates on the one hand the patient's abilities, interests and resources and on the other hand difficulties, issues or problems. Family members (including the patient) are asked to complete this individually, and the patient is encouraged to include items pertaining to his relatives. The lists are then pooled and information from earlier assessments, for example initial interviews or questionnaires are used by the therapist to identify further issues of concern. It is often necessary to probe for patient strengths, for example what were the patient's interests before the illness? Are the family overlooking patient abilities as too ordinary to mention, but which may be important for future plans, for example the ability to drive or a particular work skill? An example of a strengths/needs list is given in Table 4.4.

Intervention

1. The needs of the family are reviewed and rank ordered by the family in terms of priority and being realistic to achieve in the short term. It is important that the needs are seen as important to the patient, or are linked to other needs which have higher priority for him or her. For example, doing the housework may have priority for the relatives, whereas the patient may only be concerned with getting his or her own accommodation in the case of a parental household. The patient may see that improving say cooking skills would be an advantage and a step

Table 4.4 Example of a strengths/needs list and goal plan for a teenage girl living with her parents

Strengths	Problems/Issues areas for change	Needs
Interests music, clothes, reading, tennis, seeing friends, watching "soaps" on TV, *Abilities* 'O' levels and good academic record at school, typing, driving licence, cooking skills, good listener and enjoys helping others *Resources* parents, sister and several friends and relatives keen to help; school helpful to assist her return	*parents won't leave me alone in house *worry about missing school *feeling tired & lethargic *overweight spends a lot of time in bed, doing very little when up, avoiding friends and relatives, not interested in personal appearance	1. Parents to discuss and plan to go out without daughter 2. Return to school 3. Review tiredness 4. Reduce weight 5. Get back to reasonable getting up/bedtimes 6. Engage in more activities 7. Get back to seeing friends/relatives 8. Take more interest in personal appearance

* problems identified by the patient

towards independent living whereas cutting the grass may hold no interest or incentive.
2. After identifying the need, the strengths list is scanned for approaches that might be used to meet the need.
3. A goal is then set and stated in clear behavioural terms and where necessary it is broken down into small quickly attainable steps.
4. The relatives' and patient's participation in the goal step is reviewed be this an active, facilitating, or passive role—the latter being desirable if the relative's response is intrusive or fosters dependency.
5. At the next session progress with the goal step may be reviewed, efforts reinforced, goals changed, abandoned or new steps commenced.

In using goal setting with schizophrenic patients it is important to incorporate prompts into the execution of plans and also to maximise the reinforcing value of achieving goal steps: a common difficulty for patients is in initiating behaviour and the patient may feel that the effort required to perform a task may not be equal to the subjective value of the goal. Hence the importance of beginning with small steps which achieve goals of importance to the client. Any failure to achieve the goals should be viewed as a planning failure, since one otherwise risks reducing the low self efficacy of the patient and further diminishing their "motivation", and possibly in making the relatives feel that the patient "is not trying".

SOME CONCLUDING COMMENTS

The above guidelines are intended for working with individual families. We know rather less about the efficacy of working with groups of relatives, and there do seem to be problems of maintaining relatives' attendance at group meetings. Even with individually planned sessions, many of the reviewed studies have families who decline help or who quickly drop out, and where patients in these families have been followed up, they appear to have a poor prognosis (Smith and Birchwood, 1990). A commitment to working with the family over an extended time period is important, with a nine months to a year time frame of weekly/fortnightly then monthly appointments, followed by less frequent but regular contact. Engaging the family in interventions may be more difficult in cases of longstanding illness, where relatives have had little previous support, and have become alienated from services. A collaboration between relatives, patients and practitioners is required to extend the optimism of research findings into clinical practice.

REFERENCES

Barrowclough, C. and Tarrier, N. (1984) Psychosocial interventions with families and their effects on the course of schizophrenia: a review. *Psychological Medicine*, **14**, 629–42.

Barrowclough, C. and Tarrier, N. (1987) A behavioural family intervention with a schizophrenic patient: a case study. *Behavioural Psychotherapy*, **15**, 252–71.

Barrowclough, C. and Tarrier, N. (1990) Social functioning in schizophrenic patients. I: The effects of expressed emotion and family intervention. *Social Psychiatry and Psychiatric Epidemiology*, **25**, 125–9.

Barrowclough, C., Tarrier, N., Watts, S., Vaughn, C., Bamrah, J.S. and Freeman, H. (1987) Assessing the functional value of relatives' reported knowledge about schizophrenia. *British Journal of Psychiatry*, **151**, 1–8.

Birchwood, M. and Smith, J. (1987) Schizophrenia and the family. In: Orford, J. (ed.), *Coping with Disorder in the Family*, Lawrence Erlbaum, London.

Birchwood, M., Smith, J., Cochrane, R., Wetton, S. and Copestake, S. (1990) The social functioning scale: the development and validation of a scale of social adjustment for use in family intervention programmes with schizophrenic patients. *British Journal of Psychiatry*, **157**, 853–9.

Cardin, V.A., McGill, C.W. and Falloon, I.R.H. (1986) An economic analysis: costs, benefits and effectiveness. In: Falloon, I.R.H. (ed.), *Family Management of Schizophrenia*, John Hopkins University Press, Baltimore.

Cheek, F.E., Laucius, J., Mahnoke, M. and Beck, R. (1971) A behavior modification training programme for parents of convalescent schizophrenics. In: Rubin, R. (ed.), *Advances in Behaviour Therapy*, Vol. 3, Academic Press, New York.

Creer, C. and Wing, J.K. (1974) *Schizophrenia in the Home*, National Schizophrenia Fellowship, Surbiton.

Dawson, M.E., Liberman, R.P. and Mintz, L.I. (1989) Sociophysiology of expressed emotion in the course of schizophrenia. In: Barchoz, P. (ed.), *Sociophysiology of Social Relationships*, Oxford University Press, New York.

Ehlert, U. (1989) Psychosocial intervention for relatives of schizophrenic patients. In: Emmelkamp, P., Everaed, W., Kraaimaat, F. and van Son, M. (eds), *Advances In Theory and Practice in Behaviour Therapy*, Swets & Zeitlinger, Amsterdam.

Fadden, G., Kuipers, I. and Bebbington, P. (1987) The burden of care: the impact of functional psychiatric illness on the patient's family. *British Journal of Psychiatry*, **150**, 285–92.

Falloon, I.R.H. and Pederson, J. (1985) Family management in the prevention of morbidity of schizophrenia: the adjustment of the family unit. *British Journal of Psychiatry*, **147**, 156–63.

Falloon I.R.H., Boyd, J.L., McGill, C.W., Razani, J., Moss, H.B. and Gilderman, A.M. (1982) Family management in the prevention of exacerbations of schizophrenia. *New England Journal of Medicine*, **306**, 1437–40.

Falloon, I.R.H., Boyd, J.L. and McGill, C. (1984) *Family Care of Schizophrenia*, Guilford Press, New York.

Falloon, I.R.H., Boyd, J.L., McGill, C.W., Williamson, M., Razani, J., Moss, H.B., Gilderman, A.M. and Simson, G.M. (1985) Family management in the prevention of morbidity of schizophrenia: clinical outcome of a two year longitudinal study. *Archives of General Psychiatry*, **42**, 887–96.

Goldberg, D. (1972) *The Detection of Psychiatric Illness by Questionnaire*, Maudsley Monographs No. 21, Oxford University Press, London.

Goldiamond, I. (1974) Towards a constructional approach to social problems:

ethical and constitutional issues raised by applied behaviour analysis. *Behaviourism*, **2**, 1–84.

Goldstein, M.J., Rodnick, E.H., Evans, J.R., May, P.R. and Steinberg, M.R. (1978) Drug and family therapy in the aftercare of acute schizophrenia. *Archives of General Psychiatry*, **35**, 1169–77.

Hatfield, A.B. (1987) The expressed emotion theory: why families object. *Hospital and Community Psychiatry*, **38**, 341.

Hogarty, G., Goldberg, S., Schooler, N.R., Ulrich, R.F. and EPICS Collaborative Study Group (1974a) Drug and sociotherapy in the aftercare of schizophrenic patients. II: Two year relapse rates. *Archives of General Psychiatry*, **31**, 603–8.

Hogarty, G., Goldberg, S., Schooler, N.R. and EPICS Collaborative Study Group (1974b) Drug and sociotherapy in the aftercare of schizophrenic patients. III: Adjustment of non-relapsed patients. *Archives of General Psychiatry*, **31**, 609–18.

Hogarty, G., Schooler, N.R., Ulrich, R.F., Mussare, F., Ferro, P. and Herron, E. (1979) Fluphenazine and social therapy in the aftercare of schizophrenic patients. *Archives of General Psychiatry*, **36**, 1283–94.

Hogarty, G., Anderson, C.M., Reiss, D.J., Kornblith, S.J., Greenwald, D.P., Javan, C.D. and Madonia, M.J. (1986) Family psychoeducation, social skills training and maintenance chemotherapy in the aftercare treatment of schizophrenia. 1: One-year effects of a controlled study on relapse and expressed emotion. *Archives of General Psychiatry*, **43**, 633–42.

Hogarty, G., Anderson, C.M. and Reiss, D.J. (1987) Family psychoeducation, social skills training and medication in schizophrenia: the long and the short of it. *Psychopharmacological Bulletin*, **23**, 12–13.

Hudson, B. (1975) A behaviour modification project with chronic schizophrenics in the community. *Behaviour Research and Therapy*, **13**, 339–41.

Kellner, R. and Sheffield, B.F. (1973) A self-rating scale of distress. *Psychological Medicine*, **3**, 101–6.

Kottgen, C., Sonnichsen, I., Mollenhauer, K. and Jurth, R. (1984) Results of the Hamburg Camberwell family Interview study, I–III. *International Journal of Family Psychiatry*, **5**, 61–94.

Krawiecka, M., Goldberg, D. and Vaughan, M. (1977) A standardised psychiatric assessment scale for rating chronic psychotic patients. *Acta Psychiatrica Scandinavica*, **55**, 299–308.

Leff, J. and Vaughn, C. (1985). *Expressed Emotion in Families: Its Significance for Mental Illness*, Guilford Press, New York.

Leff, J., Kuipers, L., Berkowitz, R., Eberlein-Fries, R. and Sturgeon, D. (1982) A controlled trial of intervention in the families of schizophrenic families. *British Journal of Psychiatry*, **141**, 121–34.

Leff, J., Kuipers, L., Berkowitz, R. and Sturgeon, D. (1985) A controlled trial of social intervention in the families of schizophrenic patients: Two year follow-up. *British Journal of Psychiatry*, **146**, 594–600.

Leff, J., Berkowitz, R., Shavit, A., Strachan, A., Glass, I. and Vaughn, C. (1989) A trial of family therapy v. a relatives group for schizophrenia. *British Journal of Psychiatry*, **154**, 58–66.

Leff, J., Berkowitz, R., Shavit, A., Strachan, A., Glass, I. and Vaughn, C. (1990) A trial of family therapy v. a relatives group for schizophrenia: Two-year follow-up. *British Journal of Psychiatry*, **157**, 571–7.

Lefley, H.P. (1989) Family burden and family stigma in major mental illness. *American Psychologist*, **44**, 556–60.

Reynolds, I. and Hoult, J. (1984) The relatives of the mentally ill: a comparative trial of community-oriented and hospital-oriented psychiatric care. *Journal of Nervous and Mental Disease*, **172**, 480–9.

Smith, J. and Birchwood, M. (1990) Relatives and patients as partners in the management of schizophrenia: the development of a service model. *British Journal of Psychiatry*, **156**, 654–60.

Tarrier, N. (1989) Electrodermal activity, expressed emotion and outcome in schizophrenia. *British Journal of Psychiatry*, **155** (Suppl. 5), 51–6.

Tarrier, N. and Barrowclough, C. (1987) A longitudinal psychophysiological assessment of a schizophrenic patient in relation to the expressed emotion of his relatives. *Behavioural Psychotherapy*, **15**, 45–57.

Tarrier, N., Barrowclough, C., Vaughn, C., Bamrah, J.S., Porceddu, K., Watts, S. and Freeman, H. (1988) The community management of schizophrenia: a controlled trial of a behavioural intervention with families to reduce relapse. *British Journal of Psychiatry*, **153**, 532–42.

Tarrier, N., Barrowclough, C., Vaughn, C., Bamrah, J.S., Porceddu, K., Watts, S. and Freeman, H. (1989) The community management of schizophrenia: a two year follow-up of a behavioural intervention with families. *British Journal of Psychiatry*, **154**, 625–8.

Tarrier, N., Lowson, K. and Barrowclough. C. (1991) Some aspects of family interventions in schizophrenia. II: Financial considerations. *British Journal of Psychiatry*, **159**, 481–4.

Terkelsen, K. G. (1983) Schizophrenia and the family: II. Adverse effects of family therapy. *Family Process*, **22**, 191–200.

Test, M.A. and Stein, L.I. (1980) Alternatives to mental hospital treatment. *Archives of General Psychiatry*, **37**, 409–12.

Turpin, G., Tarrier, N. and Sturgeon, D. (1988) Social psychophysiology and the study of biopsychosocial models of schizophrenia. In, Wagner, H. (ed.), *Social Psychophysiology: Perspectives on Theory and Clinical Application*, John Wiley, Chichester.

Vaughan, K., Doyle, M., McConaghy, N., Blaszczynski, A., Fox, A. and Tarrier, N. (in press (a)) The Sydney intervention trial: a controlled trial of relatives' counselling to reduce schizophrenic relapse. *Social Psychiatry and Psychiatric Epidemiology*.

Vaughan, K., Doyle, M., McConaghy, N., Blaszczynski, A., Fox, A. and Tarrier, N. (in press (b)) The relationship between relatives' expressed emotion and schizophrenic relapse: An Australian replication. *Social Psychiatry and Psychiatric Epidemiology*.

Vaughn, C. (1986a) Comments on Dulz and Hand. In: M.J. Goldstein, I. Hand and K. Hahlweg (eds), *Treatment of Schizophrenia: Family Assessment and Intervention*, Springer-Verlag, Berlin.

Vaughn, C. (1986b) Patterns of emotional response in the families of schizophrenic patients. In: M. J., Goldstein, I. Hand and K. Hahlweg (eds), *Treatment of Schizophrenia: Family Assessment and Intervention*, Springer-Verlag, Berlin.

Chapter 5

Teaching Social and Coping Skills

JEROME V. VACCARO AND LISA ROBERTS

INTRODUCTION

While there is abundant evidence that the positive symptoms of schizophrenia—such as hallucinations, delusions and thought disorders—respond to antipsychotic medications, negative symptoms are less responsive to pharmacotherapy and may even be worsened by such medications. These deficit symptoms—apathy, amotivation, social withdrawal—impair schizophrenic individuals' abilities to establish and maintain themselves in the community. Social skills deficits prevent these individuals from successfully engaging in necessary tasks such as negotiating social relations, self-managing their illnesses, engaging in recreational activities, managing finances and performing basic self-care. It has been observed that some of these deficits begin in the premorbid phase of the illness, suggesting that for many skills, inadequate initial learning has taken place. Other sources of the deficits include inadequate learning during florid psychotic periods and atrophy of skills through disuse.

During the past decade, social skills training has become increasingly popular as a treatment for individuals with schizophrenia. There is evidence that social skills training, when carefully designed and delivered, increases patients' knowledge and skill levels (Wallace and Liberman, 1985). There is also evidence that the effects of social skills training extend to the prevention of relapse, with some suggesting as much as a halving of relapse rates (Hogarty, 1984). These findings are promising, but caution should be exercised in suggesting generalization of these data to the general population of individuals with schizophrenia, partly due to the variability of social skills training interventions (Benton and Schroeder, 1990), and to the early stage of research findings. With this mixture of enthusiasm and prudence, we would like to suggest a model of mental illness which can guide treatment efforts.

Innovations in the Psychological Management of Schizophrenia.
Edited by Max Birchwood and Nicholas Tarrier. © 1992 John Wiley & Sons Ltd

Table 5.1 Benefits of the therapeutic alliance in the treatment of schizophrenia

1. Facilitates the patient's engagement and continuity in therapy.
2. Promotes acceptance of the adherence with pharmacotherapy.
3. Permits the "active ingredients" of therapy to work.
4. Integral to the success of case management and continuity of care.
5. Enables therapists to obtain higher quality assessment information from patient and relatives for planning treatment.
6. Engages patient in more active collaboration in treatment planning and participation.
7. Humanizes the helping relationship and enables therapists to focus on patient's adaptive qualities.
8. Alliance is strengthened by the therapist's being supportive, active, consistent, pragmatic, flexible, and reality-oriented.

STRESS–VULNERABILITY MODEL OF MENTAL ILLNESS

Psychosocial interventions for schizophrenia can be guided by a multidimensional, interactive model of the disorder that considers stress, vulnerability, and protective factors. According to this model, symptoms and their associated social disabilities are the result of stressors impinging upon a person's enduring psychobiological vulnerability. The noxious effects of stress superimposed on vulnerability can be modulated or prevented by protective factors, either among the personal resources of the individual (e.g. maintenance antipsychotic medication, social competence) or the individual's social environment (e.g. supportive and tolerant family members, responsive community treatment services).

The significance of this multifactorial stress–vulnerability–protective model of symptom formation lies in the emphasis given to the therapeutic potential of psychosocial interventions that strengthen the vulnerable individual's coping capacities and social support system. While antipsychotic medication remains the single most important protective factor against stress-induced relapse, upwards of 30–40% of schizophrenic patients who are compliant with medication still relapse within a year (Hogarty, 1984). Negative or deficit syndromes in schizophrenia are not very responsive to antipsychotic medication; furthermore, drugs cannot teach life and coping skills required for successful adaptation to community life (Falloon and Liberman, 1983). New and effective psychosocial treatments, spirited by this multifactorial conception of schizophrenia, have been developed and validated for schizophrenia, in combination with antipsychotic drug maintenance strategies (Liberman and Mueser, 1989).

PSYCHOLOGICAL TREATMENT OF SCHIZOPHRENIA

Psychosocial treatments can be organized according to their focus, locus and modus, as well as to their therapeutic goals and objectives. The *focus* can be on the individual, in groups, families or a total milieu. The *locus* of therapeutic efforts can be the hospital, private office, clinic or community support program. The *modus* can derive from one or more explicit or implicit theoretical orientations, such as behavioral or psychodynamic. It is recognized that there may be considerable overlap among modalities of treatment and that much of the therapeutic impact of any psychiatric treatment derives from non-specific effects that are inherent in therapy that is offered in a credible, hopeful and positive manner (see Table 5.1). At any point in time, multiple foci, loci and modalities may be harnessed to implement a comprehensive treatment plan.

A wide spectrum of therapeutic goals and objectives can comprise psychosocial interventions: for example, emotional insight, skill development and family problem-solving are relevant aims of different modalities. Thus, the design, implementation and evaluation of psychosocial interventions requires reference to three distinctly different domains; for instance, family therapy designed to improve communication skills (*focus*) may be provided in the home (*locus*), with a behavioral orientation (*modus*).

Social skills

The general concept of social skills (e.g. interpersonal behaviors) is broadened in current training approaches to include affective, cognitive and motoric domains of functioning (Liberman, 1990). Social skills are those factors which allow an individual to cope effectively with a variety of life circumstances. These skills—such as verbal and non-verbal communication, and perceptions of interpersonal contacts—allow individuals to successfully mediate social interactions and attain desired goals. Deficits in social and independent living skills are prevalent among schizophrenic individuals. These include deficiencies in non-verbal communication skills such as eye contact, posture and facial expression as well as inadequate problem-solving abilities (Liberman, 1982).

Joe is a 27-year-old man who was diagnosed as schizophrenic at the age of 18. He was referred to a social skills training group by his psychiatrist because he was unable to socialize and meet new friends despite a desire to do so. During his first session, he was asked to describe and then enact a scene in which he had recently tried to speak with someone. He recounted a situation in which he had recently been in a cafeteria and tried to start a conversation with a young woman.

In the role play exercise, Joe was seen to make no eye contact with the woman he attempted to engage, and to pace back and forth as he started the conversation. He expressed his frustration, saying "This is exactly what happens every time. I get nervous, and I feel that if I look at the other person, she may get the wrong idea about my intentions."

When considering interpersonal communication and problem-solving abilities, it is useful to characterize the nature of an individuals social skills deficits as to the extent of impairment in his or her *receiving, processing* and *sending skills*. The schizophrenic individual may, as a result of attentional and concentration impairments, be unable to receive adequately information and cues from the environment. Positive psychotic symptoms such as hallucinations and delusions may also impede reception. Once cues are received, there may be deficiencies in the way in which the individual generates, evaluates and chooses response options. Such processing difficulties are quite common among schizophrenic individuals. The final stage in the communication process, in which effective social responses are transmitted, involves complicated sets of abilities in the domains of verbal and non-verbal skills. This phase in the process is that which identifies many schizophrenic individuals as impaired to the casual observer—for example, appearing flat in responses to others and exhibiting poor conversational abilities.

Scott is a 23-year-old man who was diagnosed as schizophrenic at the age of 18. He currently complains that he has no friends, and his family notes that he rarely engages anyone in conversation unless he is approached first. During the interview, he is found to be very isolated and to exhibit flat affect, poor eye contact, and little facial expression. He speaks barely above a whisper. He says that when he tries to engage with others he becomes overwhelmed when more than one person in a room is speaking, or when someone seems excited or angry. His family confirms his poor ability to tolerate much social stimulation.

Scott also says that he becomes easily confused when engaged in conversation, and that his attention tends to wander when he tries to concentrate. He is unable to read a book for more than one or two pages without getting lost in his thoughts. Finally, he complains that "I never get my point across to my family when I tell them things."

Scott exhibits many of the skills deficits common among schizophrenic individuals—poor verbal and non-verbal communication skills, information processing difficulties, and deficient problem-solving abilities. That these deficits are prevalent is no surprise; what we must ask ourselves is what is the best way to begin to remediate these problems. We can approach this dilemma from the vantage point of psychiatric rehabilitation, whose goals are the minimization of symptomatic impairments, enhancement of social and coping skills, and modification of living environments—

in short, the provision of social prostheses for these individuals. The ultimate goal, of course, is the amelioration of disabilities so that handicap is limited.

Social skills training: a modular approach

The most highly structured form of psychosocial therapy for schizophrenic individuals is social skills training. The goals are explicit (e.g. to teach basic conversation skills), the session agendas are usually planned in advance, the procedures are often derived from a manual, and *in vivo* and homework assignments are emphasized to spur generalization (Falloon, et al., 1990). The group format provides vicarious learning opportunities through observation of peers, a "buddy system" for completing homework and amplified reinforcement from peers.

Controlled studies, using both within-subject and group experimental designs, have yielded convergent findings regarding the efficacy of social skills training. These findings are summarized in Table 5.2 and can be found in greater detail in other publications (Falloon and Liberman, 1983; Gunderson et al., 1984; Hogarty, 1984; Liberman and Mueser, 1989). With its documented effectiveness in improving instrumental and conversational skills as well as in reducing relapse, social skills training will be a modality deserving of increased research and clinical interest in the coming years. To promote the clinical application of social skills training, the techniques have been made "user friendly" by packing them in modules,

Table 5.2 Findings from research on social skills training for schizophrenics

1. A wide variety of instrumental and affiliative skills can be learned in specific training situations.
2. Moderate generalization of acquired skills to similar situations outside the training site can be expected, but generalization is less with more complex social relationship skills.
3. When patients are encouraged to use the skills they have learned in training sessions in their natural environments, and when they are reinforced by their peers, relatives and caregivers for employing their skills, generalization is enhanced.
4. Skills are learned tediously or little at all by patients who are floridly symptomatic and highly distractible.
5. Patients consistently report decreases in social anxiety after training.
6. Durability of acquired skills depends upon duration of training and retention is unlikely to occur if training is less than 2–3 months of at least twice-weekly sessions.
7. Social skills training, when provided for 3 months to a year and integrated with other needed psychiatric services (e.g. medication) reduces relapse and improves social functioning.

comprising a Trainer's Manual, Patient's Workbook, and Demonstration Videocassette.

The modules are packaged for ready use by clinicians, ensuring reliability in their delivery. Each of the modules is goal-specific, targeted to areas relevant to community living. For example, modules are available to convey knowledge and skills necessary to self-manage effectively medications and symptoms of psychiatric illness, independently engage in grooming and self-care, start and maintain conversations, and engage in recreation and leisure activities. Each of the modules is divided into skill areas, in which the requisite skills for achieving the goals of the module are taught. For example, the skill areas in the medication management module are:

1. understanding the benefits of antipsychotic medication;
2. knowing correct self-administration of medications;
3. recognizing side effects of medications;
4. negotiating with health care providers; and
5. understanding the benefits of long-acting injectable medications.

Each of the skill areas proceeds through the seven learning activities depicted in Table 5.3. In the introduction, participants are acquainted with the material which will be covered in coming sessions. This is followed by a series of videotaped vignettes which depict the material to be learned. Upon viewing segments of the tape, participants are asked a series of questions to ensure that learning has indeed taken place.

For instance, Keri, Patrick and James watch a segment of the Symptom Management Module in which a patient (John) and his mother meet with John's therapist and doctor (Dr Martin). The scenes in the video depict the skills needed to identify warning signs of relapse and to enlist the help of others. The group leader then asks "Keri, what did Dr Martin want to talk to John about?" Keri responds, "How they could manage John's schizophrenia better so that hopefully he can prevent a relapse." The group leader reinforces appropriate responses, and if necessary, shapes patients' responses until the hoped-for response is achieved.

Table 5.3 Learning activities in skill areas

1. Introduction to the skill area.
2. Videotaped vignettes with questions and answers.
3. Role play.
4. Problem solving: resource management.
5. Problem solving: outcome problems.
6. *In vivo* exercises.
7. Homework assignments.

In the ensuing section, participants engage in role play scenes in which they demonstrate they have learned the material presented in the preceding vignettes. This affords the clinician the opportunity to again assess whether the specific material has been grasped, and see the participants "in action" as they demonstrate their verbal and non-verbal communication skills. Through modeling, role play and rehearsal with constructive feedback, participants are encouraged to improve their skills. It is best for these role play activities to be videotaped, affording participants the benefit of immediate and concrete feedback on their performance.

After each set of skills has been accurately role-played, participants engage in a process wherein they learn to obtain and manage the resources necessary to carry out their newly acquired skills. For example, once a participant has learned about side effects of medications, and how to speak with a health care provider about those problems, he must determine how he will get access to a telephone to make an appointment with the doctor, access to transportation to get to the doctor's office and the time necessary to perform these activities. Each of the necessary resources is then evaluated to decide what are the advantages and disadvantages of using or accessing it.

Inevitably, participants will encounter obstacles, or outcome problems, as they attempt to use their newly-obtained skills. For example, once they have learned how to assess their side effects and speak with the doctor, they may be turned away by a busy clinic as they seek access to their doctor. For each of the outcome problems, the clinician reads a description of an attempt to use the skill and the obstacle encountered in the environment. Then the clinician prompts participants to consider what alternatives they have in redressing the situation. This problem-solving process is aided by the use of a form depicting the steps outlined in Table 5.4. By teaching participants to use this problem-solving method systematically, they become more flexible and better able to meet their daily living needs.

Its is clear that skills learned in classrooms or clinic settings will not be maintained unless there are opportunities and encouragement for participants to use these skills in their natural environments. *In vivo* exercises provide occasions for participants to leave the training group and use the

Table 5.4 The problem solving method

1. Decide that a problem exists and define it clearly.
2. Identify the alternative solutions to the problem.
3. Evaluate the advantages and disadvantages of each solution.
4. Choose the best option or options.
5. Identify the necessary resources to carry out the chosen solution.
6. Pick a time and carry out the solution.

skills under the watchful eye of the clinician, who observes, prompts, encourages and provides positive feedback to the participant. For example, the participant might speak with the program doctor about medications with the trainer in attendance. Finally, participants independently perform the skills they have learned. As the intent of the training experience is for participants to function independently, this represents the ultimate step in the training process. Optimally, their performance is evaluated through their providing tangible proof of having completed the assignment. For example, if the assignment is to see a doctor about medication, the participant might bring back the doctor's card with confirmation that the appointment was kept and the assigned material discussed.

Social skills training: the successful living approach

In addition to the highly structured modular format, there are lesser structured approaches to delivering social skills training. One of these is the Successful Living Group described by Hierholzer and his colleagues (Hierholzer and Liberman, 1986) in which principles and practice of social skills training are utilized to teach participants the problem-solving skills they need to negotiate daily living. This type of group may be used to set treatment and rehabilitation goals, as depicted in the following case vignette.

Danny, Diana and Bill are all engaged in a community clinic's treatment program. They are diagnosed as schizophrenic and have serious social and problem-solving skills deficits. They were all sent to the Successful Living Group in order to help them plan their treatment and rehabilitation over the next year. The first group begins with Jenny, the group leader, introducing herself and then having the group members introduce themselves. Jenny then provides an overview of the group, saying that their efforts will be directed at having the participants design comprehensive goal lists so that they and their clinicians may begin to "custom tailor" approaches which are fashioned to redress the difficulties they identified and make progress toward their life goals.

Danny is the first to speak. He says that it is important for him to have "decent relationships with my family and friends, so I can count on them and they can count on me". Other group members agree that this generic goal is germane to their own struggles, and add other general goals: to be free from psychiatric symptoms, to work steadily at a job, and to maintain safe and stable housing. Next, each of the group members articulates specific objectives they must reach if they are to successfully attain their goals.

The Successful Living format is used for the phase of treatment and rehabilitation in which participants work on achieving their goals. It is also used as an ongoing intervention designed to generalize the effects of the more structured modular approach described previously. For these purposes, meetings are held once or twice each week, and the problem-solving approach outlined in Table 5.4 is employed so that participants can describe and resolve their difficulties. The following vignette characterizes this type of interaction.

Harry is referred to the Successful Living Group in order to help him plan his upcoming discharge from the hospital, where he has been for the past three weeks. He tells the group that he is very frustrated in his dealings with his mother, with whom he lives. He has been in therapy for many years in an effort to resolve their difficulties, and says that they are "constantly fighting. It's like we never stop arguing, even about the most ridiculous things". The group leader asks Harry to carefully describe the most recent of these arguments, and Harry tells the group that the last severe argument occurred when he was admitted to the hospital.

He had come home from his volunteer job at the library, and said hello to his mother. She has a hearing impairment, and did not hear him when he first addressed her. He continued to try to gain her attention, to no avail. Finally, when she did recognize his efforts, he was quite angry and was raising his voice. He recounts that he was furious that she "didn't just solve this problem and get a hearing aid, because we talk about it all the time". Harry had repeatedly insisted that she get a hearing aid, but she has refused to do so.

Harry and the other group members then discussed ways in which he might solve this interpersonal problem. After weighing the advantages and disadvantages of a series of proposed alternatives, he selected one which he thought might work for him. He role played the conversation he planned to have with her, and the group offered suggestions as to how he might improve his method of communicating. In a follow-up session, Harry reported success in his interaction with his mother.

SUMMARY AND CONCLUSIONS

The treatment of individuals with schizophrenia has seen many changes over the past four decades. The time for unidimensional and reductionistic solutions to the myriad impairments and disabilities associated with schizophrenia is past. The neurobiological and socioenvironmental determinants of this disorder require a multi-faceted approach to treatment and rehabilitation, integrating pharmacologic and psychosocial techniques. In fact, the efficacy of psychosocial treatments of schizophrenia almost always requires concomitant pharmacotherapy. Antipsychotic drugs appear to exert their primary effect on cognitive disorganization, hallucinations and delusions, but have less impact on impairments in psychosocial functioning. The opposite seems to be the case with educational and behavioral forms of psychosocial therapies. In combination, their beneficial impact on the clinical needs of the schizophrenic patient is additive. New low-dose neuroleptic drug strategies appear to capitalize on the protective benefits of structured and behaviorally-oriented therapies such as social skills training, allowing individuals with schizophrenia to cope with ambient stress while receiving less antipsychotic medication (Wirshing et al., 1990).

To be maximally effective, our biomedical and psychosocial interventions must be embedded in systems of care which presume that care for schizophrenic individuals must be long term or life long, and comprehensive and continuous in character. Not only must there be a wide spectrum of service options, but we must also be alert to the changing needs of this population. For this reason, ongoing detailed assessment of functioning must accompany diagnostic and symptomatic assessment. The important arena of *functional assessment* should address the roles a person wishes to occupy, the environmental impediments to attainment of these roles and the behavioral strengths and deficits the individual brings to the pursuit of these aims (Vaccaro, Pitts and Wallace, 1991). This approach demands that our clinical practices assume more flexible stances, altering levels and types of interventions as clinical needs dictate.

The most effective psychosocial treatment—whether provided in individual, group or family therapy, inpatient ward or community program—contains elements of practicality, problem-solving of everyday challenges, socialization and vocational activities, and specific goal orientation. A supportive and positive therapeutic relationship is central, and should infuse all treatment contacts. Psychosocial treatment should be longterm, as its benefits do not become apparent before 12 months and are even greater after 2 years. It is likely that future research will establish the benefit of indefinite psychosocial support and training in the long-term management of schizophrenia. Just as neuroleptic drugs are most effective in maintaining symptomatic improvement when continued indefinitely, it is not surprising that psychosocial treatments are similarly optimized by continuity.

Innovations that can be expected during the next decade for the treatment of persons with schizophrenia and other disabling and chronic mental disorders are heralded by current trends described in this chapter. Briefly stated, they include the following:

1. *Modular skills training*, organized with treatment manuals, patient workbooks and demonstration videos, will become available for widespread use and will encourage much greater patient participation in a psychoeducational approach to treatment and rehabilitation. Patients will become empowered, through learning community adaptation skills, to be more assertive and effective advocates for their needs, whether they be in the areas of housing, medical treatment, psychiatric treatment, personal finances, social service entitlements or vocational rehabilitation. Modular packages will also be developed to address needs of subpopulations of schizophrenic patients, such as those dually diagnosed with schizophrenia and drug dependence.

2. *Functional assessment* encourages clinicians to identify individuals' behavioral assets, excesses and deficits which help or hinder social and occupational role functioning. This helps individuals with schizophrenia to set and achieve goals which enhance their quality of life. These functional assessments will become more focused, carefully defined, and packaged for ready use by clinicians.
3. The benefits of *combining previously validated interventions,* such as case management and skills training, will be realized. Combining assertive case management and social skills training provides patients with "life coaches" who teach patients the skills necessary to maintain community tenure. Research currently underway will better define the potential benefits of adding novel pharmacotherapeutic approaches, such as minimal effective dosing, to social skills training. The cross-fertilization of such new technologies promises to enhance patients' coping skills, their ability to maintain themselves in the community and ultimately their quality of life.
4. Our *understanding of the cognitive impairments* in schizophrenia will continue to grow and direct the design of new psychosocial treatments. This will lead to the development of even more specific interventions. Probes of higher specificity will lead to earlier identification of illness and allow clinicians to strengthen coping and competence before the onset of illness or before the devastating social consequences of "chronicity" set in.
5. *Penetration of vocational rehabilitation technology and clubhouse techniques* into mental health systems will lead to more effective placement in occupational settings, and improve patients' self perception and their abilities to lead more productive lives.
6. *Patients dually diagnosed with schizophrenia and drug dependence,* now estimated at over half of the schizophrenic population, will force closer collaboration between mental health and substance abuse treatment systems. Intervention technologies such as relapse prevention (Marlatt and Gordon, 1985) and the twelve-step process (Alcoholics Anonymous and others) will be increasingly adapted to the special needs of this population. Advances in these technologies will infuse future developments in social skills training and augment this approach.
7. *Clinicians will involve families more in treatment planning and decision-making,* leading to greater treatment effectiveness as unnecessary clashes among patients, clinicians and families are avoided.

REFERENCES

Benton, M.K. and Schroeder, H.E. (1990) Social skills training with schizophrenics: a meta-analytic evaluation. *Journal of Consulting and Clinical Psychology,* **58**, 741–7.

Falloon, I.R.H. and Liberman, R.P. (1983) Interactions between drug and psychosocial therapy in schizophrenia. *Schizophrenia Bulletin*, **9**, 44–55.

Falloon, I.R.H., Krekorian, H., Shanahan, W.J., Laporta, M. and McLees, S. (1990) The Buckingham project: a comprehensive mental health service based upon behavioural pychotherapy. *Behavior Change*, **7**, 51–7.

Gunderson, J.G., Frank, A., Katz, H.M., Vannicelli, M.L., Frosch, J.P. and Knapp, P. (1984). Effects of psychotherapy in schizophrenia. *Schizophrenia Bulletin*, **10**, 564–98.

Hierholzer, R.W. and Liberman, R.P. (1986). Successful living: a social skills and problem-solving group for the chronic mentally ill. *Hospital and Community Psychiatry*, **37**, 913–18.

Hogarty, G.E. (1984) Depot neuroleptic: the relevance of psychosocial factors. *Journal of Clinical Psychiatry*, **2**, 36–42.

Hogarty, G.E., Anderson, C.M., Reiss, D.J., Kornblith S.J., Greenwald D.P., Javna C.D. and Madonia, M.J. (1986) Family psychoeducation, social skills training and maintenance chemotherapy. *Archives of General Psychiatry*, **43**, 633–42.

Liberman, R.P. (1982) Assessment of schizophrenics symptoms. *Schizophrenia Bulletin*, **8**, 62–84.

Liberman, R.P. (ed.) (1990) *Psychiatric rehabilitation of chronic mental patients*, American Psychiatric Press, Washington, D.C.

Liberman, R.P. and Mueser, R.T. (1989) Psychosocial treatment of schizophrenia. In: H.I. Kaplan and B.J. Sadock (eds), *Comprehensive Textbook of Psychiatry*, 5th ed, Williams & Wilkins, Baltimore.

Marlatt, G.A. and Gordon, J.R. (eds) (1985) *Relapse Prevention: Maintenance Strategies in Addictive Behaviour Change*, Guilford Press, New York.

Vaccaro, J.V., Pitts, D.B. and Wallace, C.J. (1991) Functional assessment. In: R.P. Liberman (ed.), *Handbook of Psychiatric Rehabilitation*, Pergamon, Elmsford, New York.

Wallace, C.J. and Liberman, R.P. (1985) Social skills training for schizophrenics: a controlled clinical trial. *Psychiatry Research*, **15**, 239–47.

Wirshing, W., Eckman, T., Liberman, R.P. and Marder, S. (1990) Management of risk of relapse in schizophrenia. In: C.A. Tamminga and S.C. Schulz (eds), *Scientific Advances in Schizophrenia*, Raven Press, New York.

Chapter 6

Early Intervention

MAX BIRCHWOOD, FIONA MACMILLAN AND JO SMITH

INTRODUCTION

Early intervention in schizophrenia is a much-discussed ideal with an appealing simplicity, yet its conceptual and practical underpinnings remain limited. *When* early intervention should take place, *what* it should seek to change and *how* it should do so, are crucial issues which can barely be answered at the moment.

This chapter will concentrate on a limited but nevertheless important component of early intervention: namely, the availability of strategies to prevent or abort an impending episode of acute schizophrenia. Emphasis is laid upon co-operation of psychological and medical approaches, describing in detail the theoretical background and practical intervention strategies which are presently being developed.

The prevention or amelioration of relapse is important for the future well-being of the individual with schizophrenia. It is known that each relapse brings with it an increased probability of future relapse, residual symptoms and accompanying social disability (World Health Organisation, 1979). Even an ideal combination of pharmacological and psychosocial intervention does not ablate the potential for relapse (Hogarty et al., 1986). Studies of first episode patients suggest that early intervention before or during the first episode may have a disproportionate impact on future vulnerability to relapse compared to future episodes. The Northwick Park study (Macmillan et al., 1986) followed up 253 first episode patients over 2 years, of which 120 took part in a placebo-controlled trial of maintenance neuroleptic medication. The period of time between the individual's loss of well-being and presentation to services and time in treatment combined ("duration of untreated illness") was carefully documented; they found that the shorter the duration of untreated illness, the less likely the patient was to relapse over the following 2 years. Duration

Innovations in the Psychological Management of Schizophrenia.
Edited by Max Birchwood and Nicholas Tarrier. © 1992 John Wiley & Sons Ltd

of untreated illness is to some degree associated with insidious onset which predicts a poor outcome; but in many cases relates to serendipitous factors determining the promptness of access to care. The clear implication is that the more quickly schizophrenia is recognised and intervention initiated, the greater the chances of survival become. Reducing this apparently critical period is no easy task, since there are known to be a number of filters that operate between the first experience of distress or disorder and presentation to specialist services (Goldberg and Huxley, 1980). Ian Falloon and colleagues in the rural area of Buckingham in the UK, are attempting to meet this problem by training GPs in the early recognition of (first episode) schizophrenia, thus prompting rapid medical and psychosocial intervention. The Buckingham project represents an innovative approach to early intervention which is presently being evaluated and whose outcome could have profound implications for service provision.

Other efforts have therefore concentrated on the less ambitious goal of early intervention to abort an impending relapse in individuals with an existing history of vulnerability to schizophrenia. Although such individuals may be well known to services, clinicians may have only modest ability to anticipate the potential for relapse. In a small study of 14 patients, Pyke and Seeman (1981) demonstrated the practical difficulty in predicting the potential for relapse when they exposed patients on maintenance therapy to a 6-week period free of drug treatment, repeated at 6-monthly intervals, aimed to reduce or discontinue the maintenance therapy. The cohort was drawn from ordinary clinical practice, including some individuals with tardive dyskinesia, some who were well and symptom-free, and a small group with residual symptoms who insisted on participation against the judgement of the clinicians. Eight patients suffered recurrences, four of whom required inpatient treatment. One patient who had been symptom-free and well for 11 years on small doses of oral neuroleptic suffered an acute relapse 3 months after discontinuation, another who participated against the advice of clinicians, remained well and symptom-free for two and a half years following discontinuation.

Studies of very large groups exposed to dose manipulations of neuroleptic therapy (Kane, Woerner and Sarantakos, 1986) suggest that the response of individuals is difficult to predict. Kane suggests that elucidation of subgroups is necessary to determine those individuals who may remain well on minimal doses. This is extremely difficult in clinical practice and may confound routine use of low-dose strategies.

Although clinicians may be only modest predictors of relapse potential in individuals, this does not prevent early recognition of loss of well-being, nor preclude early intervention. McCandless-Glincher et al. (1986) studied 62 individuals attending for maintenance therapy, and enquired about their recognition of and response to reduced well-being. The patients were drawn from those routinely attending two medical centres; their age range (20–75 years) with a mean illness duration of 28 years, suggests that such a group would be well represented in ordinary clinical practice. Sixty-one said they could recognise reduced well-being; of these thirteen relied upon others to identify symptoms for them. Nine were assisted by others and thirty-six identified the problem themselves. The majority (fifty out of sixty-one) of patients initiated some change in their behaviour when they recognised reduced well-being, including engaging in diversionary activities, seeking professional help and resuming or increasing their neuroleptic medication. Only three of this group had ever been encouraged to self-monitor by mental health professionals, and a further seven had received encouragement from relatives. Thus these schizophrenic patients had initiated symptom-monitoring and a range of responses almost entirely at their own initiative.

In essence, there may be a relatively untapped pool of information which is not being accessed adequately enough to initiate early intervention, except perhaps by patients themselves. If individuals can recognise and act on symptoms suggestive of reduced well-being, then it is possible that patterns of prodromal episodes heralding relapse may be apparent and identifiable. Studies of prodromes of relapse have been conducted in research centres which lend support to this possibility which we now review.

STUDIES OF PRODROMES

Clinical studies

While reports of clinical studies lack observational rigour and objectivity they have provided important insights into the phenomenology of decompensation. The most common approach is the detailed case study that retrospectively gathers information after a relapse, from the patient and family members (e.g. Chapman, 1966). Past reviewers of the early literature (Donlan and Blacker, 1975; Docherty et al., 1978) distinguished four sequential stages of relapse. Although the clinical literature is not sufficiently powerful to clearly support the validity of these stages and their suggested sequential relationship, they provide a useful framework for descriptive purposes.

The first stage, described by many authors, is a feeling of loss of control over cognitive and perceptual processes. McGhie and Chapman (1961), Bowers (1968) and Freedman and Chapman (1973) describe cases where the individual is initially aware of heightened mental efficiency, creativity and general well-being. Birchwood et al. (1989) described a patient who abruptly discontinued medication due to a sensation of well-being, only to relapse; and a further two cases who experienced a similar feeling of well-being prior to the onset of decompensation. However, this "euphoria" quickly subsides as the individual begins to experience a diminution of control over cognitive–perceptual processes. This is described in most of the clinical reports as a feeling of over-stimulation, involving a difficulty in preventing internal or external events invading consciousness (e.g. Chapman, 1966). Visual, proprioceptive and time distortions are common resulting in visual illusions and feelings of derealisation and depersonalisation "... irrelevant thoughts and feelings appear from nowhere and cannot be separated from more meaningful ones ... the patient becomes a passive recipient ... past memories and present occurrences, varying in length, relevance and emotional tone that run through his mind, leaving him fearful and perplexed" (Donlan and Blacker, 1975, p. 324). Perhaps not surprisingly it has been reported that patients will consult their physicians with vague, diffuse symptoms which are suggested to be the result of activated biological systems (Offenkrantz, 1962).

The onset of depressive-like symptoms is widely reported in the second stage and is regarded by some as a psychological reaction to deteriorating mental processes. These include low mood, lowered self-esteem, vegetative signs and social withdrawal (Cameron, 1938; Stein, 1967; Donlan and Blacker, 1975). Chapman's (1966) classic study notes an absorbing self-concern and preoccupation with aberrant mental functions and experiences. The uncertainty this creates may be responsible for obsessional rituals which Chapman notes as characteristic of the prodrome in some of his patients. Those with prior experience of relapse may feel a sense of foreboding; this, in the context of intact insight, may be the trigger for self-administration of medication observed by Brier and Strauss (1983) and McCandless-Glincher et al. (1986). Such changes were clearly associated with impairment of role performance.

Some authors describe a further third stage characterised by impulsivity, exaggeration of normal emotions and an inability to exercise control over the expression of personal thoughts. "She began atypically to lose her temper and spend money freely ... she bought an automobile and drove it impulsively without a licence ... (she acted) in a rebellious urge to obtain what she wanted for her life" (Docherty et al., 1978). The disinhibition tends to be progressively more primitive, including sexuality, rage, demands for attention and concerns about death ["I'm not afraid of anyone anymore, I hate everyone, I hate good, I'm going to burn the world" (Donlan and Blacker, 1975)].

Many of the cases described in the clinical studies suggest a fourth stage which includes experiences of "pre-psychotic" thinking: these include delusional mood, ideas of reference, a sense that one's thoughts have an alien quality and losing trust in people. Perceptual misinterpretations are frequently reported and delusional-like explanations may be entertained to make sense of these experiences.

The clinical studies do not reveal a homogeneous picture of prodromes of schizophrenia partly because they are based on observations of over 30 patients taken in different epochs by clinicians schooled in different psychiatric traditions. There is some consensus in observation of pre-psychotic changes (anxiety/agitation and dysphoria) but less agreement in respect of other "borderline" symptoms (disinhibition and "pre-psychotic" thinking). However, it is possible that the transition to full relapse may be as variable *between* subjects as the characteristics of an episode itself. The strong emphasis on phenomenology in these studies has shown that early signs of relapse are inappropriately caricatured as "neurotic" symptoms—i.e. in terms of Foulds' (1976) notion of a hierarchy of psychiatric illness, according to which schizophrenia, at the top of the hierarchy, will concurrently incorporate dysphoria, anxiety and other neurotic symptoms. The loss of control over normal mental processes is widely observed and probably plays a significant role in the genesis of "neurotic" symptoms giving them a unique character. In fact, in the retrospective study by Hirsch and Jolley (1989 see below), "fear of going crazy" was the most prevalent early symptom reported by 70% of their relapsing patients.

The clinical studies have offered a set of hypotheses for further examination. They have not provided information about the duration of prodromes, the validity of the "stages", their sequential relationship, nor the survival of insight. All of these aspects are prerequisites for clinical application.

Retrospective studies

The interview study by Herz and Melville (1980) in the USA attempted systematically to collect data from patients and relatives about early signs of relapse. It is widely regarded as definitive since they interviewed 145 schizophrenic sufferers (46 following a recent episode) as well as 80 of their family members. The main question, "could you tell that there were any changes in your thoughts, feelings or behaviours that might have led you to believe you were becoming sick and might have to go into hospital?", was answered affirmatively by 70% of patients and 93% of families. The overall agreement between patients and families was 66%. The study did not, however, determine the reasons for the discrepancy between patients and family members.

Generally the symptoms most frequently mentioned by patients and family members were dysphoric in nature: eating less (53%), trouble concentrating (70%), troubled sleep (69%), depression (76%) and seeing friends less (50%) . The most common "early psychotic" symptoms were hearing voices (60%), talking in a nonsensical way (76%), increased religious thinking (48%) and thinking someone else was controlling them (39%).

A similar British study (Birchwood et al., 1989) interviewed relatives of 42 CATEGO "S" schizophrenic patients recently admitted or discharged from inpatient care. All relatives recalled "early signs" but 19% could not specify when they occurred. Table 6.1 summarises results of this study together with parallel data from Herz and Melville (1980). There is considerable agreement in the content of the early signs although somewhat less in their relative frequency. Both studies concur in finding "dysphoric" symptoms the most commonly prevalent. In the Herz and Melville study although more families than patients reported the presence of early signs, there was considerable concordance between patients and families in the content and relative significance of early symptoms. There was substantial agreement between patients that non-psychotic symptoms such as anxiety, tension and insomnia were part of the prodrome but less agreement as to the characteristics of the earliest changes. Fifty per cent of the patients felt

Table 6.1 Percentage of relatives reporting early signs.

	Birchwood et al. (1989) ($n = 42$)		Herz and Melville (1980) ($n = 80$)	
Category	%	Rank*	%	Rank*
Anxiety/agitation				
Irritable/quick tempered	62	2(eq)	—	—
Sleep problems	67	1	69	7
Tense, afraid, anxious	62	2(eq)	83	1
Depression/withdrawal				
Quiet, withdrawn	60	4	50	18
Depressed, low	57	5	76	3
Poor appetite	48	9	53	17
Disinhibition				
Aggression	50	7(eq)	79	2
Restless	55	6	40	20
Stubborn	36	10(eq)	—	—
Incipient psychosis				
Behaves as if hallucinated	50	7(eq)	60	10
Being laughed at or talked about	36	10(eq)	14	53.8
"Odd behaviour"	36	10(eq)	—	—

* There were many other symptoms assessed. Percentage reporting only shown for parallel data.

that the characteristic symptoms of the prodrome were repeated at each relapse. A number of these patients also reported that many of the non-psychotic symptoms persisted between episodes of illness, an important issue to which we shall return below.

Both studies carefully questioned respondents about the timing of the onset of the prodrome. Most of the patients (52%) and their families (68%) in the Herz and Melville study felt that it took more than a week between the onset of the prodrome and a full relapse. Only 10% of patients and families believed that the time period was less than a day. Similarly, Birchwood et al. (1989) found that 59% observed the onset of the prodrome one month or more prior to relapse, and 75% two weeks or more. Nineteen per cent were however unable to specify a time scale.

These studies systematise relatives' and patients' experiences of the prodromal period, finding the characteristic symptoms to be predominantly non-psychotic, and of sufficient duration to enable the implementation of an early intervention strategy. Such a strategy would require the compliance of the patient, which might not always be forthcoming without sustained insight. Heinrichs et al. (1985) examined the survival of insight retrospectively in a group of 38 DSM-III schizophrenics who had relapsed. A systematic retrospective case note analysis indicated that insight was present in 63% of relapses, a figure confirmed by an independent interview with the responsible clinicians. They also found that retention of insight predicted a much better response to early intervention. In those with early insight, 92% responded well to rapid intervention, as compared to only 50% without early insight.

Prospective studies

The true predictive significance of prodromal signs can only be clearly established with prospective investigations. Such studies need to examine three issues: (a) Whether prodromes of psychotic relapse exist; (b) to what extent there are similarities and differences to those identified in the clinical and retrospective studies, and (c) how often the "prodromes" fail as well as succeed to predict relapse (i.e. "sensitivity" and "specificity"). The clinical implications of this research will largely depend on the degree of specificity which early signs information affords. In particular a high false positive rate will tend to undermine the use of an early intervention strategy that uses raised doses of neuroleptic medication since in such cases, patients will have been needlessly exposed to additional medication.

The first prospective study of prodromal signs was reported by Marder et al. (1984a). In the course of a study comparing low and standard dose maintenance medication, patients were assessed on a range of psychiatric symptoms at baseline, 2 weeks later, monthly for 3 months and then every 3 months. Relapse was defined as the failure of an increase in medication to manage symptoms following a minor exacerbation of psychosis/ paranoia ratings. Thus under this definition it is not known how many genuine prodromes were *aborted* with medication and whether those that responded to medication were similar to those that did not. Of the 41 DSM-III chronic schizophrenic men who took part in the study, 14 relapsed. Patients were assessed using a standard psychiatric interview scale (BPRS—Overall and Graham, 1962) and a self-report measure of psychiatric symptoms (SCL-90: Derogatis et al., 1973). Changes in scores "just prior to relapse" were compared with the average ("spontaneous") change for a given scale during the course of the follow up period. Marder et al. (1984a) found increases in BPRS depression, thought disturbance and paranoia and SCL-90 scores for interpersonal sensitivity, anxiety, depression and paranoid ideation prior to relapse. Marder et al. note that the changes they observed were very small (equalling 2 points on a 21-point range) and probably not recognisable by most clinicians. A discriminant function analysis found the most discriminating ratings were paranoia and depression (BPRS) and psychotism (SCL-90). They suggest "such a formula if used in a clinic could probably predict most relapses although there would be a considerable number of ... false positives" (p. 46). While this study strongly supports the presence of the relapse prodrome, and some of the characteristics described by Herz and Melville (1980), it was unable to control for timing. The last assessment before relapse varied from between 1 and 12 weeks, weakening the observed effects. One would anticipate the prodrome to be at its maximum in the week or two prior to relapse; assessments carried out prior to this would measure an earlier and weaker stage of the prodrome, or miss it entirely.

Subotnik and Nuechterlein (1988) considerably improved upon the Marder study by administering the BPRS bi-weekly to 50 young recent onset schizophrenic patients diagnosed by RDC criteria. Twenty-three patients relapsed and their BPRS scores 2, 4 and 6 weeks prior to the relapse were compared with their scores in another 6-week period not associated with relapse and with scores of a non-relapse group ($N=27$) over a similar period. This research found that BPRS Anxiety–Depression (which includes depression, guilt and somatic concern) and Thought Disturbance (hallucinations and delusions) were raised prior to relapse. Increases in "odd thought content" were more prominent as relapse approached (2–4 weeks prior to relapse). The contrast with the non-relapsed patients revealed a rise in low-level "psychotic" symptoms as part of the prodrome, but not of the non-psychotic items (depression, somatic concern, guilt, etc.). This suggests that the non-psychotic symptoms are sensitive to relapse but not specific to it. If however, they were followed by low-level psychotic symptoms, then this study suggests that relapse is more probable. It is also possible that elevations in anxiety–depression may be predictive in certain individuals. Subotnik and Nuechterlein note: "... mean elevations in prodromal symptoms were small ... 0.5–1.00 on a 7-point scale ... but in three patients no prodromal symptoms were present ... in several others they did not begin to show any symptomatic change until 2–4 weeks prior to relapse ... thus lowering the magnitude of the means" (p. 411). These results support clinical observation, that the nature and timing of prodromal signs are like relapse itself—not universal, but including considerable between-subject variability. Nevertheless Subotnik and Neuchterlein reported that a discriminant function using two BPRS "psychotic" scales correctly classified 59% of relapses and 74% of non-relapse periods, suggesting a false positive rate of 26%.

Hirsch and Jolley (1989) in the course of an early intervention study measured putative prodromes ("neurotic or dysphoric episodes") in a group of 54 DSM-III schizophrenics using the SCL-90 and Herz's Early Signs Questionnaire (ESQ; Herz, Szymonski and Simon, 1982). Patients and their key workers received a one-hour teaching session about schizophrenia, particularly concerning the significance of the "dysphoric" syndrome as a prodrome for relapse. This enabled them to recognise "dysphoric episodes", a task made more feasible as all subjects were symptom-free at the onset of the trial. At each dysphoric episode, the SCL-90 and the ESQ were administered and then weekly for two further weeks; otherwise each was rated monthly. Relapse was defined as the re-emergence of florid symptoms including delusions and hallucinations. Seventy-three per cent of the relapses were preceded by a prodromal period of dysphoric and neurotic symptoms within a month of relapse. These prodromes were defined clinically but confirmed by SCL-90 scores which were similar to those reported by the other two prospective studies and included depression, anxiety, interpersonal sensitivity and paranoid symptoms. Interpretation of this study is complicated by the design in which half the subjects received active and half placebo maintenance medication and all patients showing signs of dysphoric (prodromal) episodes were given additional active medication (Haloperidol, 10 mg per day). Dysphoric episodes were much more common in the placebo (76%) than in the active group (27%) but the prompt pharmacological intervention does not allow us to ascertain whether these dysphoric episodes were part of a reactivation of psychosis (i.e. true prodromes) aborted by medication and to what extent these included "false positives" related, perhaps, to the use of placebo.

This study confirms the existence of a prodromal period of approximately 4 weeks duration characterised by non-psychotic symptoms including:

(a) mild depression or dysphoria, anxiety and interpersonal sensitivity; and
(b) low-level psychotic symptoms including suspiciousness, ideas of reference and a feeling that the individual does not "fit in" with others around him.

One interesting result of the study arose from the administration of the ESQ interview questionnaire designed by Herz and Melville and reproduced in Table 6.2. This shows the importance of symptoms of dysphoria/depression and general blunting of drives and interests and highlights the phenomenological experience of psychotic decompensation, which are not generally part of the psychopathology examined by BPRS and SCL-90. Experiences such as "increased perceptual intensity", "puzzlement about objective experience", "racing thoughts" and "loss of control" and "fear of being alone" capture the phenomenological schemas which were described so lucidly in the clinical studies.

A further prospective study conducted by the authors (Birchwood et al., 1989) involved the development of a scale designed to tap the specific characteristics of the prodrome rather than that of general psychopathology. Construction of the scale was informed by the previous retrospective study reported and underwent extensive psychometric validation. Birchwood et al. (1989) developed scales to be completed by both the patient and an observer (e.g. relative, carer, hostel worker). There were four concerns (relating to the clinical application of early signs monitoring) that influenced this development. First the identification of early signs by a clinician would require intensive, regular monitoring of mental state at least bi-weekly which is rarely possible in clinical practice. Second, some patients choose to conceal their symptoms as relapse approaches and insight declines (Heinrichs and Carpenter, 1985). Third, many patients experience persisting symptoms, cognitive deficits or drug side-effects which will obscure the visibility of the prodromes. Indeed the nature of a prodrome in patients with residual symptoms (in contrast to those who are symptom-free) has not been studied and is important since in clinical practice the presence of residual symptoms is the norm. Fourth, the possibility is raised that the characteristics of prodromes might vary from individual to individual and that this information may be lost in scales of general psychopathology and group designs in research studies.

The authors developed an ongoing system of measurement, where patients and observers completed the scale fortnightly; at out-patient clinic attendance, with a community psychiatric nurse or through the mail.

Appendix ①

Table 6.2 Frequency of emergent symptoms during prodromal episodes (Herz Early Signs Questionnaire). Reproduced from Hirsch and Jolley (1989)

Emergent symptom	Prodromal episodes (n = 44) (%)
Fear of going crazy	70
Loss of interest	60–70
Discouragement about future	
Labile mood	50–60
Reduced attention and concentration	
Preoccupation with one or two things	
Feelings of not fitting in	40–50
Fear of future adversity	
Overwhelmed by demands	
Loss of interest in dress/appearance	
Reduced energy	
Puzzled/confused about experience	
Loss of control	
Boredom	
Thoughts racing	
Indecisiveness	
Distanced from friends/family	30–40
Feeling that others do not understand	
Disturbing dreams	
Loneliness	
Reduced sex drive	20–30
Fear of being alone	
Increased energy	
Increased perceptual intensity	10–20
Increased sex drive	
Depersonalisation	
Religious preoccupation	
Ideas of reference	0–10
Elevated mood	
Risk taking	

These data were then plotted in an ongoing fashion (Figure 6.1). It was reasoned that the behavioural observations by the observers might provide additional information if the individual under-reported or lost insight. *Changes* in baseline levels were readily apparent, which is particularly important if the individual experiences persisting symptoms.

The authors reported the investigation of 19 young schizophrenic patients diagnosed according to the broad CATEGO "S" class. All except

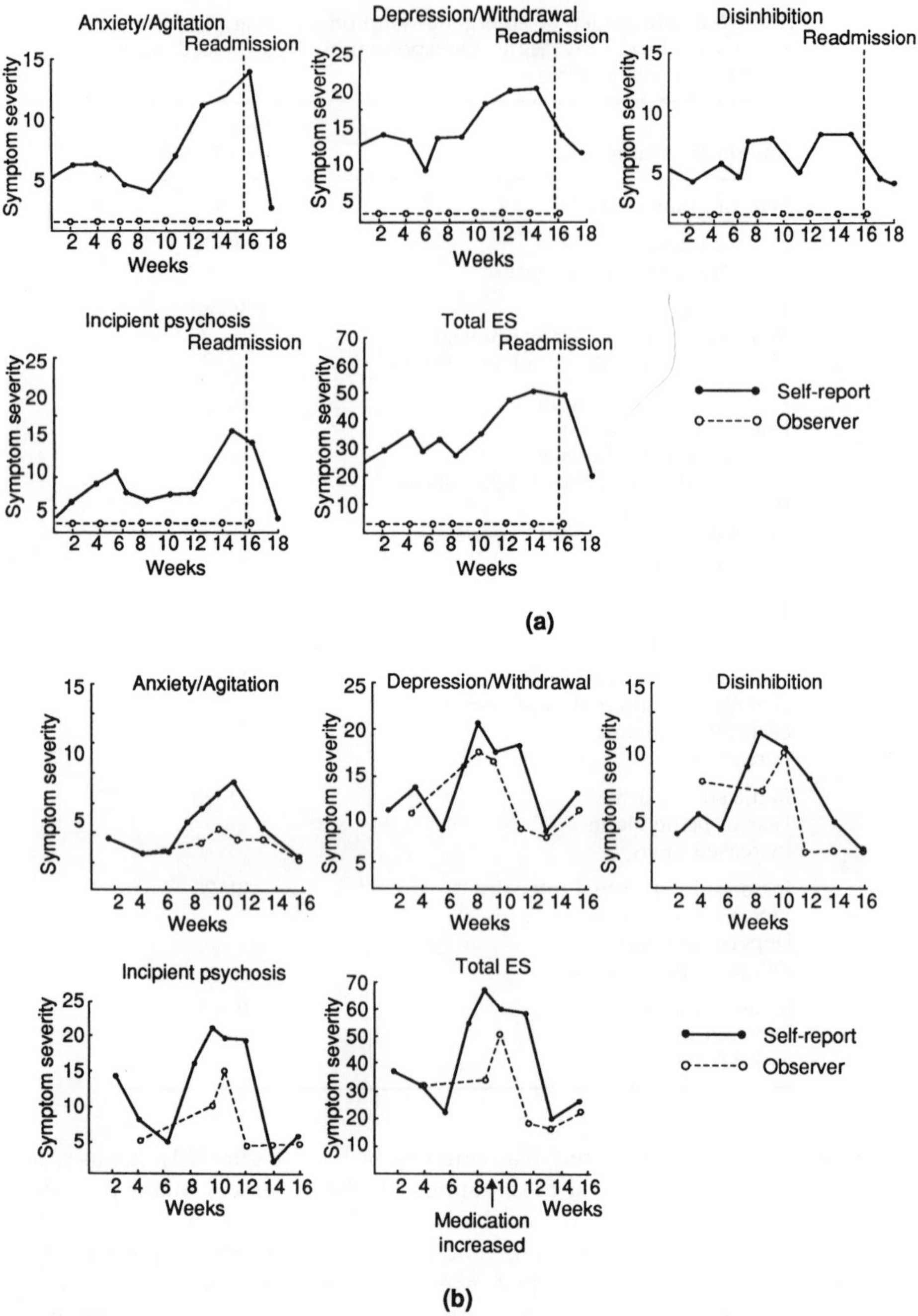

Figure 6.1 Five prodromes detected using the ESS scales.

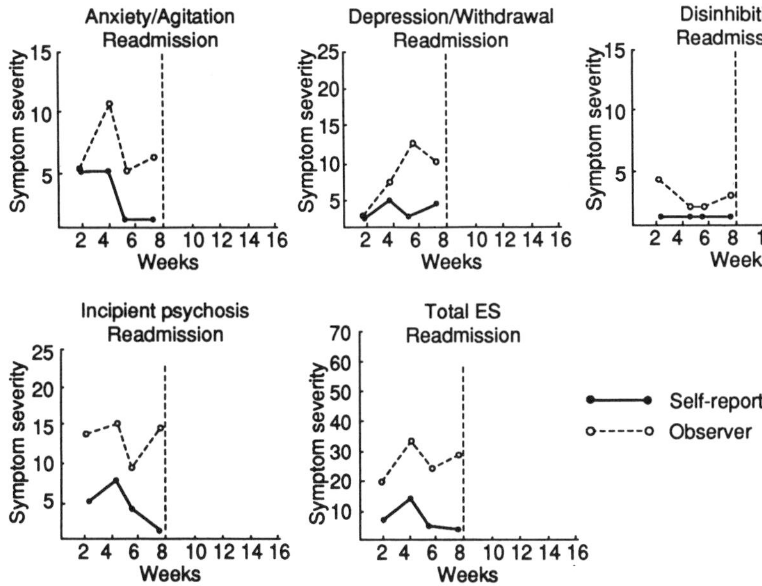

(c)

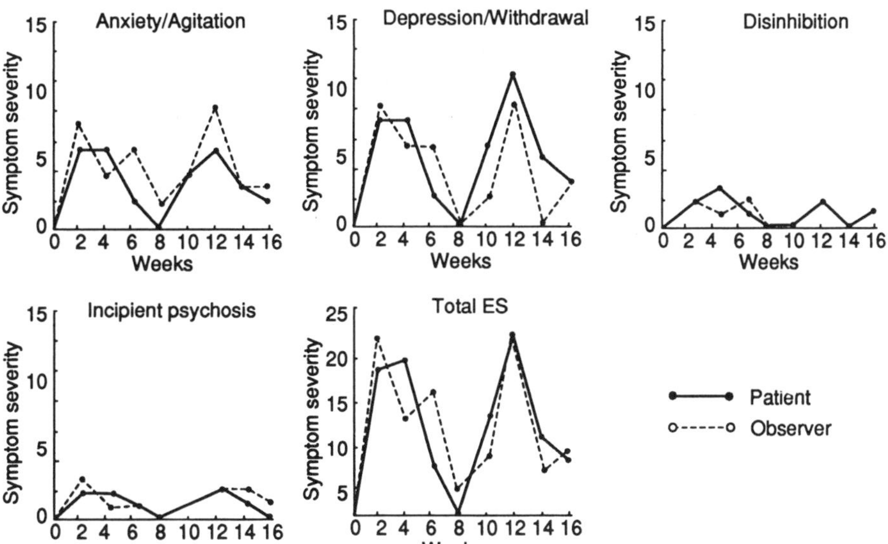

(d)

Figure 6.1 (continued).

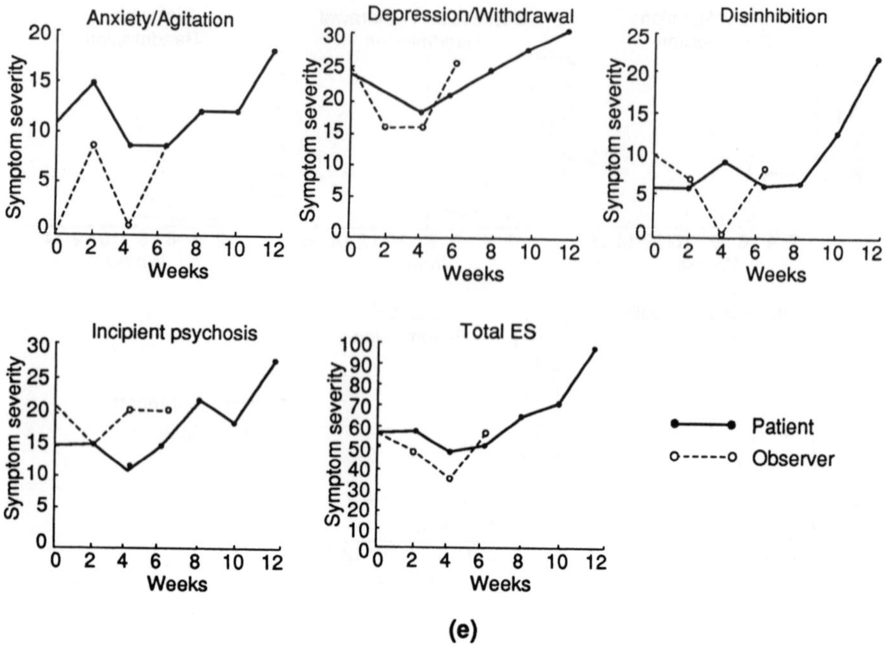

Figure 6.1 (continued).

one were on maintenance medication and monitored in the context of a routine clinical service and were not involved in a drug trial. Eight of the 19 relapsed in the course of 9 months and of these, 50% showed elevations on the scales between 2 and 4 weeks prior to relapse. A *post hoc* defined threshold on their scale (> or <30) led to a sensitivity of 63%, specificity of 82% and an 11% rate of false positives.

This study was a clinical investigation to see how prodrome monitoring might be applied in the clinical setting and to examine in more detail idiopathic aspects of the prodromes. Figure 6.1 show some of the results of individual prodromes. Figure 6.1a is that of a young male who relapsed 16 weeks following discharge. In this case the first change was that of dysphoria/withdrawal which was apparent 5 weeks prior to relapse. After 1–2 weeks he became steadily more agitated and within 2 weeks of relapse, low level ("incipient") psychotic symptoms appeared. Disinhibition was unaffected. In contrast the individual shown in Figure 6.1b reported dysphoria/withdrawal and incipient psychotic symptoms simultaneously together with signs of disinhibition; anxiety/agitation did not peak until somewhat later. It is interesting to note that the observer's behavioural observations showed striking concordance to self-report in respect of dysphoria but lagged behind by up to 2 weeks in respect of the behavioural concomitants of incipient psychosis. These two examples also reveal an apparent *improvement* in well-being just prior to the onset of the prodromes. The third case (Figure 6.1c) is a young male where the rise in anxiety/agitation, dysphoria and incipient psychosis were noted by the observer, but the individual reported a slight rise in symptoms followed immediately by a sharp fall, presumably due to loss of insight. Case four (Figure 6.1d) demonstrates a definite rise in the scales which returned to base line 4 weeks later and was not followed by a relapse. While the scores did not rise above the 30-point threshold, the apparent rise might be regarded as a "false alarm". This particular individual had learnt he had secured employment which seemed to be associated with a feeling of well-being noted by the individual and his mother; as the start of his job approached, his symptoms increased then returned to baseline a few weeks after the start of his job. What was witnessed here was probably the impact of a stressful life event that on this occasion did not culminate in relapse.

The patients in this study were drawn from an outpatient clinic. Many had residual symptoms which were reflected in their baseline scores: Case 1 had moderate negative symptoms and partial delusions; Case 2 also had moderate negative symptoms and heard a "voice" that she knew was part of her illness; Case 3 was asymptomatic. Clinically the detection of a prodrome in those with residual symptoms is not easily done by reference to absolute scores: comparisons with a baseline are clearly valuable here. The issue is raised as to how *severe* residual symptoms need to be before the concept of "relapse" and therefore of a "prodrome" becomes meaningless. In the cases we have monitored, prodromes have been apparent in those with "mild to moderate" residual positive or negative symptoms but only if some insight continues to be available. In case 5 (Figure 6.1e) a young female continued to hear voices which caused her considerable distress. She had retained some insight but steadily lost it as she found the voice content increasingly plausible. Two weeks prior to this she became more withdrawn and self absorbed and her psychotic symptoms became more generalised.

Continuing questions

The results of the four prospective studies are consistent with the clinical and retrospective studies, particularly supporting Herz and Melville's (1980) seminal investigation. The studies all found that psychotic relapse was preceded by non-psychotic, "dysphoric" symptoms including anxiety, dysphoria, interpersonal sensitivity/withdrawal and low-level psychotic thinking including ideas of reference and paranoid thoughts. In two of these studies (Marder et al., 1984a; Hirsch and Jolley, 1989) the observations were confounded with a targeted medication strategy, so it was not clear how many of their putative prodromes were actually false positives. It is also possible that the use of an early intervention strategy exaggerated the magnitude of the recorded prodromes. Under normal conditions the baseline levels of psychopathology would be increased in the non-relapsed patients by transient fluctuations in dysphoric symptoms which were not part of a relapse (i.e. the false positives) which might respond to medication, thus reducing the contrast between relapsed and non-relapsed groups.

The possibility of between-subject variability in the nature and timing of prodromes will however act to reduce their apparent amplitude in group studies. Subotnik and Nuechterlein (1988) reported that, some patients showed no prodromal symptoms. Among the patients that did show prodromal signs, some were elevated 6 weeks prior to relapse while in others this occurred a full month later, thus lowering the mean value for the whole group within the time frames (6, 4 or 2 weeks prior to relapse). The study by Birchwood et al. (1989) raises further potential complications as not only does it reveal differences in the amplitude and timing of symptoms, but also that the pattern of prodromal symptoms shows subject variability: some may "peak" on anxiety symptoms, others on disinhibition, and so forth.

The prospective studies have thus raised a number of questions. They have confirmed the existence of prodromes of psychotic relapse, but their limitations have not enabled a clear picture to emerge of the true predicative significance of apparent early warning signs. If the work of Birchwood et al. (1989) is borne out, then group studies in the mould of Subotnik and Nuechterlein (1988) would be inherently limited as they could not capture the apparent qualitative and quantitative differences between patients in their early signs symptoms. This is supported by Subotnik and Nuechterlein's finding that greater prediction came when patients were compared against their own baseline rather than that of other patients. It may be more appropriate to think of each patient's prodrome as a personalised "relapse signature" which includes core or common symptoms together with features unique to each patient. If an individuals relapse signature can be identified, then it might be expected that the overall predictive power of "prodromal" symptoms will be increased. Identifying the unique characteristics of a relapse signature can only be achieved once a relapse has taken place; with each successive relapse further information becomes available to build a more accurate image of the signature. This kind of learning process has been acknowledged by patients (Brier and Strauss, 1983) and could be adapted and developed by professionals and carers as well.

An issue not directly examined in the prospective studies concerns the existence of a prodrome of relapse where the individual continues to experience significant residual symptoms. Where the patient experiences continued negative symptoms such as anergia, alogia and withdrawal, a prodrome presumably will involve an apparent *exacerbation* of these symptoms as shown in some of the cases in Figure 6.1. Where individuals continue to suffer from symptoms such as delusions and hallucinations, a "relapse" will involve an exacerbation of these symptoms; whether these relapses will also be preceded by prodromes of a similar character is unknown. Patients in the Hirsch and Jolley (1989) and Subotnik and Nuechterlein (1988) studies were generally symptom free; there was somewhat more variability in residual symptoms than in the Birchwood et al. (1989) and Marder et al. (1984a) studies. In view of the large numbers of patients with even moderate residual symptoms, this issue deserves serious and careful examination.

Patients participating in the prospective studies generally were young (18–35 years) with a relatively brief psychiatric history. Such individuals are more prone to relapse and tend to be recruited at acute admission or because they were thought to be appropriate for low dose or intermittent drug strategies (c.f. Hirsch and Jolley, 1989). The application of this methodology to older, more stable individuals is another important area for further investigation.

EARLY INTERVENTION STUDIES

In this section we shall review studies which have used neuroleptic drugs as the main vehicle of early intervention. Brier and Strauss (1983) and McCandless-Glincher et al. (1986) presented evidence that individuals believe they not only have ability to recognise early signs of relapse, but also to initiate methods of self-control. This area has received little systematic attention in the literature and should do so; however, as the prodrome phenomena occupies only a brief time window the conditions for psychological research and treatment are not ideal. Nevertheless, this is an avenue which must be pursued (see Birchwood, 1992).

All the drug studies have involved withdrawing patients from maintenance regimes, monitoring clinical state and providing brief pharmacotherapy at the onset of a prodrome. This paradigm has been chosen with the goal of minimising drug exposure, and therefore side-effects, without prejudicing prophylaxis rather than as a means of further controlling relapse. This issue will be returned to at the conclusion of this section.

Herz, Szymonski and Simon (1982) were the first group to use an intermittent approach in an open pilot study of a small sample of patients withdrawn from maintenance therapy. Over a 9-month period, 11% of the sample relapsed which compares favourably with results of relapse on maintenance therapy from other studies. This team are presently engaged in a comparison of patients maintained on active or placebo maintenance medication and given (intermittent) medication at the onset of a prodrome (Herz et al., 1989). On the preliminary data they present, there was no difference between groups in the severity or duration of prodromes, although the placebo group had *more* prodromes. Few hospitalisations had occurred at the time of their preliminary report.

The best controlled study using this paradigm is that of Jolley and Hirsch (1989) and Jolley et al. (1990) in which 54 stabilised, asymptomatic and thus highly-selected patients were randomly assigned to active or placebo maintenance therapy conditions, with both receiving early drug intervention which involved the administration of 5–10 mg daily of Haloperidol. Each patient was given a starter pack of 3 days of oral medication if they were unable to make contact with the research team at the early sign of relapse. Patients received a brief educational session on entry to the study about prodromes and early intervention. Great reliance was placed on patients to recognise the early signs of relapse. Outcome at one year revealed that significantly more patients experienced prodromal symptoms in the intermittent group (76%) than in the control group (27%) which was accompanied by an increased rate of relapse in the intermittent group (30% versus 7%). However, the groups did not differ in readmission, use of compulsory detention or total duration of hospital stay, suggesting that severe relapse was not affected and was indeed low in both groups. Extrapyramidal side effects were reduced in frequency and severity, particularly akathisia, parkinsonism, sedation and gait. Tardive dyskinesia increased from 32% to 55% in the control group and reduced slightly in the intermittent group (29% to 24%). As anticipated by some observers of the first report (e.g. Harrison, 1989) results at 2 years were at variance with the first year and largely disappointing: relapse was more frequent (50% versus 12%) and more severe in the intermittent group. Total exposure to neuroleptics was reduced by 60% in the intermittent group reflected in a much reduced severity of extrapyramidal side effects, but with no impact on social functioning. During the first year of the study, 73% of relapses were preceded by identified prodromal symptoms; during the second year this fell to 25%. As reliance was placed on patients and families to identify and seek assistance for prodromal symptoms, this suggests "... that the single teaching session at the start of the study does not provide patients and families with an adequate grasp of the intermittent paradigm ... ongoing psychoeducational intervention should be an essential component of further studies ..." (p. 841).

Carpenter et al. (1990) report the outcome of a study of similar design to Jolley and colleagues in which continuous and intermittent medication regimes were contrasted in a sample of 116 patients randomly assigned to groups but not under double-blind conditions. Thus 57 patients in the targeted group were withdrawn from maintenance therapy and compared to 59 who were not. Both groups received early intervention as in the Jolley study determined by the presence of clinically defined prodromes. Unlike the Jolley study, subjects were not specifically selected as good candidates for drug withdrawal and were engaged in the trial following a period of hospitalisation; thus scores on the BPRS and social functioning scales indicated "... moderate signs and symptoms and moderate impairment of social and occupational functioning" (p. 1144); and in addition the sample were young (mean age 28 years) with a 6-year illness history and only a small number in employment. Results did not support the intermittent regime. Patients experienced a higher rate of hospitalisation (53% vs 36%) and survival analyses indicated that continuous medication was superior throughout the 2 years of the trial. Hospital admissions were however regarded as "brief" in both groups and no other differences were noted between the groups in clinical or social functioning at two years. However, the greater number of hospitalisations in the intermittent group was associated with a lower rate of employment at two years. Drug exposure was lower in the intermittent group but data on side-effects were not reported. Not only was the intermittent regime less effective, but it was also less popular too: 50% refused to continue with the regime (vs. 20% in continuous treatment), presumably due to the higher rate of prodromes and hospitalisation and perhaps patients also found the responsibility placed on them to recognise relapse an excessive one.

In evaluating the results of these studies, a distinction must be drawn between the utility of the paradigm *per se* (i.e. intervention at the onset of a prodrome) and the particular application of this approach in terms of the design and methodology of each study. Experimental designs ask specific questions and hitherto the early intervention studies have asked only whether a targeted regime alone yields comparable prophylaxis to one which combines maintenance *and* targeting with the benefit of minimising side effects. The answer to this is clearly negative. A variant of this design might contrast targeting alone with a maintenance regime alone; this design would have greater clinical validity but raise methodological problems.

Other designs will address different questions. A comparison of continuous with targeted and continuous regimes would inform whether early intervention provides additional prophylaxis to the standard regime. A comparison of "standard" dose maintenance regime with a combined low dose and targeted regime would examine whether the increased risk inherent in this drug reduction manoeuvre can be offset by early intervention. With regard to the first design, the study of Jolley et al. (1990) finds an unusually low rate of relapse over 2 years in the group receiving continuous and targeted regimes (12%) suggesting a possible additive effect. This possibility has yet to be adequately tested. A study by Marder et al. (1984b, 1987) bears upon the second design. In this study patients were assigned to a low (5 mg) or standard (25 mg) dose regime of fluphenazine decanoate every 2 weeks and at the first sign of exacerbation the dose was doubled. If this failed patients were considered to have relapsed, which occurred in 22% taking the lower dose and 20% on the higher dose with fewer side effects in the former. Marder et al. (1984, 1987) found that lower doses carried a greater risk of relapse, but these were not "serious" and were eliminated once the clinician was permitted to double the dose at the onset of a prodrome (the survival curves of the doseage groups were not different under targeted conditions). Although "low" dose strategies do carry an increased risk of relapse, they have yet to be properly tested in the context of a targeted regime and the results of Marder do give cause for optimism. Since it is now widely accepted that maintenance doses in clinical practice may be far higher than necessary and may actually reduce prophylaxis (Teicher and Baldessarini, 1985), a double-blind evaluation of targeting in the context of a lower dose maintenance regime would seem to be the next logical research step.

The methodology used to identify relapse prodromes has relied heavily upon patients' skill and their initiative to alert services. Jolley and Hirsch have suggested that a brief educational session is insufficient for patients to grasp the intermittent paradigm; and the high dropout rate noted by Carpenter, Heinrichs and Hanlan (1987) underlies its unpopularity. This experience suggests that it is unrealistic to expect patients to shoulder this responsibility alone and is best shared with services. It is for this reason that the authors are using a more proactive method of monitoring for prodromes in which the burden of early recognition and intervention is shared (Birchwood, Macmillan and Smith, 1991).

In conclusion, early intervention in the form of targeted (intermittent) regimes are severely cautioned by existing studies. Future studies should pay greater attention to the methodology used to identify prodromes so that the burden is shared with services. The use of the early intervention paradigm in other contexts (e.g. low dose regimes) and specifiable subgroups needs further research. The possibilities are numerous and important and offer the clinician much greater flexibility in clinical management.

EARLY INTERVENTION PROCEDURES

Selecting suitable subjects

Individuals with a history of repeated relapse or who are at high risk, for reasons of drug non-compliance, use of a low dose maintenance regime, living alone or in a high EE family environment, may be appropriate. Patients showing severe or early signs of Tardive Dyskinesia may also be considered. Those individuals already in receipt of very high doses of maintenance medication may not be suitable for early intervention based on raised drug dose, since in this context higher doses are likely to meet with diminishing returns. Other procedures for early intervention based on psychosocial measures might be considered in such cases. For those with quite severe drug refractory persisting positive symptoms, discriminating a prodrome against such a background is likely to prove extremely difficult (indeed its very existence is questionable) and early intervention becomes less meaningful in this context. The absence of insight may preclude an individual's acceptance of an early intervention strategy. Indeed the ultimate test will be the individual's acceptance of the approach, which in our experience has much to do with his or her dislike of the dislocation which relapse/readmission can cause, as well as fear of the experience itself. The availability of a close relative or carer to corroborate self-report can maximise information about prodromal signs but must be selected in collaboration with the individual. Further, the kind of early intervention strategy which is to be considered will influence subject selection. An intermittent strategy in the context of withdrawal from maintenance medication will be safe perhaps only in 40% of cases: Jolley and Hirsch (1989) excluded 60% of patients on this basis and Chiles, Sterchi and Hyde (1989) found that only one-third (34.8%) of chronic schizophrenic patients attending a Mental Health Centre were eligible. As discussed earlier, those electing to continue with maintenance medication may still benefit from a targeted strategy involving medication given at the onset of a prodrome. In these cases a low dose maintenance regime might be considered.

Engagement and education

Early intervention rests on the close co-operation between patient, carer/relative and professionals. In common with many interventions outlined in this book, an ethos of trust and "informed partnership" between these groups must be developed (Smith and Birchwood, 1990). Education about prodromes and early intervention opportunities needs to be provided

Table 6.3 Early signs interview: relatives' version

Stage one: Establish date of onset/admission to hospital and behaviour at height of episode

"On what date was X admitted to hospital?"
  Prompt: date, day, time; contemporary events to aid recall

"When did you decide X needed help?"
  Prompt: date

"What was X's behaviour like at that time?"
  Prompt: What kind of things was X saying?
    What kind of things was X doing?

Stage two: Establish date when change in X was first noticed

"So X was admitted to hospital weeks after you decided X needed help ..."

"Think back carefully to the days or weeks before then"

"When did you first notice a change in X's usual behaviour or anything out of the ordinary?"
  Prompt: Nature, time of change

"Were there any changes before then, even ones which might not seem important?"

Stage three: Establish sequence of changes up to relapse

"I'd like to establish the changes that took place after that up to (date) when you decided X needed help"

"What happened next (after last change)?"
  Prompt: Was this a marked change?
    When did this happen?
    Can you give me some examples?
    Repeat question until point of relapse is reached

Stage four: Prompting for items not already elicited

"During this build up to X's relapse/admission to hospital ..."

"Was X unusually anxious or on edge?"
  Prompt: When did you notice this?
    Prompt items from relevant early signs checklist

"Did X seem low in spirits?"
  Prompt: as above

"Did X seem disinhibited (excitable, restless, aggressive, drinking, etc.)?"
  Prompt: as above.

"Did X seem suspicious or say/do strange things?"
  Prompt: as above.

Stage five: Summary

"Let me see if I'm clear on what happened before X's admission"

"X was admitted on (date), (number) weeks after you decided X needed help; X was (describe presentation)"

"You first noticed something was wrong on (date) when X
(describe behaviour) ... then X began to ..."
(Complete description of prodrome)

"Have I missed anything out?"

which might be given in the context of general educational intervention about psychosis (Smith and Birchwood, 1985, 1987; Birchwood, Macmillan and Smith, 1991). Education must emphasise that some responsibility is being placed on the individual and relative to recognise a potential relapse and to initiate treatment. Engagement and compliance will be enhanced where the client has a stable, trusting relationship with individuals in the mental health services. As the experience of Jolley et al. (1990) illustrates, this requires psychoeducation to be a continuous feature of this relationship.

Identifying the relapse prodrome and time window for early intervention

Precise information about the individual's prodrome or "relapse signature" may be obtained through careful interviewing of patient or relative about the changes in thinking and behaviour leading up to a recent episode. This must be fed back to patient and carer and carefully documented by the case manager to enable a more accurate discrimination of any future prodrome.

An interview used by the authors to identify the relapse prodrome is shown in Table 6.3. This involves five stages. The first establishes the date of onset of the episode and the time between this and any admission. The second establishes the date when a change in behaviour was *first* noticed; and in the third and fourth stages the sequence of subsequent changes is established using specific prompts if necessary. Finally, the prodrome is summarised. An example of such a prodrome is shown in Table 6.4.

Monitoring for prodromes

Predicting (and therefore controlling) an impending relapse is greatly enhanced by closer monitoring of a possible prodrome. In addition, those with residual symptoms, severe drug side-effects or unstable symptoms will benefit from closer observation as the establishment of a baseline will facilitate the discrimination of a prodrome from the background "noise". The prodrome it sketches will also bring greater definition to the "signature", thus providing patient, carer and professional with a learning opportunity to improve prediction on any subsequent relapse.

The items in Table 6.1 have been developed into a series of interval scales by Birchwood et al. (1989) and incorporated into a monitoring system in which patient and observer make fortnightly observations plotted on a graph. The frequency of observation can be increased should there be any cause for concern. Figure 6.1a–d illustrate some data arising from this

Table 6.4 Results of a prodrome interview

Informant:	Parents
Admitted:	25/5/90
Relapse:	March 1990 (first episode)
Change first noted:	October 1989

Early sign	Category	Period prior to relapse (weeks)
Spending more time alone in bedroom	W	12–20
Avoiding contact with family; talking less	W	
Stopped interests/hobbies —listening to music and drawing wild life	W	
Stopped work—"people were picking on him". Accused friends of same	IP	
Neglecting personal hygiene—not washing, changing clothes	W	8–12
Stood in front of mother naked	D	
Stealing money from family	D	
Irritable and argumentative toward family	D	
Accusing family of reading his mind	IP	4–6
Said he thought the phone was being interfered with	IP	
Laughing for no reason	IP	
Very preoccupied with TV —sat and stared but not appear to be watching	IP	

A: Anxiety/agitation W: Withdrawal/dysphoria D: Disinhibition IP: Incipient psychosis.

method. A series of decision rules has been developed and form the basis of an early intervention study presently in progress.

A sense of ownership over these data should be created in the minds of patients and their families so that responsibility for initiating early intervention is a shared one; for example in the author's work, regular updated copies of the graphs are provided for participants. Educating patients and relatives about early signs of relapse, feeding back to them information from the early signs interview, and collaboration in monitoring, should significantly raise the likelihood of early detection and therefore intervention.

Selecting a targeted dose

The selection of a targeted dose of neuroleptics will depend on many factors; but ultimately the final choice is largely empirical in terms of what is known to be effective for a given patient. In the Jolley and Hirsch (1989) trial, the selected sample of stable, symptom-free patients without maintenance medication received a targeted dose of between 5–10 mg/day of oral Haloperidol for up to 2 weeks. Among a representative *clinical* sample it is difficult to be prescriptive. The dosage of medication effective during a recent relapse can serve as a guide, starting with the minimum dose used and, if necessary, working upwards.

Crisis counselling

Once a prodrome has been declared, the individual and family need intensive support. The psychological reaction to a loss of well-being, and the possibility that this may herald a relapse, places a significant strain on both parties, which, if unchecked, could accelerate the decompensation process. The availability of support, quick access to the team, the use of stress management and diversionary activities will help to mitigate these effects (Brier and Strauss, 1983). It is possible that a relapse may be triggered by a stressful life event; if so, counselling should be directed towards its resolution. For example, the individual depicted in Figure 6.1e revealed an abrupt change in his early signs record associated with the stress of starting a new job (at week 12 on the graph). (The possibilities for early *psychological* intervention are discussed in Birchwood, 1992.)

IMPLICATIONS AND CLINICAL APPLICATIONS

The clinical application of early signs monitoring offers considerable opportunity for improving care. However, if the encouraging results of the early intervention studies employing targeted medication are to be realised in clinical practice, careful thought must be given to the identification of individual "relapse signatures", the design of monitoring methodology and the nature of the service response to secure these advances for the well-being of patients.

The relationship between early signs of decompensation and actual psychotic relapse remains unclear. There is unlikely to be a simplistic relationship and evidence suggests that false positives and negatives will occur. We have discussed a number of means to improve the specificity of early signs information using additional information relating to idiosyncratic signs for a given individual.

Experienced staff, engaged in long-term clinics supporting patients often have years of regular contact with a client, and can provide useful information concerning certain key changes which in themselves might go unnoticed, but for a given individual may be highly predictive of relapse. The fuller "relapse signature" that is thus obtained can be incorporated into the early signs monitoring procedure and used as a hypothesis to predict specific idiosyncratic signs which will occur at a subsequent relapse of a given individual. Any additional early signs information observed at this relapse can be added to the signature, thereby increasing the accuracy of prediction with each relapse.

Monitoring methodology

The strategy of close monitoring by highly trained personnel is impractical in routine care. On the other hand, the use of close monitoring by staff for particular target groups, with a high relapse risk is limited by the ability to reliably select high potential relapse risks. The methodology adopted by Birchwood et al. (1989) harnessing the experiences of patients and their carers in a routine service setting may be possible to apply clinically. This offers the potential for documenting information relating to early signs of relapse for a substantial group of patients, with relatively limited input of professional time. However, it is still probable that a substantial group of patients, who retain very little insight or where loss of insight occurs very early in decompensation, may be unable or unwilling to entertain self-monitoring and are also least likely to consent to observation by another. There are no easy solutions to these problems, although education about the illness may, in some cases, improve insight and key people in the individuals life can be trained to monitor and recognise specific early warning signs and to initiate preventative strategies such as increasing medication, or seeking professional help promptly if relapse is predicted.

Notwithstanding its potential therapeutic value, the notion of self-monitoring does raise a number of concerns about sensitising patients and carers to disability, promoting the observations as critical responses, burdening individuals and carers further with requests for repetitive information at frequent intervals, or increasing the risk of self-harm in an individual who becomes demoralised by an impending relapse. There is no real evidence that self-monitoring is likely to increase the risk of self-harm; indeed, florid and uncontrolled relapse may be more dangerous and more damaging. Engaging patients and carers more actively in the management of the illness may also promote a sense of purposeful activity and have therapeutic benefits *per se*. The repetitive nature of the procedure may be self-defeating in the long term and indeed wasteful in well-stabilised patients. Instituting monitoring at times of stress may be a reasonable alternative to continuous monitoring. Those individuals who develop expertise of monitoring through a number of relapses may develop and sharpen the signature in the minds of professionals and carers alike. Despite the many limitations, if early signs monitoring fulfils even part of its promise, it may for many patients with recurrent episodes, promote learning and lead to increased opportunity for combined efforts to control exacerbations due to stress.

The service response

For the group of patients who routinely attend clinical appointments, information from monitoring by patients and carers has an identified route of access. If this route were formalised it might be possible to ensure clear responses from the service. However, not all patients attend services and the move away from an institutional model is likely to further devolve care away from centralised services. The difficulty in accessing traditional psychiatric services was well documented by Creer and Wing (1974) and Johnstone et al. (1984), a decade later, describe patchy access to care with particular problems for relocated patients and families. The implementation of case management for the long-term mentally ill may ensure constant service links at a distance, but the utilisation of psychiatric services during critical periods will necessarily require information concerning early signs of relapse to be adequately assessed and harnessed (Shepherd, 1990).

The nature of the service response to information concerning early signs of decompensation is still an open question. Most clinical trials have employed pharmacological interventions upon recognition of early signs of decompensation (Jolley and Hirsch, 1989). Within defined cohorts (as in clinical trials) the use of targeted medication has not been sufficient to cope with individual variation. In the clinical setting, where there is a very wide range of maintenance therapy and where the dose and duration of targeted medication is likely to be vary considerably between individuals, targeted medication would require to be individually tailored. However the implementation of strategies that are already recognised by patients and carers as useful would often be entirely appropriate. Indeed the work of McCandless-Glincher et al. (1986) is particularly encouraging since it suggests that very nearly all patients recognise loss of well-being and the majority institute some change in behaviour at their own initiative in response to this, including engaging in diversionary activities, seeking professional help or resuming and increasing neuroleptic medication. In the face of this information, individuals might be encouraged to employ self-management strategies, e.g. stress management procedures or symptom control strategies (Brier and Strauss, 1983) to initiate preventative actions in terms of increasing the frequency of day-centre attendance, requesting brief admission or enlisting professional support to assist in symptom management. To achieve these ends may require radical service change in the direction of the development of a more responsive and flexible service than currently exists. The resultant service envisaged would need to be proactive rather than reactive and responsive to the needs and concerns of individuals and their carers particularly if these alternative preventative strategies are to be viable.

In summary, routinely monitoring early signs to identify individual relapse signatures opens the possibility for individuals to recognise and act on symptoms suggestive of reduced well being and to initiate early intervention strategies to prevent relapse. However, if the promising results of the research studies are to be systematically applied and incorporated into routine clinical practice a viable system of monitoring needs to be established in order to access information routinely and accurately. The service structure also needs to be adapted in order to facilitate this and to be able to respond flexibly and promptly when relapse is predicted. It is to this end that the authors research efforts are devoted.

REFERENCES

Berkowitz, R., Shavit, N. and Leff, J. (1990) Educating relatives of schizophrenic patients. *Social Psychiatry and Psychiatric Epidemiology*, **25**, 216–20.

Birchwood, M. (1992) Practice Review. Early intervention in schizophrenia: theoretical background and clinical strategies. *British Journal of Clinical Psychology* (in press).

Birchwood, M., Smith, J., Macmillan, F., Hogg, B., Prasad, R., Harvey C. and Bering S. (1989) Predicting relapse in schizophrenia: the development and implementation of an early signs monitoring system using patients and families as observers. *Psychological Medicine*, **19**, 649–56.

Birchwood, M., Macmillan, F. and Smith, J. (1992) Early signs of relapse in schizophrenia: monitoring methodology. In: D. Kavanagh (ed.), *Schizophrenia: an Interdisciplinary Handbook*, Chapman and Hall, London.

Bowers, M.B. Jr. (1968) Pathogenesis of acute schizophrenic psychosis—an experimental approach. *Archives of General Psychiatry*, **19**, 348–55.

Brier, A. and Strauss, J.S. (1983) Self control in Psychiatric Disorders. *Archives of General Psychiatry*, **40**, 1141–5.

Cameron, D.E. (1938) Early schizophrenia. *American Journal of Psychiatry*, **95**, 567–78.

Carpenter, N.T., Heinrichs, D.W. and Hanlon, T.E. (1987) A comparative trial of pharmacological strategies in schizophrenia. *American Journal of Psychiatry*, **144**, 1466–70.

Carpenter, W.I., Hanlon, T.E., Heinrichs, D.W., Summerfelt, A.T., Kirkpatrick, B., Levine, J. and Buchanan, R.W. (1990) Continuous versus targetted medication in schizophrenic outpatients: outcome results. *American Journal of Psychiatry*, **147**, 1138–48.

Chapman, J. (1966) The early symptoms of schizophrenia. *British Journal of Psychiatry*, **112**, 225–51.

Chiles, J.A., Sterchi, D. and Hyde, T. (1989) Intermittent medication for schizophrenic outpatients: who is eligible? *Schizophrenia Bulletin*, **15**, 117–20.

Creer, C. and Wing, J. (1974) *Schizophrenia at Home*, National Schizophrenia Fellowship, Surbiton, Surrey, UK.

Davis, J.M. (1975) Overview: maintenance therapy in psychiatry: I. Schizophrenia. *American Journal of Psychiatry*, **132**, 1237–45.

Derogatis, L., Lipman, R. and Covi, L. (1973) SCL-90: an outpatient psychiatric rating scale—preliminary report. *Psychopharmacology Bulletin*, **9**, 13–17.

Docherty, J.P., Van Kammen, D.P., Siris, S.G. and Marder, S.R. (1978) Stages of onset of schizophrenic psychosis. *American Journal of Psychiatry*, **135**(4), 420–6.

Donlan, P.T. and Blacker, K.H. (1975) Clinical recognition of early schizophrenic decompensation. *Disorders of the Nervous System*, **36**, 323–30.

Eckman, T.A., Liberman, R.P., Phipps, C. and Blair, K. (1990) Teaching medication management skills to schizophrenic patients. *Journal of Clinical Psychopharmacology*, **10**, 33–8.

Foulds, G.W. (1976) *The Hierarchical Nature of Personal Illness*, Academic Press, London.

Freedman, B. and Chapman, L.J. (1973) Early subjective experience in schizophrenic episodes. *Journal of Abnormal Psychology*, **82**(1), 45–54.

Goldberg, D. and Huxley, P. (1980). *Mental Illness in the Community*, Tavistock, London.

Harrison, G., (1989) Brief intermittent neuroleptic prophylaxis for selected schizophrenic outpatients. *British Journal of Psychiatry*, **155**, 702–6.

Heinrichs, D., Cohen, B. and Carpenter, W. (1985) Early insight and the management of schizophrenic decompensation. *Journal of Nervous and Mental Disease*, **173**, 133–8.

Heinrichs, D.W. and Carpenter, W.T. (1985) Prospective study of prodromal symptoms in schizophrenic relapse. *American Journal of Psychiatry*, **143**(3).

Herz, M.I., Szymonski, H.V. and Simon, J. (1982) Intermittent medication for stable schizophrenic outpatients. *American Journal of Psychiatry*, **139**, 918–22.

Herz, M.I., Glazer, W., Mirza, M., Mostest, M. and Hafez, H. (1989). Treating prodromal episodes to prevent relapse in schizophrenia. *British Journal of Psychiatry* (suppl. 5), 123–7.

Herz, M.I. (1985) Early signs questionnaire (personal communication).

Herz, M. and Melville, C. (1980) Relapse in schizophrenia. *American Journal of Psychiatry*, **137**, 801–12.

Hirsch, S.R. and Jolley, A.G. (1989) The dysphoric syndrome in schizophrenia and its implications for relapse. *British Journal of Psychiatry* (suppl. 5), 46–50.

Hogarty, G.E., Anderson, C.M. and Reiss, D.J. (1986) Family psychoeducation, social skills training and maintenance chemotherapy in the after care treatment of schizophrenia: I. One year effects of a controlled study on relapse and expressed emotion. *Archives of General Psychiatry*, **43**, 633–42.

Jolley, A.G. and Hirsch, S.R. (1989) The Dysphoric Syndrome in schizophrenia and its implications for relapse. *British Journal of Psychiatry*, **155**, 46–50.

Jolley, A.G., Hirsch, S.R., Morrison, G., McRink, A. and Wilson, L. (1990). Trial of brief intermittent neuroleptic prophylaxis for selected schizophrenia outpatients: clinical and social outcome at two years. *British Medical Journal*, **301**, 847–52.

Johnson, D.A.W., Pasteski, G., Ludlow, J.H., Street, K. and Taylor, R.D.W. (1983) The discontinuance of maintenance neuroleptic therapy in chronic schizophrenic patients. *Acta Psychiatrica Scandinavica*, **67**, 339–52.

Johnstone, E.C., Owens, D.G.C., Gold, A., Crow, T. and Macmillan, J.F. (1984) Schizophrenic patients discharged from hospital: a follow up study. *British Journal of Psychiatry*, **145**, 586–95.

Kane, J.M., Woerner, M. and Sarantakos, S. (1986) Depot neuroleptics: a comparative review of standard intermediate and low dose regimes. *Journal of Clinical Psychiatry*, **47**(5), (suppl. May), 30–3.

Marder, S.R., Van Putten, T., Mintz, J., McKenzie, J., Lebell, M., Faltico, G. and May, R.P. (1987). Low and conventional dose maintenance therapy with Fluphenazine Decanoate. *Archives of General Psychiatry*, **44**, 518–21.

Marder, S., Van Putten, T., Mintz, J., Labell, M., McKenzie, J. and Faltico, G. (1984a) Maintenance therapy in schizophrenia: new Findings. In: J. Kane (ed.), *Drug Maintenance Strategies in Schizophrenia*, pp. 31–49, American Psychiatric Press, Washington, D.C.

Marder, S.R., Van Putten, T., Mintz, J., McKenzie, J., Lebell, M., Faltico, G. and May, R.P. (1984b) Costs and benefits of two doses of fluphenazine. *Archives of General Psychiatry*, **41**, 1025–29.

McCandless-Glincher, L., McKnight, S., Hamera, E., Smith, B.L., Peterson, K. and Plumlee, A.A. (1986) Use of symptoms by schizophrenics to monitor and regulate their illness. *Hospital and Community Psychiatry*, **37**, 929–33.

McGhie, A. and Chapman, J. (1961) Disorders of attention and perception in early schizophrenia. *British Journal of Medical Psychology*, **34**, 103–16.

Macmillan, J.F., Crow, T.J., Johnson, A.L. and Johnstone, E.C. (1986) The Northwick Park first episodes of schizophrenia study. *British Journal of Psychiatry*, **148**, 128–33.

Offenkrantz, W.C. (1962) Multiple somatic complaints as a precursor of schizophrenia. *American Journal of Psychiatry*, **119**, 258–9.

Overall, J.E. and Graham, D.R. (1962) The brief psychiatric rating scale. *Psychological Reports*, **10**, 799–812.

Owens, D.G.C. and Johnstone, E.C. (1980) The disabilities of chronic schizophrenia: their nature and factors contributing to their development. *British Journal of Psychiatry*, **136**, 384–95.

Pyke, J. and Seeman, M.D. (1981) 'Neuroleptic Free' intervals in the treatment of schizophrenia. *American Journal of Psychiatry* **138**(12), 1620–1.

Schooler, N.R. (1986) The efficacy of antipsychotic drugs, and family therapies and the maintenance treatment of schizophrenia. *Journal of Clinical Psychopharmacology*, **6**, 115–95.

Shepherd, G., (1990) Case management. *Health Trends*, **22**, 59–61.

Smith, J. and Birchwood, M. (1985) *Understanding Schizophrenia*, West Birmingham Health Authority, Health Promotion Unit.

Smith, J. and Birchwood, M. (1987) Specific and non-specific effects of educational intervention with families living with a schizophrenic relative. *British Journal of Psychiatry*, **150**, 645–52.
Smith, J. and Birchwood, M. (1990) Relatives and patients as partners in the management of schizophrenia. *British Journal of Psychiatry*, **156**, 654–60.
Stein, W. (1967) The sense of becoming psychotic. *British Journal of Psychiatry*, **30**, 262–75.
Subotnik, K.L. and Nuechterlein, K.H. (1988) Prodromal signs and symptoms of schizophrenic relapses. *Journal of Abnormal Psychology*, **97**, 405–12.
Tarrier, N., Barrowclough, C. and Vaughn, C., et al. (1988) The community management of schizophrenia: a controlled trial of behavioural intervention with families to reduce relapse. *British Journal of Psychiatry*, **153**, 532–42.
Teicher, M.H. and Baldessarini, R.J. (1985), Selection of neuroleptic dose. *Archives of General Psychiatry*, **42**, 636–7.
World Health Organisation (1979) *The International Pilot Study of Schizophrenia*, Chichester: Wiley.

Chapter 7

Management and Modification of Residual Positive Psychotic Symptoms

NICHOLAS TARRIER

INTRODUCTION

In the 1950s the development of neuroleptic medication resulted in great advances in the management of schizophrenia. The effectiveness of these drugs to reduce the positive symptoms of schizophrenia is well established (Davis, 1975; Davis et al., 1980), however, up to 30% to 40% of schizophrenic patients will relapse on medication (Leff and Wing, 1971; Johnson et al., 1987). Furthermore, a considerable number of patients will continue to experience persistent delusions and hallucinations (Curson et al., 1985, 1988; Harrow and Silverstein, 1977; Silverstein and Harrow, 1978). Thus despite the apparent effectiveness of neuroleptics, psychotic symptoms still persist and exacerbations and relapses occur frequently. These drugs also produce undesirable and unpleasant side-effects in a considerable number of patients who may default or poorly adhere to their medication regimens as a result. Because of these difficulties other methods of controlling psychotic symptoms have been investigated.

An area of psychological input which is beginning to attract attention is the management of individual psychotic symptoms. This approach can be important in two circumstances:

1. when patients continue to experience persistent residual symptoms which are not responding further to medication; and
2. when alternatives to medication are required: this may occur when patients are particularly susceptible to medication side effects, notably tardive dyskinesia or when adherence to medication is poor or non-existent. The literature has mainly focused on the first circumstance.

Innovations in the Psychological Management of Schizophrenia.
Edited by Max Birchwood and Nicholas Tarrier. © 1992 John Wiley & Sons Ltd

The aim of this chapter is to review treatment methods which have previously been used in the psychological management of psychotic symptoms and to describe in more detail a treatment programme devised by the author.

SYMPTOM MANAGEMENT METHODS

Assessment issues

Although the assessment of individual psychotic symptoms would seem a relatively easy task, it is beset with difficulties. Symptom recognition and measurement have been used principally for the purpose of psychiatric diagnosis and to a lesser extent for the identification of relapse. There has been much less interest in the measurement of symptoms *per se*. Multidimensional assessment of hallucinations and delusions is therefore still in its infancy and the development of such assessment methods describing the parameters of psychotic symptoms is a priority for future research endeavours.

A review of psychological treatments

A number of approaches have been reported that attempt to treat psychotic symptoms through psychological means. These approaches are reviewed briefly below.

Contingency management

Methods based on the operant tradition of psychology have been used to manipulate rewards and punishments contingent on specified behaviours. This method has reached its zenith in institutional settings in the token economy (e.g. Paul and Lentz, 1977). Contingency management has also been used to decrease the behavioural correlates of hallucinations and delusions.

A number of methods have been used including social reinforcement (Ayllon and Haughton, 1964; Liberman et al., 1973; Bulow, Oei and Pinkey, 1979), time out (Davis et al., 1976), social interference (Alford and Turner, 1976; Turner, Herson and Bellack, 1977; Alford, Fleece and Rothblum, 1982), punishment (Bucher and Fabricatore, 1970; Anderson and Alpert, 1974; Turner, Herson and Bellack, 1977; Fonagy and Slade, 1982; Belcher, 1988) and negative reinforcement (Fonagy and Slade, 1982).

Although positive results have frequently been reported, there are a number of problems with these approaches:

1. Improvements are rarely long lasting or resistant to extinction.
2. Improvements do not generalise to other settings and situations.
3. While these reports are usually of chronic patients in institutional settings in which some control over contingencies can be maintained, applicability in community settings must be doubtful.
4. The manipulation of contingencies requires overt behaviour to reinforce or punish and in this way overt behavioural correlates of hallucinations and delusions are eliminated or reduced.

Since psychotic symptoms are experiential and largely private mental events, patients may be learning not to talk about their symptoms rather than the symptoms themselves being reduced. Despite these problems and the fact that contingency management alone may have limited general value, especially in the era of community care, operant principles will be an important component of any treatment programme.

Stimulus control

A number of case reports have attempted to accurately identify and then modify antecedent conditions to the occurrence of psychotic symptoms. The results are somewhat mixed with some positive (Slade, 1972, 1973; Nydegger, 1972) and some negative results (Slade, 1973; Watts et al., 1973). The approach appears to be dependent on the patient's ability to identify accurately either internal or external antecedents and this may not be possible with all patients. However, it is suggested that this is a promising approach with suitable patients.

Control of auditory input

This treatment approach, designed to eliminate auditory hallucinations, involves the manipulation of auditory input and is based on theories which have hypothesised an important relationship between external (physical) stimuli and perception of internal (mental) phenomena (e.g. West, 1962; Horowitz, 1975; Slade, 1976). A number of case studies have reported successful interventions using this approach (Green, Glass and O'Callaghan, 1980; Feder, 1982; Green, Hallett and Hunter, 1983; James, 1983; Birchwood, 1986; Morley, 1987).

Biofeedback

Biofeedback has rarely been used with schizophrenic patients, however Schneider and Pope (1982) report on an intriguing use of EEG biofeedback.

They attempted to train nine patients to produce EEG patterns that resembled those associated with neuroleptic-induced clinical improvement. Significance within session changes were observed but there were no session to session changes. Unfortunately no assessments were made of any dimension of psychopathology so the clinical utility of such a procedure cannot be assessed.

Cognitive modification

Self-Instructional Training (SIT). Meichenbaum and his colleagues produced a treatment programme for schizophrenic patients which involved training the patient in self-instruction in on-task behaviour (Meichenbaum and Cameron, 1973). Initial reports demonstrated improvements in task performance, an increase in "healthy talk" and a decrease in "sick talk" (Meichenbaum and Cameron, 1973; Meyers, Mercatons and Sirota, 1976). Other reports, however, have failed to replicate these findings (Gresen, 1974; Margolis and Shemberg, 1976). In a more recent study Bentall, Higson and Lowe (1987) reported improvements in task performance but these showed poor generalisation to other tasks and there was no evidence of superiority of SIT compared to problem solving training.

Belief modification. Cognitive therapy methods which modify patients' beliefs and attitudes have been used very successfully over the last decade to treat a wide range of psychological disorders (e.g. Hawton et al., 1989). The use of cognitive belief modification methods to treat delusional beliefs predates this more widespread use with non-psychotic disorders (Beck, 1952; Watts, Powell and Austin, 1973). Watts and his colleagues in a series of controlled case studies demonstrated that belief modification reduced the severity of the abnormal belief whereas relaxation and systematic desensitisation to social situations (a stimulus control method) did not. Following on from this study a controlled trial of belief modification versus belief confrontation demonstrated the superiority of the former (Milton, Patwa and Hafner, 1978). In some patients confrontation appeared to result in the strengthening of delusional beliefs. Other case studies have also reported positive results for this method (Hole, Rush and Beck, 1979; Hartman and Cashman, 1983; Alford, 1986; Chadwick and Lowe, 1991).

Modification of cognitive processes

The modification of cognitive processes can be distinguished from cognitive modification as the latter attempts to change conscious and dysfunctional beliefs while the former attempts to address the problems of cognitive and information processing deficits which are assumed to underlie the schizophrenic disorder. A considerable amount has been written on the potential usefulness of modifying basic cognitive processes as a treatment procedure (see Brenner, 1986; Gross, 1986; Magaro, Johnson and Boring, 1986; Spaulding, 1986). However in clinical terms this area is still in its infancy. A number of case studies have reported on multi-element programmes aimed at facilitating cognitive processes (Adams et al., 1981; Spaulding et al., 1986) and Brenner and his colleagues in Bern have reported on a controlled trial of a multi-faceted programme including: cognitive differentiation, social perception, verbal communication, social skills and problem-solving (Brenner et al., 1990). This programme has been shown to be superior to placebo and control groups on a number of tests of cognitive performance and measures of general psychopathology after treatment and at 18 months follow-up. Although the rationale for this approach is plausible, there is still a lack of understanding about cognitive processes and how they relate to schizophrenic symptoms and whether poor cognitive task performance is an index of a basic underlying disorder or a consequence of the schizophrenic illness. Similarly does improvement in task performance with training reflect an improvement in the underlying cognitive deficits or a training effect? Furthermore, do these methods reduce individual hallucinations and delusions and if so what are the mechanisms of change? These questions are unresolved, however, in the light of the considerable research literature on cognitive deficits in schizophrenia this approach is worthy of further investigation.

Self-management

A number of studies have utilised a variety of self-management procedures in which patients monitor their experiences, identify them as being illness-related or not, implement a procedure to reduce symptoms when present and reinforce themselves for their successes. Such procedures have been reported to occur naturally in some patients (Breier and Strauss, 1983) and one case report suggested monitoring alone was sufficient to reduce hallucinations (Baskett, 1983). Other approaches which have included elements of self-management have been, use of thought stopping (Erickson, Darnell and Labeck, 1978; Lamontagne, Audet and Elie, 1983) and the self-administration of shock (Weingaertner, 1971). Neither of these methods demonstrated any significant clinical effect. One well-controlled study of an inpatient self-control programme did show a decrease in symptoms, however, these returned to baseline levels once the patient was discharged from hospital (Alford, Fleece and Rothblum, 1982).

Coping strategies

A number of studies have examined whether schizophrenic patients who experience persistent psychotic symptoms make any attempt to cope with these symptoms. Coping in this sense refers to cognitive and behavioural efforts to control or master the symptoms or to minimise the distress caused by them. The consistent finding from these studies has been that the majority of patients (range: 67–100%) do use active coping with varying degrees of success (Falloon and Talbot, 1981; Breier and Strauss, 1983; Cohen and Berk, 1985; Tarrier, 1987; Carr, 1988).

These naturalistic studies on the use of coping strategies have suggested that symptoms such as delusions may not be completely impervious to non-pharmacological intervention and systematic training in coping methods could be a productive method of management. This approach clearly has features in common with self-management and also includes other methods such as self-instruction and stimulus control. Three characteristics which tend to distinguish this approach are:

1. There is an attempt to use and build on coping methods already used by the patient. Hence the patient's current coping repertoire is assessed and utilised.
2. Secondly, *in vivo* practice is encouraged: that is during training in coping the patient is encouraged to simulate or even bring on the symptoms and practise the coping strategies and as homework to enter situations in which symptoms usually occur with the aim to practise coping strategies.
3. Lastly, training in coping is not restricted to the application of a single technique but may include an array or combinations of individual coping strategies.

Fowler and Morley (1989) report on five case studies, in which patients were asked to continually monitor their mood states, the frequency of symptoms and three aspects of psychotic experience: the extent to which they could control their symptoms, the extent to which they believed their symptoms to be true and the extent to which they were distressed by their symptoms. One patient showed a marked overall improvement and three others showed improvements on their perceived ability to control their symptoms.

A SPECIFIC TREATMENT METHOD BASED ON COPING STRATEGIES

The remainder of this chapter will describe a treatment method based on a behavioural analysis of psychotic symptoms and the patient's coping strategies. It involves training and practice in specified coping methods.

Clinical report

Tarrier et al. (1990) reported case studies of two schizophrenic patients who received what the authors termed Coping Strategy Enhancement (CSE). This involved the careful behavioural analysis of the patient's symptoms including the antecedents and consequences. The patient was first given a detailed rationale of the approach. If the patient lacked insight then the intervention focused on the alleviation to any distress caused by their symptoms. One symptom was targeted and a strategy to cope with it was selected. The strategy was then systematically practised under increasingly more difficult conditions in the treatment session and later as homework. Cognitive strategies were first demonstrated overtly by the therapist, then practised overtly and lastly covertly by the patient. Training in behavioural strategies was through role playing or guided practice. If the strategy was successful another symptom was selected for treatment; if not then the patient was trained in a further coping strategy and so on. The two patients treated in this manner both showed considerable improvements in their symptom. At the six month follow-up one patient had continued to improve while the second had shown some deterioration from his post-treatment level but improvements from the pretreatment were still apparent.

Evaluation

In an ongoing controlled trial to reduce residual and persistent psychotic symptoms being carried out by the author and his colleagues, CSE is being compared to problem solving (PS)(Tarrier (1987), Note 1). CSE follows the same procedure as described in this chapter. Problem-solving is used as the control treatment using the following procedure. The patient is given the rationale for PS, the procedure is initially practised on a neutral task (e.g. a simple game such as draughts or noughts and crosses) with the therapist firstly modelling the use of overt self-instruction to outline the possible alternative moves and their consequences. A move is then selected and implemented on the basis of the evaluation of the positive and negative consequences of each alternative. This procedure is then practised by the patient overtly and then covertly. A similar procedure is then applied to a standard problem (e.g. how to make new friends). Finally, the patient is asked to apply the PS method to problems that they are experiencing at that time. It will be evident from the descriptions of these two treatments (i.e. CSE and PS) that CSE directly focuses on symptom reduction while PS focuses on broader areas of functioning.

Patients were recruited into the study if they:

1. had had a diagnosis of schizophrenia (including first rank symptoms);
2. they were still experiencing psychotic symptoms which were not responding to medication;
3. they had been ill for at least 6 months;
4. they were living in the community, and
5. were between the ages of 16 and 65.

Patients were randomly allocated to one of two treatment limbs (CSE or PS). Both groups received 10 sessions of the appropriate treatment over a 5-week period. Fifty per cent of subjects in each limb were first entered into a 5-week waiting/no treatment period before treatment started. This allowed the waiting time period to act as a control condition.

In each treatment limb 50% of patients were allocated to high expectancy, in which the positive benefits of the treatment were continually emphasised and the remainder were allocated to neutral expectancy. The manipulation of expectancy of treatment outcome was performed to assess the effect of non-specific factors in the intervention. In a previous study involving the use of applied relaxation training (ART) in the treatment of generalised anxiety, expectations of treatment success were found to be responsible for some of the treatment effect (Tarrier and Main, 1986). Little appears known about the possible effect of such non-specific factors in psychological treatment approaches with schizophrenic patients. Assessment was carried out at pre-waiting period (if appropriate), pretreatment, post-treatment and at 6-month follow-up. The assessment battery included:

1. Psychotic symptoms were elicited using the PSE (Wing, Cooper and Sartorius, 1974) and a number of dimensions were then rated: severity was rated on a 7-point scale (from absent to extremely severe) based on the BPRS scales of unusual thought content or hallucinations (Lukoff, Nuechterlein and Ventura, 1986); conviction of belief, preoccupation with the symptom and interference in functioning caused by the symptom were measured using the method described by Brett-Jones, Garety and Hemsley (1987). At post-treatment and follow-up the PSE was repeated and change scores (Tress et al., 1987) calculated for any psychotic symptom that had been present at pretreatment.
2. Global psychopathology was assessed by use of the Psychiatric Assessment Scale (PAS; Krawiecka, Goldberg and Vaughan, 1977) this rates the following 8 items on a 5-point scale: depression, anxiety, delusions, hallucinations, incoherence of speech, poverty of speech, flat affect and retardation.

3. Social functioning was assessed by means of the Social Functioning Scale (SFS)(Birchwood et al. 1990).
4. Coping strategies were assessed for frequency and efficacy.
5. The problem-solving abilities of the patient were measured on a standardised task.
6. The credibility of the treatment and the patient's expectancy of its success were also assessed after the first session during which the rationale had been given; and the patient's subjective estimate of the benefit of the treatment was assessed at the post-treatment assessment.

At the time of writing 43 patients had been assessed as suitable for the study. Of these nine (21%) had refused to participate. Thirty-four patients had been allocated, fourteen to PS and twenty to CSE. Of these twenty-one had completed treatment, thirteen had completed follow-up and thirteen had completed a waiting/no treatment period. This study is as yet incomplete and any results presented at this stage should be viewed with a certain amount of caution. However, preliminary analyses indicate the following: If the symptom severity score is aggregated across symptoms for each patient then the CSE group show statistically significant improvements over treatment in symptom severity, whereas no significant change is seen in the PS group or over the waiting/no treatment period. Two (22%) patients in the PS limb show a complete remission of symptoms at post-treatment, however, no other patients show a greater than 50% improvement. In the CSE limb seven (58%) patients show an improvement of 50% or more and two (17%) of these show a complete remission of symptoms at post-treatment. Patients in the CSE limb show a decrease in preoccupation, conviction and interference of their symptoms but only the latter reaches significance. Patients receiving PS show a decrease in the strength of conviction of belief in their symptom and preoccupation with their symptoms, only the latter of which reached significance. Both treatment groups show a non-significant decrease in depression and the CSE group show a significant decrease in anxiety. However, neither treatment appears to affect social functioning. There were no changes over the waiting/no-treatment period on any of these measures.

Patients receiving neutral expectancy showed a decrease in symptom severity that just reached significance, while the high expectancy group just failed to reach significance. Hence expectancy does not appear to be an influential factor.

The results at this point indicate a superiority of CSE over PS which in turn is superior to no treatment. We await the completion of the study to see if these improvements are maintained. Research in this area is still at an early stage and there are many important clinical and theoretical questions that need to be addressed. One important direction will be to integrate research on cognitive deficits typically found in schizophrenia and how these relate to the practice of cognitive therapy.

Clinical procedure

Assessment

Standardised assessment measures have already been discussed in the section on CSE evaluation. In addition, a thorough assessment of the patients symptomatology and coping skills should be covered through a semi-structured interview.

Antecedent and coping interview

The nature of the symptoms. A thorough knowledge of the patient's current psychopathology is required and each psychotic symptom should be clearly defined. The Present State Examination (Wing, Cooper and Sartorius, 1974) is a suitable instrument for eliciting such symptoms. During the interview each symptom should be elicited and the frequency, the duration, and intensity of each symptom should be ascertained. This information can be obtained by asking general questions such as "how often do you hear the voices talking about you?" and then asking about a specific day, e.g. "how many times did you hear the voices yesterday?" Also the duration of each episode of symptoms should be obtained by asking for how long the voices were heard. This line of questioning will probably elicit a range of time periods and should be followed by questions concerning what would be the usual or typical time period. Similarly the severity of each episode should be asked about through questioning on the loudness of the hallucinations or the strengths of the delusional ideas, how easy or difficult they were to ignore or how preoccupying they were when experienced.

Elicit the accompanying emotional reactions. Initially general questions concerning the accompanying emotional reaction should be asked such as "how do you feel when this happens?" and "how does this affect you?" Prompts can also be used such as "do you feel frightened/nervous/angry/fed up/sad, etc?" Once a general emotional reaction to the experience of the psychotic symptom has been elicited, then attempts should be made to obtain more specific examples in terms of somatic sensations, cognition and behaviour. Somatic sensations can be elicited by questioning about how the patient feels physically and prompts can be given concerning specific sensations, for example, "do you experience: your heart beating fast?/your muscles tensing up?/your hands sweating?/butterflies in your stomach?, etc. Similarly, cognitive reactions can be elicited by initially asking general questions such as "what goes through your mind when you feel this way/or hear these voices?" It is important to pick up examples the interviewee may give and use these to make suggestions that elicit further examples. Behavioural reactions can be obtained by asking what the patient does when she/he has their experiences. Questions should then be asked concerning whether these are typical reactions, for example, "do you always feel/think/act like this?", "what else happens?" The interviewer should continue to probe for other alternatives once the first few examples have been elicited. Probe questions should be used to help elicit the patient's account of the emotional consequences of the symptoms and the acceptance of a "yes" response without an account of how the patient felt should be avoided. During this line of questioning, examples and evidence of coping strategies may also be given and these should be noted and used as prompts later in the interview.

Elicit antecedents. Questions should now be asked concerning the occurrence of any antecedent or precipitating context for each symptom in turn. Example questions include: "can you tell when (the symptom) is going to occur?", "how do you know?", "when does (the symptom) happen?", "what happens before you experience (the symptom)?" Attempts should be made to elicit: where the person is, what they were doing, who else was there, and so on. Probes should be made to elicit external or environmental stimuli so as to assess regular and consistent antecedents to the symptom. If a number of antecedents are elicited then common elements or characteristics should be ascertained. Once external stimuli have been assessed, then questions should be asked concerning internal stimuli such as physical sensations especially feelings of tension, and cognitive stimuli, e.g. a particular train of thought. When both external and internal antecedents have been elicited possible relationships should be examined, for example do certain internal stimuli always occur in the presence of specific external ones? For example, does the patient frequently feel anxious in social situations which precipitate delusions of reference? Questions concerning apparently obvious antecedents should also be asked, for example, do delusions of receiving messages from the TV only occur when the TV is on. Careful attention should also be paid to whether lack of stimulation (e.g. being alone or inactive) or overstimulation (e.g. being in social situations) act as precipitant. Lastly, it is important to assess how easily the patient can identify antecedents as this may have implications for facilitating treatment.

Elicit consequences. In eliciting the consequences of the symptom we are attempting to ascertain the longer-term consequences and not the immediate emotional reactions. That is what the person does in response to the symptoms. Questions should be asked concerning what happens after the symptom has occurred. If the patient repeats their emotional reaction then ask what happens after that or how they deal with their emotions. Here we are looking for examples of the effects of experiencing the symptoms such as social withdrawal and avoidance or reductions and restrictions in the patients behavioural repertoire. These consequences are frequently passive coping attempts which result in behavioural and social difficulties.

Elicit active coping. This part of the interview attempts to find out how the patient tries to master the symptoms. As before, initially ask general questions and use this information along with any information obtained earlier in the interview to probe for specific coping strategies. For example, such questions as: "how do you cope with this?", "how do you react to (the symptom)?", "what do you do to make yourself feel better?", "is there anything you can do to get rid of (the symptom)?" are useful probes. Attempt should be made to get the patient to describe their coping in terms of changes in physical sensations, cognitive processes or actions. For example, "is there anything you can do to help yourself by feeling a certain way? (e.g. relaxing)", "how do you do this?" If the patient answers in the affirmative, then follow-up with further probes such as "are there any other ways in which you can relax?" Similarly with cognitive strategies, "can you help yourself by thinking in a certain way or telling yourself certain things?" Care should be taken to ascertain the function of the cognitive strategy: does the patient restrict or narrow the range of items already in attention or is attention switched to another subject? Likewise, behavioural strategies should also be assessed, for example by asking: "can you help yourself by doing something?" Here the actual behaviour should be elicited and the opportunities for its implementation, (e.g. by changing the environment or social context). For example, if the patient indicates that engaging in social interaction is effective then ask about the opportunities to do this. Furthermore, ask about common functions of different strategies, for example, if it appears that social engagement is distracting then ask about other methods of distraction (e.g. "can you distract yourself in other ways?"). Table 7.1 classifies coping strategies.

Effectiveness of coping. When a list of coping strategies has been defined, attempt to assess the effectiveness of each. For example, ask "when you (specify the strategy), how much help is this?" Rate each strategy as negligible, moderate or very effective. Strategies that are inconsistently effective should only be rated as negligible or moderate. To be rated as very effective a strategy should be consistently effective and stable across time. The

Table 7.1 Classification of coping strategies

1. Cognitive strategies

(a) Attention Switching
The process of focusing attention on to a stimulus which was not already in attention, e.g. distraction

(b) Attention Narrowing
The process of reducing the range of attention

(c) Self-Statement
The process of using covert verbal behaviour to either direct behaviour or re-attribute the cause of an experience or event.

2. Behavioural strategies

(a) Increased Activity Levels
The action of increasing activities which do not require social interaction, e.g. exercise, walking

(b) Increased Social Activity
The action of initiating social engagement

(c) Decreased Social Activity
The action of disengaging from social interaction or avoiding social interaction. (The short-term use of social engagement may be a useful coping method, however, social avoidance resulting in withdrawal and isolation should be classified as a negative consequence and not encouraged)

(d) Reality Testing
Actions which lead to the testing of various causal explanations of events or their interpretation

3. Sensory strategies
Strategies which involve the modification of sensory input

4. Physiological strategies
Strategies which involve the modification of physiological states. These can be appropriate e.g. relaxation or breathing control, or inappropriate e.g. alcohol or drug abuse.

patient's ability for training in coping should also be assessed, that is, whether she/he uses coping strategies already but inconsistently. If coping results in variable success, elicit under what conditions this variability occurs.

In conclusion. Lastly check that (1) the range of symptoms has been completely assessed; (2) where a symptom has been identified, then its occurrence, emotional response, antecedents, consequences and coping responses have been completely assessed. At this point a comprehensive picture of the determinants of the patient's psychotic experience and his/her attempts to deal and cope with them should have been built up. As in cognitive-behaviour therapy an accurate and detailed analysis of the problem and its determinants is essential for successful intervention. The interview also serves the function of building a rapport and relationship with the patient and to demonstrate that you take his or her experience seriously, even if you do have a different explanation of the cause.

Potential problems. The probability of the success of this behavioural assessment of psychotic symptoms is increased if the symptoms are discrete, easily identified and viewed as being illness-related. A lack of insight into the nature of the symptoms is less of a problem if the patient recognises the distress these experiences and thoughts can cause even if she/he regards their content as true. The rationale of reducing distress is then frequently acceptable to the patient as a rationale for intervention. Greater difficulty will be encountered if symptoms appear to be diffuse and vague, the patient's accounts of them appear unreliable or varying or when the patient is severely thought disordered or confused. In these cases detailed analysis may prove extremely difficult and more general information may have to be accepted.

Treatment using coping strategy enhancement (CSE)

The aim of CSE is to systematically teach the patient the use of effective coping strategies to reduce the frequency, intensity and duration of the residual psychotic symptoms and their emotional consequences. The assessment interview should produce detailed and individualised data concerning the patient's symptoms, their maintaining factors and his/her coping. The data should be used as a basis for generating interventions based on knowledge of antecedents and coping.

Education and rapport building

As with all cognitive behavioural interventions an approach of "collaborative empiricism" should be adopted. To enhance this collaborative endeavour between the therapist and the patient it is advisable to provide the patient with detailed information about schizophrenia and the rationale for this treatment approach. Such information can be obtained from appropriate texts (e.g. Barrowclough et al., 1985; Barrowclough and Tarrier, 1992). It is likely that some patients will reject some or all of this information. The therapist should not dismiss the patient's personal explanation of his or her experience, but rather suggest that they agree to differ at this point with a view to putting the different explanations to experimental test at a later stage. Later, appropriate predictions can be generated from the therapist's illness model and the patient's personal model which should be tested out in reality (see later in the text). At this early stage, however, both parties should agree to focus on reducing the associated stress experienced by the patient.

Procedure

1. From the assessment information a target symptom should be selected on the basis of either ease of treatment (i.e. the symptom which has clearly identified and modifiable antecedents, for which the patient has clearly identified or partially successful or appropriate coping strategies) or being of high priority (i.e. causing the patient considerable distress or disruption to functioning).
2. Select an appropriate coping strategy from those that occur naturally or one which seems most appropriate or potentially successful (Table 7.1).
3. Again explain the rationale to the patient and obtain feedback indicating that the patient has understood the rationale.
4. Put the coping strategy into action, where possible using the antecedents to the symptoms as contextual cues.
   (a) Where appropriate systematically practice the coping strategy within the session:
      (i) first practice the strategy in isolation, asking the patient to rate on a 0–10 scale how easy/successful they were with the implementation;
      (ii) generate the symptom or alternatively simulate the symptom in imagination and implement the coping strategy, again asking the patient to rate ease/success. Continue until the patient's rating of ease and success of use is high and stable.
   (b) When a coping strategy is difficult to practice within the session then:
      (i) clearly stipulate the required procedure in behavioural terms and conditions under which it is to be implemented;
      (ii) verify through feedback that the patient is fully aware of the strategy and conditions under which it should be used;
      (iii) practice this procedure in imagination;
      (iv) set self-directed *in vivo* practice as homework tasks.
5. Instruct the patient in how to monitor and record the implementation of the strategy. Set explicit and appropriate homework exercises involving the use of coping strategies in real life situations. Homework exercises should gradually become more complex and difficult.
6. During the next session verify that the strategy was implemented and assess its success through examination of records and by direct questioning. If the strategy was successful then reinforce the patient with praise and encouragement and give booster practice. If it was not implemented then return to stage 1. If it was not successful then assess the possible reasons, modify the intervention accordingly and

re-implement. If there is no improvement then select a new target symptom.
7. Implement at least two strategies for each symptom before selecting a new target symptom. Further strategies can also be added later if required.

Attempt to achieve a consistent and stable approach and not one characterised by short and general advice. Patients may require long and detailed training in coping methods before change is produced in their symptoms. It should be remembered that non-psychotic patients frequently hold irrational beliefs with great conviction which are difficult to modify, therefore psychotic patients can be expected to change at an even slower rate.

Case example

Tom experienced unpleasant and hostile auditory hallucinations mainly describing his actions and his thoughts. They occurred when he was out of the house, in public places, in queues and at the shops. He would also experience these voices when alone and inactive at home, usually in the evening and at night. These experiences would make him feel frightened and angry. He also experienced feeling that other people could read his mind, this was especially true of teenagers whom he thought were "out to get him". Generally, he did not experience any such symptoms at home during the day, in the company of his parents with whom he lived or when at the day hospital which he attended twice a week. He found his experiences exceedingly distressing and consequently he avoided going out of the house if at all possible and he found the journey to the day hospital very difficult and frightening. He frequently failed to attend or occasionally he took a taxi which was a strain on his limited finances. At home he did little except watch the television and occasionally help his retired parents around the house. He tried to shout back and argue with the voices, especially when he was at home, and he would occasionally get into arguments with teenagers and schoolchildren while travelling to the day hospital. On one occasion Tom had hit a teenage boy while on the bus as he had thought that he was going to be attacked. Objectively, however, Tom's assault was unprovoked. Tom said that he did try to think of other things to distract himself but this was usually unsuccessful.

The first situation to be targeted was the experience of auditory hallucinations at home. These occurred mainly during the evenings and at night when he was alone in his room. It was first suggested that he should avoid spending long periods alone in his room during the evenings. As an alternative he should spend more time with his parents and if possible engage them in conversation. Goals were set for spending specified time periods with his parents and to attempt suitable conversation with them. This resulted in the reduction of time spent in the precipitating situation but Tom still experienced the voices when he went to bed. Coping in this situation was broken down into three elements:

1. reattributing the experience as illness-related and not due to a group of people gathering outside his window;

2. allowing himself to relax instead of getting angry and tense;
3. instructing himself not to respond to the voices but to continue with his relaxation.

Firstly, Tom was taught a quick version of autogenic relaxation which concentrated on "letting go" of tension, controlled breathing and self-instruction to relax. Secondly, Tom was taught to relabel the voices as illness-related. This involved using the onset of the auditory hallucinations as a stimulus to repeat relabelling statements. These statements were: "the voices aren't real", "they're a symptom of the illness", "they cannot hurt me". These statements were written down on a cue-card and Tom memorised them during the session. The therapist then simulated the auditory hallucinations in response to which Tom repeated aloud the three statements. After the first practice Tom rated on a 11-point scale (0 = "cannot do it" to 10 = "no trouble, completely successful") how easy he had found this. In fact he had found this task quite difficult (a score of 3) and he had muddled his statements. Practice continued until Tom correctly repeated the statements and scored at least 7 on three consecutive trials. The complete procedure was then repeated with Tom repeating the statements covertly instead of aloud and then again with Tom imagining the voices instead of the therapist simulating them.

The next stage was to use the successful repetition of the relabelling statements as a cue to implement relaxation. This again was practised under simulated conditions until a success criterion was achieved. Lastly, the maintenance and reality-test component was taught. Tom believed the voices came from people who were outside his window and were planning an imminent attack. By getting angry and shouting back at them he believed that he had prevented an actual physical attack. Distraction was unlikely to be successful unless this belief was challenged. Tom and the therapist agreed to put this belief to the test. If the voices were real and Tom's belief true then a failure to argue should result in an attack. If the therapist's view that the voices were a symptom of his illness was true then no attack should occur. The third element of the coping sequence were statements aimed at maintaining relaxation and preventing a reply to the voices, e.g., "If I just concentrate on my breathing, I'll be OK", "I mustn't reply". Tom's homework was to spend the evening in the presence of his parents and then to implement the coping sequence outlined above when he retired to his room.

When Tom was seen again 3 days later it transpired that this sequence had been partially successful. The first 2 nights he had managed not to shout back at the voices, but he had done so on the third night. Tom agreed that he had not been attacked and although his belief in the voices being real was still strong, he felt greatly relieved and much less concerned for his own safety. The difficulty with the programme appeared to be in maintaining distraction and physical relaxation over an extended period of time while not attending to the voices. Further distraction strategies were therefore required.

Tom was asked to think of an activity or situation that he liked doing or enjoyed. He chose having a meal in a favourite café in Blackpool. This was where he spent his holidays and the situation had a lot of positive memories for him. He was asked to describe the situation in detail while creating a mental image of himself having his favourite meal. This was practised until he could easily produce and maintain a mental image of the situation. The previous training procedure was then repeated with Tom switching his attention to this positive mental image after repeating the relaxation maintaining self-statement to himself. He was then instructed to use the extended procedure for coping with the hallucinations that occurred in the evenings.

This modified procedure proved much more successful in maintaining distraction.

A similar procedure was implemented to deal with the psychotic experiences Tom had while travelling to the day centre. Training in a similar package of coping strategies was performed with the therapist firstly verbalising the delusional ideas that people at the bus stop could read his thoughts, were talking about him and were going to "get him". These overt verbalisations were used as cues to implement the coping package, when the success criterion was achieved the procedure was repeated with Tom imagining the delusional thoughts. As homework Tom was instructed not to avoid travelling to the centre by public transport but to use this difficult situation as a training exercise for implementing the coping strategies. As before attention was focused on modifying the emotional and behavioural sequelae of the psychotic phenomena on the basis that these formed an emotional and behavioural complex which maintained the occurrence of the psychotic symptoms and were also strong inhibiters of appropriate on-going behaviour which compromised his quality of life.

It should be clear from this example that a detailed behavioural analysis of the patients symptomatology and systematic training in coping strategies is essential. It may also be the case that coping strategies and behavioural testing are not powerful enough to remove the delusional belief but may remove the emotional and behavioural consequences of that belief. For example another patient would experience auditory hallucinations of voices shouting obscenities. She experienced these on one occasion while attending a church social and became convinced that other attenders had heard the voices and believed that it was her blaspheming. She became convinced that she was being shunned because of these transgressions and decided that she could not attend any further meetings. Besides causing her considerable distress these meetings were her only social activity. The therapist accepted her beliefs as being possible and predicted that if she did attend a further meeting the other women would make their disapproval evident. An alternative explanation was also advanced and this was that the voices were part of her illness and that she had misinterpreted the social cues at the meeting because of her distress. This explanation would predict that if she attended further meetings and concentrated on controlling her anxiety there would be no social censure. Putting these two explanations to the test she found that she was welcomed to the meetings as before. In the week following she agreed that her belief had been wrong. A number of weeks later, however, she said that she was firmly convinced that the other women had heard the voices but this no longer caused her any distress and she continued to attend church meetings with evident enjoyment. In this case the hallucinations and their delusional interpretations were not permanently eradicated but the consequential emotional distress was alleviated and social withdrawal and isolation prevented.

Potential problems and difficulties in implementation

To achieve success with this therapeutic strategy the patient must be engaged and maintained in treatment for a sufficient time to teach them the appropriate skills and to ensure that these skills are implemented appropriately and consistently. There are a number of potential problems that may arise with this patient population.

1. Initial engagement can be difficult and some time may be necessarily spent building up a personal relationship with the patient before assessment and treatment can be initiated. It should be remembered that schizophrenia frequently renders the sufferer intolerant of social stimulation. Hence the duration of sessions may, at least at first, be quite short. Recognition that the patient's experiences and their interpretation of them are very real to the patient will help to build rapport. Practical arrangements such as seeing the patient at home or at a day centre or drop in centre may also facilitate initial engagement.
2. Many patients may retain absolute conviction in their delusional beliefs. Since a confrontational approach is likely to discourage engagement attention should be focused on the negative emotional consequences of these experiences and the positive effect that the alleviation of such distress will have for the patient.
3. Since many patients have chronic illnesses the approach of psychiatric staff to the patient's self-report of their symptoms is frequently to ignore them. Hence the assessment and treatment procedure detailed here may have the effect of encouraging the patient to talk about their symptoms. It is therefore important to pay careful attention to the changes in contingencies and their consequences that this programme may bring about.
4. A time limited treatment programme may be inappropriate for some patients who will need involvement for an extended period of time. Other patients should be provided with regular booster sessions to maintain treatment benefits.
5. Symptom management programmes should be integrated with other intervention programmes to meet the individual needs of the patient. For example, it may be desirable to combine both the CSE programme with a Problem-Solving programme so as to address wider areas of functioning. Similarly interventions focused on living skills (see Chapter 7) could be incorporated to expand the patient's behaviour repertoire and level of functioning.
6. Emotional difficulties such as depression are common in patients suffering from schizophrenia and may also need to be addressed.
7. Other factors may also affect the variation in symptom level. These may be internal and require pharmacological intervention or external such as the level of stress in the home environment and may require a psychosocial intervention with the patient's relatives (see Chapter 9).
8. Strategies for maintenance of coping skills should be programmed into the overall treatment approach, this may involve the collaboration of relatives or other direct care staff or psychiatric personnel.

CONCLUSIONS

In conclusion there is reasonable evidence that careful and systematic intervention designed to improve symptom management can result in improvements in drug resistant symptoms. These benefits, especially when integrated into a comprehensive treatment plan can improve the quality of life of patients suffering from schizophrenia.

REFERENCES

Adams, H.E., Malatesta, V., Brontley, P.J. and Turkat, I.D. (1981) Modification of cognitive processes: a case study of schizophrenia. *Journal of Consulting and Clinical Psychology*, **49**, 460–4.

Alford, B.A. (1986) Behavioural treatments of schizophrenic delusions: a single-case experimental analysis. *Behavior Therapy*, **17**, 637–44.

Alford, G.S. and Turner, S.M. (1976) Stimulus interference and conditioned inhibition of auditory hallucinations. *Journal of Behavior Therapy and Experimental Psychiatry*, **7**, 155–60.

Alford, G.S., Fleece, L. and Rothblum, E. (1982) Hallucinatory–delusional verbalisations: modification in a chronic schizophrenic by self-control and cognitive restructuring. *Behavior Modification*, **6**, 421–35.

Anderson, L.T. and Alpert, M. (1974) Operant analysis of hallucination frequency in a hospitalised schizophrenic. *Journal of Behavior Therapy and Experimental Psychiatry*, **5**, 13–18.

Ayllon, T. and Haughton, E. (1964) Modification of symptomatic verbal behavior of mental patients. *Behaviour Research and Therapy*, **2**, 87–97.

Barrowclough, C. and Tarrier, N. (1992) *Families of Schizophrenic Patients: Cognitive Behavioural Intervention*, Chapman and Hall, London.

Barrowclough, C., Tarrier, N., Watts, S., Vaughn, C. and Freeman, H.L. (1985) *Information for Relatives about Schizophrenia*, North West Fellowship, Warrington.

Baskett, S.J. (1983) Tardive dyskinesia and treatment of psychosis after withdrawal of neuroleptics. *Brain Research Bulletin*, **11**, 173–4.

Beck, A.T. (1952) Successful out-patient psychotherapy of a chronic schizophrenic with a delusion based on borrowed guilt. *Psychiatry*, **15**, 305–12.

Belcher, T.L. (1988) Behavioural reduction of overt hallucinatory behaviour in chronic schizophrenics. *Journal of Behavior Therapy and Experimental Psychiatry*, **19**, 69–71.

Bental, R.P., Higson, P. and Lowe, C.F. (1987) Teaching self-instruction to chronic schizophrenic patients: efficacy and generalisation. *Behaviour Psychotherapy*, **15**, 58–76.

Birchwood, M. (1986) Control of auditory hallucinations through occlusion of monoaural auditory input. *British Journal of Psychiatry*, **149**, 104–7.

Birchwood, M., Smith J., Cochrane, R., Wetton, S. and Copestake, S. (1990) The social functioning scale: the development and validation of a scale of social adjustment for use in family intervention programmes with schizophrenic patients. *British Journal of Psychiatry*, **157**, 853–9.

Breier, A. and Strauss, J.S. (1983) Self-control in psychotic disorders. *Archives of General Psychiatry*, **40**, 1141–5.
Brenner, H.D. (1986) On the importance of cognitive disorders in treatment and rehabilitation. In: J. Strauss, W. Boker and H. D. Brenner (eds), *Psychosocial Treatment of Schizophrenia*, Hans Huber, Bern.
Brenner, H.D., Kraemer, S., Hermanutz, M. and Hodel, B. (1990) Cognitive treatments in schizophrenia. In: E.R. Straube and K. Hahlweg (eds), *Schizophrenia: Concepts Vulnerability and Intervention*, Springer-Verlag, Berlin.
Brett-Jones, J., Garety, P. and Hemsley, D. (1987) Measuring delusional experience: a method and its application. *British Journal of Clinical Psychology*, **26**, 257–65.
Bucher, B. and Fabricatore, J. (1970) Use of patient administered shock to suppress hallucinations. *Behavior Therapy*, **1**, 382–5.
Bulow, H., Oei, T.P.S. and Pinkey, B. (1979) Effects of contingent social reinforcement with delusional chronic schizophrenic men. *Psychological Reports*, **44**, 659–66.
Carr, V. (1988) Patients' techniques for coping with schizophrenia: an exploratory study. *British Journal of Medical Psychology*, **61**, 339–52.
Chadwick, P. and Lowe, F.L. (1991) The measurement and modification of delusional beliefs. *Journal of Consulting and Clinical Psychology*, **58**, 225–32.
Cohen, C.I. and Berk, B.S. (1985) Personal coping styles of schizophrenic out-patients. *Hospital and Community Psychiatry*, **36**, 407–10.
Curson D.A., Barnes, T.R.E., Bamber, R.W., Platt, S.D., Hirsch, S.R. and Duffy, J.D. (1985) Long term depot maintenance of chronic schizophrenic outpatients. *British Journal of Psychiatry*, **146**, 464–80.
Curson, D.A., Patel, M., Liddle, P.F. and Barnes, T.R.E. (1988) Psychiatric morbidity of a long stay hospital population with chronic schizophrenia and implications for future community care. *British Medical Journal*, **297**, 819–22.
Davis, J.M. (1975) Overview: maintenance therapy in psychiatry: I. Schizophrenia. *American Journal of Psychiatry*, **13**, 1237–54.
Davis, J.M., Schaffer, C.B., Killian, G.A., Kinard, C. and Chan, C. (1980) Important issues in the drug treatment of schizophrenia. *Schizophrenia Bulletin*, **6**, 70–87.
Davis, J.R., Wallace, C.J., Liberman, R.P. and Finch, B.E. (1976) The use of brief isolation to suppress delusional and hallucinatory speech. *Journal of Behavior Therapy and Experimental Psychiatry*, **7**, 269–75.
Erickson, E., Darnell, M.H. and Labeck, I. (1978) Belief treatment of hallucinatory behaviour with behavioural techniques. *Behavior Therapy*, **9**, 663–5.
Falloon, I.R.H. and Talbot, R.E. (1981) Persistent auditory hallucinations: coping mechanisms and implications for management. *Psychological Medicine*, **11**, 329–39.
Feder, R. (1982) Auditory hallucinations treated by radio headphones. *American Journal of Psychiatry*, **139**, 1188–90.
Fonagy, P. and Slade, P. (1982) Punishment vs negative reinforcement in the aversive conditioning of auditory hallucinations. *Behaviour Research and Therapy*, **20**, 483–92.
Fowler, D. and Morley, S. (1989) The cognitive–behavioural treatment of hallucinations and delusions: a preliminary study. *Behavioural Psychotherapy*, **17**, 267–82.
Gresen, R. (1974) The effects of instruction and reinforcement on a multifaceted self-control procedure in the modification and generalisation of behaviour in schizophrenia. Unpublished Ph.D. thesis, Bowling Green University (cited by Margolis and Shemberg, 1976).

Green, W.P., Glass, A. and O'Callaghan, M.A. (1980) Some implications of abnormal hemisphere interaction in schizophrenia. In: J. Gruzelier and P. Flor-Henry (eds), *Hemisphere Asymmetries and Psychopathology*, Macmillan, London.

Green, W.P., Hallett, S. and Hunter, M. (1983) Abnormal interhemispheric specialisations in schizophrenic and high risk children. In: P. Flor-Henry and J. Gruzelier (eds), *Laterality and Psychopathology*, Elsevier, Amsterdam.

Gross, G. (1986) Basic symptoms and coping behaviour in schizophrenia. In: J. Strauss, W. Boker and H.D. Brenner (eds), *Psychosocial Treatment of Schizophrenia*. Hans Huber, Bern.

Harrow, M. and Silverstein, M.L. (1977) Psychotic symptoms in schizophrenia after the acute phase. *Schizophrenia Bulletin*, **3**, 608–16.

Hartman, L.M. and Cashman, F.E. (1983) Cognitive–behavioural and psychopharmacological treatment of delusional symptoms: a preliminary report. *Behavioural Psychotherapy*, **11**, 50–61.

Hawton, K., Salkovskis, P.M., Kirk, J. and Clark, D.M. (1989) *Cognitive Behaviour Therapy for Psychiatric Problems*. Oxford University Press.

Horowitz, M.J. (1975) A cognitive model of hallucinations. *American Journal of Psychiatry*, **132**, 789–95.

Hole, R.W., Rush, A.J. and Beck, A.T. (1979) A cognitive investigation of schizophrenic delusions. *Psychiatry*, **42**, 312–19.

James, D. (1983) The experimental treatment of two cases of verbal hallucinations. *British Journal of Psychiatry*, **143**, 515–16.

Johnson, D.A.W., Ludlow, J.M., Street, K. and Taylor, R.D.W. (1987) Double blind comparison of half-dose and standard dose flupenthixol decanoate in the maintenance treatment of stabilised out-patient schizophrenics. *British Journal of Psychiatry*, **151**, 634–38.

Krawiecka, M., Goldberg, D. and Vaughan, M. (1977) A standardised psychiatric assessment scale for rating chronic psychotic patients. *Acta Psychiatrica Scandinavica*, **55**, 299–308.

Lamontagne, Y., Audet, N. and Elie, R. (1983) Thought stopping for delusions and hallucinations: a pilot study. *Behavioural Psychotherapy*, **11**, 177–84.

Leff, J.P. and Wing, J.K. (1971) Trial of maintenance therapy in schizophrenia. *British Medical Journal*, **iii**, 599–604.

Liberman, R.P., Teigan, J., Patterson, R. and Baker, V. (1973) Reducing delusional speech in chronic paranoid schizophrenics. *Journal of Applied Behavior Analysis*, **6**, 57–64.

Lukoff, D., Nuechterlein, K.H. and Ventura, J. (1986) Manual for Expanded Brief Psychiatric Rating Scale (BPRS). *Schizophrenia Bulletin*, **12**, 594–602.

Magaro, P.A., Johnson, M. and Boring, R. (1986) Information processing approaches to the treatment of schizophrenia. In: R.E. Ingram (ed.), *Information Processing Approaches to Clinical Psychology*, Academic, London.

Margolis, R. and Shemberg, K. (1976) Use of self-instruction for the elimination of psychotic speech. *Behavior Therapy*, **7**, 668–71.

Meichenbaum, D. and Cameron, R. (1973) Training schizophrenics to talk to themselves: a means of developing attentional control. *Behavior Therapy*, **4**, 515–34.

Meyes, A., Mercatons, M. and Sirota, A. (1976) Use of self-instruction for the elimination of psychotic speech. *Journal of Consulting and Clinical Psychology*, **44**, 480–2.

Milton, F., Patwa, V.K. and Hafner, J. (1978) Confrontation vs belief modification in persistently deluded patients. *British Journal of Medical Psychology*, **51**, 127–30.

Morley, S. (1987) Modification of auditory hallucinations: experimental studies of headphones and earplugs. *Behaviour Psychotherapy*, **15**, 240–51.

Nydegger, R.V. (1972) The elimination of hallucinatory and delusional behaviours by verbal conditioning and assertive training: a case study. *Journal of Behavior Therapy and Experimental Psychiatry*, **3**, 225–7.

Paul, G. and Lentz, R. (1977) *Psychological Treatment of Chronic Mental Patients. Milieu versus Social Learning Programmes*, Harvard University Press, Cambridge, Mass.

Schneider, S.J. and Pope, A.T. (1982) Neuroleptic-like electroencephalographic changes in schizophrenics through biofeedback. *Biofeedback and Self-Regulation*, **7**, 479–90.

Slade, P.D. (1972) The effects of systematic desensitisation auditory hallucinations. *Behaviour Research and Therapy*, **10**, 85–91.

Slade, P.D. (1973) The psychological investigation and treatment of auditory hallucinations: a second case report. *British Journal of Medical Psychology*, **46**, 293–6.

Slade, P.D. (1976) Towards a theory of auditory hallucinations: outline of an hypothetical four-factor model. *British Journal of Social and Clinical Psychology*, **15**, 415–23.

Silverstein, M.L. and Harrow, M. (1978) First rank symptoms in the post acute schizophrenic: a follow-up study. *American Journal of Psychiatry*, **135**, 1481–6.

Spaulding, W.D., Storms, L., Goodrich, V. and Sullivan, M. (1986) Application of experimental psychopathology in psychiatric rehabilitation. *Schizophrenia Bulletin*, **12**, 560–77.

Tarrier, N. (1987) An investigation of residual psychotic symptoms in discharged schizophrenic patients. *British Journal of Clinical Psychology*, **26**, 141–3.

Tarrier, N. and Main, C. (1986) Applied relaxation training (ART) with patients suffering from generalised anxiety and panic attacks: the efficacy of a learnt coping strategy on subjective reports. *British Journal of Psychiatry*, **149**, 330–6.

Tarrier, N., Harwood, S., Yusopoff, L., Beckett, R. and Baker, A. (1990) Coping Strategy Enhancement (CSE): a method of treating residual schizophrenic symptoms. *Behavioural Psychotherapy* **18**, 283–93.

Tress, K.H., Bellenis, C., Brownlow, J.M., Livinston, G. and Leff, J.P. (1987) The Present State Examination Change rating scale. *British Journal of Psychiatry*, **150**, 201–7.

Turner, S., Herson, M. and Bellack, A. (1977) Effects of social disruption, stimulus interference and aversive conditioning on auditory hallucinations. *Behaviour Modification*, **1**, 249–58.

Watts, F.N., Powell, G.E. and Austin, S.V. (1973) The modification of abnormal beliefs. *British Journal of Medical Psychology*, **46**, 359–63.

Weingaertner, A.H. (1971) Self-administered aversive stimulation with hallucinating hospitalised schizophrenics. *Journal of Consulting and Clinical Psychology*, **36**, 422–9.

West, L.J. (1962) A general theory of hallucinations and dreams. In: L.J. West, (ed.), *Hallucinations*, Grune & Stratton, New York.

Wing, J.K., Cooper, J.E. and Sartorius, N. (1974) *Measurement and Classification of Psychiatric Symptoms: an Instruction Manual for the PSE and Catego Programme*, Cambridge University Press.

Chapter 8

Management of Long-term Impairments and Challenging Behaviour

LORNA HOGG AND JOHN HALL

Long-term impairments and challenging behaviour are not new problems facing clinicians working with people who have a diagnosis of schizophrenia. The need to activate people demonstrating long-term impairments such as lethargy and slowness was one of the main principles underlying the development of the asylum in the nineteenth century. Also it might be argued that the recently coined term "challenging behaviour" is no more than a euphemism for the aggressive, bizarre, personally and socially disruptive behaviour which has always been a feature noted in association with schizophrenia. What have changed, however, are the politics and philosophies underpinning the care of people with schizophrenia and it is these that have necessitated changes in the management of people with schizophrenia (Shepherd, 1991).

Changes in care practices which have had a major impact on the management of long-term impairments and challenging behaviour include the loss of beds in acute and long-term care wards where people presenting with such behaviour were once to be found. Such changes have led to a reduction in the average length of stay, and an increase in the use of alternative day-care and residential options. Treatment at home, where possible, is now strongly encouraged and patients with long-term problems are discharged to a wide range of community facilities. Whereas once all services required to meet patients' needs were brought together on one site, the psychiatric hospital, now they are often scattered across the community (Häfner, 1985).

The drive towards community care has had major implications for the care of people with schizophrenia. For example, many authors have argued that it has led to an increase in the numbers of people with schizophrenia to be found in homeless populations and prisons (Lamb, 1984)

Innovations in the Psychological Management of Schizophrenia.
Edited by Max Birchwood and Nicholas Tarrier. © 1992 John Wiley & Sons Ltd

where staff are ill-equipped to cope with the problems they present (Hogg, Hall and Marshall, 1990). It has been suggested that shelters for the homeless are simply taking over the role of the traditional psychiatric hospital (Bassuk, Rubin and Lauriat, 1984) and the difficulty staff in these settings have in managing actively disturbed people has been used as an argument for a return to "asylum" for such people (King's Fund Forum, 1987).

Recent interest in challenging behaviour can in part be attributed to the management problems such behaviour presents within inadequate and underfunded community contexts, and possibly also within a context of low public tolerance compared to hospital settings, rather than any new set of problems. Thus clinicians already experienced in the assessment and treatment of behavioural problems within hospital settings will find many of their skills very useful in managing challenging behaviour in community settings.

Consistent with the belief that knowledge and techniques learned within traditional hospital settings have much to contribute to the management of problem behaviours within community settings, one of the main aims of this chapter is to pull together what has been learned from tried and tested methods such as token economy procedures, milieu approaches, and structured individual programmes. Details of how to carry out some treatments are given. A further important aim of the chapter is to consider more recent developments in assessment and treatment, in particular drawing on work developed in relation to other problem areas and client groups, such as cognitive-behaviour therapy approaches to the understanding and management of problems within general adult populations (Hawton and Kirk, 1989).

The chapter is split into four main sections covering the nature and definitions of the problems of both long-term impairments and challenging behaviour; assessment; goal setting; and therapeutic interventions. The importance of considering aspects of settings as well as carer and patient variables in relation to planning successful interventions will be referred to throughout the chapter.

DEFINITIONS OF THE PROBLEMS

In this section the main problems which can be categorised as long-term impairments and challenging behaviour in schizophrenia will be outlined and discussed in relation to clinical issues. Other aspects of schizophrenia such as positive psychotic symptoms will not be addressed directly here (see Chapters 1 and 7 for further information on this topic).

Long-term impairments

A list of the main long-term impairments is given in Table 8.1.

Long-term impairments can be very distressing both for the individuals experiencing loss of functioning and for their carers. For sufferers, persistent impairments very often have a major impact on social functioning and ability to achieve life goals. If unaddressed, impairments such as lethargy, loss of pleasure in relationships, and difficulty conversing can result in previously active, enthusiastic, sociable people becoming withdrawn, slowed up and friendless. For example, a young newly diagnosed schizophrenic man trying hard to continue with a course at college was devastated by his difficulties in concentrating and persisting with course exercises which ultimately, sadly, resulted in his dismissal from the course. This was a tremendous blow to his self-esteem.

The impact of impairments on carers, especially families, can be equally catastrophic. In addition to the extra burden placed on them by having to be more active and make more decisions themselves to compensate for their impaired relative, the emotional impact can be devastating. Often families are much more distressed by their relatives' all-pervasive low mood and loss of drive than by their bizarre or disturbed behaviour. Creer and Wing (1974) report that the most frequent needs of schizophrenic patients living with families in their sample were for management of negative symptoms and difficulties with social performance.

The benefits of ameliorating such undermining symptoms can be great. They include increased self-esteem and improved quality of life. Therapeutically it is important to detect and address these problems as early as

Table 8.1 Long-term impairments in schizophrenia

Restricted expression of emotion
Limited range of facial expression; poor eye contact; loss of expressive gestures; lack of inflections in speech; poor emotional responsivity
Speech impairment
Poverty of speech; limited content of speech; blocking; increased latency to respond
Underactivity/apathy
Loss of energy; poor self-care; difficulty persisting with activities; lack of initiative; slowed movements
Loss of pleasure
Loss of interest in sex; abandonment of recreational interests and activities; loss of interest in friendships; loss of intimacy
Attentional impairment
Poor concentration; distractibility

possible to prevent secondary handicaps, and also because it is much easier to help someone to maintain existing social contacts and interests than to develop new ones at a later date.

Research into effective psychological management techniques for dealing with long-term impairments is particularly important as to date no anti-psychotic medication has been found which makes much impact (Bebbington and McGuffin (1988) give a useful review of pharmacological treatments of schizophrenia).

Challenging behaviour

A list of the most commonly occurring challenging behaviours in schizophrenia is found in Table 8.2.

A crucial aspect of understanding and working with challenging behaviour is the need to consider the behaviour within the context in which it presents. By definition, it is as much a function of carers' perceptions of behaviour and estimation of available coping resources as it is of the behaviour itself. For example, the behaviour of a mentally ill person is more likely to be perceived as "challenging" by an untrained member of staff working alone on night duty in a large hostel for the homeless, than by a team of experienced nurses in a small well-equipped unit.

It is important to distinguish between behaviour which is dangerous and that which is bizarre. Both types of behaviour constitute a challenge, and interfere with community integration. Dangerous behaviour, however, such as violence to others, to property, and self-injurious behaviour might be given a higher priority than bizarre behaviour, due to its destructive and potentially life-threatening nature.

One of the main problems of people labelled as "difficult to place" who

Table 8.2 Challenging behaviours in schizophrenia

Aggression
Physical assault on other people; damage to property; self-injury
Antisocial behaviour
Shouting or screaming; swearing; spitting; recurrent and uncontrolled vomiting; smearing of faeces; stealing
Sexually inappropriate behaviour
Nakedness in public; exposure of genitals; masturbation in public; sexual harassment/assault
Bizarre behaviour
Stereotypic behaviour, e.g. rocking; odd speech, e.g. nonsense or jumbled up words; unusual gait and hand movements; altered routines, e.g. sleeping during the day; unrestrained eating and drinking, including dangerous substances

often end up in hostels for the homeless in the community, is assault. The incidence of violence in schizophrenia reported in the literature varies greatly, a recent paper estimated the range as 8–45% (Volavka and Krakowski, 1989). Variation in reported figures has been found to be related to such factors as type of schizophrenic disorder, stage of hospital admission and cultural factors. Noble and Rodger (1989) found that incidents of violence recorded in a hospital register were more likely to have been committed by someone with the diagnosis of schizophrenia, hallucinating or deluded at the time, who had been admitted to hospital repeatedly in the past. In one report of a sample of difficult-to-place people it was suggested that violence often occurred in association with drug or alcohol abuse and was usually preceded by a period of build-up of tension (Elmore Committee, 1987). These findings suggest the importance of understanding the context in which violence occurs even in relation to psychotic patients.

ASSESSMENT

A structured approach to problem management requires careful and comprehensive assessment. In this section those methods considered to be particularly helpful in assessing long-term impairments and challenging behaviour will be outlined. It is important to stress that the assessment methods covered are not alternatives; with most patients a range of methods will be necessary. For example, if a patient is newly admitted to a ward with behavioural and emotional problems such as anger and aggression towards other residents in a group home, it would be important to interview the patient to understand his perspective, and also, if possible, interview others living in the group home and care staff or relatives recently in contact. After a period of observation it might be useful to complete a general behaviour-rating scale to consider the problem within a wider context. Also, systematically recording details of further incidents of anger or aggression as they occur would be important as actual events may differ from the patient's and others' accounts and important clues as to the maintenance of the problem may be uncovered. As far as possible a full and detailed assessment should always precede any treatment interventions including changes in medication as these will alter the problem and may obscure information crucial to the understanding and effective management of the problem.

Prior to selecting assessment methods it is important to consider their usefulness in relation to monitoring progress in treatment. Some measures should be included that can be easily used repeatedly and are sensitive to change.

Interviewing the patient

Unfortunately the value of interviewing people with schizophrenia who are disturbed or impaired continues to be underestimated. Approaches which involve doing things to people as opposed to working *collaboratively* with them predominate. Perhaps the greatest obstacle to developing effective methods for managing challenging or impaired behaviour is the difficulty carers and clinicians have in understanding the meanings people with schizophrenia attach to particular events and therefore why they react in ways which are perceived as problematic.

There is a recent and growing body of evidence that even severely disabled psychiatric patients can respond consistently and reasonably to questions asked in the context of an interview. MacCarthy, Benson and Brewin (1986) questioned a group of severely handicapped psychiatric day-patients about their perceptions of their skills, motivation to perform tasks, current problems and coping resources. They found that patients were able to respond reasonably and consistently to questions.

Clinicians therefore should not assume that impaired patients either do not have an opinion or are unable to express it. They may, however, have to become much more inventive in devising ways of assessing disturbed or impaired patients and working collaboratively with them. Interventions developed in collaboration with patients and those directly involved in their care are much more likely to be perceived positively and therefore more likely to be successful than attempts to change people without their cooperation.

Long-term impairments

More information may be obtained if the style and structure of the interview are adapted to take account of individuals' specific impairments. Adaptations include: speaking more slowly and clearly; keeping sentences short and simple; avoiding the use of abstract language; keeping the interview time short (approximately 20 minutes); and allowing adequate time for people who take a long time to answer questions.

When interviewing patients who say very little and take a long time to respond it can be tempting to ask *closed* questions such as "Do you feel bored?", "Would you like help getting to occupational therapy?". Although it may seem as though more information is gathered this way in less time and with less stress being placed on individuals, the information gathered is unlikely to be accurate as it probably reflects the interviewer's concerns more than the patient's. It is worth persisting with *open* questions such as "How are you feeling at the moment?", "What do you think of occupational therapy?", or "How do you think you might be able to get to occupational therapy more easily?". Open questions require more than a "yes" or "no" answer and therefore elicit more useful and detailed responses. If patients are very impaired and fail to respond at all, or consistently say "I don't know" despite repeated attempts at interview and involving carers who know the patient well, then providing some options to enable the patient to express themselves might be helpful. For example, the question "What do you think of occupational therapy?", could be followed up with "Do you like going there or is it boring?". Be careful not to give impaired patients too many possible options as their attention span may be limited and too many alternatives can be overwhelming.

Challenging behaviour

It is extremely important for the clinician to consider personal safety in conducting an interview with a patient who may be aggressive. It may be appropriate to ensure that another professional is with you, that you leave the door open or simply that someone else is informed of the interview and remains within earshot should you need help. In preparing the setting ensure that your exit is not blocked, and in particular that the patient is not sitting between you and the door, should you need to leave quickly. Depending on your knowledge of the patient you may want to remove any objects that could easily be thrown or used as weapons, prior to commencing the interview.

Although important to consider safety, it is rare for patients in most clinical settings to become aggressive during an interview. If this is a frequent occurrence then transfer to a more secure environment where such behaviour can be safely contained, while assessed, should be considered. With most potentially aggressive patients it is possible to manage the interview in such a way as to minimise the risk of anger becoming uncontrollable, by being sensitive to cues and responding quickly and skilfully. Also, the expression of anger by a patient in a session can be very valuable and is one of the best ways of accessing the source of the anger, in particular patients' thoughts/beliefs which may underpin the problem. To access these it is worth saying to patients at the moment they start to show any anger, "I see that you are beginning to feel angry. It might help me to understand your upset if you could tell me what is going through your mind just now?"

Most of us, from our own personal and social experiences, are aware of the signs of someone becoming angry. They usually include agitation, increased breathing, sweating, flushed appearance, louder and faster speech. The following suggestions can be helpful in preventing a patient's anger from escalating:

1. continue to speak in a calm, controlled way;
2. try to move in a predictable and relaxed manner, avoid making sudden or rapid movements;
3. avoid the use of statements that may be interpreted as confrontation, e.g. "You seem a bit sensitive about that";
4. increase empathic statements such as "I can see why that might upset you" and "I'm sorry that you're so upset".

A list of important areas to cover in the interview is given in Table 8.3. Obviously all areas do not have to be covered in one interview, and with many patients much of the information may have to be obtained from interviewing others, case notes and direct observation. The areas listed in Table 8.3 do not have to be covered in the order in which they are listed. It is important to be flexible. The major objective for the first interview should be to relate well to the patient such that they enjoy the interaction,

Table 8.3 Patient interview schedule

Problem details
Nature of the problem; context in which it occurs (where, when, who with); frequency of occurrence; duration of episodes; details of other related problems

History of the problem
Time of onset; events associated with the onset; course since it developed (particularly clarify reasons surrounding an increase or decrease in the problem)

Previous attempts at solution
Details of solutions tried by patient and relatives/friends; details of past professional help; success of previous attempted solutions (particularly what the patient did or did not find helpful and why).

Current coping resources
Current management of problems (by patient or others); success of current coping strategies; appropriateness of current coping strategies (spending 15 minutes lying down might be a more appropriate way of staying calm than drinking alcohol); availability of personal resources (e.g. ability to see another perspective or other solutions)

Motivation to change (patient's own views)
Benefits of changing; importance of changing; ease of changing; negative consequences of changing (e.g. fear that others may take advantage if stop being aggressive); advantages of staying the same (e.g. withdrawing may reduce demands from others)

Other areas
Social contacts; interests/hobbies; contacts and state of relationships with relatives; occupation/daytime activity; any other additional worries/problems

feel happy to speak with you again, feel able to express their views, and also feel that their views are respected by you, however negatively they believe them to be evaluated by others.

Interviewing carers

In addition to interviewing the patient, it is important to interview others who may have a role in maintaining the problem or simply be able to give an accurate and detailed description. This might include relatives, friends, residential and day-care staff. Interviewing others is particularly important when it is difficult to relate to the patient themselves, perhaps because they are too impaired or uncooperative.

It is important to obtain as good a description of the problem as possible from observers, encouraging them to avoid fuzzy descriptions of the sort: "Sally has been a bit aggressive lately". Such a description does not give any useful information about the form the aggression takes, e.g. verbal or physical, how serious it is, how frequent it is, where and when it usually occurs, at what or whom it has been directed and so on. It is particularly useful, in doing this, to review details of recent examples of the problem as these are likely to be more objective than a general summary. General comments can be a useful adjunct to this, however, giving valuable information about how the reporter perceives or interprets events. If a relative/friend/carer persistently appraises events very negatively this might also become a focus for therapy, particularly if the person concerned is in high contact with the patient or is perceived by the patient as being very important (see Chapter 4).

Rating scales

Standardised rating scales can be useful in assessing both long-term impairments and challenging behaviour. They are particularly helpful for the following purposes:

1. selecting groups of patients for a specific purpose such as for a treatment programme, group, or hostel;
2. monitoring progress, either on an individual, group, or ward basis;
3. identifying specific problems for further, more detailed, assessment;
4. evaluating the contribution of specific interventions such as a change in medication or psychological treatments.

Rating scales differ in the extent to which they measure general or specific behaviour, and also according to whether they are intended for completion by the patient or others such as staff and relatives. Staff-completed scales typically are either completed by care staff on the basis of observation of day-to-day living, or on the basis of an interview. All are useful.

The Rehabilitation Evaluation Hall And Baker (REHAB) scale (Baker and Hall, 1983) and the Manchester Scale (Krawiecka, Goldberg and Vaughan, 1977) are useful for general screening of patients. Used together they cover most aspects of functioning. REHAB is split into two sections: Deviant Behaviour and General Behaviour. The Deviant Behaviour section covers such problems as verbal and physical aggression, self-injury and sexual offensiveness. The General Behaviour section includes social and speech skills, self care, activity levels, domestic skills and use of community facilities such as cafés and buses. Raters are trained over a 3-week period. Ratings are then based on one week's direct observation. (Direct observation in this context means paying special attention to the patient rather than constantly observing them. Constant observation, in addition to being very time-consuming, can also affect the patient's behaviour. The rater should, however, also take note of events which have occurred when they were off-duty by asking other staff.)

The Manchester Scale is completed by a professional rater on the basis of behaviour observed at interview, responses to questions during an interview, verbal reports of carers and case records. It has eight items covering different aspects of mental state including impairments such as poverty of speech, slowness, and flattened affect. It involves rating degree of disturbance, each on a 5-point scale.

A range of rating scales are available for specifically assessing long-term impairments. The Scale for the Assessment of Negative Symptoms (SANS) (Andreasen, 1981) is perhaps the best known. It is a very detailed scale. It covers five main areas of negative impairment together with a general rating. Patients are rated on each item using a 0–5 scale of severity. The scale has good reliability.

Other rating scales which are not specifically designed for use with this client group, but nevertheless can be very useful include the Beck Depression Inventory (Beck et al., 1961), Hopelessness Scale (Beck et al., 1974), Spielberger Anger Inventory (Spielberger et al., 1983), and the Social Situations Questionnaire (Trower, Bryant and Argyle, 1978). These scales are all completed by the patient. Given that they are not standardised on patients with long-term impairments and challenging behaviour they cannot be used to compare populations but are very useful for within-subject comparisons. They cover specific problem areas as their names suggest. The presentation of items may have to be modified on these scales for use with impaired patients in particular. For example, items may need to be read out and responses recorded by the interviewer. This may also be the case for patients with literacy or numeracy problems.

Although rating scales are useful, they are no substitute for the detailed assessment of specific problems when planning intervention programmes. The nature of challenging behaviour in particular is often very idiosyncratic and it is important to assess the specific maintaining factors for each problem, as well as the exact nature and extent of the problem, so that changes can be readily monitored.

Detailed assessment of specific problems

Detailed objective assessment of problems can serve two main purposes: first, the establishment of a baseline of the extent of a problem against which change can be compared, and second, clarification of the factors maintaining a particular problem essential to effective problem management.

Baseline recording

Methods of recording a baseline obviously depend on the nature of the problem, such as frequency of occurrence. For example, social withdrawal, one of the most common long-term impairments, often occurs for relatively long periods at a time. Clearly it would be a gross waste of time to have a member of staff sitting with a stop watch recording the amount of time a particular patient spent engaged in a specific type of social contact each day for a week. In such cases time sampling, a technique involving recording predefined behaviour at specific regular prearranged points in time, might be a better method of establishing a baseline. Similarly, a checklist is a quick and easy way of monitoring self-care: a carer would simply have to unobtrusively scan the patient at particular prearranged points in the day to check problem aspects of self-care such as that zips and buttons are correctly fastened. Interval recording is often the technique of choice for discrete problems such as shouting, spitting or sexual harassment. The observer might record whether or not the behaviour has occurred within a predefined time period broken into smaller units, such as every 2 minutes within a 10-minute period every hour. Again this is a much more efficient use of time than continuous observation and recording. Interested readers should consult Barker (1982) for other useful details of how and when to use different methods of behavioural recording.

Assessing maintaining factors

Assessing maintaining factors is important in planning an effective treatment programme. For example, just as we may be aware that we eat or smoke too much, but unaware of the exact times and situations when we do overeat or smoke, so people with schizophrenia, and their carers, may be aware of the existence of problems but less aware of the surrounding contingencies. Knowing that you tend to smoke after a meal or when feeling anxious is invaluable information when it comes to cutting down. You could plan some alternative pleasant activity after meals and learn other ways of dealing with anxiety.

A useful way of obtaining detailed objective information about a specific problem is to get the patient and/or carers to record in a diary incidents of the problem behaviour as they occur, or as soon after as possible. An example of a basic diary for staff to record incidents of aggressive behaviour is given in Figure 8.1 on page 199. Diaries with the same headings can be used for both groups. The sooner details are recorded the more likely they are to be accurate. It is important to include details of events preceding the occurrence of the problem (*antecedents*) as problems usually occur within a specific context, which is not always clear from verbal reports often given long after the event has taken place. For example, a patient may attack the television only in response to thoughts that the TV is transmitting harmful rays to him, or another patient may doze off to sleep in a particular environment that she finds boring. In both these situations the behaviour being investigated may at an initial glance appear as though it occurred spontaneously, but becomes more understandable when details of the patients' thoughts, other behaviour and the situation are recorded.

A list of general factors which should be considered in trying to assess the context within which problems occur is given in Table 8.4. Some relevant questions to consider in relation to identifying important factors are given in this table. This list is not exhaustive. Information gained from interviews both of patients and carers is crucial in planning specifically what to monitor in relation to any target problem.

Table 8.4 Contextual factors to consider in detailed assessment

Facts to consider	Relevance
Physical environment	where is the person?, is the environment too hot/cold/—cramped/empty?
Social environment	who else is there?, how well do they get on together?, what are the others present saying/doing?
Activity	what is the person being assessed doing?, is the task too difficult/easy/boring?
Physiological state	are there any internal physical factors that might be making a contribution, e.g. drugs (check prescribed and illicit), alcohol, pain, obesity, thyroid problems?
Cognitive state	what is the person thinking/feeling just prior to or during the occurrence of the behaviour?

It is also important to record details of events immediately following the problem (*consequences*) as these can have a maintaining role. For example, if vomiting in a conspicuous place such as the ward sitting room results in someone dashing over to clean up the mess, fuss over the person who has been sick and make them a cup of tea, then this might encourage that person to continue to vomit in the sitting room rather than cope with the problem themselves in the toilet. In assessing possible relevant consequences consider the same areas outlined in Table 8.4. For example: does a change of environment follow incidents of the behaviour?; how do others react?; is there any consequent change in activity?; how does the person feel immediately after the event, both physically and emotionally?; and what are the resultant thoughts?

A basic diary suitable for recording contingencies could have four columns headed antecedents, concurrent events, behaviour, and consequences. These categories could be subdivided to include the more specific information suggested in Table 8.4 as appropriate. The format of diaries should be altered according to the nature of the problem being assessed. Limitations may be imposed on what can be recorded by aspects of settings such as the suitability of the layout for direct observation, or specific individual difficulties such as poor literacy and numeracy skills. Assessment forms and diary record sheets should always be easily readable, clear and understandable to those required to complete them, be unobtrusive, and take a minimum amount of time and effort to fill in, otherwise the chances are they will simply not be completed. These factors may be particularly important in units where staff:patient ratios are low and staff turnover high, as motivation to use structured approaches, which are often perceived as very time consuming, can be low.

Detailed assessment of long-term impairments

The importance of asking patients how important, and how difficult, they perceive tasks to be has been established by MacCarthy, Benson and Brewin (1986). They found that patients were less likely to engage in activities that they perceived as being unimportant or difficult. The range of tasks offered and degree of interest to patients are also important to clarify. The nature of the environment can be an important stimulator. Smaller, more personal, attractive and interesting rooms are more stimulating. Similarly, sitting with other withdrawn, inactive, emotionally flattened people may help to maintain low levels of activity and social engagement. Problems such as overeating, especially high carbohydrate foods, just before activities and tiredness may be relevant. Recent reports suggest unusually high rates of obesity and medical or physical complaints in chronic schizophrenia sufferers (Gopalaswamy and Morgan, 1985; Honig et al., 1989; Vieweg et al., 1989).

Staff factors can also be related to inactivity. Low staff levels often result in minimal individual attention especially for those not making requests, and not causing any trouble. Patients may feel neglected and this may trigger beliefs about being worthless, and hopelessness about the prospect of their lives changing, which then undermine any attempts to change. Staff attitudes about the hopelessness of trying to encourage impaired patients may also be an important maintaining factor.

Detailed assessment of challenging behaviour

Assessing thoughts and feelings are crucial here. Many acts of aggression are preceded by thoughts of having been insulted or rejected, often linked to the very low self-esteem of such patients. Anger has been found to be the most common emotion preceding aggression. Thoughts may be delusional. For example, a patient might hit his mother if troubled by the delusional belief that she is Satan come to take his soul. However, it would be very wrong to assume that all aggression in schizophrenia is maintained by the illness. The association between occurrences of the problem behaviour and thought disorder needs to be established for each individual using diaries as indicated above.

Other factors that can be associated with challenging behaviour include overcrowding, noise levels, temperature (either too hot or too cold), pain, tiredness, the use of alcohol or disinhibiting drugs and sexual arousal.

Case illustrations are given at the end of the chapter of assessment strategies used in the detailed assessment of two patients, one with problems primarily in the area of long-term impairments and the other with predominantly challenging behaviour.

GOAL SETTING

A comprehensive assessment of most people with schizophrenia will reveal a range of needs at any one point in time. Obviously it would not be practical to try to tackle all areas at once, particularly when working with schizophrenic patients presenting with long-term impairments such as poor concentration and motivation. Limitations may also be imposed by carers, such as time available. In addition to these factors, altering too many variables at once, even if achievable and successful, will confound so many factors that interpretation of results and planning a maintenance programme will be made impossible.

In general, in prioritising goals, it is useful to allocate a higher priority to those problems that (a) are most likely to respond to treatment, (b) will require the least effort, (c) will take relatively less time to change, (d) occur most frequently, and (e) are likely to bring about the greatest improvements in the quality of life of the individual concerned, other patients and carers. For example, a self-care problem might be given a high priority if improvement in the problem might mean that other patients will spend more time socially with the person. Also, reducing a problem with violence might be important to target if it means that the person can then be considered for placement in a group home in the community. Although expectations of change should be realistic, the gains for this client group, their carers and therapists of achieving some, even small, change relatively quickly cannot be understated. Expectations of patients and opportunities can change radically and often further change becomes possible as everyone's motivation increases. It is sensible to limit the number of goals for each patient at any one time. Obviously the optimum number of goals will vary depending on individual factors and the nature of the problems being addressed. However, 4–5 goals at any one time is probably a reasonable maximum.

THERAPEUTIC INTERVENTIONS

In this section, for ease of reference, interventions will be split into the broad categories of: milieu approaches and staff practices; group behavioural regimes; individual behavioural approaches; and cognitive–behavioural developments. The ordering of these categories of intervention reflects their chronological development.

Consistent with the previous section on assessment, the possible interventions outlined in this section are not linked with problems in a prescriptive way. As the purpose of assessment is essentially to generate possible hypotheses about how problems are being maintained for each individual, so the purpose of treatment is to test out these hypotheses in a systematic way in order to establish exactly how the problems are being maintained. Thus in the psychological treatment of challenging behaviour and long-term impairments, as with other psychological problems, it is crucial to be flexible and be guided by information revealed in the assessment of each individual rather than base treatments on general preconceived ideas about the nature of challenging behaviour or long-term impairments. Such an empirical and individually-tailored approach is much more likely to be successful. Thus any one intervention may be appropriate for more than one problem; altering aspects of a ward milieu in the direction of increasing privacy and attractiveness of washroom areas may both be an appropriate intervention for increasing motivation to wash regularly in someone with long-term impairments and reducing verbal abuse and aggressiveness in someone displaying this form of challenging behaviour in relation to washing. It follows also that any one problem such as lethargy may be maintained by any number of different factors or combinations of factors such as obesity, boredom, lack of confidence, depression. The choice of intervention has to depend on the hypothesised reason(s) for the continuation of the problem.

Milieu approaches and staff practices

A therapeutic milieu will be regarded here as the physical and social environment in which people live, including the attitudes and practices of carers. It can usefully be regarded as an important backdrop against which detailed individual and group programmes can be developed. In this section, those aspects of milieu which have an impact on the problems of long-term impairments and challenging behaviour will be considered. Unfortunately, very little research has been conducted into the effects of experimentally manipulating aspects of the physical environment on impaired and challenging behaviour, so what will be presented here are some suggestions for good clinical practice.

Long-term impairments

A well-known risk with patients presenting with long-term impairments is that of under-stimulation (Wing and Brown, 1970), which may exacerbate negative impairments. On the other hand, "total push" therapy, advocated by Myerson (1939), has been linked to over-arousal and re-emergence of positive symptoms. The experimental evidence for this remains sparse, however. Clearly achieving a balance between structured activities and free leisure time is important.

A combination of consistency, particularly in terms of staffing and routines, and opportunities to take part in interesting and enjoyable activities, where the chances of succeeding are high, is probably the best environment for people with long-term impairments.

Creating a friendly, accepting, low-stress, atmosphere in day-care and residential facilities is also helpful. This might include pleasant decoration, and the organisation of furniture to facilitate interaction between residents. Seats positioned around the walls of rooms or lined up in front of the television are not conducive to interaction.

In relation to staff attitudes, optimism is a key variable. While most staff want the best for the patient, they are unlikely to invest themselves in an active treatment regime unless they believe that change is likely to occur. Underestimating patients' true level of functioning can help maintain long-term impairments such as lethargy and apathy by limiting opportunities. Levels of optimism in staff can, however, be taught and fostered (Moores and Grant, 1977).

Challenging behaviour

In creating a therapeutic milieu for people with challenging behaviour, it is important to try to minimise the possible sources of stress which may aggravate, and together with some specific stressor, such as a critical comment or disappointment, lead to an aggressive incident. The consistent presence of experienced staff on a unit can help prevent problems emerging. Privacy and the provision of personal space are also important. Overcrowding is likely to lead to short tempers. Other stressors such as an unacceptable noise or temperature level can also affect behaviour. It is particularly important to consider issues such as "ward restrictiveness", which can be assessed by the hostel–hospital practice profile of Wykes (1982). Essentially this relates to the degree to which ward practices are designed to permit and foster independence in patients. This would include such factors as whether patients have the freedom to choose when they want to go to bed or rise in the morning, whether they can only use their bedrooms at specific times and whether staff control the radio and television.

The provision of secure locker space and locks on bathroom doors are important for the protection of others, if stealing and sexually inappropriate behaviour are likely. Other aspects of safety need to be considered in any setting catering for people who may exhibit challenging behaviour. These would include the removal of heavy or sharp objects that could be used as weapons, providing flexiglass windows, installation of an effective alarm system and unobtrusive means by which staff can observe the behaviour of patients fairly continuously.

Group behavioural regimes

Group behavioural regimes are procedures for the management of groups of patients which apply predominantly behavioural treatment methods. The best known example is the "Token Economy" (TE). Although now rarely found in its pure form, there are a number of projects reported in the literature which combine principles of the TE with a therapeutic milieu consisting of many of the features outlined above (Hall, 1991). This combination seems to be very effective in the community management of new long-term patients with problems of impairments and challenging behaviour. Since TEs are still useful in the management of such patients (they have played a major part in the development of detailed individual programmes, in clarifying what are some of the principal therapeutic factors in ward regimes, and in leading to more effective monitoring and evaluation measures) the principles and procedures of this approach will be outlined in this section.

TEs in their modern form were initially based explicitly on operant-conditioning theory, and were seen as the creation of conditioned responses by the use of secondarily conditioned reinforcers (tokens), which gave access to primary reinforcers. They were inspired mainly by the work of Ayllon and Azrin (1968) described in their classic book.

A Token Economy is a therapeutic procedure, where the attainment of a pre-specified target by the patient is followed by the delivery of a "token", which itself gives access to a menu of reinforcers. The form of the token (whether plastic disc, simulated money, star chart or holes punched in a ticket) is not in itself important. Giving the token to the patient is usually accompanied by delivery of social reinforcement and constructive informational feedback. For example, a patient working on social skills who greets a member of staff appropriately might be told, "Well done, Jim. I really liked the way you smiled as you said Good Morning to me." In addition to the general positive, accepting tone of this interaction, the patient's attention is drawn to the important aspects of the skill he is trying to acquire thus helping him refine the skill. A TE programme can be designed for a group of patients, or for an individual. The term TE by itself does not define the precise learning processes occurring within the TE programme. For example, a TE for overactive young adults in a day centre would be different in many respects from a TE for withdrawn older patients in a high-dependency setting.

The target behaviours in a TE are defined so that they can be clearly recognised by the direct-care staff of the programme, and are sub-divided, so that wherever possible a graded series of sub-goals is constructed, leading to the final target. Attainment of sub-goals is then linked to a token tariff, so that a specified value of tokens is attached to achieving each sub-goal—for example, two tokens for initiating conversation with another patient.

A procedure is then devised to exchange the tokens for the "back-up" or so-called "primary" reinforcers, which may be sweets, cigarettes or soft drinks obtained through a ward shop, or privileges such as access to a day-room or to a single room. Very sophisticated weighting of token values and design of "economic" procedures, such as interest on unspent tokens and exchange-controls with the outside cash economy(!), can be introduced.

A considerable number of both clinical and experimental papers were published throughout the 1970s, including large-scale comparative studies (pre-eminently the volume by Paul and Lentz, 1977) and carefully designed detailed studies (Hall, Baker and Hutchinson, 1977) which looked at the influence of different therapeutic factors in bringing about the positive results universally found. The relative importance of a number of general therapeutic factors, such as the overall level of social interaction, and agreement on therapeutic goals, which are not specific to TEs, has been clarified by these studies. A number of comprehensive reviews of TE practice have been published (see Kazdin, 1982; Hall and Baker, 1986).

This research has found that the rate of response of individual long-term patients varies, with some patients responding to the general therapeutic factors, present in any active treatment milieu, some responding specifically to the token programme, and some being non-responders under the most ingenious variations of the programme possible.

The series of studies by Paul and Lentz gives details of the design of assessment and therapeutic procedures, and also contains the most robust comparative effectiveness study, showing that the social learning (TE) programme was more effective than a therapeutic-community-type programme. Other studies have looked at the specific contribution to effectiveness of contingent token reinforcement, as opposed to the contribution of other therapeutic factors implicitly present in a TE. The best conclusion is that the specific effectiveness is probably due to the informational exchange and social reinforcement system set up, rather than to the value of tokens as conditioned reinforcers. To the extent that tokens are helpful for chronic schizophrenic patients, it is not necessary for them to provide access to the back-up reinforcers, i.e. to give access to sweets, privileges and so on, thus removing a potential ethical dilemma.

Elements of a therapeutic milieu, such as giving patients choice over the activities in which they engage, and encouraging patient groups, can readily be integrated with other specific behavioural components of a TE regime. Problem-solving sessions can be integrated with a TE on an individual or group basis. Garety and Morris (1984) describe how individual behavioural procedures can be integrated into a positive therapeutic milieu in a hostel in the community. This combination of approaches is probably the best for managing very impaired patients or those demonstrating challenging behaviour within a community context.

Individual behavioural approaches

Long-term impairments

In working with long-term impairments there is a need to differentiate between problems caused by skills deficits, where interventions might take the form of teaching new skills, and problems largely caused by poor motivation to perform skills which already exist in the individual's repertoire. Many people suffering from schizophrenia become ill during early adulthood and therefore may not have learned appropriate skills, for example for interacting with adults of the opposite sex (a competence issue). Alternatively, skills such as dressing, washing and table etiquette are less likely to be performed if lack of motivation or insensitivity to others' feedback is a problem (a performance issue). Obviously this tends to highlight the problems of institutional settings in that often patients who mix with socially, or eat with, other patients, may not be exposed to very appropriate models or realistic expectations and feedback.

If the problem is primarily a skills deficit, then techniques for teaching new behaviours would form appropriate interventions, such as modelling, rehearsal, practice and feedback. In most instances, the effectiveness of the intervention is enhanced by using these strategies together, at least initially, in teaching patients with long-term impairments. For example, in teaching listening skills, staff members could model having a conversation and instruct the patient in the key aspects of the behaviour to imitate such as smiling, eye contact and nodding. The patient would then be encouraged to rehearse the skill and, when feeling more confident, practise it in appropriate situations. Feedback would involve drawing the patient's attention to those specific aspects of the behaviour done well and those requiring further practice. It is important that the person modelling the skills is well liked by the patient and that attention is drawn to the key components of the behaviour to be learned. Modelling is faded out once the new behaviour has been learned. Skills training has been established as an effective treatment for people with schizophrenia. See Chapter 5 for further details of this valuable approach.

In most instances where skills are not being performed by patients with chronic impairments, assessment will reveal that at some point the patient was able to perform skills appropriately but that this has simply ceased, rather than that the skills have never been acquired. In such instances strategies for increasing motivation are required rather than teaching new skills. It is important not to make assumptions in this respect, however. One of the authors had the experience of asking a long-stay patient about self-care; in answer to the question "how often do you change your toothbrush?" the patient replied very appropriately and proudly "after every visit to the dentist". Subsequent questioning revealed that his last visit to the dentist had been 18 years before!

In trying to increase motivation to perform a skill you might begin by altering antecedents. For example, if someone is very inactive during ward group activities changing the timing of activities from after a large two-course lunch to earlier in the morning might make a difference. If changing antecedents is ineffective in itself, or detailed assessment clearly indicates that the behaviour is being maintained by its consequences, then it might be more useful to begin by modifying the consequences of the behaviour. It is important to do this in a controlled way by introducing a reinforcement schedule. Introducing social reinforcement is usually the best way to start, and only proceeding to more tangible reinforcers if this is insufficient. Social reinforcement is usually effective and has the benefit of allowing easier long-term maintenance and generalisation. There is some evidence that severely impaired patients benefit more from tangible reinforcers than social ones illustrating the possibility that dominant learning mechanisms may vary with differing levels of disability (Matson, 1980). If using tangible reinforcers, it is important to pair these with social reinforcement so that the tangible reinforcers can eventually be faded out. Failure to do this can result in behaviours being bound to inappropriate contingencies.

In using reinforcers with someone who is negatively impaired and consequently has a very restricted range of experience, it is sometimes necessary to offer new experiences which can later be used as reinforcers. Another way of overcoming the problem of the very impaired patient is to use the Premack principle (selectively reinforce a low frequency behaviour with access to a high frequency behaviour). Where possible, it is important to involve patients in the choice of reinforcer as this increases the likelihood that the reinforcer chosen will be effective. Access to the selected reinforcer must be restricted to completion of the desired skill or behaviour, otherwise the reinforcer will lose its specific effect in encouraging performance of the target behaviour. In reinforcing patients it is important that this is done immediately on completion of the desired behaviour; that the reinforcement is clearly paired to the performance of the behaviour being encouraged; that the patient's attention is clearly drawn to the reason for the reinforcement; and that the behaviour is reinforced consistently, i.e. after each occurrence rather than at random. Once the behaviour has become established it is useful to reduce the frequency of reinforcement from every occurrence of the behaviour to intermittently. This mimics contingencies in the real world and is easier to maintain. The ideal end point of such an intervention is for the patient to gain intrinsic reward from performing the behaviour or for the behaviour to be reinforced naturally rather than in a contrived way.

In teaching new behaviours and increasing motivation, it is crucially important to encourage generalisation of skills from the treatment situation to the full range of situations in which the patient needs to perform the skills (Shepherd, 1990). Care should be taken to introduce different situations into the practice, especially those of particular importance to the patient.

Challenging behaviour

Unfortunately, for a number of reasons, punitive and unsophisticated approaches are often used in the management of challenging behaviours. Containment, or seclusion, is an example of such an approach. Patients are often locked in a room on their own for hours at a time. It is important to differentiate between this and time-out with which it is often confused; time-out will be discussed in detail later in this section. Other punitive strategies include excessive use of sedative drugs, and withdrawal of privileges. Nagging patients to conform to rules such as when to get out of bed, and criticism such as of poor self-care, might also be included. Such strategies are often used in the absence of more constructive attempts to encourage appropriate behaviour. The use of punishment usually reflects staff frustration rather than appropriate and effective problem management. Such approaches in addition to being unethical can in fact lead to a worsening of the problem. The effects of hostility and criticism on relapse in schizophrenia are considered in Chapter 4.

Potentially more effective techniques for reducing unwanted behaviours include altering the contingencies of the behaviour, such as time-out or differential reinforcement of other behaviour (either incompatible behaviour or behaviour that constitutes a reduction in the problem).

Time-out can be an effective way of managing very disruptive behaviour such as violence, shouting, swearing, etc. particularly where the hypothesised reason for the continuation of the behaviour is that of immediate social reinforcement. Time-out is also suitable for the management of behaviour reinforced in other ways, however. For example, occasionally patients will behave in a disruptive way because they know that they will then be taken to a quiet area. It may be that bedroom areas are locked during the day and that there is no other opportunity to relax away from others. In this case continuing to deal with the behavioural problem by escorting the patient to a quiet area would clearly increase the frequency of the behaviour. A more appropriate and effective strategy might be to make a quiet area available throughout the day and manage any further incidents of disturbed behaviour by making the individual stay in the company of others. The aim of time-out is to block the association between the behaviour and its reinforcing consequences. In order to be effective, rather than punitive, this has to be conducted in quite a rigorous manner; the individual should be removed from opportunities for continuing reinforcement with the minimum of fuss (this might mean anything from escorting the person in silence to a quiet room to carrying on as though nothing strange had happened). Time-out should ideally be terminated when the patient has become quiet or stopped the undesirable behaviour. Periods spent in time-out should be very carefully monitored and should not exceed a maximum of a few minutes. If the patient repeats the same unacceptable behaviour on being returned to the reinforcing environment, then he/she should again be removed. The effectiveness of this approach rests on repeated occurrence of the behaviour without reinforcement, not on spending excessive amounts of time in seclusion. Careful consideration has to be given to the policy behind the use of time-out.

Reinforcing incompatible behaviour together with consistently not reinforcing the problem behaviour, can be a very effective technique particularly for reducing socially and sexually inappropriate behaviour, such as spitting, shouting or screaming, smearing of faeces and sexual harassment. Reinforcement should be delivered as described previously. It is important to ensure consistency in non-responding to incidents of the problem behaviour as they occur. Failure to achieve this is probably the most common reason why this technique fails. The difficulty in achieving consistency in management is one of the main drawbacks to community management where that involves care being spread across a number of different care agencies. An example of this technique would be managing incidents of screaming by selectively reinforcing speech of normal pitch and volume. It is important to stress that not reinforcing behaviour which is hypothesised to be maintained by the attention of others means behaving as though nothing has happened. Trying to ignore someone by not speaking to them, looking away, or turning your back on them can give the same message as responding directly, i.e. that you have noticed their behaviour and are distressed by it. It is also important to realise before starting such a programme that withdrawing reinforcement often results in an initial increase in the frequency, duration or severity of the target behaviour as the individual attempts to elicit further reinforcement. Such techniques should therefore not be used with dangerous behaviours. Recommencing reinforcement once the behaviour has escalated can have the very negative effect of encouraging a more severe form of the same behaviour.

Often a thorough assessment of challenging behaviour will reveal an absence of skills necessary to resolve difficulties in a more appropriate manner. Violence, or drug or alcohol abuse may be the only way that the person has of coping with extreme levels of tension or of anger. Sexual deviance can persist in the absence of skills or opportunities for developing more socially acceptable ways of expressing sexuality, in particular developing a more appropriate sexual relationship. In these situations the obvious intervention would be to work with the individual on creating opportunities for using and developing more appropriate skills, perhaps in conjunction with developing a structured way of responding to any further incidents of the problem behaviour, should they occur.

Cognitive–behavioural approaches

One of the main contributions that cognitive-behavioural approaches have made to psychological treatments in general has been to expand our understanding of problems, and in particular to provide techniques for uncovering and changing the meanings that people attach to events. Cognitive–behavioural approaches have been applied to people with schizophrenia in a very limited way so far, mainly in relation to the management of positive psychotic symptoms (see Chapter 7). In this section the possible application of such approaches to the management of negative impairments and challenging behaviour will be considered. Developments in the understanding of emotions such as anger and depression in non-schizophrenic populations in particular may have something useful to contribute to our understanding of these problems in people with schizophrenia.

Long-term impairments

Many long-term impairments are very similar to the features of depression. These include poor motivation, loss of pleasure, inactivity, poor concentration and poverty of speech. Since CBT has been found to be a very effective treatment for depression (Blackburn et al., 1981), its usefulness in the management of negative impairments should be explored. Even if neurological impairment is found to underlie long-term impairments as some authors have suggested (although the evidence for this so far remains inconclusive, Meltzer (1985)), this should not prevent attempts at understanding and trying to modify impairments by psychological means. Psychological techniques have made a tremendous impact on the management of people with neurological damage and learning difficulties. Although many people with schizophrenia do get depressed at some point in their lives, use of CBT strategies should not be restricted to people who can be diagnosed as depressed. Clinicians might like to try using CBT techniques with people who have long-term impairments in the following ways: overcoming inactivity and boredom and increasing motivation to perform tasks by activity scheduling and rating mastery and pleasure, considering pros and cons in decision-making, eliciting thoughts underlying fears about tackling new activities or meeting new people and challenging these, challenging negative beliefs about the future and the self, managing poor concentration by systematically increasing time spent focused on one task and reinforcing this, and problem-solving.

An increasing range of cognitive–behavioural treatments are being shown to have some efficacy in the treatment of people with long-term impairments. Problem solving has proved useful (Hansen, Lawrence and

Christoff, 1985). This is a technique which involves teaching patients a strategy for solving problems involving five stages: defining the problem; generating possible solutions; selecting the potentially most effective solution; implementing the chosen solution; and evaluating outcome (see Hawton and Kirk (1989) for a useful guide on how to teach problem-solving).

Self-instructional training has also been used with schizophrenics, with mixed success. Bentall, Higson and Lowe (1987) had some success in altering long-term impairments in people with schizophrenia using this technique, but the skill did not generalise to tasks unlike those used in the training. In this procedure patients are taught to control their own behaviour by instructing themselves in what to do. Initially instructions are spoken out loud, and as patients become more proficient they direct themselves silently.

A further recent development which has promise in the treatment of negative impairments is Integrated Psychological Therapy (IPT) (Brenner, 1989). IPT involves addressing both cognitive and behavioural impairments in a stepwise process. The intervention has five stages. The initial stages are directed at ameliorating more specific cognitive impairments such as attentional and perceptual difficulties. The following stages deal more with skills such as verbal communication, social skills and interpersonal problem-solving. People with schizophrenia who have received IPT have been found to improve on measures of cognitive functioning, social adjustment and psychopathology (Brenner, Hodel and Roder, 1990).

It may be that more purely cognitive approaches are only useful for people who are not severely incapacitated by their long-term impairments. However, some clinicians are currently adapting CBT techniques for use with even the most retarded of depressed in-patients with promising preliminary results (Scott, 1989) and therefore it is worth considering with impaired schizophrenics. It may be that sessions would have to be modified to accommodate individuals' capabilities. For example, briefer but more frequent sessions might be useful, as might audiotaping sessions and giving the patient the tape to listen to as a refresher between sessions. It might be helpful to have a direct carer sit in on sessions. Also, behavioural experiments could be reviewed immediately on completion by the therapist to minimise problems with recall.

Challenging behaviour

Cognitive theorists have come up with an appealing proposal for the psychological meaning underlying the emotion of anger (Beck, 1976; Burns, 1980). Essentially anger is hypothesised to arise from the interpretation of an event as breaking personal rules for appropriate conduct. As with other emotional problems, such as depression and anxiety, misinterpretation of the meaning of events, others' actions or statements, can occur, and, if misinterpreted as rule-breaking, result in anger. This, depending on individual and contextual factors, may lead to violent or threatening behaviour. In the case of schizophrenia, as mentioned earlier, anger and aggression may result from the delusional misinterpretation of events (see Chapter 7 for information on CBT for delusions). Obviously, this type of approach depends on the feasibility of establishing a collaborative relationship with the patient and the patient being able to access thoughts and understand the relationship between thoughts, feelings and behaviour. All of these can be problems with people who have schizophrenia although insurmountable problems in these areas should not be assumed.

Hahlweg (1988) found that schizophrenics reacted in a similar way to both positive and negative comments made by a relative judged to be high on emotional over-involvement. This finding suggests that the information in both instances, whether positive or negative in content, was being interpreted in a similar way by the person with schizophrenia. In addition to elaborating the possible mechanism linking emotional over-involvement with relapse, this work suggests that schizophrenics may use schemas like everyone else and interpret incoming information in relation to them. So when schizophrenics behave in an unexpected and apparently unprovoked, aggressive way it may be that their behaviour makes perfect sense from within their cognitive framework. Our inability to understand it, reflects perhaps our difficulty in accessing that individual's schemas. Thus perhaps there are two challenges in "challenging behaviour": one being to understand better the meanings which people with schizophrenia attach to events which cause them to react in such a disruptive way; the other being to help in the reinterpretation of events causing such distress, or if more appropriate, help individuals to resolve their problem in a more socially acceptable way. Perhaps one reason why we are only now beginning to view schizophrenia sufferers in this way and trying to access the meaning they attach to events, is our own long-standing assumption that behavioural disturbance in schizophrenia was simply a consequence of a disease process that has no meaning.

CASE EXAMPLES

The following case examples describe, firstly, an individual who has long-term impairments and, secondly, a patient with challenging behaviour as a major problem. They illustrate some of the ways in which inactivity and challenging behaviour can be perpetuated and the use of appropriate intervention strategies.

Case example 1

Judith is 46 years old and has been known to the psychiatric services for 21 years. She lives in a staffed group home in the community and attends Occupational Therapy at the nearby psychiatric hospital. She attends irregularly often not being out of bed and ready in time for the hospital minibus that comes to collect her each weekday morning. Staff try sporadically to get her out of bed in time which usually involves a particular staff member nagging her, getting her clothes ready for her and even pulling her out of bed. Typically when she gets to the OT department they are usually so short-staffed that she has to organise herself. Feeling exhausted from the effort of getting there (Judith is also very unfit and overweight), she slumps into a chair in the corner out of the way and proceeds to sleep off and on until lunchtime. The staff who are around are busy supervising the cooking of lunch and managing those patients who are causing trouble, or working with groups in other small activity rooms. Judith sits in the main room which is an old drab long-stay ward with chairs around the outer edge of the room. Other patients are there also but they, like Judith, are slumped in chairs, smoking or sitting with their eyes closed. Nobody is talking to each other or even sitting together.

Behavioural recording (time sampling) revealed that Judith spent on average 85% of her day at OT sitting on her own, not engaged in any activity (other than smoking) or social interaction. Interviewing Judith revealed that she felt bored at OT. None of the activities offered really interested her and the effort of organising herself seemed overwhelming. She reported that she used to like knitting, sewing and cooking but had not done any of these activities for many years and lacked confidence in her ability to try again. She, and OT staff interviewed, felt that Judith was unlikely to be helped to change much. Judith was helped to complete the Beck Depression Inventory (BDI) and this revealed a score indicative of moderately severe depression. From her rating of herself on the BDI she strongly disliked herself, believed that she looked ugly, felt that she was a failure, and found it more difficult to initiate activities and make decisions than she used to.

Interventions with Judith included getting staff at the group home to stop nagging her about getting up but instead make it more rewarding for her to get out of bed. She was rewarded by a member of staff filling her a bath with lots of bubble bath and praising her for getting up with sufficient time to make the bus. This was relatively less time consuming than previous strategies and therefore staff were able to carry it out fairly consistently until Judith took over initiating this herself. OT was also made more rewarding. One of the OT staff was given responsibility for motivating Judith. She introduced her into the cooking group and built her confidence by grading tasks to ensure success and giving her lots of praise. The physical environment at OT posed some problems but it was possible to reorganise chairs into smaller clusters and have some activities such as board games take place in the large room. Judith joined in with these. Within 2–3 months Judith was attending OT most days in the week and was actively engaged in activities, mostly involving others. Time sampling repeated at this point revealed that she was now inactive for only a daily average of 35% of her time. Judith expressed feeling happier and less lethargic and her BDI scores consequently improved. In fact it was considered that she had made so much progress that she could shortly be considered for transfer to a smaller, unstaffed group home.

Case study 2

Glen is 38 years old. He has a long history of violence dating back to his adolescence. This led to him spending 14 years in a secure hospital before transfer to the psychiatric hospital he is in at present about 3 years ago. The staff of the unit were concerned about Glen's violence both towards staff and other residents. Incidents of shouting abuse, hitting, kicking and throwing objects at people occurred on average once per week. From staff accounts of previous incidents, Glen appeared to become aggressive when encouraged to do things he did not want to do, such as take part in group activities on the ward, get out of bed in the morning and talk to people he did not know well. Staff were also concerned about Glen's isolation on the unit and inactivity; he appeared to spend a great deal of time lying on his bed staring at the ceiling.

Nursing staff were asked to record details of any incidents of aggressive behaviour that occurred. With the aid of this, a detailed account of the most recent incident was obtained. See Figure 8.1 for a copy of this Incident Record.

Glen had been brought back to hospital dirty and mildly confused, after being absent for several hours. Only three ward staff were on duty, and a new staff member had tried to bathe him, but Glen shouted and lashed out at the nurse. Staff felt that the incident had occurred because of a conflict between their attempts to care for Glen by trying to bathe him, and insensitivity to his difficulty relating to unfamiliar people caused by the pressure of a heavy work load. The situation appeared to be further aggravated by the restricted space in the bathroom in which the nurse tried to undress him. It was not possible to obtain a detailed account of the incident from Glen who became agitated whenever the subject was broached. He did, however, say that he would like to make more friends, and generally found it hard to talk to people.

It was hypothesised that Glen's agitation in social situations and aggression were caused by his difficulty in expressing himself and his unfamiliarity with strangers. The goal for therapy, agreed with Glen, was to increase his contact with others on the unit and improve his ability to communicate with people. It was felt that the interventions of choice for Glen were encouragement and reinforcement of appropriate behaviour together with the reduction of opportunities for conflict, arising out of pressuring Glen to engage in activities he appeared to find very distressing. Considerable time was then spent with Glen eliciting from him his main interests—which were listening to a particular pop-group and horse-racing. He also enjoyed reading a tabloid newspaper and was happy to recall stories he had read while being audiotaped, to give a baseline record of his clarity of speech (not helped by his missing top teeth), and duration of speech. The NART vocabulary test (Nelson, 1982) established the probable upper limit of Glen's conversational understanding, so that realistic goals could be set, when encouraging more interaction with other residents.

Glen was willing to meet with two other residents who he regarded as his friends on the unit, and it was possible to identify common interests, which included listening to another pop group and watching sports programmes on the television. Glen was encouraged to meet regularly with his friends to talk about his friends' interests, so that generalisation of improved communication could take place in the group. Glen began to look forward to these sessions, and the duration of his unprompted speech improved considerably, as timed on the tape recording. His clarity of speech did not improve as much, even when he *did* wear his dentures. Nursing staff reported that Glen became less agitated in social situations and they

INSTRUCTIONS: Record in this diary details of any incidents of problem behaviour such as shouting, hitting, kicking, scratching, and throwing things.

	Antecedents	Behaviour	Time			Consequences
Date	Where was Glen? What was happening around him?	What exactly did he do and say?	Started	Ended	Duration	What happened as a direct result of his behaviour?
6th August 1990 Sunday	He was brought back to the ward by a nurse. He had been found wandering by the river on his own, looking dirty and untidy. He couldn't say where he had been or what he was doing. He had been missing since after breakfast. He was taken to the bathroom to get cleaned up.	A nurse Glen didn't know tried to help him undress and get washed. He didn't speak at first but then shouted at the nurse and hit him in the chest.	6.20pm	6.23pm	3mins	Glen went to his room and lay on the bed. He came down at 9pm and made himself something to eat before going back to bed.

Figure 8.1 Incident record.

felt less frightened when approaching him. The incidents of violence reduced initially to once or twice a month and then less frequently as Glen's conversational ability improved and he reported gaining confidence in his ability to relate to people. Nurses also noted that Glen began to spend less time alone and inactive, lying on his bed.

CONCLUSION

Changes in philosophies of care and political decisions have always affected the tasks facing clinicians in trying to respond to the changing needs of people with long-term psychiatric disabilities. This has never been more the case than now, and many of the challenges for clinicians in managing challenging behaviour and long-term impairments result from changes in the last 30 years in the care of people with schizophrenia. In this chapter traditional approaches to the understanding and management of these problems have been reviewed as they are considered to continue to be very helpful. New developments in effective residential units in the community designed to replace the old traditional hospital wards have selectively used many of the procedures and techniques learned from traditional approaches such as the therapeutic community and token economy. The main aspects and contributions of these approaches have been reviewed. Looking to the future, there are four main ways in which approaches to the management of long-term impairments and challenging behaviour, need to develop:

1. There is a need for clinicians to continue to develop ways of effectively communicating with very distressed and impaired individuals in order to understand their experiences better, establish effective working relationships and take note of their concerns in planning treatments. This is central to any therapeutic approach.
2. Further consideration could be given to the contribution that developments in the psychological assessment and treatment of other adult emotional and behavioural disorders can make to the understanding and treatment of people with schizophrenia.
3. Given that contextual factors are crucial to the understanding of any behavioural problem, there is a need to work at understanding more fully the contexts in which problems present in order to manage them better.
4. As services become more diffuse there is a growing need to maximise coordination between the different services involved in each individual's care, such as residential and day-care regimes, and to maximise flexibility in order to minimise demands on service users.

ACKNOWLEDGEMENTS

We would like to thank Paul M. Salkovskis and Max Marshall for helpful comments on earlier drafts of this chapter.

REFERENCES

Andreasen, N.C. (1981) *Scale for the Assessment of Negative Symptoms (SANS)*, University of Iowa.

Ayllon, T. and Azrin, N.H. (1968) *The Token Economy*, Appleton-Century Crofts, New York.

Baker, R. and Hall, J.N. (1983) *REHAB: Rehabilitation Evaluation Hall and Baker*, Vine Publishing, Aberdeen.

Barker, P.J. (1982) *Behaviour Therapy Nursing*, Croom Helm, London.

Bassuk, E.L., Rubin, L. and Lauriat, A. (1984). Is homelessness a mental health problem? *American Journal of Psychiatry*, **141**(12), 1546–50.

Bebbington, P. and McGuffin, P. (1988) *Schizophrenia: the Major Issues*, Heinemann, Oxford.

Beck, A.T., Ward, C.H., Mendelson, M., Mock, J. and Erbaugh, J. (1961) An Inventory for measuring depression. *Archives of General Psychiatry*, **4**, 561–71.

Beck, A.T. (1976) *Cognitive Therapy and the Emotional Disorders*, International Universities Press, New York.

Beck, A.T., Weissman, A., Lester, D. and Trexler, L. (1974) The measurement of pessimism: the Hopelessness Scale. *Journal of Consulting and Clinical Psychology*, **42**, 861–5.

Bentall, R.P., Higson, P.J. and Lowe, C.F. (1987) Teaching self-instructions to chronic schizophrenic patients: efficacy and generalisation. *Behavioural Psychotherapy*, **15**, 58–76.

Blackburn, I.M., Bishop, S., Glen, A.I.M., Whalley, L.J. and Christie, J.E. (1981) The efficacy of cognitive therapy in depression: a treatment trial using cognitive therapy and pharmacotherapy, each alone and in combination. *British Journal of Psychiatry*, **139**, 181–9.

Brenner, H.D. (1989) The treatment of basic psychological dysfunctions from a systemic point of view. *British Journal of Psychiatry*, **155** (suppl. 5), 74–83.

Brenner, H.D., Hodel, B. and Roder, V. (1990) Integrated cognitive and behavioural interventions in the treatment of schizophrenia. *Psychosocial Rehabilitation Journal*, **13**(3), 41–3.

Burns, D.D. (1980) *Feeling Good*, New American Library, New York.

Creer, C. and Wing, J.K. (1974) *Schizophrenia at Home*. National Schizophrenia Fellowship, Surbiton, UK.

Elmore Committee (1987) Support for difficult to place people in Oxford, Elmore Community Support Team, 42 Park End Street, Oxford, UK.

Garety, P.A. and Morris, I. (1984) A new unit for long-stay psychiatric patients: organisation, attitudes and quality of care. *Psychological Medicine*, **14**, 183–92.

Gopalaswamy, A.K. and Morgan, R. (1985) Too many chronic mentally disabled patients are too fat. *Acta Psychiatrica Scandinavica*, **72**, 254–8.

Häfner, H. (1985) Changing patterns of mental health care. *Acta Psychiatrica Scandinavica*, **71** (suppl. 319), 151–64.

Hall, J.N. (1991) Ward-based rehabilitation programmes. In: F.N. Watts and D.H. Bennett (eds), *Theory and Practice of Psychiatric Rehabilitation*, John Wiley, Chichester.

Hall, J.N. and Baker, R.D. (1986) Token economies in schizophrenia: a review. In: A. Kerr and R.P. Snaith (eds), *Contemporary Issues in Schizophrenia*, Gaskell, London.

Hall, J.N., Baker, R.D. and Hutchinson, K. (1977). A controlled evaluation of token economy procedures with chronic schizophrenic patients. *Behaviour Research and Therapy*, **15**, 261–83.

Hahlweg, K. (1988) Behavioural marital therapy: the state of the art. Guest lecture presented at The Behaviour Therapy World Congress, Edinburgh.

Hansen, D.J., Lawrence, J.S.S. and Christoff, K.A. (1985) Effects of interpersonal problem solving training with chronic aftercare patients on problem solving component skills and effectiveness of solutions. *Journal of Consulting and Clinical Psychology*, **53**, 167–74.

Hawton, K. and Kirk, J. (1989). Problem solving. In: K. Hawton, P.M. Salkovskis, J. Kirk and D.M. Clark (eds), *Cognitive Behaviour Therapy for Psychiatric Problems: a Practical Guide*. Oxford University Press.

Hogg, L.I., Hall, J.N. and Marshall, M. (1990) Assessing people who are chronically mentally ill: new methods for new settings. *Psychosocial Rehabilitation Journal*, **13**(3), 7–9.

Honig, A., Pop, P., Tan, E.S., Philipsen, H. and Romme, M.A.J. (1989) Physical illness in chronic psychiatric patients from a community psychiatric unit: the implications for daily practice. *British Journal of Psychiatry*, **155**, 58–64.

Kazdin, A.E. (1982) The token economy: a decade later. *Journal of Applied Behaviour Analysis*, **15**, 431–55.

King's Fund Forum (1987) *The need for asylum in society for the mentally ill or infirm*. Consensus statement, the third King's Fund Forum, King's Fund Centre, London.

Krawiecka, M., Goldberg, D. and Vaughan, M. (1977) A standardized psychiatric assessment scale for rating chronic psychotic patients. *Acta Psychiatrica Scandinavica*, **55**, 299–308.

Lamb, R.H. (1984) Deinstitutionalization and the homeless mentally ill. *Hospital and Community Psychiatry*, **35**(9), 899–907.

MacCarthy, B., Benson, J. and Brewin, C.R. (1986) Task motivation and problem appraisal in long-term psychiatric patients. *Psychological Medicine*, **16**, 431–8.

Matson, J.L. (1980) Behaviour modification procedures for training chronically institutionalized schizophrenics. *Progress in Behaviour Modification*, **9**, 167–204.

Meltzer, H.Y. (1985) Dopamine and negative symptoms in schizophrenia: critique of the Type I–II hypothesis. In: M. Alpert (ed.), *Controversies in Schizophrenia*, Guilford Press, New York.

Moores, B. and Grant, G.W.B. (1977) Optimists and pessimists: attitudes of nursing staff towards the development potential of mentally handicapped patients in their charge. *International Journal of Nursing Studies*, **14**, 13–18.

Myerson, A. (1939) Theory and principles of the 'total push' method in the treatment of chronic schizophrenia. *American Journal of Psychiatry*, **95**, 1197–204.

Nelson, H. (1982) *National Adult Reading Test. Test Manual*. NFER, Windsor.

Noble, P. and Rodger, S. (1989) Violence by psychiatric inpatients. *British Journal of Psychiatry*, **155**, 384–90.

Paul, G.L. and Lentz, R.J. (1977) *Psychosocial Treatment of Chronic Mental Patients*, Harvard University Press, Cambridge, Mass.

Scott, J. (1989) *Advantages and disadvantages of cognitive therapy with depressed inpatients*. Paper presented at World Congress of Cognitive Therapy, Oxford.

Shepherd, G. (1990) A criterion-oriented approach to skills training. *Psychosocial Rehabilitation Journal*, **13**(3), 11–13.

Shepherd, G. (1991) Foreword: Psychiatric Rehabilitation for the 1990s. In: F.N. Watts and D.H. Bennett (eds), *Theory and Practice of Psychiatric Rehabilitation*, John Wiley, Chichester.

Spielberger, C.D., Jacobs, G.A., Russel, S. and Crane, R.S. (1983) Assessment of Anger: the State-Trait Anger Scale. In: Butcher, J. and Spielberger, C.D. (eds), *Advances in Personality Assessment, Vol. 2*, Lawrence Erlbaum, New Jersey.

Trower, P., Bryant, B. and Argyle, M., (1978) *Social Skills and Mental Health*, Methuen, London.

Vieweg, W.V.R., Godleski, L.S., Mitchell, M., Hundley, P.L. and Yank, G.R. (1989) Abnormal diurnal weight gain among chronically psychotic patients contrasted with acutely psychotic patients and normals. *Psychological Medicine*, **19**, 105–9.

Volavka, J. and Krakowski, M. (1989) Schizophrenia and violence. *Psychological Medicine*, **19**, 559–62.

Wing, J.K. and Brown, G.W. (1970) *Institutionalism and Schizophrenia*, Cambridge University Press.

Wykes, T. (1982). A hostel-ward for 'new' long-stay patients: an evaluative study of 'a ward in a house'. *Psychological Medicine Monograph Supplement 2* (ed. J.K. Wing), 59–97, Oxford University Press.

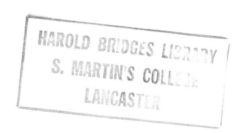

HAROLD BRIDGES LIBRARY
S. MARTIN'S COLLEGE
LANCASTER

Part 3

Services

Chapter 9

Models of Continuing Care

TONY LAVENDER AND FRANK HOLLOWAY

INTRODUCTION

This chapter reviews models of continuing care for people suffering from severe long-term mental health problems. The discussion is therefore not limited to services for those who are diagnosed as suffering from schizophrenia, although invariably this is the most frequent diagnosis among samples of the "old" and "new" long-stay inpatients and the "new long term" living in the community (Wainwright, Holloway and Brugha, 1988; Patrick et al., 1989; Clifford et al., 1991).

The chapter begins with a historical overview of community care services. Developments during the 1980s are discussed, and concerns commonly expressed about current provision are reviewed. The essential components of a continuing care service are then presented. The chapter closes with an attempt to identify future trends. The focus is on mental health services in Britain. Similar trends in policy and provision can be identified throughout the West (Mangen, 1988) and relevant literature from Europe, North America and Australia is presented.

THE HISTORY OF MENTAL HEALTH CARE IN THE COMMUNITY

Public mental health services originated as a philanthropic response to the needs of "pauper lunatics". During the early nineteenth century asylums functioned as therapeutic institutions. "Moral treatment" in small, humanely-run, institutions produced impressive discharge and cure rates (Bockhoven, 1954). From the mid-1800s the increasingly extensive network of local asylums entered what has been described as their "long sleep".

Patient numbers expanded rapidly, and cost containment became a major priority (Scull, 1979). Even during this era of "custodial care" there

Innovations in the Psychological Management of Schizophrenia.
Edited by Max Birchwood and Nicholas Tarrier. © 1992 John Wiley & Sons Ltd

was some interest in the care of patients released into the community, as evidenced by the founding of the Mental Aftercare Association in 1879. Since the 1920s there has been a progressive move towards "community care", gathering pace following the Second World War (Martin, 1984a; Ramon, 1988).

A variety of intellectual undercurrents have shaped the community care movement (Ramon, 1988). An important factor was the "psychologisation" of everyday life that was associated with increased interest in Freud's thought which began during the 1920s and gathered momentum during the Second World War. The idea that everyone was potentially abnormal given adequate stress gained currency, and this may have increased tolerance within the community towards abnormal behaviour (Ramon, 1988). The therapeutic community movement stemmed from attempts by military psychiatrists to rehabilitate psychiatric casualties of war by engaging them in the treatment process (Bion, 1989). The movement began to have an impact on traditional mental hospitals, which had left local authority control with the founding of the NHS in 1948, during the 1950s. Medical Superintendents introduced an "open door" policy, which meant both literally opening the doors of wards within the hospital and figuratively making discharge (and readmission) of patients easier and more frequent (Ramon, 1988). In some hospitals rehabilitation wards were established, and the then novel techniques of occupational therapy were applied (Bennett, 1983).

At the same time psychiatric hospitals, and other institutions, were criticised as environments that produced apathy and physical and mental deterioration among residents (Barton, 1959). The highly complex relationship between social environment and psychiatric disorder has subsequently been the subject of considerable research (e.g. Wing and Brown, 1970; Vaughn and Leff, 1976; Brown and Harris, 1978; Goldstein and Caton, 1983; Falloon and Liberman, 1983; Shepherd, 1988). However, this body of empirical evidence has been less influential than the simplistic message that institutions are both dehumanising and largely responsible for the disabilities of their residents (Jones and Fowles, 1984).

During the 1960s and 1970s a series of scandals broke out when the quality of care in mental illness and mental handicap hospitals was found to have deteriorated to an unacceptable degree (Martin, 1984b). Common themes were identified in the official enquiries that resulted; these included the isolation of institutions and the staff groups within them, a failure of professional leadership and general management, lack of resources and inadequate training of staff (Martin, 1984b). These scandals served "to reinforce the developing view that the large institutions were self-evidently harmful" (Thornicroft and Bebbington, 1989). It is not, however, clear that the underlying causes of institutional failure have been adequately understood by critics of the institution.

A further medicalisation of mental illness followed the introduction of effective drug treatment for depression and schizophrenia during the 1950s (Scull, 1984). Psychiatry moved into the District General Hospital (DGH). This move was predicated on the belief by politicians that major mental illnesses could now be cured (Scull, 1984, p. 81). Outpatient and day-care expanded, although the community support available to patients and carers in the new pattern of services was often inadequate (Brown et al., 1966). Community psychiatric nursing (CPN) emerged in the 1950s and has subsequently expanded steadily to become an essential component of every District Psychiatric Service. Conflicting models for CPN services emerged. There remains an unresolved tension between the CPN as a member of a multidisciplinary psychiatric team and as an independent practitioner working in primary care (Royal College of Psychiatrists, 1980; Conway-Nicholls and Elliott, 1982; Martin, 1984a). The available evidence does not, however, favour the independent practitioner model (Woof and Goldberg, 1988).

During the 1960s and early 1970s a rejection of traditional concepts of "mental illness" was articulated in the vivid writings of the "antipsychiatrists" (Sedgwick, 1982). Hospitalisation for episodes of "acute mental distress" was rejected in favour of psychotherapeutic approaches and communal living, in which sufferers would be supported by the lay people with whom they lived. More recently the "primary consumer" movement has had an increasingly influential voice. This may become an attempt to liberate the subjects of a system that is seen to serve the needs of the professional rather than the user, adopting the ideas and terminology of "antipsychiatry" (Brown, 1981; Chamberlain, 1988). The concept of empowerment of service users and the practice of advocacy are becoming increasingly significant within mental health services (Royal College of Psychiatrists, 1989). The necessity for an advocate to be independent of the service system has been stressed (Sang, 1989). There is growing interest in incorporating the views of users into the planning process (Kingsley and Towell, 1988). This occasionally takes tangible form.

Normalisation has been increasingly influential amongst managers and clinicians in services for people with severe learning difficulties and more recently the mentally ill (Kingsley and Towell, 1988). The principles of normalisation (Wolfensberger, 1972), or social role valorisation (Wolfensberger, 1983) are the subject of intense controversy (Garety, 1988). There has been no dispassionate review in the proposition that "all human services (and particularly those serving people who are subjected to discrimination, are marginalised or devalued) should aim to enable users to reach as valued a social position as possible" (Wainwright, Holloway and

Brugha, 1988). Normalisation principles have been developed into a very powerful training tool that can also serve as a framework for service evaluation (Wolfensberger and Glen, 1973; O'Brien and Tyne,1981; Wolfensberger and Thomas, 1983; Kingsley, Towell and McAusland, 1985).

One common element of the community care movement has been a tendency to deny the severity and persistence of the disabilities experienced by many people who suffer from long-term mental health problems. The terminology used to identify sufferers from "long-term mental health problems" to "chronic mental illness" is a cause of controversy and confusion (Bachrach, 1988; Lavender and Holloway, 1988). Illness-language may be seen as devaluing and excessively "medical". In reality contemporary psychiatric thinking emphasises the interaction between the biological, the psychological and the social (Falloon and Liberman, 1983; Wing, 1983).

There also appears to have been a rather naive view of what the terms "community" and "community care" actually mean (Hawks, 1975; Abrams, 1977). Enthusiasm for community-based work and the use of non-specialist resources was prevalent among the increasing number of social workers recruited and trained to staff the burgeoning social services departments that were formed in 1971 (Martin, 1984a). Ironically this anti-professional stance coincides with the politically powerful perspective that in some sense the community should be providing for its own. By implication responsible citizens should be so arranging their lives and finances that they can receive support from friends and relatives and purchase professional care when the need arises.

Radical commentators have pointed out that in reality a major motivating behind community care has been the fiscal crisis of welfare that affects all Western countries (Jones and Fowles, 1984; Scull, 1984). This crisis has led to a general policy emphasis towards targeting resources at those who are deemed to need them most. Financial considerations have also played a large part in the decision to close hospitals.

CONTINUING CARE IN THE 1980s: INFLUENCES AND FAILURES

The pace of change in mental health services in Britain accelerated rapidly during the 1980s (Ramon, 1988). A small number of psychiatric hospitals actually closed, and plans for more closures were energetically pursued. The development of the "dowry", a financial mechanism that allowed money to move with patients discharged into the community, was highly significant (Mahoney, 1988). However, hospital inpatient services continued to consume more than 80% of Hospital and Community Health Services revenue (Taylor and Taylor, 1989). Despite the isolated examples of cooperation between the health service and local authority social service departments that could be identified (Audit Commision, 1986), Government initiatives to improve inter-agency working by means of joint finance largely failed. Joint finance seems in particular to have bypassed the needs of the mentally ill. The proportion of social service department expenditure devoted to the mentally ill increased but remained extremely low (HMSO, 1989a; Taylor and Taylor, 1989).

Legislative changes

The British 1983 Mental Health Act, largely a product of libertarian concerns over compulsory detention in hospital, required local authorities to train "Approved Social Workers" who would make assessments for admission and were charged with considering alternative sources of help in the community. Although it offered some encouragement to the rediscovery of a mental health specialism within social services, the Act did nothing concrete to encourage community-based services (Ramon, 1988).

Much more influential on the pattern of provision, particularly but not exclusively for the elderly, was a change in social security regulations. This resulted in an explosion in the use of supplementary benefit board and lodging monies to subsidise people living in private and voluntary residential and nursing homes. Government monies became available to pay charges for residential care, up to a stipulated limit for a locality. These rules may have acted as a perverse incentive against the development of domiciliary services by health and social service authorities (Audit Commission, 1986). There is evidence that the need to maximise revenue from welfare benefits may have influenced the plans to provide some British mental hospitals destined for closure (Mahoney, 1988; NUPRD, 1989).

Problems with community care

The policy of community care attracted vociferous criticism (Scull, 1984). The National Schizophrenia Fellowship (NSF), an advocacy group composed largely of carers, described the realities of community care as "The Sham Behind the Slogan" (NSF, 1984). The NSF perspective was one of the relatively frequent tragic stories of individual neglect and family suffering. Examples cited include sons killing their mothers during a psychotic breakdown, and severely disabled individuals apparently being left to wander the streets or live in unsuitable boarding house accommodation (Taylor and Taylor, 1989).

The report "Making a Reality of Community Care" (Audit Commission, 1986) reviewed progress towards the British Government's stated objective of promoting community care for the elderly, mentally ill, mentally handicapped and people with physical disability. It found that progress towards community care had been slowest for mentally ill people. The reduction in NHS residential provision had outstripped the build-up of community resources. There were gross geographical variations in services. Funding arrangements both for the NHS and Local Authorities worked against the development of community services, with local authorities that are progressive actually suffering financial penalties. There was a lack of bridging finance to ease the transition between hospital-and-community-based services. Joint planning between Health and Local Authorities was in disarray, with fragmented responsibility for the development of community-based services. Organisational arrangements for delivering community care at the local level were exceedingly complex, with the many agencies involved working to quite different priorities. Staffing arrangements for the new services were inadequate. There had been a failure to address training needs both within the declining institution and in the new services. A decade of persuasion and exhortation from central government following the White Paper *Better Services for the Mentally Ill* (HMSO, 1975) had had little impact on the delivery of community-care services. The Audit Commission consequently recommended that a new organisational framework be developed that would remedy these problems.

This powerful critique of the organisational aspects of community care policies serves as a background for discussion of the practical problems of community care for people with long-term mental health problems. Complaints have included inadequate resources; perverse incentive towards residential care; poor quality of care and quality of life for chronically mentally ill people; inappropriate diversion of mentally ill people into the criminal justice system; community care policies causing homelessness; community care policies resulting in unacceptable family burden; and poor coordination of care to the individual patient/client.

There is very little systematic data available on the quality of the supports that have been provided to people with long-term mental health problems, even the special group who return to the community after prolonged periods of inpatient care. Indeed there has been a startling lack of clarity about what should be provided. For patients who have been in hospital discharge planning may take place but may be naive, unrealistic and fail to take account of the range of social and medical needs experienced by patients (Caton, Goldstein and Serrano, 1984). Day-care, seen as an essential component of service, varies in quantity throughout Britain and is also probably of very variable quality (Brewin, Wing and Mangen, 1988; Wainwright, Holloway and Brugha, 1988). There is however no doubt that day care users value what is provided (Holloway, 1989).

For many former psychiatric hospital residents in America, community care came to mean "transinstitutionalisation" rather than "deinstitutionalisation" (Mangen, 1988). Patients regarded as institutionally dependent and/or untreatable were discharged into non-psychiatric nursing homes. This has been particularly true for the elderly (Talbott, 1988). Poor quality of care has been documented in the nursing home sector in America and West Germany (Brown, 1985; Kunze, 1985). A controlled trial of nursing home care versus traditional inpatient care for elderly mentally ill residents of Veterans' Administration Hospitals found that the decreased costs of nursing home care were achieved at the expense of poorer clinical outcome for the patients (Linn et al., 1985). In America less dependent patients have moved into Board and Care Homes, which may in some cases provide an acceptable alternative (Lamb, 1979). However, "For the long-term hospitalised patient, the move [from hospital to community] is usually into a boarding home facility.... These facilities are for the most part like small long-term state hospital wards isolated from the community. One is overcome by the depressing atmosphere ... because of the passivity, isolation and inactivity of the residents" (Lamb and Goertzel, 1971).

The scant available information suggests that most people are glad to have left hospital, whatever dissatisfactions they may have with their current situation (Johnstone et al., 1984; Kay and Legg, 1986; Lehman, Possidente and Hawker, 1986; Gibbons and Butler, 1987; Perkins, King and Hollyman, 1989). American studies into the quality of life of people with long-term mental health problems have indicated that severe difficulties are experienced in a variety of life domains (Lehman, 1983). Outcomes of relocation for former long-stay hospital residents are extremely variable. Anecdotal evidence suggests that those who were best-adjusted to life in the hospital, with a secure niche within the hospital community and relatively high status within the patient hierarchy, fare relatively badly (Marlowe, 1976; Holloway et al., 1988).

Community care and prisons

It has been claimed that the decrease in the numbers of long-stay and acute psychiatric inpatient beds in Britain has resulted in an increase in the numbers of mentally disordered people in prison (Rollin, 1977; Bluglass, 1988; Scannell, 1989). Although individual patients may have been rejected by catchment area psychiatric services, often because of difficulty in containing severely disturbed behaviour within the District General Hospital (DGH) inpatient unit or a shortage of inpatient beds, there is no evidence of an excess of psychotic illnesses among prisoners (Coid, 1984). A further study of psychiatric morbidity in the prison population is under way

(Bluglass, 1988). This may show a marked increase in the prevalence of psychosis amongst prisoners on remand. Reluctance by catchment area psychiatrists, particularly those working in DGHs rather than mental hospitals, to accept mentally disordered remand prisoners for treatment has been documented (Coid, 1988a). Prisoners with long term mental health problems and severe social disabilities were particularly likely to be rejected. It would appear that neither the Regional Secure units that were opened for the more difficult mentally abnormal offenders nor contemporary DGH acute units can adequately address the needs of people with severe and long-term problems.

Lack of appropriate long-term residential provision, including long-term hospital care, may well have led to patients with severe illnesses or continuing vulnerability being discharged without adequate support and subsequently coming to the notice of services by offending. Coid (1988b) noted the desperate lengths some chronically disabled individuals went to in order to receive care. Attitudes of staff towards mentally disordered offenders vary markedly, and there is evidence that patients may be inappropriately labelled as psychopathic, personality disordered or violent as part of the process of rejection by services (Coid, 1988b).

Homelessness

Homelessness among the mentally ill in the USA has been a major political issue (David, 1988). The reported prevalence of schizophrenia among samples of homeless persons has varied from 2% to 37% (Susser, Struening and Conover, 1989). A careful study of men admitted to municipal shelters in New York identified 17% as having a definite or probable diagnosis of psychosis. A firm diagnosis of schizophrenia was made in 8%, while 58% had a history of substance abuse (Susser, Struening and Conover, 1989). Shelters for homeless people have been described as "open asylums", which accept people who lack any relationship with traditional support systems (Bassuk, Rubin and Lauriat, 1984). These people are not being adequately helped by local psychiatric services (Lamb, 1984), or other social services agencies (Bassuk, Rubin and Lauriat, 1984). Consequently specialised treatment services for the homeless have been advocated (Jones, 1986; Susser, Struening and Conover, 1989).

There is evidence that psychosis and alcohol abuse are common among users of night shelters and the few remaining large homeless hostels in Britain (Weller et al., 1987; Timms, 1989). There is, however, controversy over the relationship between the decline in hospital beds for the mentally ill and the well-documented increase in homelessness among the mentally ill in Britain and the United States (Garety and Toms, 1990). A causative relationship has been argued (Weller, 1986), although a review of the case notes of any large psychiatric hospital with a reception centre in the catchment area is likely to identify patients who became long-stay decades ago after prolonged periods of homelessness. In England and Wales the discharge of patients from inpatient psychiatric care who are "Homeless and Vulnerable" under the 1977 Housing Act, and therefore liable to be offered temporary accommodation by local authority housing departments, is a part of everyday clinical practice in certain inner-city areas. Although there is an undoubted lack of specialised non-hospital residential accommodation for the mentally ill, the fact that former hospital residents become homeless is largely a reflection of the general housing crisis in Britain.

Family burden

Community care implies to some not care "in the community" but care "by the community" (Ramon, 1988). In effect this may mean shifting the burden of care from the state to relatives (MacCarthy, 1988). This is despite evidence that the pattern of community supports is changing, with a decline in the numbers of people living with or close to relatives, a decline in traditional neighbourhoods, increasing isolation among some minorities and demographic changes altering the balance of carers to those in need (Audit Commission, 1986, p. 10). Early studies into community-oriented services indicated that this pattern of care was associated with an increased level of burden among relatives compared with traditional services which responded to disturbed behaviour by prolonged, even life-long, hospital admission (Grad and Sainsbury, 1968; Hoenig and Hamilton, 1969). More recent studies of highly community-oriented services that attempt to minimise usage of hospital beds have shown that these services either result in similar levels of burden compared to contemporary hospital-oriented practice (Fenton, Tessier and Struening, 1979) or are associated with decreased burden (Test and Stein, 1980; Hoult, 1986) It appears that the standard psychiatric service of the 1970s and 1980s offered poor support following an inpatient admission, in contrast to the community-oriented services that provided long-term support to the sufferer and carers, including appropriate intervention in crises.

The coordination of care

One area of particular concern has been the lack of continuity of care for chronically mentally ill people, who are faced with a complex and confusing service system. One solution was the introduction of "case management" services. These aim to improve the continuity and coordination of care, its accessibility, accountability and efficiency (Intagliata, 1982; Clifford and Craig, 1988; Renshaw, 1988; Kanter, 1989). Given the well-documented reluctance of staff working in the community to address the needs of the chronically mentally ill (Borus, 1981; Mollica, 1983), opinion also began to favour the use of specialised "continuing care" teams to coordinate care for the people with long-term and socially disabling mental illnesses who lived within a defined geographical area (Holloway, 1988; Lehman, 1989). The "continuing care team" and its relationship to case management are discussed in more detail below and in Chapter 11.

In Britain, experimental "community care" projects were shown to decrease the need by frail elderly people for local authority residential care and to delay admission into long-term hospital care. Social worker case managers were employed who held budgets that could purchase paid helpers who provided practical and emotional support (Challis and Davis, 1986). This important finding, which is not strictly relevant to mental health services, was to shape subsequent government thinking about community care for the whole range of client groups (HMSO, 1989a, 1989b).

Policy developments

The 1980s closed with major British Government initiatives affecting both community care and the NHS (HMSO, 1989a, 1989b). The community-care proposals identified local authority social services departments as the agency with lead responsibility for all community care client groups. This appears unrealistic since in 1989 the local authority spending in England and Wales on the mentally ill was 1/36th that of the National Health Service (Taylor and Taylor, 1989). To confuse matters further the proposals made a distinction between an individual's needs for "health" care, which remained an NHS responsibility, and their "social" care, the responsibility of the local social services authority. This distinction makes little sense to those working within health services who have for many years realised that mental health problems are the result of an interaction between "social" and "health" domains. Effective treatment and care therefore requires a programme of interventions that include both "social" and "health" components. By working together local service providers might mitigate the unfortunate consequences of the artificial health/social care divide. Without such cooperation it is conceivable that the health service contribution to community care will actually decrease, as providers retrench to traditional bed-oriented styles of working.

A major aim of policy was to make services more cost-effective. To this end the purchaser of services (commissioning health authority or local authority social services department) was separated from the service provider (HMSO, 1989a, 1989b). The community-care proposals envisaged a "mixed economy of care" within which providers in the statutory, private and voluntary sector would compete. The relationship between purchaser and provider was to be regulated by service contracts. The long-term efficacy of this policy is open to doubt (Knapp, 1988). Contracting for services for the mentally ill has been markedly successful in a demonstrative project in the USA (Stein, Diamond and Factor, 1990). It is however, unlikely that services will have much of a market from which to choose. Reliance on private sector providers, working in isolation to tight budgets, must in any case be a cause of concern given experience in the USA (Mollica, 1983; Brown, 1985; Talbott 1988).

It has been argued that a central authority planning and directing a service system should act as a contractor of services rather than a service provider because any provider will substitute the needs of its employees for the needs of its clients as the organisation's primary goal (Stein, Diamond and Factor, 1990). This is not particularly plausible. There is a danger that if the purchaser/provider distinction is adhered to rigidly those in direct contact with people in need might be removed from the planning process. Purchasers would then lack the relevant information about what to buy. Effective organisational change requires the involvement of the people who must implement it (Georgiades and Phillimore, 1975), and direct care staff are vital stakeholders in the system. Their voice should be heard within the planning process, along with the voices of the consumers and carers (NIMH, 1987). Distancing providers from planning may result in the deprofessionalisation of community-care services and an increased split between hospital and community care. One possible way forward is for commissioners and providers to come together to plan services and agree arrangements for the monitoring and evaluation of services.

COMPONENTS OF CONTINUING CARE

A number of publications have set out in a programmatic fashion the components of an ideal "continuing care" service (MIND, 1983; Richmond Fellowship, 1983; NIMH 1987). However, despite numerous examples of good practice, there are few blueprints available for a comprehensive service that can readily be copied. (An interesting exception is the model developed in Madison, USA to provide a comprehensive service for schizophrenic patients living in an affluent urban/rural community (Stein, Diamond and Factor; 1990).) Components of the service that can be confidently identified include a planning structure; adequate information systems; multidisciplinary teams to organise, coordinate and in part provide care; structured day activities; residential services; and access to care during crises. Other significant elements of a comprehensive service include support for carers, access to welfare rights advice and advocacy systems.

Service planning

The development of high quality services requires leadership and clarity of vision. This has often been lacking partly because of the complex needs of the "continuing care client" and partly because of current interagency and interprofessional rivalries. Planning must involve all the relevant stakeholders (NIMH, 1987; Kingsley and Towell, 1988) which means that a planning group should be multidisciplinary and bring together both users and the relevant agencies. To be effective the group must include people who are innovative, understand the workings of the local health and social services, have the means to make plans a reality and have a direct knowledge of the needs of the client group. Members must also have the time and ability to undertake the necessary strategic and operational planning tasks. These range from developing a "vision" for the service to the minutiae of opening a project. (see Chapter 12 for a full review.)

Commentators in the United States have argued that a central authority should be responsible for planning the service system, with responsibility for all patients in the catchment area and control over public monies for the client group (NIMH, 1987; Lehman, 1989; Stein, Diamond and Factor, 1990). In Britain, health authorities (responsible for "health" component of the community care) must assist local social services authorities (responsible for the "social" component) in the production of a "Community Care Plan" (HMSO, 1989a), but mechanisms for this joint planning are left to local negotiation.

Early on in the planning process the "philosophy" or aspirations of the service should be defined and an outline of its future shape should be produced. Differences between planning group members in their views about the nature of "long-term mental illness" or "severe mental health problems" should be acknowledged and as far as possible resolved at this stage. The subsequent service plans should be based on an appreciation of the local epidemiology and take account of existing provision. They should reflect local geography, including such mundane factors as the patterns of public transport, and should have a realistic chance of acceptance given local circumstances. Wide consultation should follow, with adjustment of plans in the light of reasoned comment. The opinions and support of those involved in implementing the plans should be sought.

Information systems

Health authorities in Britain are now required to maintain a register of patients suffering from mental illness who are in need of continuing health and social care (HMSO, 1989a). Existing services lack adequate information systems. A register of those in need would seem to be an appropriate starting point to the planning process (Wing, 1972), and a potentially important mechanism for ensuring that people do not fall through the cracks of a complex service system. Traditional psychiatric case registers have contributed much to the epidemiological understanding of mental illnesses (see, for example, Wing and Hailey (1972), Gibbons, Jennings and Wing, (1984) and Walsh (1985)). These case registers were somewhat cumbersome, and were certainly not designed with the needs of practitioners and managers in mind. Technological advances have made it possible to develop "tailor-made" information systems based on micro-computers (Shepherd, 1988). A number of interesting projects have attempted to utilise this emerging technology to monitor the activity of a service system and the pattern of service contacts by individuals and to act as an aid to care planning (Fagin and Purser, 1986; Gibbons, 1986; Taylor and Bhumgara, 1989; Henderson, 1990). The introduction of a nationwide network of computerised registers of "people in need" is, however, fraught with both ethical and practical problems. The civil-libertarian aspects of being included on a register of vulnerable people, which might have serious implications for a person's future prospects of employment and access to financial services, have not been clearly addressed.

There is little difficulty in identifying data that might usefully be included on a register. The major stumbling block to the development of a clinically-relevant register is the amount of time required to input the data (Taylor and Bhumgara, 1989). This might suggest to the sceptic that registers should be as unambitious in scope as possible, merely including very basic sociodemographic, diagnostic and service contact data. Maintaining even a limited data-set is a formidable task. It is technically feasible for registers to serve other functions, including the facilitation of report writing and the assessment of the outcome of service contact (Taylor and Bhumgara, 1989). This technology currently appears to work best in the hands of enthusiasts who produce a system designed to meet local needs. To date no computerised system has been shown to be useful in more than one locality or over an extended period of time.

The continuing care team

An effective multi-disciplinary team with a clear system for coordinating care is now seen as the hub of any service for people with long-term mental health problems (Holloway, 1988; Lehman, 1989; Stein, Diamond and Factor, 1990). This "continuing care" team needs to be multi-disciplinary because the client's needs are invariably multi-faceted, requiring expert assessment and intervention in social, psychological and medical areas. No single profession has the range of skills to provide an overall package of high quality care. It would be impossible to train a generic mental health worker to have an adequate level of knowledge and skills to intervene across the whole spectrum of needs. Good care occurs when the multidisciplinary team works together with the client to assess needs and priorities and then plan and implement a programme of care. This programme must be reviewed and revised regularly, if necessary over many years.

The current panacea for the ills of community care is the case manager. A number of potential models of case management exist (Clifford and Craig, 1988; Bachrach, 1989). The term case management is not well thought of by user groups. People dislike being identified as a case. Key working has been suggested as an alternative, although it may not adequately convey the range of responsibilities that the literature generally assigns to the case manager. The concept of the continuing care team fits well with the development of a case management system.

In order to carry out the case management function the team needs to organise itself to provide a coordinated package of care to each client. Thus a comprehensive assessment of the client's needs should come first. Assessment should include life skills (cooking, budgeting, personal hygiene, laundering, etc.), symptomatology and how it affects the client's life, social circumstances (housing, employment, social support and social life) and finances (Watts and Lavender, 1984). A number of team members will usually be involved in the assessment, including the person who will go on to function as the case manager (or "key worker"). The assessment will enable a package of care to be devised which will include therapy, treatment, advice and support in the areas of identified need. The case manager will coordinate this package of care and usually offer some direct care. The case manager inevitably therefore straddles the purchaser/provider divide.

The case manager will often involve other members of the continuing care team in the provision of care, but will also have to ensure that other agencies (e.g. the housing department, benefits offices, sheltered employers, adult education services) make their contribution. Staff must develop positive, supportive relationships with clients, as well as teaching them practical survival skills in real-life settings (Stein and Test, 1980). The service needs to be responsive 24 hours a day to requests from clients and carers (Finlay-Jones, 1983). A policy of assertive outreach is required to prevent people from falling through the cracks in the system. An important function of the case manager is to monitor the success of the package of care that was initially devised, and, with advice from the client and other members of the continuing care team, make any alterations that are required.

The team base, from which the case management system will operate, can provide a place where the client and other agencies involved in the care package can meet to coordinate and review their activities. The process of reviewing the function of the team is clearly central to the provision of a high-quality service. Clifford et al. (1989) provide an overview of the methods that have been used to monitor quality of care. Service management, care practices and treatment outcome all require evaluation. The QUARTZ system attempts to intervene at an organisational level to ensure the commitment and involvement of both managerial and direct care staff in the process of evaluation (Clifford et al. 1989). It also provides a set of evaluative schedules.

The team itself should offer its members both professional advice and a supportive group of colleagues who can help them deal with the personal stresses that are integral to work with a disadvantaged and disabled client group. Such support should help avoid the problems of staff "burn-out" and the high turnover of staff which often prevents teams from providing the long-term coordinated care that is an essential component of a high quality service (Test and Stein, 1980). Issues of recruitment, retention and career development are of crucial importance in all forms of community mental health care.

An important adjunct to any continuing care service is a strong system of client advocacy. Sang (1989) has described a number of working models. These have as a common element the activities of an individual (the advocate) who acts on behalf of or with the client to help obtain the best possible care, and helps make the client's wishes known to service providers. Many standard lists of the case management tasks include the role of advocate. This shows a misunderstanding of advocacy, since the advocate must always be independent of the services.

The model of the continuing care team put forward in this section argues against a strict distinction between purchasers and providers of services. Effective coordination of an agreed package of care is more than a bureaucratic exercise. It requires the active involvement of workers who have developed a therapeutic relationship with the client (Kanter, 1989).

Community-based teams operating in this way can be highly effective in preventing hospital admission and are generally preferred by clients and carers when compared with more traditional services (Stein and Test, 1980; Hoult, 1986). It is, however, important to emphasise that continuous care teams can only complement other elements of the service system. Like case management, the team is no panacea for community care. Forming and sustaining a team presents a considerable challenge to service managers, who must both offer the necessary support and guidance and allow the team to develop an identity that crosses traditional professional boundaries.

Structured day activities

Work plays a central role in the lives of most people. Employment not only has "manifest" functions (e.g. monetary benefits), but also significant "latent" functions (e.g. structuring time, providing shared experiences and social contacts and enforcing activity) (Jahoda, 1981). Unemployment may lead to apathy, loss of social contact and loss of self-esteem (Warr, 1984). The Three Hospitals Study, which investigated the relationship between the quality of care and the clinical status of women diagnosed as suffering from schizophrenia, found that the more time patients spent doing nothing the more apathetic and withdrawn the patients were (Wing and Brown, 1970). Changes in the social environment were associated with changes in negative psychotic symptoms.

A key element in the influential "Fountain House" philosophy of psychosocial rehabilitation is the significance of productive activity and the opportunity for gainful employment for even the most disabled psychiatric client (Beard, Propst and Malamud, 1982). Any continuing care service should address users' needs for employment (in the sense of opportunities for paid work). A range of employment opportunities are required from access to open employment, through sheltered placements in ordinary firms to specialist sheltered work schemes (Pilling, 1988). Numerous isolated examples of good practice exist; a recent MIND publication listed over 300 work schemes currently operating in Britain (Stuart, 1990). Overall, however, provision is poor. Innovative and successful schemes reflect the local economy, and have tended to move away from the light industrial assembly work of traditional Industrial Therapy. Opportunities for training are also vital, and must take account of the particular problems of people with psychiatric disabilities, who may require additional support and time to complete a training scheme. In general it is important that such services are locally based, enable clients in valued work and, as far as possible, help them integrate with "ordinary" members of the community (Pilling, 1988). The location and appearance of sheltered work provision must be appropriate to its function. The product range must be marketable, and be sufficiently interesting to produce that a workforce is retained. Work schemes must assess their clients effectively and continuously, offering opportunity routes to waged employment.

Most "continuing care" clients are either unwilling or unable to engage in employment. This partly reflects the current benefits system, which can heavily penalise those seeking work, and partly the lack of local opportunities. Many people are too severely disabled by their psychiatric symptoms or lack confidence and skills required to tackle the ladder to open employment. For those not in employment traditional psychiatric day-care may offer structured activities that provide the latent functions of work (Holloway, 1989), with consequent psychological benefits to the attender. Increasingly emphasis is being put on facilitating the use of mainstream services, such as adult education classes, recreation centres and local community centres. Some people may just want a welcoming place where they can meet other people and have a cheap meal. Others may benefit from a highly structured programme of activities either within a day unit or at a number of different locations. As opportunities for day activities expand in a locality, the need for coordination between units increases; this is an obvious function of the continuing care team.

Although emphasis is rightly placed on the social significance of day care, activities can help users to develop new skills (such as shopping, cooking, budgeting, interpersonal skills) and develop their social networks. Befriending schemes can complement formal day-care by offering a vital opportunity for clients to develop new relationships (Sang, 1989). The day unit can be a place where specific therapies (individual, group, family, behavioural) take place. Some attenders receive much needed personal care whilst others require close monitoring of their mental state (Holloway, 1988). Day-care may, in certain circumstances, provide an acceptable alternative to inpatient admission during periods of psychiatric crisis (Creed, Black and Anthony, 1989).

Residential services

The majority of people suffering from long-term mental health problems live either alone or with their families. Only a small minority make use of specialist residential services, partly because these services are pitifully inadequate. There are a number of useful literature reviews on residential care for the mentally ill (e.g. Carpenter, 1978; Garety, 1988; Gibbons, 1988). Unfortunately contemporary information on the quality of residential care in Britain is lacking. It is only recently that the rundown of large psychiatric hospitals has been accompanied by careful assessment of residents' needs and the subsequent development of a network of residential provision (NUPRD, 1989). A spectrum of support, from intensively staffed units to supported independent housing within the community, is required to replace the traditional hospital (NUPRD, 1989). Assessment measures are now available to quantify local need within this spectrum (Clifford, 1988; Mullhall, 1989).

Despite a broad consensus over what is required the planning and development of residential provision is often marked by arguments over competing philosophies or ideologies of care. Protagonists may adopt a civil libertarian, anti-institutional stance (Bachrach, 1978), they may emphasise the provision of a rehabilitative environment that facilitates skills development (Watts and Bennett, 1983, 1991; Shepherd, 1984) or they may espouse the tenets of social role valorisation with its concern that the individual be facilitated to adopt valued social roles (Wolfensberger, 1983). Although these differences have considerable value in raising significant issues, it is important that the evolving residential services take account of the nature of severe psychiatric disability, which is not necessarily a product of the institution and the "medical model".

Some hospital patients prove particularly hard to place, often as a result of previous or continuing aggressive, sexually inappropriate or otherwise socially unacceptable behaviour (NUPRD, 1989). Such "challenging behaviours" are hard to define and are certainly context-dependent (see Chapter 8); as a result the epidemiology of the problem is totally obscure. The traditional solution is the large mental hospital, with its locked wards and extensive campus. A small number of "Hospital Hostels", set up to provide an alternative to the traditional mental hospital, have been extensively researched. They have been found to provide an acceptable standard of care within a relatively homely environment and an improved quality of life to residents (Garety and Morris, 1984; Gibbons and Butler, 1987; Simpson, Hyde and Farager, 1989). However, hospital hostels are not a comprehensive alternative since some residents cannot be adequately contained within these settings. Other models include an "asylum community" on a hospital campus (Wing and Furlong, 1986) which could cater for "patients with special needs". Attempts have been made to characterise the potential users of such a campus, who might include people who are elderly, demented and behaviourally disturbed; people with coexisting learning difficulty and major mental illness; people who are brain-damaged and assaultative; those suffering from functional psychoses who are assaultative; and people who are diagnosed as suffering from chronic schizophrenia and present socially unacceptable or self-injurious behaviours (Gudeman and Shore, 1984). At the other philosophical extreme lies the provision of "ordinary housing" for two to four "challenging" residents in intensively staffed houses on ordinary streets. This latter model has been applied with some success to services for people with learning difficulties (Mansell, 1986). There is also an expanding network of private psychiatric hospitals that offer (at a price) treatment and containment for those difficult to place patients who cannot be provided for within their localities.

With the exception of the hospital hostels, evaluations of residential alternatives to hospital care are largely unavailable. A number of studies are now under way. American experience calls into question the role of nursing homes as an alternative to hospital care for elderly people with chronic mental illnesses (Mollica, 1983; Brown, 1985; Talbot, 1988). Clinical outcomes in this context may be closely correlated with expenditure (Linn et al., 1985). Foster-care, landlady and family placement schemes are useful components of a residential care system (Linn, Klett and Caffey, 1982; Anstee, 1985; Howat et al., 1988). The traditional group home seems less relevant to current demand, which is for independent living with the necessary support. Unfortunately the many innovative schemes have been inadequately evaluated. For those with greater needs, emphasis is now on various forms of supported housing within which non-professional workers provide "social care" for residents. The intensity of staffing and professional back-up to these "ordinary housing" schemes varies, as does the organisational context of the scheme (NUPRD, 1989). It is as yet unclear how viable innovative alternatives to the traditional mental hospital that are based on the ordinary housing model will prove to be in the long term. One major difficulty of the ordinary housing model is its high unit costs when compared with traditional services which enjoy some economies of scale. Management of these dispersed services, that are often in the voluntary sector, is also problematical.

The major barrier to the development of residential services is lack of adequate revenue and, even more acutely, capital funding (Mahoney, 1988). Constraints are likely to be exacerbated, at least in the short term, by changes in the financing of "social care", including residential, day and domiciliary services, which is to be channelled through the local authority social service department (HMSO, 1989a). Budgets will not be ring-faced against competing demands on limited local authority resources, and may in any case not reflect the degree of local psychiatric morbidity. Unless services are defended at a local level it is difficult to be optimistic about the immediate future for new forms of residential care in Britain, despite a recent explosion of innovative developments.

Dealing with crises

Continuing care clients are prone to recurrent crises because of exacerbation in psychiatric symptomatology and breakdown in social supports. Community-based teams that include experienced mental health professionals can be highly effective in preventing hospital admission when an acute crisis occurs (Hoult, 1986). A central issue is whether, when a crisis cannot be contained, use should be made of existing acute psychiatric in-patient facilities or alternative facilities should be developed. Busy acute wards in a DGH unit may provide a highly stressful environment and therefore exacerbate psychotic symptomatology while failing to maintain instrumental skills (see Chapter 3). Acute unit staff, unused to people with continuing disability, are also likely to have difficulty in judging when a patient whose symptoms respond only partially to treatment can appropriately be discharged.

A number of options need to be explored to improve the care of long-term clients who are in acute crisis. The simplest is to improve liaison between the continuous care team and the acute unit. The need for admission may be identified in advance. Clear aims for inpatient care may be identified and the continuing care team may remain involved in management decisions throughout the inpatient episode. Alternatively, separate inpatient services might be provided for patients with long-term disabilities. This would only be practical in districts where psychiatric morbidity is particularly high. The importance of respite services for people with long-term mental health problems, long acknowledged in the care of elderly people suffering from dementia, has not been adequately recognised (Talbott and Glick, 1986). Interestingly a "respite house" has been included in the plans for the replacement of a mental hospital (NUPRD, 1989), although the operation of respite services for the mentally ill has not been adequately evaluated.

FUTURE DIRECTIONS

Much is now understood about the failings of previous service delivery systems (Martin, 1984b). Unfortunately past failures are often explained in terms of the prevailing ideology; the very real needs of the client group and care staff are often ignored. Although current rhetoric in Britain rightly emphasises the importance of the individualised assessment of the needs of people in receipt of continuing care services (HMSO, 1989a), there are grounds for severe concern about the future. It is possible that the understandable attempts to promote cost-effective services will result in a diminution in the real resources available to provide care for people with long-term mental health problems. Other more politically favoured client groups may gain. The transfer of responsibility for "social care" to local authorities represents a major challenge to health care professionals, who will be required to develop new skills in consultancy with the plethora of providers what will emerge within the "mixed economy of care". The service system in Britain is likely to become more fragmented, at a time when the need for an integrated local mental health authority has at last been recognised in the USA (NIMH, 1987; Lehman, 1989).

Continuing care teams may be allowed to combine the case management function outlined in "Caring for People" (HMSO, 1989a) with direct clinical care. This tenuous possibility, together with increasing involvement in the needs of the long-term mentally ill shown by general practitioners (Kendrick, 1990) and the stirring of a primary consumer movement anxious to ensure good quality services provide the only elements of optimism in an otherwise depressing view of the future. It is all too likely that depleted hospital services will struggle to care for patients in isolation from cash-limited social care services, within which the lack of mental health expertise is not alleviated by awareness of resources within the local community. Clinicians and managers with responsibility for local health, housing and social services need to work together if quality services for people with long-term mental health problems are to emerge from the decaying asylums.

REFERENCES

Abrams, P. (1977) Community care; some research problems and priorities. *Policy and Politics*, **6**, 125–51.

Anstee, B.H. (1985) An alternative form of community care for mentally ill; supported lodging schemes ... a personal view. *Health Trends*, **17**, 39–40.

Audit Commission (1986) *Making a Reality of Community Care*, HMSO, London.

Bachrach, L.L. (1978) A conceptual approach to deinstitutionalisation. *Hospital and Community Psychiatry*, **29**, 573–8.

Bachrach, L.L. (1988) Defining chronic mental illness: a concept paper. *Hospital and Community Psychiatry*, **39**, 383–8.

Bachrach, L.L. (1989) Case Management; toward a shared definition. *Hospital and Community Psychiatry*, **40**, 883–4.

Barton, R. (1959) *Institutional Neurosis*, John Wright, Bristol.

Bassuk, E.L., Rubin, L. and Lauriat, A. (1984) Is homelessness a mental health problem? *American Journal of Psychiatry*, **141**, 1546–50.

Beard, J.H., Propst, R. and Malamud, T.J. (1982) The Fountain House model of psychiatric rehabilitation. *Psychosocial Rehabilitation Journal*, **5**, 47–53.

Bennett, D. (1983) The historical development of rehabilitation services. In: F.N. Watts and D. Bennett (eds), *The Theory and Practice of Psychiatric Rehabilitation*, John Wiley, Chichester.

Bion, W.R. (1989) *Experiences in Groups*, Routledge, London.

Bluglass, R. (1988) Mentally disordered prisoners; reports but no improvements. *British Medical Journal*, **296**, 1757.

Bockhoven, J.S. (1954) Moral treatment in American psychiatry. *Journal of Nervous and Mental Diseases*, **124**, 167–94 and 292–320.

Borus, J. (1981) Deinstitutionalisation of the chronically mentally ill. *New England Journal of Medicine*, **305**, 339–42.

Braucht, G.N. and Kirby, M.W. (1986) An empirical typology of the chronically mentally ill. *Community Mental Health Journal*, **22**, 3–21.

Brewin, C.A., Wing, J.K., Mangen, S.P., Brugha, T.S., Maccarthy, B. and Lesage, A. (1988) Needs for care among the long-term mentally ill; a report from the Camberwell High Contact Survey. *Psychological Medicine*, **18**, 443–56.

Brown, G.W., Bone, M., Dalison, B. and Wing, J.K. (1966) *Schizophrenia and Social Care*, Oxford University Press, London.
Brown, G.W. and Harris, T. (1978) *Social Origins of Depression*, Tavistock, London.
Brown, P. (1981) The mental health patients' rights movement and mental health institutional change. *International Journal of Health Services*, **11**, 523–40.
Brown, P. (1985) *The Transfer of Care; Psychiatric Deinstitutionalisation and its Aftermath*, Routledge and Kegan Paul, London.
Carpenter, M.D. (1978) Residential placement for the chronic psychiatric patient; a review and evaluation of the literature. *Schizophrenia Bulletin*, **4**, 384–98.
Caton, C., Goldstein, J., Serrano, O. and Bender, R. (1984) The impact of discharge planning on chronic schizophrenic patients. *Hospital and Community Psychiatry*, **35**, 255–62.
Challis, D. and Davis, B. (1986) *Case Management in Community Care*, Gower, Aldershot.
Chamberlain, J. (1988) *On Our Own*, MIND, London.
Clifford, P., Charman, A., Webby, A. and Best, S. (1991) Planning for Community Care: longstay populations of hospitals scheduled for closure. *British Journal of Psychiatry*, **158**, 190–6.
Clifford, P. (1988) *Community Placement Questionnaire*, NUPRD, London.
Clifford, P. and Craig, T. (1988) *Case management systems for the long-term mentally ill. A proposed inter-agency initiative*, NUPRD, London.
Clifford, P., Leiper, R., Lavender, A. and Pilling, S. (1989) *Assuring the Quality of Mental Health Services; The QUARTZ System*, Free Association Books, London.
Coid, J. (1984) How many psychiatric patients in prison? *British Journal of Psychiatry*, **145**, 78–86.
Coid, J. (1988a) Mentally abnormal prisoners on remand; I—Rejected or accepted by the NHS? *British Medical Journal*, **296**, 1779–82.
Coid, J. (1988b) Mentally abnormal prisoners on remand; II—Comparison of services provided by Oxford and Wessex regions. *British Medical Journal*, **296**, 1783–4.
Conway-Nicholls, K. and Elliott, A. (1982) North Camden community psychiatric nursing service. *British Medical Journal*, **285**, 859–61.
Creed, F., Black, D. and Anthony, P. (1989) Day hospital and community treatment for acute psychiatric illness: a critical appraisal. *British Journal of Psychiatry*, **154**, 300–10.
David, A. (1988) On the street in America. *British Medical Journal*, **296**, 1016.
Fagin, L. and Purser, H. (1986) Development of the Waltham Forest Local Mental Health Care Register. *Bulletin of the Royal College of Psychiatrists*, **10**, 303–6.
Falloon, I.R.H. and Liverman, R.P. (1983) Interactions between drug and psychosocial therapy in schizophrenia. *Schizophrenia Bulletin*, **9**, 543–54.
Fenton, F.R., Tessier, L. and Struening, E.L. (1979) A comparative trial of home and hospital psychiatric care: one year follow-up. *Archives of General Psychiatry*, **36**, 1073–9.
Finlay-Jones, R. (1983) The practice of psychiatry in the community. *Australian and New Zealand Journal of Psychiatry*, **17**, 107–8.
Fisher, M., Newton, C. and Sainsbury, E. (1984) *Mental Health Social Work Observed*, Allen and Unwin, London.
Garety, P. and Morris, I. (1984) A new unit for long-stay psychiatric patients; organisation, attitude and quality of care. *Psychological Medicine*, **14**, 183–92.
Garety, P. (1988) Housing. In: A. Lavender and F. Holloway (eds), *Community Care in Practice*, John Wiley, Chichester.

Garety, P. and Toms, R.M. (1990) Collected and neglected: are Oxford hostels for the homeless filling up with disabled psychiatric patients? *British Journal of Psychiatry*, **157**, 269–72.
Georgiades, N.J. and Phillimore L. (1975) The myth of the hero innovator and alternative strategies for organisational change. In: C.C. Kiernan and F.D. Woodford (eds), *Behaviour Modification with the Severely Retarded*, Associated Scientific Publishers, Amsterdam.
Gibbons, J. (1986) *Coordinated Aftercare for Schizophrenia; the Community care information unit*, University Department of Psychiatry, Royal South Hants Hospital, Southampton.
Gibbons, J. (1988) Residential care for mentally ill adults. In: I. Sinclair (ed.), *Residential Care: the Research Reviewed*, HMSO, London.
Gibbons, J.S. and Butler, J.P. (1987) Quality of life for 'new' long-stay psychiatric in-patients: the effects of moving to a hostel. *British Journal of Psychiatry*, **151**, 347–54.
Gibbons, J., Jennings, C. and Wing, J.K. (1984) Psychiatric Care in Eight Register Areas, 1976–1981. *Psychiatric Case Register*, Knowle Hospital, Fareham, Hants.
Goldstein, J.M. and Caton, C.L.M. (1983) The effects of the community environment on chronic psychiatric patients. *Psychological Medicine*, **13**, 193–9.
Grad, J. and Sainsbury, P. (1968) The effects that patients have on their families in a community and a control psychiatric service. *British Journal of Psychiatry*, **114**, 265–78.
Gudeman, J.E. and Shore, F. (1984) Beyond deinstitutionalisation: a new class of facilities for the mentally ill. *New England Journal of Medicine*, **311**, 832–6.
Hawks, D. (1975) Community care; an analysis of assumptions. *British Journal of Psychiatry*, **127**, 276–85.
Henderson, A. (1990) The monitoring of psychiatric patients. *Nursing Standard*, 25 April, 28–31.
Her Majesty's Stationery Office (1975) *Better services for the Mentally Ill*, HMSO, London.
Her Majesty's Stationery Office (1989a) *Caring for People*, HMSO, London.
Her Majesty's Stationery Office (1989b) *Working for Patients*, HMSO, London.
Hoenig, J. and Hamilton, M.W. (1969) *The Desegregation of the Mentally Ill*, Routledge and Kegan Paul, London.
Holloway, F. (1988) Day care and community support. In: A. Lavender and F. Holloway (eds), *Community Care in Practice*, John Wiley, Chichester.
Holloway, F. (1989) Psychiatric day care; the users' perspective. *International Journal of Social Psychiatry*, **35**, 252–64.
Holloway, F., Booker, D., Mill, S., Siddle, K. and Wilson, C. (1988) Progress and pitfalls in the move out of hospital. *The Health Service Journal*, 11 August, 910–12.
Hoult, J. (1986) Community care of the acutely mentally ill. *British Journal of Psychiatry*, **149**, 137–44.
Howat, J., Bates, P., Pidgeon, J. and Shepperson, G. (1988) The Development of Residential Accommodation in the Community. In: A. Lavender and F. Holloway (eds), *Community Care in Practice*, John Wiley, Chichester.
Intagliata, J. (1982) Improving quality of care for the chronic mentally disabled: the role of case management. *Schizophrenia Bulletin*, **8**, 655–74.
Jahoda, M. (1981) Work, employment and unemployment; values, theories and approaches in social research. *American Psychologist*, **36**, 184–91.
Johnstone, E.C., Owens, D.G.C., Gold, A., Crow, T.J. and Macmillan, J.F. (1984). Schizophrenia patients discharged from hospital: a follow-up study. *British Journal of Psychiatry*, **145**, 586–90.

Jones, B. (1986) *Treating the Homeless; Urban Psychiatry's Challenge*, American Psychiatric Press, Washington.
Jones, K. and Fowles, A.J. (1984) *Ideas on Institutions*, Routledge and Kegan Paul, London.
Kanter, J. (1989) Clinical case management: definition, principles, components. *Hospital and Community Psychiatry*, **40**, 361–8.
Kay, A. and Legg, C. (1986) *Discharged to the Community*. A review of housing and support in London for people leaving psychiatric care, Housing Research Group, The City University.
Kendrick, T. (1990) The challenge of the long-term mentally ill. *Royal College of Practitioners' Members' Reference Book*, pp. 283–6. Royal College of Practitioners, London.
Kingsley, A., Towell, D. and McAusland, T. (1985) *Up to Scratch: Monitoring to Maintain Standards*, Kings Fund College, London.
Kingsley, S. and Towell, D. (1988) Planning for High-quality Local Services. In: A. Lavender and F. Holloway (eds), *Community Care in Practice*, John Wiley, Chichester.
Knapp, M. (1988) Searching for efficiency in long-term care, deinstitutionalisation and privatisation. *British Journal of Social Work*, **18**, Supp., 151–71.
Kunze, H. (1985) Rehabilitation and institutionalisation in community care in West Germany. *British Journal of Psychiatry*, **147**, 261–4.
Lamb, H.R. (1979) The new asylums in the community. *Archives of General Psychiatry*, **36**, 129–34.
Lamb, H.R. (1984) Deinstitutionalisation and the homeless mentally ill. *Hospital and Community Psychiatry*, **35**, 899–907.
Lamb, H.R. and Goertzel, V. (1971) Discharged mental patients—are they really in the community? *Archives of General Psychiatry*, **24**, 29–34.
Lavender, A. and Holloway, F. (1988) Introduction. In: A. Lavender and F. Hollaway (eds), *Community Care in Practice*, John Wiley, Chichester.
Lehman, A.F. (1983) The well-being of chronic mental patients. *Archives of General Psychiatry*, **40**, 369–73.
Lehman, A.F. (1989) Strategies for improving services for the chronic mentally ill. *Hospital and Community Psychiatry*, **40**, 916–20.
Lehman, A.F., Ward, N. and Linn, L.S. (1982a) Chronic mental patients: the quality of life issue. *American Journal of Psychiatry*, **139**, 1271–6.
Lehman, A.F., Reed, S.K. and Possidente, S.M. (1982b) Priorities for long term care: comments from board and care residents. *Psychiatric Quarterly*, **54**, 181–9.
Lehman, A., Possidente, S. and Hawker, F. (1986) The quality of life of chronic patients in a state hospital and in community residences. *Hospital and Community Psychiatry*, **37**, 901–7.
Linn, M.W., Klett, C.J. and Caffey, E.M. (1982) Relapse of psychiatric patients in foster care. *American Journal of Psychiatry*, **139**, 778–83.
Linn, M., Gurel, L., Williford, W.O., Overall, J., Gurland, B., Laughlin, P. and Barchiesi, A. (1985) Nursing home care as an alternative to psychiatric hospitalization. *Archives of General Psychiatry*, **42**, 544–51.
MacCarthy, B. (1988) The Role of Relatives. In: A. Lavender and F. Holloway (eds), *Community Care in Practice*, John Wiley, Chichester.
Mahoney, J. (1988) Finance and Government Policy. In: A. Lavender and F. Holloway (eds), *Community Care in Practice*, John Wiley, Chichester.
Mangen, S. (1988) Implementing Community Care: an International Assessment.

In: A. Lavender and F. Holloway (eds), *Community Care in Practice*, John Wiley, Chichester.
Mansell, J. (1986) *Developing Staffed Housing for People with Mental Handicaps*, Costello, London.
Marlowe, R. (1976) When they closed the doors at Modesto. In: P.I. Ahmed and S. Plog (eds), *State Mental Hospitals: What Happens When They Close?*, Plenum Press, New York.
Martin, F.M. (1984a) *Between the Acts*, Nuffield Provincial Hospitals Trust, London.
Martin, J.P. (1984b) *Hospitals in Trouble*, Blackwell, Oxford.
MIND (1983) *Common Concern*, MIND, London.
Mollica, R.F. (1983) From asylum to community: the threatened disintegration of public psychiatry. *New England Journal of Medicine*, **308**, 367–73.
Mullhall, D.J. (1989) *Functional Performance Record*, NFER-Nelson, Windsor.
National Institute of Mental Health (1987) *Towards a model plan for a comprehensive community-based mental health system*, Administrative Document. US Department of Health and Human Services.
National Schizophrenia Fellowship (1984) Community care: the sham behind the slogan. *Bulletin of the Royal College of Psychiatrists*, **8**, 112–14.
National Unit for Psychiatric Research and Development (1989) *First Interim Report of the Cane Hill Closure Research Team*, NUPRD, London.
O'Brien, J. and Tyne, A. (1981) *The Principle of Normalisation: a Foundation for Effective Services*, CMH/CMHERA, London.
Patrick, M., Higgit, A., Holloway, F. and Silverman, M. (1989) Changes in an inner city psychiatric in-patient service following bed reduction: a follow-up of the East Lambeth 1986 Survey, *Health Trends*, **21**, 121–3.
Perkins, R.E., King, S.A. and Hollyman, J.A. (1989) Resettlement of old long-stay psychiatric patients: the use of the private sector. *British Journal of Psychiatry*, **155**, 233–8.
Pilling, S. (1988) Work and the Continuing Care Client. In: A. Lavender and F. Holloway (eds), *Community Care in Practice*, John Wiley, Chichester.
Ramon, S. (1988) Community Care in Britain. In: A. Lavender and F. Holloway (eds), *Community Care in Practice*, John Wiley, Chichester.
Renshaw, J. (1988) Care in the Community: individual care planning and case management. *British Journal of Social Work*, **18**, Supp., 79–105.
Richmond Fellowship (1983) *Mental Health and the Community*, Richmond Fellowship Press, London.
Rollin, H.R. (1977) 'Deinstitutionalisation' and the Community: fact and theory. *Psychological Medicine*, **7**, 181–4.
Royal College of Psychiatrists (1980) Community Psychiatric Nursing. A discussion document by a working party of the Social and Community Psychiatry section. *Bulletin of the Royal College of Psychiatrists*, **4**, 114–18.
Royal College of Psychiatrists (1989) Patient advocacy—Report for Public Policy Committee. *Psychiatric Bulletin*, **13**, 715–16.
Sang, B. (1989) The Independent Voice of Advocacy, In: A. Brackx and C. Grimshaw (eds), *Mental Health Care in Crisis*, Pluto, London.
Scannel, T.D. (1989) Community care and the difficult and offender patient. *British Journal of Psychiatry*, **154**, 615–19.
Scull, A.T. (1979) *Museums of Madness*, Penguin, Harmondsworth, Middlesex.
Scull, A. (1984) *Decarceration: Community Treatment and the Deviant*, Polity Press, Cambridge.
Sedgwick, P. (1982) *Psychopolitics*, Pluto Press, London.

Shepherd, G. (1984) *Institutional Care and Rehabilitation*, Longman, London.
Shepherd, G. (1988) The Contribution of psychological interventions to the management of chronic schizophrenia. In: P. McGuffin and P. Bebbington (eds), *Schizophrenia: the Major Issues*, Heinemann, London.
Simpson, C.J., Hyde, C.E. and Farager, E.B. (1989) The chronically mentally ill in community facilities: a study of quality of life. *British Journal of Psychiatry*, **154**, 77–82.
Sinclair, I. (1988) Residential Care for Elderly People. In: I. Sinclair (ed.), *Residential Care: the Research Reviewed*, HMSO, London.
Stein, L.I. and Test, M.A. (1980) Alternative to mental hospital treatment. I. Conceptual model, treatment program and clinical evaluation. *Archives of General Psychiatry*, **37**, 392–7.
Stein, L.I., Diamond, R.J. and Factor, R.M. (1990) A System Approach to the care of Persons with Schizophrenia. In: M.I. Herz, S.J. Keith and J.P. Docherty (eds), *Handbook of Schizophrenia*, Vol. 5, Psychosocial Therapies, Elsevier, Amsterdam.
Stuart, M. (1990) Working Out. *The Mind Guide to Employment Projects*, MIND, London.
Susser, E., Struening, E.L. and Conover, S. (1989) Psychiatric problems in homeless men. *Archives of General Psychiatry*, **46**, 845–50.
Talbott, J.A. (1988) Nursing homes are not the answer. *Hospital and Community Psychiatry*, **39**, 115.
Talbott, J.A. and Glick, I.D. (1986) The inpatient care of the chronically mentally ill. *Schizophrenia Bulletin*, **12**, 129–40.
Taylor, J. and Bhumgara, K. (1989) The Safety Net Project. *Psychiatric Bulletin*, **13**, 677–9.
Taylor, J. and Taylor, D. (1989) *Mental Health in the 1990's: from Custody to Care?* Office of Health Economics, London.
Test, M.A. and Stein, L.I. (1980) Alternative to mental hospital treatment. III. Social costs. *Archives of General Psychiatry*, **37**, 409–12.
Thornicroft, G. and Bebbington, P. (1989) Deinstitutionalisation—from hospital closure to service development. *British Journal of Psychiatry*, **155**, 739–53.
Timms, P.W. (1989) Homelessness and mental illness. *Health Trends*, **21**, 70–1.
Vaughn, C.E. and Leff, J.P. (1976) The influence of family and social factors on the course of psychiatric illness. *British Journal of Psychiatry*, **129**, 125–37.
Wainwright, T., Holloway, F. and Brugha, T. (1988) Day care in an inner city. In: A. Lavender and F. Holloway (eds.), *Community Care in Practice*, John Wiley, Chichester.
Walsh, D. (1985) Case registers for monitoring treatment outcome in chronic functional psychoses. In: T. Helgalson (ed.), *The Long-term Treatment of Functional Psychoses*, Cambridge University Press.
Warr, P. (1984) Job Loss, Unemployment and Psychological well-being. In: V.L. Allen and E. van der Vliert (eds), *Role Transitions*, Plenum Publications, New York.
Watts, F.N. and Bennett, D. (1983) *The Theory and Practice of Psychiatric Rehabilitation*, John Wiley, Chichester.
Watts, F.N. and Bennett, D. (1991) *The Theory and Practice of Psychiatric Rehabilitation*, 2nd edition, John Wiley, Chichester.
Watts, F.N. and Lavender, A. (1984) Rehabilitation Investigation. In: G. Powell and S. Lindsay (eds), *Handbook of Clinical Psychology*, Gower, London.
Weller, M.P.I. (1986) Does the community care? *Public Health*, **100**, 76–83.
Weller, B., Weller, M. and Coter, R. (1987) *Crisis at Christmas 1986, Lancet*, **i**, 533–54.

Wing, J.K. (1972) Principles of evaluation. In: J.K. Wing and A.M. Hailey (eds), *Evaluating a Community Psychiatric Service*, Oxford University Press.
Wing, J.K. (1983) Schizophrenia. In: F.N. Watts and D. Bennett (eds), *The Theory and Practice of Psychiatric Rehabilitation*, John Wiley, Chichester.
Wing, J.K. and Hailey, A.M. (1972) *Evaluating a Community Psychiatric Service*, Oxford University Press.
Wing, J.K. and Brown, G.W. (1970) *Institutionalism and Schizophrenia*. Cambridge University Press.
Wing, J.K. and Furlong, R. (1986) A haven for the severely disabled within the context of a comprehensive psychiatric community service. *British Journal of Psychiatry*, **149**, 449–57.
Wolfensberger, W. (1972) *The Principle of Normalization in Human Services*. National Institute of Mental Retardation, Toronto.
Wolfensberger, W. (1983) Social role valorization: a proposed new term for the principle of normalization. *Mental Retardation*, **21**, 234–9.
Wolfensberger, W. and Glen, L. (1973) Programme analysis of Service Systems (PASS); a method for the quantative analysis of human services. *Handbook of the National Institute of Mental Retardation*, Toronto.
Wolfensberger, W. and Thomas, S. (1983) Program analysis of Service Systems' Implementations of Normalization Goals (PASSING). *Normalization Criteria and Rating Manual*, 2nd edn, Canadian Institute of Mental Retardation.
Woof, K. and Goldberg, D.P. (1988) Further observations on the practice of community care in Salford: Differences between community psychiatric nurses and mental health social workers. *British Journal of Psychiatry*, **153**, 30–7.

Chapter 10

Family Interventions: Service Implications

Jo Smith

INTRODUCTION

Recent years have witnessed a marked revival of interest in the family of individuals with schizophrenia, particularly in the light of observations that the family environment may be an important predictor of relapse following discharge from hospital. The impressive research on "Expressed Emotion" (Brown, Birley and Wing, 1972; Vaughn and Leff, 1976) revealed that the presence of critical, hostile or emotionally over-involved attitudes, expressed at the time of admission to hospital, is a powerful predictor of subsequent relapse. Awareness that family members were often bearing the brunt of responsibility for community aftercare and that specific characteristics of the family environment may be unhelpful, led to the development of family intervention programmes designed to support the family, prevent relapse and foster social recovery of the individual with schizophrenia. Indeed, seven family intervention studies have been completed in Britain and the USA (see Chapter 4) which have provided convincing evidence for their effectiveness (supplementary to normal clinical practice and active medication) in reducing relapse risk for the individual and in modifying the emotional climate of the family, at least in the short term (see Table 10.1). However, it remains unclear whether these interventions can alter the course of schizophrenia in the long term.

Despite consistent demonstration of the validity of the concept of EE and strong evidence from well-designed intervention studies that relapse can be prevented by manipulating social and environmental factors (Kuipers and Bebbington, 1988), there has been little change in service provision for individuals and their relatives and few developments in terms of the dissemination of necessary skills to clinicians. As with all innovations, one expects a time lag between empirical validation of treatment methods and

Innovations in the Psychological Management of Schizophrenia.
Edited by Max Birchwood and Nicholas Tarrier. © 1992 John Wiley & Sons Ltd

Table 10.1 Family intervention studies*: percentage relapse rates

Study	n	Follow-up 9 or 12 months	24 months
Goldstein and Kopeikin (1981)†			
family intervention	25	0	—
routine treatment	28	16	—
Leff et al. (1982, 1989)			
family intervention	12	8	20
routine treatment	12	50	78
family therapy	12	8	—
relatives groups	6	17	—
Kottgen et al. (1984)			
family intervention	15	33	—
control (high EE)	14	43	—
control (low EE)	20	20	—
Falloon et al. (1985)			
family intervention	18	6	17
individual intervention	18	44	83
Hogarty et al. (1986)			
family intervention	21	19	—
social skill training	20	20	—
combined intervention	20	0	—
control	17	41	—
Tarrier et al. (1988, 1989)			
family intervention	25	12	33
education only	14	43	57
routine treatment	15	53	60

* All subjects in these studies were in receipt of neuroleptic medication.
† The follow-up period for this study was 6 months.

their adoption and implementation by practitioners. The family interventions reported to date have largely been specialised well-resourced projects carried out by highly motivated research teams. They have successfully established and refined methods of intervening with individuals and families. However, the experience gained from these, in terms of intervention possibilities, has yet to influence ordinary clinical practice or to be integrated with the routine management of the illness by psychiatric services. The time is now overdue for family interventions to begin to influence clinical practice (Kuipers and Bebbington, 1985) and is particularly timely in view of the increasing trend towards community-based psychiatric services.

The integration of family interventions into existing clinical practice requires a change in practice and demands careful planning in terms of mental health resources, staff training and evaluation in order to ensure that the overall quality of these interventions is maintained and that they are accessible to those individuals and families who most need it (Smith and Birchwood, 1990). This chapter considers some of the major issues that need to be addressed when attempting to integrate psycho-social interventions within a routine psychiatric service and describes some of the recent attempts to apply family interventions in everyday health service settings.

CONSIDERATIONS IN THE DEVELOPMENT OF FAMILY SERVICES

Problems in engaging families

Attempts to engage new families in intervention does not always meet with success, which is surprising in view of the well-documented burdens that they face (Gibbons et al., 1984). Indeed, data from a number of studies suggest that there are a substantial group of individuals and relatives who are difficult to engage in intervention at the outset and others who are poor and inconsistent compliers. Non-engagement figures from six of the published family intervention studies range from 14% to 29% (see Table 10.2). The Hogarty et al. (1986) intervention is the largest well-controlled study to date and probably gives a more accurate picture of true non-engagement, at least in the United States. However, non-engagement figures for family intervention conducted in a service setting are considerably higher. The figure for our own sample (Smith, 1991) identified 38% of relatives who initially declined the offer of help and a further 16% who subsequently withdrew in the early stages of assessment and intervention, comprising an overall non-engagement rate of 54%. Similarly, McCreadie et al. (1991) reported that a staggering 73% of relatives failed to engage in

Table 10.2 Adherence to family intervention

Study	% Refusing	% Withdrawing	% Non-engagement
Hogarty et al. (1986)	13	11	24
Leff et al. (1982)	18	*	18†
Leff et al. (1989)	4	26	29
Falloon et al. (1985)	7	7	14
Goldstein and Kopeiken (1981)	*	8	8†
Tarrier et al. (1988, and personal communication)	14	†	14†
Smith and Birchwood (1991)	38	16	54
McCreadie et al. (1991)	51	22	73

* Not reported.
† All those withdrawing were included in the analyses.

treatment, comprising 51% of relatives who refused intervention and a further 22% who having initially agreed to intervention subsequently failed to attend the educational seminars or relatives' groups offered. It is worth noting that in both of the latter studies, unlike previous family interventions, intervention was offered to all families independent of EE status (i.e. including low EE families) when patients were not always subject to acute admission.

From a service perspective, it is important that factors contributing to non-engagement are elucidated and attempts are made to try and address the problem and create a family service that is both "user-friendly" and accessible to the widest range of individuals and families that elect to take up the offer of help. There may be several potential reasons for non-engagement. McCreadie et al. (1991) noted four principal reasons for refusing intervention: denial of family needs; stigma and embarrassment; resignation to the situation; and pride preventing admission of the need for help. Smith and Birchwood (1990) identified three further possible reasons: the perception of the offer of help as "treatment" with the implication that the family has in some way failed; denial of illness particularly with first admission patients (who formed 45% of the patient sample); and lack of understanding concerning the rationale and personal relevance of family intervention. Factors contributing to non-engagement clearly need further clarification and validation. However, any service would need to take constructive action to address potential contributory factors and might consider the following measures to try and improve engagement and adherence to intervention:

1. *to adopt a vigorous outreach policy* where the service is pro-active rather than referral-based, offers home-based help and repeats the offer of assistance and support during the course of the illness following initial refusal or treatment drop-out. This might be achieved using a case management type service where the needs of individuals and their carers are regularly reviewed and followed up in the long term (Tarrier and Barrowclough, 1990);
2. *to educate and train "front-line" professionals* to increase their awareness of the needs of families and to improve their skills and confidence in providing information and ongoing support, while also encouraging families to make use of specialist help and advice services as appropriate;
3. *to develop a service which is accessible to the widest range of families* who may choose to use it by, for example, employing interpreters or workers from a similar culture and ethnic origin as appropriate;
4. *to offer a non-judgemental approach* which acknowledges the problems families may face and the constraints within which they are operating and offers help and support to jointly overcome these difficulties;

5. *to work in "partnership" with families* from the outset of contact, ensuring families are informed and actively involved in all aspects of the treatment and care of their relative and working with family members to define their needs and plan how these needs might best be met.

Use of expressed emotion as the major criterion for intervention

It has been suggested and often assumed that high EE families should be the priority focus of a family service (e.g. Leff et al., 1982). This has much to commend it, since high expressed emotion does predict certain kinds of behaviour (critical, over-involved, hostile, rejecting) and is strongly associated with relapse. Furthermore, comparison of the needs of high and low EE families reveals that high EE families are coping with higher levels of disturbed behaviour and often less effectively than their low EE counterparts while individuals from high EE households tend to be more socially impaired (Smith, 1991). However, Vaughn (1986) suggested that an "atypical" group of low EE relatives may exist who do not fit the characteristic EE profile and who are not calm, tolerant, coping individuals. This is supported by Smith, Birchwood and Cochrane (1991) who identified a low EE "high need" group who had high needs on at least one index of family stress, burden or coping. The identification of a low EE "high need" group supports the notion that interventions based on a high EE/high risk, low EE/low risk dichotomy may not be satisfactory. It is clear that low EE may not always offer an optimal living environment or epitomise good coping. Indeed, some low EE families may have needs and burdens similar to those observed with high EE relatives. This information needs to be incorporated into family interventions, particularly if one is to identify "atypical" low EE families that might otherwise be overlooked.

A sizeable minority of relatives spontaneously revert from high to low EE with time (Dulz and Hand, 1986; Hogarty et al., 1986; Tarrier et al., 1988) probably related to changes in behavioural disturbance (Brown, Birley and Wing, 1972). Some low EE relatives also become high EE over time (Tarrier et al., 1988; Smith, Birchwood and Cochrane, 1991). These observations support the view that expressed emotion may be a characteristic of interactions between individual and family variables (Birchwood, Hallett and Preston, 1988). This highlights the need for family services to adopt a dynamic assessment process and to continue interventions over a longer term given that measures of need or risk can change with phases of the disorder or emerge as a consequence of increasing chronicity or with hospital readmission (Brown, Birley and Wing, 1972).

The use of expressed emotion as the sole risk criterion may be particularly inappropriate with a younger, more acute patient group. High EE appears to be an emergent characteristic associated with chronicity (Brown, Birley and Wing, 1972) and the discriminative power of EE with respect to relapse, at least in the early phase of the disorder, is poor (Leff and Brown, 1977; MacMillan et al., 1986). The definition of high EE (at risk) usually depends on the identification of those individuals who have already experienced relapse and readmission. Thus with younger, more acute patients the level of prediction achieved using the measure of EE is likely to be low (Smith, 1991) and to change with time, with increasing numbers of high EE relatives emerging with increasing chronicity. The goal of reducing EE may be less crucial in the early phases of the disorder. Instead, with this particular group, interventions might more profitably focus on improving family coping and social adjustment enabling the individual to be more resistant to stressful events, reducing family tensions and fostering more helpful, tolerant attitudes (associated with low EE and lower relapse risk) independent of whether the family and patient are formally classified as high EE.

High EE may predict relapse and return of symptoms but may not necessarily predict social or family outcome with comparable specificity. It may be that other variables predict other outcomes. For example, level of behavioural disturbance was found to be highly associated with improvements in family burden, tolerance and coping (Smith, 1991). The role of EE in promoting or constraining social functioning is unclear: high EE may not necessarily predict poor social outcome and low EE families may not necessarily possess the skills to promote social reintegration and maintain well-being. Indeed, in our own family intervention study, individuals living in low EE households showed a *deterioration* in interpersonal functioning at nine months follow-up (Smith, 1991). Similarly, some low EE families may actively resort to management strategies characterised by disengagement and distancing (Birchwood and Smith, 1987; Birchwood and Cochrane, 1990) which may promote withdrawal and poor social adjustment (Vaughn, 1986).

In summary, the limitations of high expressed emotion as a measure of risk or need and the identification of a "high need" low EE group does highlight the need, when providing a service to families, to carefully assess the specific assets and needs of *all* families when considering who might profit from intervention and to look beyond simple diagnostic labels or *a priori* indices of risk such as high EE. Specifically, there is a need to consider low EE families when planning family interventions. Low EE relatives who appear benign by one criterion may not be by another (Vaughn, 1986) and in the absence of information, advice and support may have the capacity to become stressed, critical or over-involved with changing circumstances.

Continuity of intervention

A rise in relapse rates was observed at 2 years follow-up in all of the family intervention studies. This suggests that if we are to maintain the benefits of family intervention it may be necessary to provide extended follow-up where individuals and families receive "booster" sessions or even continuous intervention (Wallace and Liberman, 1985; Tarrier and Barrowclough, 1990) perhaps in the context of case management (see Chapter 11). Medication is considered to be most effective in controlling relapse if continued over long periods of time. It is, therefore, not unreasonable to consider that the impact of family intervention, in combination with drug treatment, may similarly be optimal if continued long term for some individuals and their carers. The level of clinical and social functioning of the individual at a particular point in time reflects a snapshot of the family environment, social network, vulnerability and personal coping which is prone to change, particularly in young people. There are also likely to be clinical interactions among these various factors which will determine the clinical and social status of the individual at a given point in time. The commitment to *long-term* intervention with families may ensure that the benefits are maintained and allow flexibility in responding to the changing needs of individuals and families over time. This is an issue that needs to be considered when contemplating routine services to families particularly in terms of staff training and resource allocation. A service structure needs to be devised to ensure this continuity and which does not depend on individuals or research teams. Some such possibilities are considered in the concluding section.

Service delivery issues

It has been suggested that family interventions are no more time consuming that ordinary treatment and may actually result in financial savings (Cardin, McGill and Falloon, 1986; Tarrier, 1991). However, they do tend to make heavy demands on resources in terms of personnel and time which must be offset against savings that accrue from fewer readmissions (Tarrier, 1991). If family interventions are to be effectively implemented in clinical practice, to ensure that help of a requisite quality reaches those who require it, there is a need for both an investment of resources and an adequate system of staff training and supervision. This demands sufficient numbers of appropriately trained staff to deliver the service and the availability of "tutors" with experience in family interventions who are able to disseminate skills to staff through a structured programme of training and to provide ongoing support and supervision. The provision of necessary back-up resource materials such as booklets, videos and training manuals will also be important. The dissemination of skills raises the issue of quality control. It is vital that the approaches do not become devalued or diluted in the process of training or delivery. Continued monitoring and evaluation of all aspects of the service is therefore vital to identify the crucial components of family intervention, to ensure that intervention objectives continue to be fulfilled and to assist in maintaining the long-term efficacy, quality and continuity of family intervention within a routine psychiatric service.

Importance of needs-led, goal-defined interventions

Examination of the different intervention packages reveals a variety of descriptive labels used, for example: "psycho-education" (e.g. Hogarty et al., 1986); "family therapy" (e.g. Goldstein and Kopeikin, 1981; Leff et al., 1989); "relatives' groups" (e.g. Leff et al., 1982, 1989); "communication skills and problem-solving" (e.g. Falloon, et al., 1985); "behavioural treatment" (e.g. Tarrier et al., 1988, 1989); and "social skills training" (e.g. Wallace and Lieberman, 1985; Hogarty et al., 1986). The majority of intervention studies, with the exception of the Falloon and Tarrier studies, have largely been intuitive or exploratory in nature. They lack a clear rationale to guide their design and appropriate measures of change, apart from reductions in EE, as indicators of success. This is important if one is to gauge whether the intervention is proceeding correctly and also makes the procedures difficult to replicate. Intervention content should be *needs-oriented* in a service setting, logically relating to the specific needs of individuals and their families in adjusting to the emergence of schizophrenia. In this way, interventions can be individualised and remain flexible to respond to the broad spectrum of potential needs, particularly important if interventions are not EE focused. A clearly articulated model, with goal oriented steps, facilitates dissemination to other professionals and assists the service provider in monitoring how the intervention is proceeding.

Despite variations in content and rationale, family interventions include several common components which might be embraced within a service framework. These include: patient and family education, symptom monitoring to prevent relapse and more intensive family intervention (comprising structured support, communication skills training and the development of coping and problem-solving skills). The availability of a range of intervention opportunities allows the clinician to adjust interventions in response to specific needs and attributes of individuals and families. This enables clinicians to incrementally offer additional interventions conditional upon the cumulative impact and effectiveness of previous interventions, allowing a "minimum/maximum" approach to intervention. This helps to make intervention more efficient by only offering as much as is desired or needed. Some families may only need a few education sessions, while others, whose coping skills are poor, may need extended education and more systematic intensive family intervention and problem-solving training. Relapse monitoring could be initiated to protect those individuals who are particularly vulnerable to stress-induced relapse and might also be used to enable clinicians to titrate and refine a combination of psycho-social intervention and maintenance medication according to individual need. The use of a variety of outcome measures allows one to evaluate in more detail the specific value of each intervention element with different individual and family needs.

Integration with community resources and rehabilitation policy

Family intervention is not an alternative model of care, but a significant advance which needs to be integrated with existing community provision and coordinated with other care. In order to ensure coordination and continuity of care, close liaison needs to be maintained with key professionals involved in the care of the individual to ensure that the goals of family intervention are in line with overall treatment and rehabilitation plans for a given individual. Conversely, it is equally important that families are viewed as an important and valuable resource in the management of schizophrenia and that both the individual and the family are encouraged to be actively involved in treatment and after-care plans.

Family intervention is not a panacea for the community management of schizophrenia especially since the long-term outcome of family intervention remains uncertain. It is therefore important that families are given knowledge of and access to a comprehensive system of community and specialist support services such as leisure and day-care opportunities, sheltered employment schemes, self-help support groups and financial assistance. Engagement in other services may be a crucial mediating factor in the effectiveness of family intervention. This is particularly important if "burn-out" and other adverse consequences for the family are to be avoided which may arise when families are left with the burden of care without the supporting context of a rational comprehensive system of case management, rehabilitation and community services.

IMPLICATIONS FOR SERVICE PROVISION

In view of the issues described earlier, it is suggested that an effective service should aim to meet the following requirements:

1. *Actively engage families*, adopting a vigorous outreach policy which is pro-active rather than referral based; includes home-based help and where offers of assistance are repeated following initial refusal or non-compliance.
2. *Ensure that family needs are understood and responded to sympathetically* by front-line professionals within a framework which encourages partnership in solving "problems for families" rather than the treatment of "problem families".
3. *Be "needs"- rather than "EE"-led* where interventions are based on a clear assessment of need and delivered in a structured logical framework of goal-oriented steps, with improvements in family coping and adjustment and client social adjustment as the primary goals of intervention.
4. *Offered in the context of a service structure providing long-term support* where both the intensity and content of intervention are adjusted according to individual need.
5. *Ensure ongoing training and support of "front line" professionals* through an intensive programme of staff training and provision of appropriate resource materials such as booklets, videos and training manuals.
6. *Maintain service efficiency and quality* by establishing a system of ongoing supervision for trained staff and routinely monitoring and auditing all aspects of the service in relation to planned outcomes.
7. *Ensure that family interventions are integrated into existing rehabilitation policy and overall community service provision* to facilitate coordination and continuity of care in the context of a long-term intervention plan.

SERVICE MODELS IN PRACTICE

The application of family intervention methods to clinical practice is still severely limited. However, in this section, some service innovations which attempt to integrate family intervention into mainstream psychiatric treatment are briefly described to show how these considerations can inform routine clinical practice and service provision. In recent years, seven different initiatives across the United Kingdom have been reported in the literature. These are briefly described with particular attention to the service requirements outlined earlier. The majority are still in the process of being evaluated and are presented here as potential models of service provision, although acknowledging the lack of evaluative data to support their efficacy.

One of the best models of cognitive behavioural family intervention implemented at a primary care level is provided by Falloon and his colleagues (1990) who describe the "Buckingham Project". This is a comprehensive mental health service for the management of mental illness (including schizophrenia) where close collaboration between primary and secondary care services enables severe mental disorder to be recognised and treated at an early stage of development and distressing acute symptoms to be ameliorated or even prevented. A multi-disciplinary team of highly trained mental health specialists work alongside existing primary care teams to support families and primary care workers. Training in current intervention strategies is provided weekly via half-day workshops and group supervision of cases is ongoing to ensure that competent skills are developed and maintained. Individual needs including those of care-givers are assessed and reviewed every 3 months. Key elements of intervention include long-term case management, early signs detection and intervention, extensive education of patients and care-givers, behavioural family management and home-based intensive treatment (including daily activity schedules, social and inter-personal skills training, stress management and problem-solving training). The programme uses an assertive outreach and ensures active involvement of individuals and families in treatment plans and intervention. Treatment is provided within the context of existing community resources and where unavailable, efforts are made to develop resources through community agencies. A comprehensive 5-year evaluation is underway but incomplete. Initial reports (Falloon et al., 1989) suggest that it may aid clinical and social recovery and reduce family burden and personal costs to the family and GPs. An analysis of the monetary costs suggests that it is not cheaper than hospital care but is highly competitive and may have considerably greater therapeutic impact.

Tarrier and his colleagues (Tarrier et al., 1988, 1989) similarly attempted to implement and integrate behavioural family intervention as a clinical service in Salford, Manchester, UK. They aimed to evaluate a number of interventions in terms of their efficacy in reducing relapse rates as well as assessing the viability of delivering family intervention as part of a hospital-based mental health service. The intervention incorporated an education programme, prophylactic medication and a stress management component intended to reduce environmental stress and tension within the home environment and meet individual patient needs. Family intervention was incorporated within a broader community-based comprehensive service for the management of schizophrenia and involved close partnership between clinicians and families. One shortcoming of the project is that they incorporated measures of EE as the primary indicator of service need, which may be unnecessary or even undesirable in a clinical setting. They did, however, use multiple outcome measures. They reported a reduction in relapse rates, associated with changes in EE from high to low, over a 9-month post-discharge period and improvements in social functioning (Tarrier et al., 1988). Two-year follow-up indicated that benefits were maintained although a rise in relapse rates was observed after two years where intervention was not continued (Tarrier et al., 1989). They also calculated direct costs and found that family intervention resulted in a 26% financial saving compared to routine treatment (Tarrier, 1991).

A similar service in West Birmingham, UK (Smith and Birchwood, 1990) involved the establishment of the Family Centre for Advice, Resources and Education with a remit to develop and evaluate interventions for individuals with schizophrenia and their families within the context of a routine urban psychiatric service. The Centre was set up as an independent service but aimed to be fully integrated with existing treatment services offered to individuals with schizophrenia, in terms of rehabilitation policy, finance, professional resources and the development of community-oriented service provision.

The service did not use high EE or acute admission as an entry point or index of need. The Centre routinely initiated contact with individuals and their families at multiple entry points to the wider psychiatric service. Service availability was not determined by referral or specific requests for help but was offered routinely to all families as one component of the psychiatric service. Once an offer of help had been accepted, the specific needs of the individual and his family were assessed. The service was entirely needs-based and attempted to meet a range of needs, within a framework of partnership, through the variety of services which were offered. These included information about schizophrenia for individuals and families (Smith and Birchwood, 1987; Birchwood, Smith and Cochrane, 1991), help in coping and living with schizophrenia (Smith, 1991), training individuals and families to recognise early warning signs of relapse (Birchwood et al., 1989) and teaching self-management of persisting symptoms (Birchwood, 1986). Close liaison was maintained with key professionals involved with a particular individual, through joint working and regular case reviews, to ensure coordination and continuity of care and ensure that the goals of family intervention were consistent with overall treatment and rehabilitation goals for a given individual. The centre maintained close contact with community statutory and voluntary agencies (for example, day-care and sheltered employment facilities) relevant to the particular needs of individuals and their families. The Centre provided ongoing training for front-line professional staff through in-service workshops designed to highlight the needs of families and to train them to respond to the information and emotional needs of families, as well as reducing the practical burdens of schizophrenia. Trained tutors were identified as supervisors to whom staff could relate directly for information, support and supervision while continued maintenance of the Family Centre as a central resource ensured that the dissemination of skills did not dilute the intervention or prejudice its quality. Back-up information materials were available in the form of a teaching pack with a training manual, video and information booklets (Smith and Birchwood, 1987; Birchwood, Smith and Cochrane, 1991). All aspects of the service were closely monitored and evaluated to ensure that intervention objectives were being fulfilled and that the quality of service provision was maintained. Preliminary data support the value of the service in improving understanding about schizophrenia and reducing family burden and stress although having limited impact in terms of reducing relapse rates and improving social functioning.

More recently, the West Birmingham Service has been embraced within the range of services offered by the "Archer Centre", to people with long-term mental illness, within a case management model. The multi-disciplinary team of specialist workers trained in family intervention methods provide specialist support to staff in community mental health teams, working with families and formal carers such as hostel staff. All workers have received specialist training in family intervention methods and are closely supervised. Services offered include: education, intensive family intervention and support, relapse monitoring and skills based work with individuals, particularly practically based ideas such as computer skills training and other employment opportunities linked to training agencies and industry.

Two further schemes operate in South Glamorgan and Southampton. The Schizophrenia Therapeutic Education Project (STEP) was established in South Glamorgan and comprises a district-wide multi-disciplinary team of trained workers consisting of psychiatrists, psychologists, nurses and CPNs who assess family referrals and work on a long-term basis for at least 2 years with individual family referrals (Abbati, Hailwood and Tanaglow, 1987). In Southampton, a multi-disciplinary group of 14 therapists comprising CPNs, psychiatric nurses, social workers, an occupational therapist, a psychologist and a psychiatrist have been specifically trained in behavioural family intervention (based on Falloon's model) to provide support to families (Whitfield, Taylor and Virgo, 1988). However, the schemes have not produced any evaluative data, to date, to support their efficacy.

Brooker (1990) describes a research project currently underway in the department of nursing at the University of Manchester evaluating the outcome of teaching psychiatric nurses to deliver psycho-social intervention to families caring for a relative with schizophrenia at home. A pilot training programme, consisting of a 30-day taught course run over a 6-month period, using tutors from the Salford family intervention service, has been completed. The aim of the course is to teach nurses to acquire a theoretical appreciation of intervention techniques, to become competent in the assessment of families, develop skills in behavioural family stress management techniques, appreciate the importance of information about the nature of the illness for individuals and their families and design appropriate education programmes, and social, occupational, vocational programmes for clients based on identified assets and needs. Trainees are taught to undertake a comprehensive assessment of family circumstances and although not specifically trained to rate EE, use a related interview measure. Each trainee works with three families. All problem-solving and intervention with families is closely monitored by the teaching team in weekly study days, using tape recorded interviews, assessment measures and self-report to facilitate supervision. Although initial reports seem promising, no firm evaluation data is yet available concerning the efficacy of this kind of family intervention training programme.

Finally, McCreadie et al. (1991) report an intervention package comprising educational seminars, relatives groups and family meetings. The intervention was offered, over a minimum of eight sessions, to an unselected group of relatives and patients living in the community by professionals working in Nithsdale, South West Scotland. They reported high levels of non-engagment and non-compliance with treatment and found no change in relapse rates or expressed emotion after intervention at 18 months follow-up. However, relatives who took part reported feeling more knowledgeable, formed a loose support network among themselves and subsequently joined local support organisations to ensure ongoing support. The authors acknowledged their lack of expertise in family intervention and admit that the interventions offered may not have been adequate or long enough. The rationale for intervention was largely intuitive, based on the earlier model provided by Leff and colleagues, in bringing high and low EE relatives together and encouraging low EE relatives to share successful management solutions. This highlights and supports the need for specialised training for professionals and a clear model or rationale for intervention, if family interventions are to be successfully applied in clinical settings.

CONCLUDING COMMENTS

The results of the family intervention studies over the past 10 years have raised expectations among both psychiatric professionals and families. Translating these advances into clinical practice represents a major challenge for psychiatric services and requires careful planning, training and integration if these achievements and the quality of these interventions are to be maintained and made available to those most in need. The successful development of effective family services, whether hospital- or community-based, needs to acknowledge and be informed by the issues raised in this chapter in order to translate theory effectively into practice. The few service models that do exist offer strong support for the feasibility and viability of establishing family intervention and disseminating skills to professionals within the context of a comprehensive psychiatric service. However, hard evaluation data is now needed to demonstrate their cost efficacy and assess whether the benefits reported by the major research studies can be reproduced when operating within the constraints of a clinical service context.

REFERENCES

Abbatti, J., Hailwood, R., Tanaglow, A. (1987) Family treatment for schizophrenia. *British Journal of Clinical Psychology*, **26**, 157–8.

Birchwood, M. (1986) The control of auditory hallucinations through the occlusion of monaural auditory input. *British Journal of Psychiatry*, **149**, 104–7.

Birchwood, M. and Cochrane, R. (1990) Families coping with schizophrenia: coping styles, their origins and correlates. *Psychological Medicine*, **20**, 857–65.

Birchwood, M., Hallett, S. and Preston, M. (1988) *Schizophrenia: an Integrated Approach to Research and Treatment*, Longman, London.

Birchwood, M. and Smith, J. (1987) Schizophrenia and the family. In: J. Orford (ed.), *Coping with Disorder in the Family*, Croom Helm, London.

Birchwood, M., Smith, J. and Cochrane, R. (1992) Specific and non-specific effects of educational intervention for families living with schizophrenia: a comparison of three methods. *British Journal of Psychiatry* (in press).

Birchwood, M., Smith, J., MacMillan, F., Hogg, B., Prasad, R., Harvey, C. and Bering S. (1989) Predicting relapse in schizophrenia: the development and implementation of an early signs monitoring system using patients and families as observers, a preliminary investigation. *Psychological Medicine*, **19**, 649–56.

Brooker, C. (1990) The application of the concept of expressed emotion to the role of the community psychiatric nurse: a research study. *International Journal of Nursing Studies*, **27**(3), 277–85.

Brown, G., Birley, J. and Wing, J. (1972) The influence of family life on the course of schizophrenic disorders: a replication. *British Journal of Psychiatry*, **121**, 241–58.

Cardin, V., McGill, C. and Falloon, I. (1986) An economic analysis: costs, benefits and effectiveness. In: I. Falloon (ed.), *Family Management of Schizophrenia*, Johns Hopkins University Press, Baltimore.

Dulz, B. and Hand, I. (1986) Short term relapse in young schizophrenics: can it be predicted and affected by family, patient and treatment?: An experimental study. In: M. Goldstein, I. Hand and K. Hahlweg (eds), *Treatment of Schizophrenia: Family Assessment and Intervention*, Springer-Verlag, Berlin.

Falloon, I., Boyd, J., McGill, C., Williamson, M., Razani, J., Moss, H., Gilderman, A. and Simson, G. (1985) Family management in the prevention of morbidity of schizophrenia: clinical outcome of a two-year longitudinal study. *Archives of General Psychiatry*, **42**, 887–96.

Falloon, I., Krekorian, H., Shanahan, W. and Laporta, M. (1989) Evaluating the benefits and costs of long-term community care. *Bulletin Royal College of Psychiatrists*, **12**, 675–6.

Falloon, I., Krekorian, H., Shanahan, W., Laporta, M. and McLees, S. (1990) The Buckingham Project: a comprehensive mental health service based upon behavioural psychotherapy. *Behavioural Change*, **7**(2), 51–7.

Gibbons, J., Horn, S., Powell, J. and Gibbons, J. (1984) Schizophrenic patients and their families: a survey in a psychiatric service based on a DGH unit. *British Journal of Psychiatry*, **144**, 70–7.

Goldstein, M. and Kopeikin, H. (1981) Short and long term effects of combining drug and family therapy. In: M. Goldstein (ed.), *New Developments in Interventions with Families of Schizophrenics*, Jossey-Bass, San Francisco.

Hogarty, G., Anderson, C., Reiss, D., Kornblith, S., Greenwald, D., Jarvna, C. and Madonia, M. (1986) Family psychoeducation, social skills training and maintenance chemotherapy in the aftercare treatment of schizophrenia. *Archives of General Psychiatry*, **43**, 633–42.

Kottgen, C., Sonnichsen, I., Mollenhauer, K. and Jurth, R. (1984) Group therapy with families of schizophrenic patients: results of the Hamburg Camberwell family interview study III. *Journal of Family Psychiatry*, **5**, 84–94.

Kuipers, L. and Bebbington, P. (1985) Relatives as a resource in the management of functional illness. *British Journal of Psychiatry*, **141**, 121–34.

Kuipers, L. and Bebbington, P. (1988) Expressed emotion research in schizophrenia: theoretical and clinical implications. *Psychological Medicine*, **18**, 893–909.

Leff, J. and Brown, G. (1977) Family and social factors in the course of schizophrenia (letter). *British Journal of Psychiatry*, **130**, 417–20.

Leff, J., Kuipers, L., Berkowitz, R., Eberlein-Fries, R. and Sturgeon, D. (1982) A controlled trial of social intervention in the families of schizophrenic patients. *British Journal of Psychiatry*, **141**, 121–34.

Leff, J., Berkowitz, R., Shavit, N., Strachan, A., Glass, I. and Vaughan, C. (1989) A trial of family therapy versus a relatives group for schizophrenia. *British Journal of Psychiatry*, **154**, 58–66.

McCreadie, R., Phillips, K., Harvey, J., Waldron, G., Stewart, M. and Baird, D. (1991) The Nithsdale Schizophrenia Surveys. VIII: Do relatives want family intervention—and does it help? *British Journal of Psychiatry*, **158**, 110–13.

MacMillan, F., Gold, A., Crow, I., Johnson, A. and Johnstone, E. (1986) Expressed emotion and relapse. *British Journal of Psychiatry*, **148**, 133–43.

Smith, J. (1991) Relatives and patients as partners in the management of schizophrenia: an evaluation of psychoeducational interventions in a dedicated service setting. Unpublished PhD thesis, University of Birmingham.

Smith, J. and Birchwood, M. (1987) Specific and non-specific effects of an educational intervention with families living with a schizophrenic relative. *British Journal of Psychiatry*, **150**, 645–52.

Smith, J. and Birchwood, M. (1990) Relatives and patients as partners in the management of schizophrenia: the development of a service model. *British Journal of Psychiatry*, **156**, 654–60.

Smith, J., Birchwood, M. and Cochrane, R. (1992) The need for care of high and low expressed emotion families. *Social Psychiatry and Psychiatric Epidemiology* (submitted).

Tarrier, N., Barrowclough, C., Vaughn, C., Bamrah, J., Porceddu, K., Watts, S. and Freeman, H. (1988) The community management of schizophrenia: a con-

trolled trial of behavioural intervention with families to reduce relapse. *British Journal of Psychiatry*, **153**, 532–42.
Tarrier, N. and Barrowclough, C. (1990) Mental health services and new research in England: implications for the community management of schizophrenia. In: A. Kales, C. Stefanis and J. Talbot (eds), *Recent Advances in Schizophrenia*, Springer-Verlag, New York.
Tarrier, N. (1991) Behavioural psychotherapy and schizophrenia: the past, the present and the future. *Behavioural Psychotherapy*, **19**, 121–30.
Tarrier, N., Barrowclough, C., Vaughn, C., Bamrah, J., Porceddu, K., Watts, S. and Freeman, H. (1989) Community management of schizophrenia: a two year follow-up of a behavioural intervention with families. *British Journal of Psychiatry*, **154**, 625–8.
Vaughn, C. (1986) Patterns of emotional response in the families of schizophrenic patients. In: M. Goldstein, I. Hand and K. Hahlweg (eds), *Treatment of Schizophrenia: Family Assessment and Intervention*, Springer-Verlag, Berlin.
Vaughn, C. and Leff, J. (1976) The measurement of expressed emotion in the families of psychiatric patients. *British Journal of Social and Clinical Psychology*, **15**, 157–65.
Wallace, C. and Liberman, R. (1985) Social skills training for patients with schizophrenia: a controlled clinical trial. *Psychiatry Research*, **15**, 239–47.
Whitfield, W., Taylor, C. and Virgo, W. (1988) Family care in schizophrenia. *Journal of Social Health*, **1**, 4–5.

Chapter 11

The Balance of Care

MATTHIJS MUIJEN

INTRODUCTION

Many changes have taken place in the structure and process of psychiatric care all over the world. The principles of psychiatric care shifted from the nineteenth-century belief that mentally ill patients require permanent protection in asylums to the conviction that users of mental-health services can function reasonably well in the community, provided support is available. The role of mental hospitals is changing from a place offering long-term care to a centre for brief, intensive treatment, being one component in a range of facilities such as day-hospitals, hostels and home-care. As a result the State Hospital population in the US declined from 559 000 in 1955 to 138 000 in 1980 (Brown, 1985) and in the UK from 148 100 in 1954 to 64 800 in 1985 (Audit Commission, 1986).

The move towards community-care began in the 1950s, coinciding with the emergence of antipsychotic medication. Hopes of greatly dwindling numbers of psychiatric patients requiring long-term care were high, as expressed by Enoch Powell, the then minister of health in 1961. Psychiatric treatment was almost exclusively provided in hospitals, and the increasing number of admissions combined with long stays meant that numbers of in-patients continued to rise. Treatments were often characterised by institutional features (Goffmann, 1961): all aspects of patients lives are conducted in the same place under the same authority; patients receive the same treatment often together; days are structured with explicit rules; and activities are designed from an institutional perspective.

The choice for the government was either a massive and very costly expansion of hospital facilities, or a transfer of care from the institutions to alternative settings. Projects were started to evaluate the feasibility of such alternatives, initially treating neurotic patients as out-patients (Carse, Panton and Watts, 1958). When this proved successful, hospital gradually

Innovations in the Psychological Management of Schizophrenia.
Edited by Max Birchwood and Nicholas Tarrier. © 1992 John Wiley & Sons Ltd

became the place of treatment for the most severely disturbed patients only, with a range of other facilities available in the community.

A second factor leading to changes in care was the lack of efficacy experienced with traditional forms of treatment, in spite of the great hopes raised by the introduction of antipsychotic medication. Studies showed that hospital treatment did not lead to better adjustment in the community after discharge (Erickson, 1975), and that about 50% of discharged patients were readmitted within a year (Anthony et al., 1972). Clinicians began to experiment with increasingly radical forms of care for the severely mentally ill, starting with short admissions, eventually leading to home-care aiming to replace hospital altogether (Braun et al., 1981; Kiesler, 1982).

After two decades opinions on community-care are as strong and divided as ever. Although it is recognised that groups of patients have benefited from less restrictive forms of care, critics have accused governments and mental-health services in many countries of patchy developments and neglect of the most vulnerable groups. These are the deinstitutionalised patients, discharged after having lived in hospital for years or decades, and the young mentally ill, often from deprived backgrounds, who in the past would have been admitted to hospital but are now at risk of neglect, since they rarely fit in with standard services (Bassuk and Gerson, 1978; Pepper, Kirschner and Rylewics, 1981; Jones and Poletti, 1985; Weller, 1989).

The UK, as most other Western countries has moved towards an implementation of community-care policies, although the ideology, process and pace differed. Many similarities can be found between the UK and the US, although changes in the US have often been more radical and earlier than those in the UK. Developments in these two countries are briefly reviewed below.

Developments in the UK

The major development after the Second World War was the foundation of the National Health Service, based on the principle of equity; good treatment for all, free at the point of entry. The first day-hospital opened in the same year (Bierer, 1951). With the introduction of the 1959 Mental Health Act community-care was endorsed by giving patients the right to choose their place of treatment, provided this would not put anyone at risk. Since then changes have been slow, but steady. In 1956 a successful experiment started which provided an out-patient service and domiciliary visits to some patients instead of admitting all requiring treatment to hospital (Carse, Panton and Watt, 1958). About 30 years later services are running which attempt to treat everybody at home, only using in-patient facilities as a last resort (Falloon and Hole, 1990; Dean and Gadd, 1989). Meanwhile, the government pursued a facilitating role, hoping that districts would develop services most suited to the needs of their population. As early as 1962 the Hospital Plan for England and Wales (Ministry of Health, 1962) proposed small scale psychiatric units; "as the majority of patients in such a unit will not require nursing in bed, their treatment and rehabilitation proceed more favourably if they can go in and out of hospital during the day and so participate in the various activities of the general community". However, no guidelines were given until 1975, when "Better Services for the Mentally Ill" (DHSS, 1975) provided target numbers for hospital and day-care places, 50 and 65 respectively for the acute mentally ill, and 20 hostel or long-stay accommodation and 60 day-places for the long-term mentally ill per 100 000 population. A shift away from mental hospitals was envisaged, with care for the acute mentally ill being provided in district general hospital units, and the long-term mentally ill receiving asylum and rehabilitation in small-scale hostels and day-centres in the community, funded by local authorities.

Ten years later the Audit Commission (1986) reported that progress had been unbalanced. The number of available hospital beds had been reduced by more than 25 000, whereas only another 3500 residential places and 9000 day-care places had been provided. The commission had also noticed a "perverse incentive" against community-care. Patients cared for in residential facilities were fully funded by state benefits, but those living at home, requiring community-care, were dependent on the scarce resources of the local authority. It was calculated that local authority expenditure had increased by only £20 million to £52 million, while an increase of £240 million was required to provide adequate services for the 17 000 patients discharged from mental hospitals. The NHS budget during this period had increased by £60 million to £900 million.

These national figures hide local variations. In Scotland the range of day-care places for the long-term mentally ill was found to vary from 0 to 0.4 per 1000 (McCready, Robinson and Wilson, 1984), whereas Camberwell in London provided 1.1 places per 1000 of the population. Even more worrying is the lack of correlation between hospital and community services (Hirsch, 1988). Rather than areas with good community services possessing few hospital beds and the other way around, those areas with most community facilities also had most hospital beds, suggesting poor coordination of planning and an inequality of resource distribution, due to local decisions on the priorities in health spending.

The lack of service integration and clarity about the responsibilities of health authorities and local services led to the White Paper *Caring for People* (DHSS, 1989), following some of the recommendations from Sir Roy Griffiths in "Community Care: An agenda for action" (Griffiths, 1988). The White Paper gives local authorities the lead role in community care, without specifying the financial aspects. The inherent risk is that the local authorities will be reluctant to commit themselves to policies they do not want and can ill afford.

Developments in the US

The National Mental Health Act of 1946 created NIMH, which was to develop new mental health programmes. This led to the Community Mental Health Centers Act, promoted by president John F. Kennedy as the "bold new approach" in his State of the Nation address in 1963. The CMHCs had to include five elements of care to qualify for federal funding: in-patient, out-patient, day-care and emergency services, consultation and education (Brown, 1985).

A parallel development was the reduction in State mental hospital residents, which accelerated during the 1960s. This was enhanced by new federal financial initiatives in 1965, Medicaid and Medicare, reimbursing cost of residence in the community, while individual states had to pay for hospital expenditure (Scherl and Macht, 1979). The intention was to stimulate the transfer of care to the "least restrictive environment", with continuing treatment provided by the CMCHs. This failed for several reasons. Firstly, state hospitals and CMCHs were funded from different sources, and were not accountable to each other. Consequently coordination of care was poor. Secondly, the CMCHs were unable to cope with the number of patients, and thirdly, the CMCHs did not consider the long-term mentally ill as their priority group. This was not only because of the glamour of prevention and psychotherapy (Stern and Minkoff, 1979), but also because of financial incentives. Federal grants were time-limited and states did not provide the extra funding required. Insurance schemes, including Medicaid and Medicare, only allowed very low ceilings for out-patient care. In contrast, private patients receiving medically approved treatments were fully reimbursed (Brown, 1985).

The failure of the CMCH movement to address adequately the needs of the mentally ill led to the development of the Community Support Program in 1977. Targeted were the non-institutionalised long-term mentally ill, estimated to number between 800 000 and 1.5 million people (Goldman, 1981). Federal money was transferred to innovative state mental health agencies to encourage statewide coordination of programmes (Tessler and Goldman, 1982). Ten functions were specified (Turner and TenHoor, 1978): identification of target population and outreach, crisis intervention, psychosocial rehabilitation, medical and mental health care, assistance with benefits, back-up support and involvement of relatives and other supporters, protection of client rights, continuity of care and case management.

Although many exciting local programmes have developed, it is unclear yet whether these can make a national impact.

Developing a balanced system of care

The problems of the UK and US are not dissimilar to those experienced elsewhere. The main issue seems to be how to translate an ideology in high quality service, offering a comprehensive range of interventions, accessible to everybody, while prioritising the severely mentally ill. In Italy, where the mental health service was changed radically by law in 1978, results were uneven, leading to good services in the well endowed north, but to neglect in the south (Jones and Poletti, 1985). Little systematic evaluation of the impact of changes in health-care on the quality of life of patients and the general population has taken place, and some ideas about the efficacy of new services may well be based on speculations.

Several model programmes suggest that day-care and home-care can minimise the need for hospital-care, with possibly some gains for patients. The evidence for this will be reviewed.

DAY-CARE

Day-care is a term used for all services providing interventions in a structured setting for less than 24 hours. This vague and all encompassing definition covers a wide range of services for many types of psychiatric patients. A global distinction can be made (Rosie, 1987) between day-hospitals, day-treatment programmes and day-centres. Day-hospitals, funded in the UK by the health services, are intended to provide active time-limited treatment of the seriously mentally ill, offering an alternative or complementary service to hospitals. Day-treatment programmes are mostly considered to be part of day-hospitals, but can be identified as offering time-limited interventions to specific groups of patients. These can include such wide ranging therapies as detoxification programmes, assertivity training or family groups, depending on the interests and commitments of the service. Day-centres, funded by social services, aim to maintain the chronically mentally ill, if necessary providing support for life.

In practice many similarities exist between highly staffed, expensive day-hospitals and the cheaper day-centres with their more basic facilities. Both tend to care for the long-term mentally ill, about 70% of whom suffer from schizophrenia. Patients attend between a day a month and 5 days a week. A national survey in the UK (Edwards and Carter, 1980) reported that turnover is higher in day-hospitals; more than half the patients at day-centres but less than one-third of day-hospital patients continued to attend for more than 2 years.

The characteristics of clients referred to, or accepted for day-care seem to depend largely on the setting of the centre (Gath, Hassal and Cross, 1973). Day-hospitals connected to large mental hospitals treat older and more chronic patients, while day-hospitals at district general hospitals care for younger patients with neurotic conditions. It is unclear whether this represents differences in patient populations between the two types of hospitals, or whether differences in staff attitudes lead to the selection of these groups.

A concern about day-care is the high drop-out rate. This can be as much as 50% after the first visit (Baekland and Lundwell, 1975), and can be due to service or patient characteristics. If day-care does not offer the interventions or support patients expect they are unlikely to return. Patient characteristics which predict drop-out from day-care are depression, low self-esteem, a diagnosis of personality disorder, living in a hostel and poor employment history. Age, sex, psychosis and chronicity of illness are not related (Bender and Pilling, 1985). The implications of patients withdrawing from treatment can be serious, since follow-up and outreach are not always included in the programmes.

Efficacy of day-care

The variety of care offered under the heading "day-care" means that a general evaluation is not possible. It has to be considered which patient groups are targeted with what objective. Three groups of studies are distinguished here: day-hospital-care as an alternative to in-patient treatment; day-hospital-care as an alternative to out-patient care and the efficacy of day-care in the maintenance of the long-term mentally ill in the community.

Day-care as an alternative to hospital-care

The first studies evaluating the use of day-hospitals were conducted as early as the late 1950s, coinciding with the emergence of psychotropic drugs (Smith and Cross, 1957; Craft, 1958). Patients suffering from neurotic conditions who were not considered to be a risk to themselves or others were allocated to day-care. A matched in-patient group was selected as a control. Little difference in outcome was found between the two groups after 12 months follow-up, although the day-care group had a slightly better social adjustment. Michaux et al., (1973), comparing patients with a serious mental illness suitable for day-care with a matched hospitalised control group from a neighbouring area without day-care facilities, found more psychopathology but better social functioning in the day-care group after 2 months, and after a year functioning continued to be superior. The matching in these studies may have biased the groups, however; for example, a larger number of the in-patient group came from a low social class (Michaux et al., 1973).

Studies which have randomised patients to either day or standard hospital-care report that day-care patients have longer community stays (Wilder, Lewin and Zwerling, 1966) and fewer readmissions (Herz et al., 1971). Day-patients showed less psychopathology and functioned better after 4 weeks follow-up, although after a year only a small advantage in social functioning could be detected (Herz et al., 1971).

These studies indicate that day-care is a valid alternative to hospital-care, but not for all patients. It was found that about 40% of all seriously mentally ill patients admitted to an in-patient unit could be cared for in a day-hospital setting without further need of in-patient care (Wilder, Levin and Zwerling, 1966; Herz et al., 1971; Creed et al., 1990). Half of these patients were diagnosed as suffering from schizophrenia. In the UK the emphasis has been on the potential of day-care in the treatment of neurotic disorders, where about 50% of emergency admissions could be transferred to day-care (Dick et al., 1985b).

Both patients (Dick et al., 1985a) and their relatives (Michaux et al., 1973) preferred day-care, rather than hospital-care. This is likely to lead to higher compliance, and may be a factor in achieving good treatment results. Furthermore, cost effectiveness studies indicate that day-treatment is considerably cheaper than hospital-care (Fink et al., 1978; Dick et al., 1985a).

Such results argue in favour of an expanded role for day-treatment in the care of many seriously mentally ill patients, although any interpretation has to be cautious. For many patients day-care is not suitable due to behavioural, physical or social problems and not all patients benefit equally from day-care. Patients suffering from schizophrenia may gain from an initial period in hospital followed by day-care, while the immediate advantages of day-care for affective and neurotic disorders is strong (Wilder, Levin and Zwerling, 1966; Michaux et al., 1973; Dick et al., 1985a). This suggests that day-care and hospital-care should be considered as complementary.

Day-care as an alternative to out-patient care

Day-hospitals can provide more intensive treatment than an out-patient clinic, and if this leads to a faster and more persistent improvement in symptoms and functioning, may balance the inherently higher costs of day-care. In a study which randomised 30 schizophrenic patients to day-hospital or out-patient treatment following admission (Weldon et al., 1979), more day-care patients were in employment after 3 months of follow-up. No differences in symptomatology or social functioning were found. Day-care activities aimed to restore vocational activities, while out-patient interventions consisted of psychotherapy, possibly underlining the importance of goal-oriented rehabilitation, rather than the setting of care. The absence of benefits on symptomatology has also been reported for a different patient group. Patients suffering from depressive, phobic or anxiety neuroses were randomly allocated to day-hospital treatment or out-patient-care, and no consistent differences between groups were found after 4, 8 and 24 months (Tyrer, Remington and Alexander, 1987). A more recent study (Dick, Sweeney and Crombie, 1991) reported greater clinical and social improvements with day-care than out-patient-care for patients with persistent anxiety and depression, however.

Since this suggests that day-hospitals have no clearly defined role in the after-care of psychotic patients and treatment of mild or moderate neurotic patients, further work is required in this field. Little attention has been given to the efficacy of well-defined short-term interventions in day-care settings for specific problem areas in the life of psychotic patients following hospitalisation.

Day-care for the long-term mentally ill

The majority of people attending day-centres and also many day-hospitals are the long-term mentally ill living in the community. Unfortunately, facilities for this group are often poorly coordinated and lacking in provisions. A survey of day-care in London found a lack of emphasis on rehabilitation, deficiencies in leisure activities and inadequate support of relatives (Wing, 1982). Individualised treatment programmes are required, but difficult to implement because of poor levels of staffing. This leads to a lack of flexibility in the activities of many facilities, often demanding either a high degree of assertivity or providing a low level of stimulation, resulting in a high drop rate with the risk of neglect. Some day-centres allow patients to use the centre as a social meeting place, and the appreciation of this by patients was expressed by an improvement in attendance.

Programmes not only affect attendance but also outcome, although little research has been done in this area. Milne (1984) compared two neighbouring day-hospitals with similar staffing levels and chronicity of patients. One centre offered directive, behavioural interventions, the other a non-directive, social interaction programme. Only the problem-solving behavioural programme led to limited improvements. In a retrospective analysis of good outcome day-centres compared with relatively poor outcome day-centres in the treatment of schizophrenia, good outcome characteristics appeared to be a low patient turnover, more behavioural and fewer psychotherapeutic interventions, the use of care plans and a key worker system (Linn et al., 1979). Differences in patient groups, higher age and more males in good outcome centres, may have been confounding variables.

The combination of day- and home-care could be of benefit to the long-term mentally ill, and it is surprising that this has not been studied. Many of the skills acquired in day-centres do not transfer to the home environment; follow-up training sessions in the home setting may result in greater generalisation of skills. Home visits can also increase the attendance at day-care facilities, with resulting reductions in relapse and improvements in community adjustment (Beard, Malamud and Rossman, 1978).

HOME CARE

Home-care aims to treat and rehabilitate patients in their own environments with the intent to maximise independent functioning and minimise handicaps. This is to be achieved by providing patients with comprehensive treatment and support-based individual needs. The teaching of daily living skills in the community is thought to minimise the need for generalisation (Marx, Test and Stein, 1973), and resulting improvements in behaviour and coping skills are more likely to be maintained than those taught in a clinical setting (Anthony et al., 1972).

A distinction can be made between the needs of the acute mentally ill without a history of hospital stay and long-term dependent patients who may have stayed in institutions for years. Home-care aims to prevent the development of a hospital dependency syndrome in the first group, while the aim for the second group is to alleviate this dependency with rehabilitation in the least restrictive setting. In practice teams will often care for a mixed client group, requiring a large number of professional skills.

Unless community care is comprehensive, patients are at risk of neglect. Community-care has to accept responsibility not only for the mental well-being of patients but also for components of care that are not traditionally part of the role of psychiatric services. These include the functions of the Community Support Programmes (Turner and TenHoor, 1978) such as continuity of care, case management and regular medical check-ups, and also the organisation of material resources, assertive support and follow-up, and active involvement of relatives in treatment and education (Stein and Test, 1980).

Evaluation of home-care

From the early 1960s onwards, several studies have evaluated home-care vs standard hospital-care for the severely mentally ill (Pasamanick, Scarpitty and Dinitz, 1967; Grad and Sainsbury, 1968). Seven of these studies randomised patients who were due to be hospitalised and followed these patients up for a year or more (Pasamanick, Scarpitty and Dinitz, 1967; Langsley, Flomenhaft and Machotka, 1969; Test and Stein, 1980; Fenton et al., 1982a; Hoult and Reynolds, 1983; Muijen et al., 1992). The studies are briefly described before their results are jointly discussed.

The project by Pasamanick, Scarpitty and Dinitz (1967) is remarkable in that it anticipates future developments, both in service ideology and study design, by about 20 years. The study was instigated in 1957, but patient intake started in Louisville in 1961, delayed by the reluctance of state hospitals to cooperate. Inclusion criteria were a diagnosis of schizophrenia, the absence of suicidal or homicidal intent, and a supportive family. The 152 patients were randomised into 3 groups: 2 home-treatment groups both receiving identical community support, but in one of these groups psychotropic medication was replaced with a placebo, and a standard hospital control group. Patients stayed in the programme for 2 years. The 7 staff members visited home treatment group patients weekly during the initial 3 months, fortnightly during the next 3-month period and monthly thereafter. Home-care was considered to be a failure if patients required admission, and at this point they were taken out of the study. Regular ratings were completed by the staff members.

Fenton et al. (1982a) used the same entry criteria in Montreal, and only 19% of all hospital admissions were eligible for randomisation into home or hospital treatment. The home-care team consisted of a part-time psychiatrist and social worker and a full-time nurse, caring for 78 patients. On average patients were visited 17 times during the one year of follow-up, most of these contacts taking place in the first month.

Family therapy was compared with hospital admission in Denver (Langsley, Flomenhaft and Machotka, 1969; Langsley, Machotka and Flomenhaft, 1971). An unknown number of family therapists conducted an average of just over 5 sessions during the first month after entry. Each group accommodated 150 patients, but the only entry criteria specified were intended hospital admission and living with a family. Follow-up ratings were completed by independent clinicians.

The most comprehensive studies were conducted in Madison, Wisconsin (Stein and Test, 1980), Sydney (Hoult and Reynolds, 1983) and Camberwell (Muijen, 1991; Muijen et al., 1992). The Camberwell and Sydney studies replicated the Madison project, so many features were similar. Inclusion criteria were intended admission for serious mental illness (schizophrenia and affective psychosis) in the absence of brain damage or primary addiction. Patients presenting with aggression, no fixed abode or no social support were accepted. The projects employed 10 staff for 65 patients in Madison, 8 staff for 60 patients in Sydney and 10 staff for 92 patients in Camberwell. All projects used an approach which integrated crisis intervention and rehabilitation; patients were visited as often as required during the year of follow-up. The research teams worked strictly independent from the clinical teams.

In spite of the considerable differences between the projects, outcomes were very similar. No study found an advantage for hospital-care in any area, but home-care led to better functioning in several studies. Patients in home-care had fewer and shorter admissions than standard-care patients. From 18% (Stein and Test, 1980) and 40% (Fenton et al., 1982a; Hoult and Reynolds,1983) to 80% (Muijen, 1991) of home-care patients required hospitalisation; the average period of admission of these patients was about 70% shorter than those of the hospital-care groups. Only in the Louisville study (Pasamanick, Scarpitty and Dinitz, 1967) were hospitalised patients from the home-treatment group admitted for a longer period than the control group. This was the only project in which clinical responsibility for patients was passed on to hospital teams on admission. In contrast, all other projects were responsible for the coordination of care at all times, possibly allowing early discharge as a result of the coordination of all resources available to patients.

Fewer psychotic symptoms were displayed by patients in the home-care groups in Sydney and Madison, but not in the other projects. No differences were found in self-esteem and leisure-time activities, but experimental patients in Madison spent more time in sheltered employment, resulting in higher earnings. In Montreal (Fenton et al., 1982a), a higher proportion of those home-care patients in employment at entry into the project had resumed work after 12 months follow-up (50%) than hospital patients (33%).

Satisfaction with home-care was higher for both patients and relatives than with hospital care in Sydney (Reynolds and Hoult, 1984) and Camberwell (Muijen, 1991). Other studies had not measured these variables. Family and community burden, measured by police contacts and suicide attempts, was not affected by type of care in any of the projects (Test and Stein, 1980; Fenton et al., 1982a; Reynolds and Hoult, 1984). Number of staff visits has been established in other studies as the major variable contributing to family satisfaction (Grad and Sainsbury, 1968; Grella and Grusky, 1989), and home-treatment is a model of care which can provide this well.

A consistent finding is the gradual loss of all gains of home-care patients who were returned to standard hospital-care at the cessation of home-treatment (Stein and Test, 1980; Davis, Dinitz and Pasamanick, 1972). Eventually no differences between the original groups could be detected, suggesting that the advantages of home-care require continuing care in order to be maintained.

An important objective is the definition of those patient groups which would benefit most from this model of care. Hoult and Reynolds (1983) separated their patient population retrospectively into those with a diagnosis of schizophrenia, patients with no previous admissions and chronic patients. The group responding best to community-care as compared to standard-care were the first admissions. Chronic patients showed relatively smaller gains with home-care, but even for this group hospital use was substantially reduced, with some clinical improvements occurring over the year. The Camberwell study (Muijen, 1991) found no differences in outcome for any diagnostic subgroups or patients with or without previous psychiatric history. No groups benefited more from hospital-care in any study.

Costs

The cost of community-care has been reported to be lower than hospital-care, with savings ranging from 1% (Muijen et al., 1992), 5% (Weisbrod, Test and Stein, 1980) and 25% (Hoult and Reynolds, 1983) to as much as 61% (Fenton et al., 1982b). However, these variations reflect differences in both methods of cost calculation and treatment models. The various projects used a cost benefit analysis (Weisbrod, Test and Stein, 1980), cost efficiency analyses (Fenton et al., 1982b; Hoult and Reynolds, 1983) and comparisons of direct treatment costs only (Pasamanick, Scarpitty and Dinitz, 1967; Langsley et al., 1968; Muijen et al., 1992). In Madison (Weisbrod, Test and Stein, 1980) the 26% higher treatment cost of community-care was compensated for by "societal benefits" such as earnings of patients. Their analysis included capital costs, but the high starting costs of community-care were disregarded. Pasamanick, Scarpitty and Dinitz (1967), Langsley et al. (1968) and Muijen et al. (1992) only measured costs of in-patient stay and community services, while Fenton et al. (1982b) and Hoult and Reynolds (1983) also calculated costs incurred by public and private agencies. Since all studies included the main cost components, such as total hospital expenditure, and since the relative costs and usage of these components were similar, the large differences in savings seem to be related to variations in the model of care, such as staff–patient ratios and intensity of care.

The consistent finding that home-care costs less than hospital-care suggests that some savings can be expected after an initial capital investment in areas such as staff training and small-scale community developments, making community-care an attractive option. Caution is advisable for several reasons. Firstly, savings in hospital expenditure can lead to higher costs elsewhere, such as day-care, hostels or social services (Borland, McRae and Lycan, 1989), with an unpredictable result. A second problem is marginal costs; closure of half a ward or half a hospital does not save half the costs because of fixed overheads. This means that a gradual implementation of community services is disproportionately expensive, encouraging the notion of wholesale closure of hospitals without the necessary evaluation of the impact of such change.

VALIDITY

Even though individual projects have demonstrated that many alternatives to standard hospital-care are effective, this in itself does not mean that these programmes can confidently be implemented elsewhere (Bachrach, 1980). The external validity of model programmes can be limited (Bachrach, 1982) due to their experimental nature. Unless evaluative and clinical methods are revealed in detail, the repeatability and relevance of the results of model programmes cannot be relied upon, and replication is unlikely to be successful. Many of the projects have identical aims, and are based on similar principles, which appear to reinforce the strength of evidence in favour of alternatives to standard-care. Major differences also exist between studies, however, both in evaluation and practice, and these are too often ignored.

Clinical and methodological issues

Although these studies all offered alternatives to standard hospital-care with the objective to improve patient functioning, differences between projects in the planning, organisation, running and evaluation of community services for the severely mentally ill can affect outcome.

The first difference is the target group which projects have chosen to care for. Specific diagnostic groups or all presenting patients, acute versus chronic illness and exclusion or acceptance of suicidal or violent patients are some of the differences between studies. Strict entry criteria guarantee a homogeneous study population with a high internal validity, but may limit generalisation. The danger of wide entry criteria is that validity may be compromised due to the heterogeneity of the patients included, not permitting any conclusions (Hennekens and Buring, 1987). Studies vary greatly in entry criteria, which means that results between studies cannot be easily compared, but this diversity may allow for an appraisal of the benefit of these interventions on a wide range of patients.

The second difference is the model of care used. Not only structural differences such as day-care vs home-care affect the efficacy of model programmes but also process variables such as a crisis intervention or a rehabilitative model. The third difference between projects are the principles of care, which operationalise the model. Patients or families may be seen, daily or monthly. Some services use case managers, others a team approach. Support may be accessible 24 hours a day or only on appointment. Care principles will partly depend on ideology and partly on practical circumstances such as funding and availability of resources. The fourth and fifth variables, staffing levels and staff mixture, are both likely to determine the type of care provided, as well as influencing quality of care. High staffing levels, frequently present at model programmes, allow for more time consuming interventions than are available to many regular services, which are often run at low budgets. A nursing team without specific therapeutic skills will differ in its approach from a multidisciplinary team, containing additional specialised staff such as psychiatrists, social workers, psychologists and occupational therapists.

A sixth factor is the support facilities available in the area. The presence or absence of day-centres, crisis-houses or hostels will greatly influence the workload of staff and quality of life of patients. As often as not such additional resources are independently run and funded, affecting the outcome of model programmes in a way which is very difficult to quantify, and rarely made explicit in the evaluation.

Two further variations between programmes which should not be ignored are time and location. A project in the US in the early 1960s can be expected to produce different findings as compared with a study from Australia in the 1980s. Many transformations in lifestyle, politics, laws, the health system, medical practice and user expectations occur within a decade in any nation, and can exist at the same time in different countries and even different areas within countries. In addition, the populations served by programmes will differ on economic, cultural and ethnic variables, making decisions about the relevance of various programmes complex.

A ninth variable is the innovative and time-limited nature of model programmes. This is linked to staff quality and morale, both of which can be decisive factors in the efficacy of any programme. Model projects are often set up by charismatic leaders, selecting motivated and highly qualified staff who are aware of the special status of the programme. This can lead to a total commitment, with private lives and holidays sacrificed for "the cause". It is unclear whether this enthusiasm can persist beyond the duration of many of these programmes, and the results of short-term evaluations are likely to be influenced by this enthusiasm which should not be depended on in a regular service. The duration of most programmes has been about a year, and this could well be a critical period for motivation. Longer periods of follow-up are required, and such studies are taking place (Marks, Connolly and Muijen, 1988).

The reported outcome of projects depends as much on clinical practice as on the methods used for evaluation. A close collaboration is required between the research and clinical team, while guarding mutual independence. These projects are at great risk of bias, since clinicians often believe in the superiority of alternative interventions before the start of the projects, a conviction which is often the stimulus for setting up these programmes. No studies have been conducted in which clinicians intended to illustrate the superiority of standard hospital-care over community-care. It is essential that evaluators are not only independent, but also dispassionate and impartial about the results and its consequences, not always an easy position when the future of services, jobs and careers can be at stake.

The quality of evaluation depends upon the data obtained. If patient numbers are too small, real benefits or drawbacks of programmes may not be measurable, leading to potentially erroneous conclusions. This is of great importance when entry criteria are broad, and a subanalysis needs to be performed. Power calculations are required, but have not been mentioned in any of the projects.

Outcome criteria differ. Few studies only measure hospitalisation and relapse, which is not meaningful in the absence of information on patient functioning (Anthony et al., 1972; Anthony et al., 1978), since rehospitalisation may be due to good follow-up, while deteriorating patients ignored in the community could be considered as a success. Most studies, however, include any of a number of other outcome data, such as psychopathology, social functioning, family burden, satisfaction, community impact and a cost analysis.

Reliable and valid rating scales are needed to measure these outcome criteria. A remarkable number of questionnaires is used. The five controlled home-care studies used about 20 different scales between them, some of them self designed, and only one scale is used in two studies.

Widely ignored is the variability of the control groups. Even though all control groups receive "standard hospital care", the type and quality of this care is unlikely to have been identical in the diverse conditions. This implies that any result depends on its own unique setting, and that the generalisation of expected improvements in patient outcome depends as much on the control treatment as on the experimental model. The issue is whether more attention to standard treatment, such as additional funding, training or more qualified staff might have negated any differences in outcome found between the two groups.

A difficult form of bias to quantify is publication bias. It is unknown how many projects have failed and why, because these results are less likely to have been published, partly due to the reluctance of clinicians to write up "failures", partly due to the refusal of journals to publish "negative" results. One study had to be discontinued because of the diffidence of clinicians to refer patients to a treatment perceived as too radical (Platt, Knights and Hirsch, 1980), but it is more than likely that other projects failed for different reasons. A new form of care cannot expect to become practice without strong advocacy and the provision of training and resources. Negative experiences are of great relevance for the planning of future community services and studies, if the repetition of mistakes is to be avoided.

Clinicians and planners intending to start a community service would be best served investigating those projects which share most characteristics with their own circumstances, and are therefore most likely to be repeatable. They must pay close attention to many structural and process variables, all of which contribute to outcome, albeit to unquantifiable degrees. Unless the changes involved in the implementation of community services have been thoroughly analysed, it seems to be hazardous to proceed.

CLINICAL EXPERIENCES

Much concern has been expressed about the low priority given to the most severely mentally ill in community mental-health centres in the US, with staff increasingly offering support to patients with relatively minor mental health problems, such as marital tensions and anxiety states, often grouped under the somewhat dismissive category "the worried well" (Zwerling, 1976; Langsley, 1980). Several factors contributed to the shift of care away from the severely mentally ill: the interest of staff in prevention and cure rather than maintenance, the higher status of psychotherapy than rehabilitation, the gradual replacement of medics with psychologists and social workers, and the lack of adequate training for mental-health workers (Fink and Weinstein, 1979; Stern and Minkoff, 1979). Little attention is given to the special demands made on staff working in community projects, with its emphasis on multidisciplinary teamwork (Bloom and Parad, 1976).

The experience of a team looking after the severely mentally ill in inner city London may not be atypical (Marks, Connolly and Muijen, 1988; Muijen, 1991; Muijen et al., 1992). The clinical team consisted of six nurses, an occupational therapist, a social worker and a psychiatrist. They worked 7 days a week, with telephone cover only during the night. A case management approach was offered to the 92 patients, with a 1 to 10 staff/patient ratio (not all patients required care constantly).

The first assessment was usually performed by a psychiatrist and another health worker. Patients were seen with available relatives and problems were identified. These varied from loneliness to disturbed behaviour endangering themselves or others. The team considered whether any interventions could solve the presenting problems in a discussion with all concerned. Medication was prescribed for most patients. A physical examination took place as early as possible. If home-care was agreed on, the patient was given a ride home and a home assessment was made. Availability of food and general living conditions was checked out and, when appropriate, neighbours and friends were informed as to how to contact the team. After the patient had settled, which could take some hours, another appointment for a home visit was made.

Early on in the programme hospital admissions were seen as failures, but gradually positive indications for the use of hospital beds were identified. Very psychotic and disturbed patients needed more structure than could be offered at home, and were often a risk to themselves or others. Brief relief could be provided for relatives in exceptional circumstances, such as parents who were worn out by too many sleepless nights. Single people were at higher risk of admission. The obvious reason for this was that no one could look after them, but this was confounded since they also tended to present with more severe problems and live in unacceptable circumstances. Finally, the lack of night staff at the DLP meant that single people had to spend the night alone if hospital admission was considered to be unnecessary, and their ability to do so was often the decisive factor.

Following admission the DLP remained responsible for their patients. The objective of hospital admission was crisis intervention only, and as soon as possible patients were taken home and cared for in their own environment. Patients were invariably delighted with the short duration of admissions.

The key-worker was responsible for the day-to-day care, which includes housing and benefits. Especially in inner city areas, accommodation can be a serious problem, with many clients homeless or living in appalling conditions. Bed and breakfast was often the only option, and was actively pursued by the team. Benefits were frequently not claimed and patients presented without any money or food. A crisis loan was sometimes offered, or patients were taken to social services. The team gave a large proportion of their time to sorting out complicated claims at benefit offices and negotiating with housing authorities. It became clear that many patients have relapsed as a result of problems in those areas, and it is likely that hospitals tend to underestimate these factors.

If home-care was arranged, visits were made as often as required. Patients and relatives could contact the DLP 24 hours a day as one of the staff was on call at night. This facility was used about once a week and has prevented some crises. Very rarely did patients have to attend an emergency clinic out of working hours, and it appears that home care was able to prevent unexpected crisis situations.

Patients suffering from a psychotic condition were assessed regularly by a psychiatrist. Feedback was also provided by nurses and treatments could be adjusted on a daily basis. The impression was that medication dosages were lower in the community than in hospital for equivalent conditions. This may have been because patients were less aroused in familiar surroundings than in hospital.

The success with patients was reflected in the very low drop-out rate. Patients may have realised that the team worked with them on their identified problems, such as finances, housing and work. Medication compliance was poor initially, but improved gradually, possibly as a result of education and the development of trust. The service has been remarkably successful in the care of ethnic minorities. Very few of this group, mostly young, male, living alone, and suffering from schizophrenia, and reported by others to be notoriously difficult to engage (Pepper, Kirschner and Rylewics, 1981), dropped out of care. Advocacy and continuing care was important.

The limitation of a community service is that it cannot provide a comprehensive range of interventions in the absence of other facilities such as day hospitals, hostels, drop-in centres and temporary accommodation. The lack of sufficient facilities can mean that too much of the burden of care has to be carried by the team, an impossible task in an impoverished inner city area. It says very much about the motivation of the staff that the service was successful in spite of these disadvantages, but it is doubtful whether this can be taken for granted in any future service.

CONCLUSION

The consistent finding that experimental community care programmes are slightly superior to standard care is promising, and implies that improvements in standard patient-care can be expected. The efficacy of short admissions, day-care and home-care for groups of patients suffering from serious mental illness has been illustrated repeatedly. Although the potential of these methods of care can be accepted, a concern remains that the success of these programmes is a characteristic of model programmes, possibly not generalisable to regular services. The comprehensive, long-term demands on a regular service are distinct from those of well-defined, short-lived projects (Bachrach, 1980).

A limitation of model programmes is the inevitably narrow scope of service evaluations. The evaluation of protects is often two-dimensional, comparing two single services for a selected group of patients in isolation, whereas regular mental health care is multi-dimensional, with many service components contributing to the care of mixed populations of patients.

We may have reached the end of the road for the first generation of studies evaluating the efficacy of community-care. These studies compare global packages of care, but do not yield further understanding on the cause of effect. Further progress is appearing from two types of studies. Firstly from those studies which narrow their scope, and aim to measure the potential benefits of specific interventions for well-defined groups of patients, such as behavioural or family interventions for patients with schizophrenia living with critical relatives (Falloon et al., 1982; Leff et al., 1982).

The other type of projects broaden their perspective, attempting to study the effect of system changes on the delivery of health-care, such as the introduction of case management (Borland, McRae and Lycau, 1989). In addition, the experience of clinicians in regular services should not be ignored. Descriptions of the planning and running of new services (Gudeman et al., 1983; Dean and Gadd, 1989, 1991) can indicate the potential of innovations in regular practice.

Eventually, a third generation of studies will aim to combine these two approaches, evaluating the integration of various care packages within different treatment approaches, until possibly an optimal form of care will emerge. It remains to be seen, however, whether a single best treatment model of general applicability will be found. Patients and countries are too diverse, and it may be necessary for any care model to be adjusted to accommodate local needs.

REFERENCES

Anthony, W.A., Buell, G.J., Sharratt, S. and Althoff, M.E. (1972) The efficacy of psychiatric rehabilitation. *Psychological Bulletin*, **78**, 447–56.

Anthony, W.A., Cohen, M.R. and Vitalo, R. (1978) The measurement of rehabilitation outcome. *Schizophrenia Bulletin*, **4**, 365–83.

Audit Commission for Local Authorities in England and Wales (1986) *Making a Reality of Community Care*, HMSO, London.

Bachrach, L.L. (1980) Overview: model programs for chronic mental patients. *American Journal of Psychiatry*, **137**, 1023–31.

Bachrach, L.L. (1982) Assessment of outcomes in Community Support Systems: results, problems and limitations. *Schizophrenia Bulletin*, **8**, 39–60.

Baekland, F. and Lundwell, L. (1975) Dropping out of treatment: a critical review. *Psychological Bulletin*, **82**, 738–83.

Bassuk, E.L. and Gerson, S. (1978) Deinstitutionalization and mental health services. *Scientific American*, **238**, 46–53.

Beard, J.H., Malamud, T.J. and Rossman, E. (1978) Psychiatric rehabilitation and long term rehospitalisation rates: the findings of two research studies. *Schizophrenia Bulletin*, **4**, 622–35.
Bender, M.P. and Pilling, S. (1985) A study of variables associated with under-attendance at a psychiatric day centre. *Psychological Medicine*, **15**, 395–401.
Bierer, J. (1951) *The Day Hospitals*, H.K. Lewis, London.
Bloom, B.L. and Parad, H.J. (1976) Interdisciplinary training and interdisciplinary functioning: a survey of attitudes and practices in community mental health. *American Journal of Orthopsychiatry*, **46**, 669–77.
Borland, A., McRae, J. and Lycan, C. (1989) Outcomes of five years of continuous intensive case management. *Hospital and Community Psychiatry*, **40**, 369–76.
Braun, P., Kochansky, G., Shapiro, R., Greenberg, S., Gudeman, J.E., Johnson, S. and Shore, M. (1981) Overview: deinstitutionalization of psychiatric patients, a critical review of outcome studies. *American Journal of Psychiatry*, **136**, 736–49.
Brown, P. (1985) *The Transfer of Care: Psychiatric Deinstitutionalization and Its Aftermath*, Routledge, New York and London.
Carse, J., Panton, N.Y. and Watt, A. (1958) A district mental health service: the Worthing experience. *Lancet*, **i**, 39–41.
Craft, M. (1958) An evaluation of treatment of depressive illness in a day hospital. *Lancet*, **ii**, 149–51.
Creed, F., Black, D., Anthony, P., Osborn, M., Thomas, P. and Tomenson, B. (1990) Randomised controlled trial of day patient versus inpatient psychiatric treatment. *British Medical Journal*, **300**, 1033–7.
Davis, A.E., Dinitz, S. and Pasamanick, B. (1972) The prevention of hospitalisation in schizophrenia: five years after an experimental program. *American Journal of Orthopsychiatry*, **42**, 375–88.
Dean, C. and Gadd, E. (1989) An inner city home treatment service for acute psychiatric patients. *Psychiatric Bulletin of the Royal College of Psychiatrists*, **13**, 667–69.
Dean, C. and Gadd, E.M. (1990) Home treatment for acute psychiatric illness. *British Medical Journal*, **301**, 1021–3.
DHSS (1975) *Better Services for the Mentally Ill*. HMSO, London.
DHSS (1989) *Caring for People*. HMSO, London.
Dick, P., Cameron, L., Cohen, D., Barlow, M. and Ince, A. (1985a) Day and full time psychiatric treatment—a controlled comparison. *British Journal of Psychiatry*, **147**, 246–9.
Dick. P., Ince, A. and Barlow, B. (1985b) Day treatment: suitability and referral procedure. *British Journal of Psychiatry*, **147**, 250–3.
Dick, P.H., Sweeney, M.L. and Crombie, I.K. (1991) Controlled comparison of day-patient and out-patient treatment for persistent anxiety and depression. *British Journal of Psychiatry*, **158**, 24–7.
Edwards, C. and Carter, J. (1980) The data of day care, National Institute for Social Work, London.
Erickson, R.C. (1975) Outcome studies in mental hospitals: a review. *Psychological Bulletin*, **82**, 519–40.
Falloon, I.R.H., Boyd, J.L., McGill, C.W., Razani, J., Moss, H.B. and Gilderman, A.M. (1982) Family management in the prevention of exacerbations of schizophrenia. *The New England Journal of Medicine*, **306**, 1437–40.
Falloon, I.R.H. and Hole, V.G. (1990) Family care as an alternative to the mental hospital. In: P. Hall and I.F. Brockington (eds), *The Closure of Mental Hospitals*, Gaskell, London.

Fenton, F.R., Tessier, L. and Struening, E.L. (1979) A comparative trial of home and hospital psychiatric care: one-year follow-up. *Archives of General Psychiatry*, **36**, 1073–9.

Fenton, F.R., Tessier, L., Struening, E.L., Smith, F.A. and Benoit, C. (1982a) *Home and Hospital Psychiatric Treatment*, Croom Helm, London.

Fenton, F.R., Tessier, L., Contandriopoulos, A.P., Nguyen, H. and Struening, E.L. (1982b) A comparative trial of home and hospital psychiatric treatment: financial costs. *Canadian Journal of Psychiatry*, **27**, 177–87.

Fink, P.J. and Weinstein, S.P. (1979) Whatever happened to psychiatry?: the deprofessionalization of community mental health centers. *American Journal of Psychiatry*, **136**, 406–9.

Fink, E.B., Longabaugh, R. and Staout, R. (1978) The paradoxical underutilization of partial hospitalizaton. *American Journal of Psychiatry*, **135**, 713–16.

Gath, D., Hassal, C. and Cross, K.W. (1973) Whither psychiatric day care?: A study of day patients in Birmingham. *British Medical Journal*, **i**, 94–8.

Goffman, E. (1961) *Asylums*, Pelican, Harmondsworth, Middlesex.

Goldman, H.H. (1981) Defining and counting the chronically mentally ill. *Hospital and Community Psychiatry*, **32**, 21–7.

Grad, J. and Sainsbury. P. (1968) The effects that patients have on their families in a community care and a control psychiatric service—a two year follow-up. *British Journal of Psychiatry*, **114**, 265–78.

Grella, C.E. and Grusky, O. (1989) Families of the seriously mentally ill and their satisfaction with services. *Hospital and Community Psychiatry*, **40**, 831–5.

Griffiths, R. (1988) *Community Care: Agenda for Action*, HMSO, London.

Hennekens, C.H. and Buring, J.E. (1987) *Epidemiology in Medicine*, Little, Brown, Boston.

Herz, M.I., Endicott, J., Spitzer, R.L. and Mesnikoff, A. (1971) Day versus in-patient hospitalization: a controlled study. *American Journal of Psychiatry*, **127**, 1371–81.

Hirsch, S.R. (1988) *Psychiatric Beds and Resources: Factors Influencing Bed Use and Service Planning*, Royal College of Psychiatrists, Gaskell.

Hoult, J. and Reynolds, I. (1983) *Psychiatric Hospital versus Community Treatment: a Controlled Study*, Department of Health, New South Wales.

Jones, K. and Poletti, A. (1985) Understanding the Italian experience. *British Journal of Psychiatry*, **146**, 341–4.

Kiesler, C.A. (1982) Mental hospitals and alternative care. *American Psychologist*, **37**, 349–60.

Langsley, D., Pittman, F., Machotka, P. and Flomenhaft, K. (1968) Family crisis therapy—results and implications. *Family Process*, **7**, 145–58.

Langsley, D.G. (1980) The community mental health center: does it treat patients? *Hospital and Community Psychiatry*, **31**, 815–19.

Langsley, D.G., Flomenhaft, K. and Machotka, P. (1969) Follow-up evaluation of family crisis therapy. *American Journal of Orthopsychiatry*, **39**, 753–9.

Langsley, D.G., Machotka, P. and Flomenhaft, K. (1971) Avoiding mental hospital admission, a follow-up study. *American Journal of Psychiatry*, **127**, 1391–4.

Leff, J.P., Kuipers, L., Berkowitz, R., Eberlein-Fries, R. and Sturgeon, D. (1982) A controlled trial of social intervention in the families of schizophrenic patients. *British Journal of Psychiatry*, **141**, 121–34.

Linn, M.W., Caffey, E.M., Klett, C.J., Hogarty, G.E. and Lamb, H.R. (1979) Day treatment and psychotropic drugs in the aftercare of schizophrenic patients. *Archives of General Psychiatry*, **36**, 1055–66.

Marks, I., Connolly, J. and Muijen, M. (1988) The Maudsley Daily Living Program. *Psychiatric Bulletin of the Royal College of Psychiatrists*, **30**, 866–71.

Marx, A.J., Test, M.A. and Stein, L.I. (1973) Extrahospital management of severe mental illness. *Archives of General Psychiatry*, **29**, 505–11.

McCready, R.G., Robinson, A.D. and Wilson, A.O.A. (1984) The Scottish survey of chronic day patients. *British Journal of Psychiatry*, **145**, 626–30.

Michaux, M.H., Chelst, M.R., Foster, S.A., Pruim, R.J. and Dasinger. E.M. (1973) Post release adjustment of day and full-time psychiatric patients. *Archives of General Psychiatry*, **29**, 647–51.

Milne, D. (1984) A comprehensive evaluation of two psychiatric day hospitals. *British Journal of Psychiatry*, **145**, 533–7.

Ministry of Health (1962) *A hospital plan for England and Wales*, HMSO, London.

Muijen, M. (1991) The outcome of the first year of the Daily Living Program: a controlled study comparing home based care with standard hospital care. PhD thesis, Institute of Psychiatry, London University.

Muijen, M., Marks, I.M., Connolly, J., Audini, B. and McNamee, G. (1992) The Daily Living Program: preliminary comparison of community versus hospital based treatment for the seriously mentally ill facing emergency admission. *British Journal of Psychiatry*, **160**, 372–8.

Pasamanick, B., Scarpitty, F.R. and Dinitz, S. (1967) *Schizophrenics in the Community*, Appleton-Century-Crofts, New York.

Pepper, B., Kirschner, M. and Rylewics, H. (1981) The young adult chronic patient: overview of a population. *Hospital and Community Psychiatry*, **32**, 463–9.

Platt, S.D., Knights, A.C. and Hirsch, S.R. (1980) Caution and Conservatism in the use of a psychiatric day hospital: evidence from a research project that failed. *Psychiatry Research*, **3**, 123–32.

Reynolds, I. and Hoult, J.E. (1984) The relatives of the mentally ill: a comparative trial of community oriented and hospital oriented psychiatric care. *Journal of Nervous and Mental Disease*, **172**, 480–9.

Rosie, J.S. (1987) Partial hospitalization: a review of recent literature. *Hospital and Community Psychiatry*, **38**, 1291–9.

Scherl, D.J. and Macht, L.B. (1979) Deinstitutionalization in the absence of consensus. *Hospital and Community Psychiatry*, **30**, 599–604.

Smith, S. and Cross, E.G.W. (1957) Review of 1000 patients treated at a psychiatric day hospital. *International Journal of Social Psychiatry*, **2**, 292–8.

Stein, L.J. and Test, M.A. (1980) Alternative to mental hospital treatment. 1, Conceptual model, treatment program and clinical evaluation. *Archives of General Psychiatry*, **37**, 392–7.

Stern, R. and Minkoff, K. (1979) Paradoxes in programming for chronic patients in a community clinic. *Hospital and Community Psychiatry*, **30**, 613–17.

Tessler, R.C. and Goldman, H.H. (1982) *The Chronic Mentally Ill: Assessing Community Support Programs*. Ballinger, Cambridge.

Test, M.A. and Stein, L.I. (1980) Alternative to mental hospital treatment. 3, Social cost. *Archives of General Psychiatry*, **37**, 409–12.

Turner, J.C. and TenHoor, W.J. (1978) The NIMH support program: Pilot approach to a needed social reform. *Schizophrenia Bulletin*, **4**, 319–49.

Tyrer, P., Remington, M. and Alexander, J. (1987) The outcome of neurotic disorders after outpatient and day hospital care. *British Journal of Psychiatry*, **151**, 57–62.

Weisbrod, B.A., Test, M.A. and Stein. L.I. (1980) Alternative to mental hospital

treatment. 2, Economic benefit–cost analysis. *Archives of General Psychiatry*, **37**, 400–45.
Weldon, E., Clarkin, J.E., Hennessy, J.J. and Frances, A. (1979) Day hospital versus outpatient treatment: a controlled study. *Psychiatric Quarterly*, **51**, 144–50.
Weller, M.P.I. (1989) Mental illness—who cares? *Nature*, **339**, 249–52.
Wilder, J.F., Levin, G. and Zwerling, I. (1966) A two year follow-up evaluation of acute psychotic patients treated in a day hospital. *American Journal of Psychiatry*, **122**, 1095–101.
Wing, J.K. (ed.) (1982) Long-term community care: experience in a London borough. *Psychological Medicine Monograph* (Supp.).
Zwerling, I. (1976) The impact of the community mental health movement on psychiatric practice and training. *Hospital and Community Psychiatry*, **27**, 259–63.

HAROLD BRIDGES LIBRARY
S. MARTIN'S COLLEGE
LANCASTER

Stein, L. I. … Economic benefit-cost analysis. Archives of General Psychiatry, 37, 400–5.

Weldon, E., Clarkin, J., Hennessy, J. and Frances, A. (1979) Day hospital versus outpatient treatment: a controlled study. Psychiatric Quarterly, 51, 144–50.

Weller, M. P. I. (1989) Mental illness—who cares? Nature, 339, 249–52.

Wilder, J. F., Levin, G. and Zwerling, I. (1966) A two-year follow-up evaluation of acute psychotic patients treated in a day hospital. American Journal of Psychiatry, 122, 1095–1101.

Wing, J. K. (ed.) (1982) Long-term community care: experience in a London borough. Psychological Medicine Monograph (Suppl. 2).

Zwerling, I. (1976) The impact of the community mental health movement on psychiatric practice and training. Hospital and Community Psychiatry, 27, 259–63.

Chapter 12

Service Organisation and Planning

KATE WOOFF

INTRODUCTION

Data for admission to psychiatric hospitals in England show that the proportion of admissions for people with a diagnosis of schizophrenia and paranoia have fallen from 22% in 1964 to 15% in 1986 (Department of Health and Social Security, 1977, 1988). Total numbers of people admitted with a diagnosis of schizophrenia have dropped slightly from 31 000 to 29 500 over the same period. As total admissions for all diagnoses over the same period rose from 155 000 to 197 000 it follows that other kinds of patients are increasingly admitted to in-patient care. If the falling proportions of admissions for schizophrenia had been accompanied by a shift in resource from in-patient to other forms of support this might be thought to represent some considerable success in the management and support for this group of patients. Because few non in-patient-based mental-health services are adequately monitored it is impossible to be certain how they are in fact performing. There is, however, evidence to suggest that as the focus of mental-health services has shifted from in-patient to community, people with a diagnosis of schizophrenia have received a smaller proportion of community-based resources than might have been expected.

Following the establishment of community mental-health centres (CMHCs) and primary-care-based community psychiatric nursing (CPN) services in the UK, the proportion of clients with long-term needs being treated, many of whom have been given a diagnosis of schizophrenia, has, in many cases, reduced (Wooff, Rose and Street, 1989; Patmore and Weaver, 1990, 1991). Further, detailed work in Salford (Wooff, Goldberg and Fryers, 1988) demonstrated that not only did the proportion of CPNs' psychotic clients decline over time but also the mean amount of CPN time devoted to clients at each contact was over 2.5 times less for those diagnosed as having a psychotic illness compared with clients with other

Innovations in the Psychological Management of Schizophrenia.
Edited by Max Birchwood and Nicholas Tarrier. © 1992 John Wiley & Sons Ltd

diagnoses or problems. The shift to community-based services spearheaded by CMHCs in the United States was also accompanied by a drift away from caring for people with psychotic illness.

Generally, this change of emphasis has been unplanned as many community-based services were in fact set up to provide care for people who would otherwise have had to be treated as hospital in-patients (e.g. schizophrenia). This chapter aims to explore the issues surrounding the apparent failure of community services to ensure that plans are translated into service practice. It argues that professionals should acknowledge their involvement in the planning process and accept responsibility for this involvement. It also describes how the application of a systematic planning approach, based on client needs rather than on health agency needs might lead to radical changes to the ways in which services are delivered. Such a change is illustrated by describing the approach followed in Salford, England.

THE PLANNING PROCESS

Recent changes in the United Kingdom (Working for Patients, 1989; Caring for People, 1989, 1990) have resulted in "purchasing" and "providing" functions in health and social services being distinguished from each other. For the first time, responsibilities for ascertaining the health needs of populations have been assigned to "purchasers" of health and social care. Perhaps because in the past "providers" have dominated service organisations, needs have tended to be defined in terms of services. As needs can be seen to be infinite, establishing needs for particular services (if no justification in terms of effectiveness or priority is required) is easy. Thus, the lack of requirement for services to demonstrate effectiveness and the failure of health authorities to specify priorities or monitor activity can be identified as key reasons why existing service networks, planned developments and management and organisational mechanisms, require urgent review.

A simple planning model suggested here is:

1. establish the size and nature of needs;
2. outline principles, aims and objectives;
3. set priorities;
4. set strategies;
5. monitor outcome;
6. adjust aims or strategies according to the results of monitoring.

That each of these components are inter-dependent and form part of a "package" cannot be over stressed. In practice, plans all too often consist of the fourth element only, although health systems which depend upon profit margins to survive may use the size of these to monitor "outcome". Not only does planning tend to focus only on strategies but also buildings and staff numbers tend to be the only strategies considered in any detail.

Establishing the size and nature of needs

Establishing the size of mental-health needs is dependent upon the definition of "mental health" or even "mental ill-health". Of all health specialties, mental health, as a result of widely differing theories and perspectives, which attempt to explain phenomena observed throughout the world, is probably the most difficult to define. Balancing needs for treatment and prevention presents a further challenge. Suffice to say, that need can be argued to be infinite and moving away from traditional service-led assessments of needs presents a formidable challenge.

In the United Kingdom health and social service information systems have generally been designed to monitor service activity in such a way as to fulfil central government demands for data and there has been a general failure to develop information systems which focus on individuals rather than service events. Where health systems are set up according to free market principles, there is virtually no possibility of monitoring routinely the health-care utilisation of specific populations unless this is done as part of a specific research programme or as part of health insurance company monitoring and cost control programmes.

Patient-based, cumulative information systems can provide data on length of time individuals and groups of individuals have remained in contact with services. The fact that only a handful of health districts in the UK will be able to produce such data, i.e. Case Register type data (TenHorn et al., 1986) underlines the fact that in the past little attempt to plan rationally has been made.

Even where adequate service information exists, it is important to recognise the extent to which individual specialist service components may or may not reflect the needs of whole populations (Goldberg and Blackwell, 1970; Shepherd et al., 1966). Goldberg and Huxley (1980) provide a health model; but, as people with mental-health problems may turn to a variety of sources for help, it is important to consider how the activities of non-health groups and agencies (voluntary groups, social services, etc.) may help to build up a picture of needs within particular communities.

It is also important to recognise that the distribution of problems will vary within planning populations. Information from United Kingdom Case Registers (Jennings et al., 1989) illustrates how the accumulation of "new" long-stay in-patients is higher in areas of population loss and social deprivation. There is also evidence that socially deprived areas will have higher proportions than average of people with severe long-term mental health problems (Neugebauer, Dohrenwend and Dohrenwend, 1980; Giggs, 1984; Freeman and Alpert, 1986; Link, Dohrenwend and Skodol, 1987; Der, 1989). The Black Report (DHSS 1980) demonstrated the general link between ill-health and social deprivation and two measures of social deprivation, the UPA8 (Jarman, 1983, 1984) and the Department of the Environment Social Index are available for local authority areas of England and Wales.

Having made some estimates of the size of the problem, it will be necessary to estimate its nature. Here again, the demographic and social characteristics of populations will be important influences. Although Census statistics tend only to be produced each decade, they nevertheless give valuable demographic and social information. Most developed countries produce detailed statistical information concerning economic and social issues such as the General Household Survey in the UK. Commercially produced packages used for company marketing purposes, for example, ACORN, which can provide information on the distribution of subcultures within specific populations may also provide useful health planning data.

In estimating the size and nature of the problem, the distinction between incidence (new cases) and prevalence (numbers existing at any specified time, e.g. on any one day, or in any one year) must be taken into account. The clinical "impression" tends to be based on case-load distributions, which most closely reflect prevalence distributions. If services and case loads are to be organised to reflect needs then the distribution of short-, medium-term and long-term patients must be estimated. The natural history of many mental-health problems remains unknown, so estimates based only on diagnostic groups will not provide all the information required to make such estimates.

Lack of detailed statistics should not preclude a review of needs from taking place. The particular group with which this book is concerned, i.e. people who have been diagnosed as suffering from schizophrenia, are, of all the clinical groups of people with mental-health problems, the most likely to be known to specialist service networks and it will be possible to undertake a manual data collection exercise. Estimates can be made by asking individual workers to list their case loads according to length of contact with services. Care should be taken, however, to ensure that people with long histories of contacts are not double-counted as they appear on more than one person's case-load list. The benefits of a manual counting exercise could be enhanced further if results were used to form the basis of a case-load monitoring system. A good background understanding of the characteristics of the populations to be served should enable published research on incidence, prevalence and clinical needs to be applied specifically.

Although the majority of people with a diagnosis of schizophrenia will be known to service providers, there is a substantial minority of clients who do not accept the "medical model" of schizophrenia and who may have dropped out of conventional models of care. They are an important group, who are likely to reject traditional services and authorities which aim to provide comprehensive care should recognise that they should offer a variety of models and approaches so that clients can make choices.

It will not be necessary in initial stages of planning to be precise about numbers. It will, however, be necessary to have a broad understanding of the relative size of particular patient groups so that their specific needs can be estimated and priorities for care identified. How those groups should be identified and described will be a matter of local choice. For example, groups might be based upon age, clinical categories, geographical location, service groups (e.g. day-patients), length of time in service contact (short-term, medium-term, long-term) or any combination of these or other factors. It is suggested here that the least helpful of these options is to describe patients in terms of service groups, which is, unfortunately, an approach which is often followed. Describing someone as, for example, a "day-patient" has several major disadvantages. It ignores the fact that individuals often use more than one type of service simultaneously; it does not describe or imply any particular needs the person may have; and it ignores the dynamics of care in that the needs of people with long-term requirements for care will vary over the course of their lifetimes.

The requirement to understand the implications of the dynamics of needs is of particular importance when services for people with a diagnosis of schizophrenia are being planned. As the focus of psychiatric services has shifted from long-term in-patient care to supporting people who remain in their own homes, there has been a tendency to use an acute psychiatric model of care. While such a model may be useful for short-term conditions, it is unsuitable for people with long-term needs. One of the most important needs can thus be taken to be the need for a systematic patient review system.

Scientific literature concerning treatment programmes, and individual needs assessments catalogue the kinds of needs which have been identified by professional workers. The views of patients and their carers (e.g. Priestly, 1979), have also been powerfully catalogued via voluntary groups such as the National Schizophrenia Fellowship and Good Practices in Mental Health. At a local level, important sources are local voluntary groups and community-health councils.

It is helpful to assign the task of identifying local needs to a specific individual or small group of individuals who are required to undertake a local needs assessment exercise. If a small group is convened, it should have an identified facilitator who is assigned responsibility for ensuring adherence to agreed timetables and it should also contain at least one service user or a member of a users' group. It should be emphasised that this will not be a once and for all exercise, that progress will be expected in stages (it is useful to identify each stage and its target date for completion) and that the exercise should not be slowed down or abandoned because it is allowed to become bogged down in detail.

It is important to start from the basics, i.e. the need for food, warmth, shelter, companionship, relief of symptoms and the retention of personal control before moving on to the more esoteric needs beloved of professionals. There can be a tendency for professionals to withdraw from the task of cataloguing needs because it is said to be too difficult and complicated, while they ignore needs which could be identified relatively easily. The tendency for professionals to ignore the basics was chillingly brought home to the author during the course of a series of workshops designed to assist planners to identify needs of people with long-term mental-health problems. Over the course of five workshops, not a single working professional identified the basic need for patients to be able to communicate with workers. Thus, the requirements for access to fluent speakers of foreign languages (important in areas where high proportions of residents do not speak English fluently) and to people who can communicate with deaf and/or blind patients were completely overlooked.

If a start is made on the basics, for example, ascertaining that a given number of people need somewhere to live, need warmth and food, require some treatment which relieves symptoms and an annual review, then progress can be made later on on a more detailed needs review. It might then be appropriate to consider where these people currently live, what their domestic circumstances are, what treatment do they currently receive, are their symptoms controlled?, etc. A review of needs will point to the components which should be included in a review system and is fundamental to the process of setting priorities.

The tendency for planning to start with a review of what services already exist and to decide how they should be expanded must be firmly resisted. The review of existing services should take place only when needs and priorities have been established. Producing estimates of the likely size and nature of mental health needs will be a time consuming and skilled activity and it must be recognised that considerable resources are required to do it properly. However, because resources should be much more effectively targeted when needs have been established, the investment in good information should be cost effective.

Principles, aims, objectives and priorities

Having formulated estimates of the size and nature of mental-health problems within a community, the next issue to be addressed concerns organisational purpose. As briefly discussed above, each local community will contain a variety of agencies, statutory and voluntary, which will have some involvement or role in offering treatment, care or support to people with mental-health problems. As need is infinite, if organisational chaos and concomitant lack of accountability is not to occur, each component of the health and social-care system must be clear about its own purpose and how that purpose relates to the purposes of the other components. For example, if the only medical services available were organised at primary-care level, the organisational purpose of general practitioners would be very different than if medical services were also available at a "specialist" level at hospitals. Each community will have its own individual mix of voluntary services; statutory services, particularly those run by local authorities will also vary in their abilities or desires to provide particular kinds of treatment and/or care.

The shift from large institutions to decentralised and dispersed services for people with mental-health difficulties, now generally accepted in developed countries as the model for the future, has been associated with changes in prevailing service principles and objectives. Specific plans, however, rarely make explicit the values and overall objectives which underpin them, even though the latter directly influence the most prosaic intentions. For example, an underlying philosophy and objective of "custody and containment" of people with mental-health problems is likely to result in the formulation of very different plans than those which would result from the philosophy and aim of encouraging maximum individual self-determination.

The need to formulate explicit principles, aims and objectives has particular force when services for people with long-term mental health problems are being planned. Because support and/or treatment are frequently required for many years, it is all too easy to lose sight of long-term goals. For example, schizophrenia can be a long-term disabling condition though it is likely that disabilities have been exacerbated by the adoption of policies which had underlying principles of "custody and containment". These principles were exemplified by the policy and practice of providing long-term custodial care in large institutions. Even when services are no longer based on long-term hospitalisation, there may be little effort made (beyond the provision of medication) to implement active treatment programmes. In these cases, an underlying philosophy of "containment" can be seen to live on in practice even though it may not be acknowledged explicitly.

Purposes and principles or values are not discrete entities, as principles inform purposes. Further, purposes and principles will underpin activity and practice. Until aims and philosophies are made explicit, performance cannot be monitored in any meaningful way as there will be no agreed criteria upon which to judge "success" or "failure". Thus, a statement which outlines organisational purpose, principles and values in relation to overall needs must be issued if organisations are to be held accountable for their activities.

As infinite resources are not available, some method of rationing or prioritising must also be adopted. In privately funded health-care systems, rationing is based upon price and ability and willingness to pay. In publicly financed systems, rationing tends to be enforced by limiting access to services. Clearly, the extent to which other organisations' purposes address the array of needs identified will influence the individual statements of organisational purpose, but even so, it is unlikely that each agency will have sufficient resources to address its stated organisational purpose to the fullest possible extent. It is, therefore, necessary to prioritise demands within each organisation. An example of how organisational purpose unlinked to priority setting can contribute to confused operational objectives can be found in relation to community mental-health centres where an organisational objective of providing a comprehensive service can result in services for people with schizophrenia being reduced as demands for services from other, larger, groups of clients are met.

While priorities may follow many models, a first priority agreed by many organisations is to save life. Thereafter, agreement is less general. In mental-health services it may be argued that high priority should be given to caring for the groups of people that other services cannot help; to supporting informal carers; to cases which are "treatable" rather than "untreatable"; to the most common conditions, or to the most uncommon conditions.

This book is about providing help for people who have been given a diagnosis of schizophrenia. It can be argued that, as this group of people are unlikely to receive specialist clinical help from any other source than the mental-health services, they should be a high priority group. Further, as major advances in treatments have been demonstrated (for example, drug therapy and family intervention) it may also be claimed that their treatments have a good record of success. Service expansions over the past decade, however, have tended to result in a widening of the boundaries of specialist care (for example, new services offering psycho-sexual counselling have been established; higher proportions of people with non-psychotic diagnoses are admitted to hospital than hitherto) rather than resulting in the provision of more help to traditional clients such as those with psychotic illnesses. We have trained the psycho-sexual counsellors but we have not trained family intervention specialists to the same extent. It is asserted here that this state of affairs has resulted, not from a well thought out and administered plan, but has resulted from a management vacuum demonstrated by the absence of relevant planning and monitoring structures and systems.

Whose principles, aims and objectives?

In many western societies the groups which have the most influence on (as distinct from responsibility for) planning belong to the "providing" professional groups who deliver the care. In the United Kingdom, groups of individual users and supporters have begun increasingly to lobby for the kinds of services they require. However, advocacy schemes are in their infancy and individual users and supporters have little opportunity to influence the kinds of help they receive other than to reject it or parts of it. The people who have the most opportunity to influence the kinds of help on offer are the individuals and groups of individuals who actually organise and deliver services. The most powerful are those who actually interact with clients.

This may be for a variety of reasons—people with mental-health problems are sometimes, because of their disabilities, unable to compete with articulate and powerful professional providers; some clients assume that professional providers "know best". However, a particularly powerful deterrent to client participation in planning is that there are few mechanisms through which they can influence what is on offer. Even in market-oriented services, real consumer choice is limited by lack of information, lack of finance and/or lack of coordinated service networks. People with psychoses are especially disadvantaged and frequently have to rely on services for many years.

Aims and objectives of service arrangements are dependent upon prevailing principles/philosophies and value systems in each society but it is likely that each individual or group of individuals within that society will have its own objectives and philosophies—at least a proportion of which will be in conflict with those of others.

The fact that, in practice, the aims and philosophies of health and other professionals influence service delivery styles and patterns more than any other single factor is perhaps one of the reasons why much service planning has so little relevance to the real needs either of whole communities or of individuals. It might be thought that in order to provide a more balanced view of what services are required, equal numbers of users and professionals should contribute to the formulation of policies and priorities through membership of management boards, planning teams, etc.

However, much resistance to such ideas may be found among professionals. This resistance will be difficult to justify if one of the principles of service provision is that services should meet needs. Until adequate consumer representation can be achieved via membership of formal decision-making bodies it will be helpful at least to invite users—both individuals and groups—to participate in *ad hoc* workshops or task centred groups which concern themselves with formulating and implementing service plans. Health-promotion activity in the mental-health field has begun lately to focus on issues of consumer empowerment.

Access to and membership of decision-making bodies should extend client involvement in strategic planning. Ensuring that individuals have more control over the services they are offered requires a different approach. Changes in the power balance between clients and professionals will demand a change in the training and socialisation of professionals, and a change in clients' attitudes. Such changes will, however, only bear fruit in the distant future. Clients with severe communication problems face particular difficulties in asserting themselves and advocacy schemes have a part to play in providing a more immediate solution. As will be discussed in more detail in the context of the Salford experience, the operation of case management systems also offer an opportunity to increase individual client involvement in formulating a care strategy.

Strategies and management arrangements

Developing contracts

Choosing appropriate strategies to achieve stated aims and objectives and priorities is the fourth stage of the planning process. The traditional separation of administrative and clinical managerial concerns has been associated with the issue of clinical freedom and professional versus managerial responsibility.

Management structures and operational policies are key components of implementation strategies, both of which affect the day to day organisation of clinical services. In the UK public sector, clinical independence has not only been defended strongly by the medical profession, but other occupational groups for example, psychologists and nurses have also claimed professional independence.

There has been no consensus reached concerning the boundaries between professional independence and management responsibility. However, as contracts between purchasers and providers become more tightly defined, the freedom of health professionals to choose whom they treat and how they treat them will lessen. Such a change will decrease the power of professionals to influence service development, but unless service users can increase their influence on service purchasers they may find that a decrease in professional power will not be accompanied by an increase in user power. The requirement to draw up contracts for the provision of health-care will, however, increase local accountability for the services purchased and provided, as health authorities not individual professionals have a duty to purchase and specify the kinds of health services they require for their population. It is important, therefore, that service-users demand the quantity and quality of services they require.

It has already been pointed out that morbidity within planning populations is likely to vary, and in order to address this issue, a notion of equity must be applied which is based on the likelihood of gaining access to treatment facilities for particular client groups.

Establishing inter-professional agreements on competencies

Not only is the assignation of management responsibility hindered by the lack of consensus on the proper division between management and clinical responsibility but also the issue of the relationships between occupational groups and the implications for clinical responsibility is a further unresolved difficulty. Should, for instance, nurses carry out instructions given by doctors or should they exercise independent professional judgements and make their own decisions concerning appropriate interventions?

These issues are relevant to all clinical specialties, but within the mental-health field, and especially for people who have been diagnosed as suffering from schizophrenia, they are of particular importance for several reasons. Needs for care are likely to go beyond the competencies of any single professional group and the permutations and combinations of care required for any individual at any one time are large. Some responsibility for coordinating these services needs to be assigned. Further complications arise because although on the one hand the underlying theoretical perspectives associated with particular occupational groups may be in conflict with each other, on the other hand there is thought to be some skill overlap between most occupational groups but there are no commonly defined skill standards agreed between them.

For example, each occupational group would be likely to claim competence in counselling skills, but there would be no agreement concerning the extent to which counselling competencies would be considered to be the same between doctors, nurses, psychologists and occupational therapists. Because there is no inter-professional agreement concerning the basic skills and competencies of individual occupational groups, operational difficulties arise. Unless basic competencies are clearly defined and understood, it will be impossible to decide which individual or profession should undertake specific caring or treatment tasks. Some courses have begun to be established which have obtained accreditation from more than one professional group. Such developments will offer important advantages in the future, but for the present, health authorities will have to seek local inter-professional agreements.

The increasing use of "open" referral systems aggravates the problem as more and more individual workers are accepting referrals for treatment and care when the referrer has no clear idea of the level of competence of the worker concerned and has insufficient information with which to make a rational choice concerning the most appropriate professional to undertake specific clinical tasks.

It is also important to distinguish between competence to prescribe a treatment and competence to carry it out. Competence to carry out a prescribed treatment programme does not confer the competence to design it. The distinction between the competence to prescribe and the competence to administer drugs is generally understood. An understanding of this distinction in relation to other therapies is less general and failure to understand its importance can have dire consequences for patients and their families. Mention has already been made of the consequences for service-delivery patterns of the increasing tendency for individual professionals to accept referrals directly from GPs and patients. The misprescription of treatments must also be acknowledged as a probable consequence of the increasing use of open referral systems if competence to prescribe has not been clearly set out and legitimated.

An example of the confusion surrounding competencies can be seen in relation to the development of community psychiatric nursing services. Early UK CPN services were set up in order to ensure greater continuity of care between hospital and community for patients with a diagnosis of schizophrenia (May and Moore, 1963). As CPN services became more established, they expanded their roles and more and more became attached to primary-care teams and accepted referrals directly from other primary-care workers. Not all CPNs received training for community work over and above their Registered Mental Nurse training. The CPN training courses were not, until more recently, skill-based so enhanced therapeutic skills could not necessarily be expected of "trained CPNs". Traditional psychiatric nurse training and experience did not equip nurses with the skills and competencies required to manage case loads (e.g. they had had no previous responsibility to admit or discharge patients from care and had not had responsibility for assessing needs for care other than for in-patient nursing care) and it can be argued that it did not train nurses to prescribe all the treatments they in fact carried out.

Nevertheless, these services were popular with general practitioners who felt there was a clear need for them and enthusiastically referred many of their patients they felt had psychological problems. In parallel with these primary-care developments, psychiatrists referred many of their patients who were maintained on depot neuroleptic drugs to CPNs, confident that this would provide the kind of community-based assistance required for their patients and their patients' supporters. It was unusual for CPN managers to have instituted any information systems which would allow CPN activity to be monitored, and as the main referrers to CPN services were vociferous in their claims that there were additional needs to be met, CPN services expanded apace.

As research evidence has emerged (Sladden 1979; Skidmore and Friend, 1984; Wooff, Goldberg and Fryers, 1988; Wooff and Goldberg, 1988) it has become clear that expectations and practice cannot necessarily be assumed to coincide. Neither GPs, psychiatrists nor nurse managers had equipped themselves with sufficient information to ensure that the services they assumed were being delivered were actually being delivered. Neither had nurse managers ensured that their staff were equipped with the skills to undertake the tasks they were assigned.

Specifying the functions of service components and ensuring choice

A confusion between objectives (where one wishes to go) and strategies (how one gets there) contributes to the lack of clarity concerning the functions of various parts of service networks. To take the example of day-care service provision, patients may be referred for day-care with no specific objective specified. If the day-care service in question has no specific function or set of functions delineated, then there can be no basis for consistent assessment of how far provision of day-care is either useful or appropriate for particular patients.

The failure to specify the functions of service components in anything other then general terms is likely to constrain the choices available both to referrers and to patients. All-purpose, generalist components can easily become purposeless, aimless dumping grounds. There is a danger that they allow referrers to avoid making specific treatment plans by providing an all-purpose option. It may also be that much needed specialist services do not develop because the generalist services are seen to plug the more obvious gaps in care.

Generalist service components (for example non-specialist day-hospitals and in-patient wards) can demonstrate clarity of purpose if all their patients have clearly documented individually negotiated treatment plans. Some specific therapies require individual treatment plans to be negotiated, formulated and their implementation monitored. Behavioural therapies are a case in point. It must be said, however, that much of the time patients are in contact with mental-health services, they are not receiving one of these therapies.

There are many care-plan models some of which are associated with particular professional groups. They generally share the following features. They must be written, the treatment or care must have clear objectives, and the nature of the professional interventions to be used and their outcomes must be specified. Although many professionals purport to use care plans, the acid test is whether one can be produced for every patient treated.

Operational policies should follow similar patterns to individual care plans though they relate to organisations rather than to individuals. They should include a statement of purpose, the range of interventions available (together with a list of staff competencies), mechanisms of referral and discharge, operational and administrative arrangements such as hours of opening, etc. lines of accountability and responsibility and information and monitoring arrangements. Each service component should have an operational policy which should be reviewed at fixed intervals. It is also a good idea for each component to produce a short annual report or review of its operation.

The way in which budgets are structured will have an important influence on the extent to which services can be tailored to meet needs. The traditional practice is to gear budgets to individual professional groups and to institutions or service components, e.g. hospital nursing budgets and community nursing budgets or psychology budgets which may relate to general health as well as psychiatric services. Such arrangements reinforce professional barriers and militate against the adoption of a flexible approach to skills and facilities provision. Further, budgets have tended to be historically-based rather than needs-based. They will thus tend to reflect past service provision rather than present or future service needs. This factor, combined with the perceived status of the large budget, virtually guarantees that budget systems based on service components and professional groupings will be inherently conservative and will be unlikely to be flexible enough to respond to changing needs with any degree of speed.

Budgets based either on client groups and/or on geographical sectors enable a more flexible approach to be pursued. Services planned and managed within geographical sectors are well placed to establish levels of morbidity, involve local people in decision-making processes and to monitor the results of service interventions. Such an approach, involving as it should, the end of budgets for individual professional groups, is likely to meet with fierce resistance from the managers of those groups. Their roles must of necessity change and their managerial responsibilities will lie in the field of the promotion of professional excellence as they will have to demonstrate their effectiveness and relevance if they are to preserve their share of service provision. The budget-holder for a specific geographical sector will have a clear responsibility for the total mental-health service provided in his or her sector.

Meeting the priorities

Although the notion of assigning priorities for care is generally accepted in theory, in practice, this concept is often applied by default rather than by design. The number and type of new patient referrals accepted on to a case load in effect implements a set of priorities. Given that the amount of work time an individual is contracted to provide is finite and that he/she is fully occupied, accepting new referrals can only occur either if existing patients are discharged at the same rate as new referrals are added and/or if the amount of time allocated to existing patients is reduced. The principles applied to case-load management thus express decisions made concerning priorities. There is a danger that the "squeeze" on resources which is likely to occur if active case-load monitoring and management is not carried out, will occur in an unplanned and unmanaged way.

Managing resources

Clarifying and delineating functions will be of little practical use if either physical resources are lacking or staff are not equipped to carry out the tasks assigned to them. A strategy must therefore include a plan to provide the resources to carry out agreed aims and objectives.

The shift from institutional care which has for so long been the declared aim of many service-planners has been hampered by the fact that the resources consumed by large mental hospitals have not been able to be released to provide a new style service. Community-based services have tended to develop using extra resources rather than resulting from a shift in resource from hospital to community.

It has long been recognised that probably the most difficult task facing those who attempt to bring about the contraction or closure of a large institution, is the relocation of hospital-based staff. Therefore, if contraction or closure is really to occur, a staff relocation strategy must be pursued actively. A more difficult problem to resolve locally concerns the availability of skills. The issue of competencies has been discussed earlier, but it is appropriate to raise it again here because skills are vital resources.

Clinical staff training is controlled by individual professional bodies. If these professions do not ensure that their members have the skills required to undertake the tasks required, local health authorities must decide either to provide supplementary training to members of the established professions, or they must decide to employ members of staff who do have the skills required whether or not they belong to one of the traditional professional groups. The ability to take this latter course is restricted by the terms and conditions of service under which health-service staff can be employed but recent changes in legislation have enabled health authorities to purchase services for their patients from outside the National Health Service network.

The emergence of care staff who are not aligned with any specific professional group is one response to perceived skill shortages although there are fears that such an approach might lead to the inappropriate use of unskilled staff. It might also be said that the increasing professionalisation of some health-care staff, particularly nurses, has created a need for staff who are willing and able to offer general help with tasks of daily living many of which have been abandoned in the rush to professionalise nursing activity.

The concept of needs assessment developed by Brewin and colleagues (Brewin et al., 1987) is directly applicable to this question. The concept of over-provision of resource is an important one. An analysis of needs based on needs for knowledge, skills and physical resources might very well not match up to what is already available. Such analyses may well reveal an over-provision of some resources—either physical or skill, and an under-provision of others. The difficulties experienced by attempting to close large mental hospitals to some extent illustrates just this point, because not only is there a physical over-provision of a large redundant building and an under-provision of more domestic type accommodation, but there is an over-provision of the skills required for custody and containment and an under-provision of the knowledge and skills required to encourage and sustain a more independent lifestyle for patients.

It is this final analysis of the gaps between what is required and what is available that is what most people understand to be the planning function. It is however, only one component of a total package and part of a dynamic process which should evolve continually. It should not always be solved by the approach which dictates that under-provision should be funded exclusively from new money but should take account of the management responsibility to shift resources used in the over-provision of some services. It is asserted here that a well-organised planning process should, if patients' needs and the delineation of skills required to meet those needs have been identified clearly, ensure that skills supply and demand are synchronised. This will involve clarifying what skills are presently available, what skills are in short supply and producing a recruitment and training strategy to meet any identified skills shortfall.

The role of care management

A tool first developed in the United States, emerges as a mechanism which combines the requirements for monitoring the needs, strategies and outcomes of care of people with long-term mental-health problems. Appropriately designed care management systems offer the opportunity to assemble clinical and social information in such a way as to allow the knowledge and experience of individual clients, their supporters and direct professional carers to be combined and analysed for whole communities.

Care management systems vary in the ways in which they are organised and managed, but have certain characteristics in common. Intagliata (1982) listed the following main components: a comprehensive assessment of needs; the development of an individual package of care to meet those needs, ensuring that the services are delivered; monitoring the quality of the services provided and offering long-term flexible support.

Clearly such systems are not only suitable for people with long-term mental health problems, but they are particularly suitable for them because of the complexities of needs an individual with an illness such as schizophrenia is likely to have. Mental-health-service development has, until relatively recently, tended to concentrate on acute service models and care-management systems, which although they impose some discipline and structure to clinical inputs do not interfere with clinical freedom to implement specific programmes of treatment. They do, however, because they monitor need, inputs and outputs, offer a vehicle both for ensuring that service activity is in line with organisational purpose and priorities and for enabling needs to be measured against service capacity to deliver. They can thus generate specifically clinical as well as management information.

The advantages and disadvantages of care management in relation to long-term mental health problems have been discussed by Shepherd (1990) who points out that they are not substitutes for resources. Where care managers see their role as resource managers rather than architects of high quality services, this must be recognised as a potential danger (Renshaw, 1988).

Monitoring and management control

Recent debates on the best ways of organising mental-health services have centred upon organisational issues such as whether community psychiatric nurses or other workers should be attached to primary-care bases and whether community mental-health centres should replace hospitals as the focuses of mental health care. Whether or not either of these organisational solutions can be considered successful will depend upon the organisational purpose of the mental-health service. Research has shown that siting mental-health workers away from hospital bases is associated with shifts away both from caring for people who have been diagnosed as suffering from schizophrenia and other clients with severe, long-term disabling conditions (Wooff and Goldberg, 1988; Wooff, Goldberg and Fryers, 1988; Patmore and Weaver, 1991). However, it is argued here that the reasons why such shifts in case load composition follow shifts of site is because organisational purpose has not been made explicit and monitoring and management control systems have not been implemented at the sites concerned.

Control of case loads emerges as a key management tool and it is of concern that case load monitoring remains the exception rather than the rule in many districts. Consultants have clear responsibility for managing their own case loads to the extent that they accept new referrals from general practitioners and discharge patients back to the care of their general practitioners when they consider it to be appropriate. However, because very few suitable information systems are in use, monitoring of consultants' case loads has been rare.

The ability to control case loads has always been associated with claims for professional autonomy and independence, and the model developed by the medical professions has been followed by newer and younger professional groups. As a consequence, not only have other professional groups failed to establish adequate monitoring arrangements but they have also, by increasingly accepting direct referrals (i.e. referrals from general practitioners, other health and social service agencies, voluntary groups and directly from clients themselves), increased the number of individuals who actively implement their own individual notions of priorities.

In contrast to health professional groups, monitoring has been an important component of social work service provision, with responsibility for this task being assigned clearly to senior social workers and social work team leaders. This acceptance of a hierarchy of responsibility for case-load management within social work contrasts markedly with the way in which community psychiatric nursing has developed. Here, an increasing trend towards the acceptance of "open" referrals, and attachment to primary-care bases has been associated with a shift away from caring for people with problems associated with a diagnosis of schizophrenia (Wooff, Rose and Street, 1989). If such a shift forms part of a managed, monitored and reviewed service plan, it may well be thought to be appropriate. When it takes "research" to demonstrate it, then it becomes clear that management arrangements are inadequate.

It might be argued that the case-load monitoring and control exercised by social services departments has acted against the interests of people with mental-health problems because mental-health care has a lower priority than, for example, child protection. This is to argue for services which do not have clear policies and priorities. While it may be true that such services might offer care to particular groups, they will do so by accident rather than design. It is difficult to hold such services to account simply because their involvement with particular clients is so haphazard. If particular client groups do not receive services because they do not belong to priority groups it is at least possible to argue either that the priorities should be changed or that resources should be made available to offer care to a wider range of client groups. As has been mentioned already, priorities must be set in order to ration finite resources. It follows that the kinds of services delivered must offer good value for money and that the monitoring process should enable some assessment of economy, efficiency and effectiveness to be made.

Having identified needs and priorities, the capacity of the organisation to deliver services which address those needs and priorities must be considered. Rather than following the approach which starts by asking the questions "what have we got and what can we do with it?" we should at this stage be in a position to ask "have we got the skills and resources to deliver what is required?"

ENSURING IMPLEMENTATION

Supply and demand in market-oriented services are regulated by the price mechanism of a "fee for service" payment. In societies such as the United Kingdom, where the vast majority of mental-health services are provided by the public sector and financed from general taxation, the extent to which finance for services is made available is dependent upon a complex process of competition for health-care funding. Further, the extent to which "health" and "social" concerns must both be addressed demands that services provided by a variety of different agencies must also be integrated and synchronised (Audit Commission, 1986).

It follows that mental-health-service planning in such a context, must address the general issue of the overall health and social needs of society; compete with other health specialties for resources and integrate services provided from a variety of non-health agencies as well as plan how to use its extant resources. In making assessments, trying to find a hostel place, deciding the interval between one appointment and the next, these "planning" activities are undertaken by professionals on behalf of their individual patients/clients on a daily basis. It thus becomes clear that professional activity, management and planning are inextricably linked and that the planning "challenge" is to ensure that strategies are devised and implemented which are based on individual clients' needs.

In practice, however, planners frequently concern themselves exclusively with deciding which of an array of bids for extra resources to support (generally bids for buildings and/or numbers of staff) and to ensuring that the necessary administrative requirements for supporting the bids are met.

They rarely concern themselves with operational policies and monitoring mechanisms as these are considered to be management issues and not their concern. Furthermore, professionals who regard themselves as being independent practitioners may consider attempts to specify operational policies or monitoring mechanisms to be management interference in clinical matters. In such a climate, where planning, management and clinical judgement are seen as distinct and exclusive areas of responsibility, there is little prospect that the services provided will be other than a reflection of individual practitioners' preferences.

This is not to argue for a "top–down" approach but rather to argue for good "bottom–up" information so that clear strategies and priorities can be agreed. The arguments do, however, come out firmly against the present system whereby the direction of services for whole populations is organised and developed on the basis of individual professional judgments and activities.

PEOPLE WITH A DIAGNOSIS OF SCHIZOPHRENIA—REDRESSING THE BALANCE

Although much of this chapter has been concerned with service organisation and planning in general, the application of the principles and ideas discussed is likely to result in improved services for people with a diagnosis of schizophrenia and other people with long-term mental-health problems.

The people in this particular client group have been adversely affected by poor service organisation and planning in two main ways. Firstly, as they formed a high proportion of people who had been in psychiatric hospitals for many years, they have suffered both from the failure to recognise them as a priority group and their consequent accumulation on "back wards", and from the lack of progress in closing these institutions. Secondly, where community services did develop, they tended to expand the boundaries of specialist psychiatric care rather than offering increased help to people with psychotic illnesses.

The failure to channel increased community support towards this obvious priority group is now beginning to be understood. It is unfortunate that such an understanding has been gained largely as a result of research activity and this fact underlines the necessity of developing urgently adequate service monitoring mechanisms. Technology has become accessible both because it has become relatively inexpensive to install and because software has become more user-friendly. An obstacle which still remains is the data-handling skill shortage. The best use of information technology for monitoring purposes is likely to come about only when teams of skilled personnel are established so that technical data-handling skills can be supplemented by knowledge of mental-health and management issues. Employing a medical secretary to input data into a commercial package just will not do. Monitoring arrangements should be specified for every service development, and should be an integral part of every development plan. If it is not, resources will continue to be utilised in an uncontrolled way and managers will have failed to discharge their duty to the general public they purport to serve.

THE SALFORD EXPERIENCE

Salford Metropolitan District is a largely urban area of North-West England. It was formed in 1974 from two adjacent areas, Salford County Borough (Salford East) and an area which had previously been part of Lancashire County (Salford West). The two parts of Salford had very different socio-demographic characteristics. Salford East had high levels of unemployment and long-term ill-health: a high proportion of its residents lived in council housing. Its population had declined from almost 250 000 in 1931 to under 100 000 in 1981. Salford West was more suburban in character and environmentally and socially more balanced. Its population had rapidly increased until 1971 .

In Salford East pioneering mental health services had been developed in the early 1960s and the local authority and health authority had close co-operative working relationships. After 1974 this cooperation extended to Salford West. A large mental hospital, situated adjacent to the health district but managed by it, provided a mixture of acute and long-stay in-patient care. Short-stay in-patient beds were also available at the local district general hospital. Out-patient facilities were well developed with most psychiatrists holding some clinics at health centres. Mental-health social workers worked within the psychiatric service and non-specialist social work support was offered by the generic social work service. Community psychiatric nurses were attached to health centres.

In 1968 a Psychiatric Case Register was established. It contained data which was patient-based and included details of in-patient, day-patient, out-patient, social work (specialist and non-specialist) and community psychiatric nursing care. It was unique in its continuous and comprehensive data collection (Fryers and Wooff, 1989).

Estimates of chronicity

An analysis of all patients seen in 1976 and 1986 who were not long-term in-patients found that 718 people (a ratio of 2.7 per 1000 total population) fulfilled the criteria. This figure represented 22% of all persons seen in 1976 who was not a long-stay in-patient. Because some patients have intermittent contact over the years, this figure is likely to be an underestimate of the extent of chronicity within the mental-health service.

Ninety-three per cent were aged less than 65 in 1976, 41% were men, 42% had a diagnosis of schizophrenia and 29% had a diagnosis of depression. The ratios per 1000 total population were 3.5 in Salford East and 2.1 in Salford West. Wide variations in the prevalence of schizophrenia in Salford had also been reported by Freeman and Alpert (1986). Comparative data from Nottingham (Nottingham Psychiatric Register, 1989) showed that fewer of a similar group of patients (25%) had a diagnosis of schizophrenia but that proportions with a diagnosis of depression were similar (27%).

Although Salford had a comprehensive mental-health service network, over the 11-year period 23% of the 718 people identified had no mental-health social work care, 29% had no CPN care, 66% had no day-hospital care, 77% had no local authority mental-health day-care, 31% had never been admitted and 5% had never had an out-patient contact. The mean number of admissions per person was 3.5 (range 0–37) and the mean number of out-patient attendances was 20.5 (range 0–99). Sixty per cent had some form of contact in each of the 11 years and approximately 10% had contact in 4 or less years.

Service aims, principles and priorities

The mental-health planning team in Salford had issued a document which set out the aims and principles of its service. Services were planned according to client group and workshops relating to each client group had been organised which had generated lists of needs and strategies for meeting those needs. People with long-term mental-health problems had been identified as a priority group. Key service principles in relation to this group were that services should be comprehensive, based on teamwork, that there should be written care plans negotiated with the client and if appropriate, with informal carers and that people should be enabled to carry on their chosen lifestyles. A network of locally based mental-health centres was planned. An important ongoing activity was to identify the quantity and quality of the skills available within Salford and the practicability of building in contractual obligations to adhere to formally agreed service principles was under discussion.

An analysis of service provision, begun with the data analysis given above, showed the following shortcomings. An acute service model was being applied to long-term problems; no formal statements of plans and objectives for individual patients were used; medical review was irregular when patients did not attend as out-patients; little help with day-to-day living tasks was given; there were no mechanisms for comprehensive staff liaison; no clarification of individual professional responsibilities; little involvement of the patient or his or her supporters in formulating personal plans and very little active therapeutic input. Other work conducted in Salford had shown that expanded community-based services had tended to extend the client-base rather than deliver extra care to clients with a diagnosis of schizophrenia (Wooff, Goldberg and Fryers, 1986, 1988; Fryers and Wooff, 1989).

Adopting strategies

A care-management system was developed in Salford as a response to this situation. Department of Health funding was used to employ a full-time system coordinator and to provide supporting computer hardware and software. Its objectives followed those laid down by the planning team and may be summarised thus. Assessment was to be comprehensive, structured and systematic; care plans were to be written, they were to involve clients and their supporters in their negotiation, they were to be circulated to all members of the professional team including general practitioners and the clients themselves; systematic monitoring and review was to be carried out. A detailed account of its function appears elsewhere (Wooff and Whitehead, 1988).

The system began in an inner city sector of Salford and covered a population of approximately 50 000. Its target group was people with long-term mental-health problems, and in particular people with a diagnosis of schizophrenia. It was decided that the professional team should be built around a core group representing psychiatrists, psychologists, occupational therapists, general social workers, mental-health social workers, community psychiatric nurses and general practitioners. Other workers involved with individual clients were also encouraged to participate. Information on reviews and care plans was stored on a microcomputer to facilitate the production of details of meeting schedules and to perform systematic analyses of documentation on patients' needs and characteristics. The system was organised and managed by a full time coordinator who had a professional background in mental-health social work but who had no responsibility for the provision of direct client care herself. The coordinator acted as organiser, facilitator, advocate, arbitrator and care-plan generator. Overall management responsibility for the project was undertaken by the Manager of the Mental Health Information Unit (KW) with guidance from a Steering Committee which consisted of senior professional managers and representatives of service-users and their supporters.

Newly referred patients were drawn into a rolling programme and initially, existing patients were referred by team members. A full list of patients who fulfilled the criteria laid down was obtained from the Mental Health Information Unit and validated. This list then formed the basis of the future programme. Assessment documents were drawn up by the Coordinator from a variety of sources. Research documentation was adapted by team members and documents evolved over time, eventually incorporating numerically coded data to facilitate analysis of needs. Two separate semi-structured assessment documents were used—one containing medical information which was completed by the psychiatrist(s) in the team, and one which covered social and non-medical mental-health topics which was completed by non-medical team members. A summary of problems and strengths concluded each assessment document.

Following assessments, the team formulated a written care plan which gave details of goals, actions required and individual responsibilities. Review dates were also included. Copies were given to team members, clients and GPs and importantly, copies were filed in hospital case notes so that should the patient be admitted to in-patient care, ward staff would be aware of the overall strategies being followed by community-based staff.

Establishing the system was not without its difficulties. Although the staff involved in the project were prepared to attempt to work as a team it quickly became apparent that there had been little collaboration between them in the past. They had already established individual ways of working and except for their work on the project they continued to function as they always had done. Consequently, participating in the case-management system involved them in additional work. However, when the team had been established for some time and real team cohesion was achieved there was a recognition that in the medium- and long-term collaboration actually reduced the work-load burden.

The mental-health social worker in the team probably undertook the largest additional burden as he/she became more involved than the other members in welfare issues and in consultation and negotiation with relatives. This underlined the deficiencies in the training of health staff in communication skills and the need for a considerable input in terms of finance, housing and so on. On a more positive note, the inclusion of an occupational therapist in the team, while increasing the personal burden on the worker concerned, resulted in much more positive liaison with local authority generic team members which in turn resulted in a much improved provision of home-care assistance and aids and adaptations.

In the early stages of the project it became apparent that the medical assessment was sometimes being completed from case notes rather than resulting from face-to-face contact. This highlighted the problems of irregular medical contact if patients did not attend for their out-patient consultation. Greater use of clinics at GP health-centres reduced the non-attendance rate and the possibility of increasing the number of home visits made by psychiatrists was under investigation.

The perceived needs for a general practitioner on the team and for patients and their supporters to participate in person were not always achieved. However, the views of GPs were actively sought by the use of a brief questionnaire, the response to which was good. The attendance of patients improved when meetings were held in health centres and when they were sent a letter of invitation by the coordinator.

It became clear that systematic working was unlikely to continue in the absence of a team coordinator, and maintaining this provision when Department of Health funding ceased became a problem. In fact, three coordinators had been employed at the time of writing and uncertainty of funding (they were all time-limited contracts) was a severe drawback.

Other possible problems inherent in such a system are that it can threaten established working practices and existing power bases which is likely to result in considerable opposition emerging from the people and professions who perceive such threats. Such systems should threaten poor standards of work but they could reinforce them if team members develop a cosy relationship and if coordinators are of poor quality. Issues which have been contained by maintaining isolated working practices will be forced into the open by the requirements of teamwork and senior managers will have to be prepared to confront and resolve these issues. The initial increased burden of work forces consideration of priorities and it may become apparent that staff priorities are not the same as clients' priorities. Here the clarity of the objectives was a vital ingredient in maintaining the system when it was under attack. Because the system evolved as a direct response to perceived service shortcomings and had the support of the Unit General Manager and other senior staff it was possible to demonstrate clearly that an attack on the system was also an attack on the agreed strategy of the Mental Health Unit. Without such support if team members begin to opt out of a system, it will collapse.

The perceived advantages of the system were that it provided a mechanism for systematic assessment of patients' needs, needs were more precisely defined, inter- and intra-professional coordination improved, more services were mobilised for this client group, responsibilities were clarified and clients and their supporters were consulted and involved more than before. As a management tool, it provided a mechanism for managing multi-disciplinary care, it provided a mechanism by which field workers' knowledge of needs could be systematically documented and drawn to the attention of planners and managers, and by the production of structured documentation it set out minimum acceptable service standards.

In spite of its drawbacks, managers felt that the system was an important mechanism for managing care. It was important for the principles driving the system to be upheld, but its detailed working methods could be adapted to the needs of other sectors of the area. A second case-management system was adopted in another sector of the city and plans to introduce such systems in other sectors were agreed.

CONCLUSION

In spite of the tendency to over complicate the nature of the planning task, the rules are simple. Plan on the basis of needs for particular client groups (we have been particularly concerned with needs of people with a diagnosis of schizophrenia and of other people with long-term mental-health problems); estimate the size of various client groups within geographical sectors; set priorities; implement appropriate management arrangements and monitor outcome.

If these simple rules are followed, there is much less likelihood that services will drift away from caring for one of the most disabled client groups. However much other groups can make valid claims for services, this group have nowhere else to turn for help. This must be recognised and professional carers and service managers must accept their responsibilities to this group of clients and their families and supporters.

REFERENCES

Audit Commission (1986) *Making a Reality of Community Care*, HMSO, London.

Brewin, C.R., Wing, J.K., Mangen, S.P., Brugha, T.S. and MacCarthy, B. (1987) Principles and practice of measuring needs in the long-term mentally ill: the MRC needs for care assessment. *Psychological Medicine*, **17**, 971–81.

Caring for People, Community Care in the Next Decade and Beyond (1989) Report to Parliament by the Secretaries of State for Health, Social Security, Wales and Scotland, Cm 849, HMSO, London.

Caring for People, Community Care in the Next Decade and Beyond (1990) Department of Health Draft Guidance CCI, 1–10.

Department of Health and Social Security (1980) *Inequalities in Health*, Report of a Research Working Group, (Black Report), HMSO, London.

Department of Health and Social Security (1977) Health and Personal Social Services Statistics for England, HMSO, London.

Department of Health and Social Security (1988) Health and Personal Social Services Statistics for England, HMSO, London.

Der, G. (1989) The effects of population changes on long-stay in-patient rates in health services planning and research, contributions from psychiatric case registers. In: J.K. Wing (ed.), *Health Service Planning and Research, Contributions from Psychiatric Case Registers*, pp. 53–7, Gaskell, London.

Freeman, H. and Alpert, M. (1986) Prevalence of schizophrenia: geographical variations in an urban population. *British Journal of Social and Clinical Psychiatry*, **4**, 67–75.

Fryers, T. and Wooff, K. (1989) A Decade of Mental Health Care in an English Urban Community: Patterns and Trends in Salford, 1976–87. In: J.K. Wing (ed.) *Health Services Planning and Research, Contributions for Psychiatric Case Registers*, pp. 31–52, Gaskell, London.

Giggs, J.A. (1984) Residential mobility and mental health. In: H.L. Freeman (ed.), *Mental Health and the Environment*, pp. 327–54, Churchill Livingstone, London.

Goldberg, D.P. and Blackwell, B. (1970) Psychiatric illness in general practice: a detailed study using a new method of case identification. *British Medical Journal*, **ii**, 439–43.

Goldberg, D.P. and Huxley, P. (1980) *Mental Illness in the Community: The Pathway to Psychiatric Care*, Tavistock, London.

Intagliata, J. (1982) Improving the quality of community care for the chronically mentally disabled: the role of case management. *Schizophrenia Bulletin*, **8**, 655–74.

Jarman, B. (1983) Identification of underprivileged areas. *British Medical Journal*, 28 May, **286**, 1705–9.

Jarman, B. (1984) Underprivileged areas: validation and distribution of scores. *British Medical Journal*, 8 December, **289**, 1587–92.

Jennings, C., Der, G., Robinson, C., Rose, S., De Alarcon, J., Hunter, D., Holliday, R. and Moss, N. (1989) In-patient statistics from eight psychiatric case registers, 1977–83. In: J.K. Wing (ed.), *Health Services Planning and Research, Contributions from Psychiatric Case Registers*, pp. 13–30, Gaskell, London..

Link, B.G., Dohrenwend, B.P. and Skodol, A.E. (1987) Socio-economic status and schizophrenia: noisome occupational characteristics as a risk factor. In: M.C. Angermeyer (ed.), *From Social Class to Social Stress: New Developments in Psychiatric Epidemiology*, pp. 82–105, Springer-Verlag, Berlin, Heidelberg.

May, A.R. and Moore, S. (1963) The mental nurse in the community. *Lancet*, **i**, 213–14.

Neugebauer, R., Dohrenwend, B. and Dohrenwend, B. (1980) Formulation of hypotheses about the true prevalence of functional psychiatric disorders among adults in the United States. In: B. Dohrenwend, B. Dohrenwend, M. Gould, B. Link, R. Neugebauer and Wuntsch-Hitzigr, *Mental illness in the United States: epidemiological estimates*, pp. 45–91, Praeger, New York.

Nottingham Psychiatric Register (1989) Personal communication.

Patmore, C. and Weaver, T. (1990) Rafts on an open sea. *Health Service Journal*, **100**(5222), 1510–12.

Patmore, C. and Weaver, T. (1991) *Community Mental Health Centres: Lessons for Planners and Managers*, Good Practices in Mental Health, London.

Renshaw, J. (1988) Care in the community: individual care planning and case management. *British Journal of Social Work*, **10**, 79–105.

Shepherd, G. (1990) Case management. *Health Trends*, **22**(2), 59–61.

Shepherd, M., Cooper, B., Brown, A.C. and Kalton, G.W. (1966) *Psychiatric Illness in General Practice*, Oxford University Press.

Skidmore, D. and Friend, W. (1984) Muddling through. *Nursing Times Community Outlook*, 9 May, 179–80.

Sladden, S. (1979) *Psychiatric Nursing in the Community: a Study of the Working Situation*. Churchill Livingstone, Edinburgh.

TenHorn, G.H.M.M., Giel, R., Gulbinat, W.H. and Henderson, J.H. (eds) (1986) *Psychiatric Case Registers in Public Health: a Worldwide Inventory 1960–1985*, Elsevier, Amsterdam.

Wooff, K. and Goldberg, D.P. (1988) Further observations on the practice of community care in Salford: differences between community psychiatric nurses and mental health social workers. *British Journal of Psychiatry*, **153**, 30–7.

Wooff, K., Goldberg, D.P. and Fryers, T. (1986) Patients in receipt of community psychiatric nursing care in Salford 1976–82. *Psychological Medicine*,**16**, 407–14.

Wooff, K., Goldberg, D.P. and Fryers, T. (1988) The practice of community psychiatric nursing and mental health social work in Salford: some implications for community care. *British Journal of Psychiatry*, **152**, 783–92.

Wooff, K. and Whitehead, C. (1988) Working together for the chronically mentally disabled. *World Health Forum*, **9**, 420–5.

Wooff, K., Rose, S. and Street, J. (1989) Community psychiatric nursing services in Salford, Worcester and Southampton. In: J.K. Wing (ed.), *Health Services Planning and Research, Contributions from Psychiatric Case Registers*, Gaskell, London.

Working for Patients (1989) Presented to Parliament by the Secretaries of State for Health, Wales, Northern Ireland and Scotland by Command of Her Majesty, January 1989, HMSO, London.

Chapter 13

The Psychological Management of Schizophrenia: into the Next Decade

MAX BIRCHWOOD AND NICHOLAS TARRIER

THEORETICAL AND CONCEPTUAL CONSIDERATIONS

No science or body of knowledge is without its controversies and conflicts, in fact it is such debates that promote the extension of knowledge. Mental health as a field of study has certainly been a trail blazer in the controversy stakes. Clements and Turpin (Chapter 2) have argued that, despite the continuing debate over the usefulness of the concept of schizophrenia and doubts about its validity, psychologists need an adequate framework for psychological formulation of the phenomena subsumed by the diagnosis of schizophrenia. Furthermore, given that mental health is a multi-agency concern, this formulation needs to be accessible to professions who have a range of backgrounds other than psychology. Vulnerability models are advanced as the most likely candidates to fit this bill at the present time. Such models as proposed by Zubin and his colleagues (e.g. Zubin and Spring, 1977; Zubin, Magaziner and Steinhaur, 1983) have the advantage of being multi-faceted and operating on a number of different levels. Although not without their detractors, these models have the *potential* to integrate data from different domains, in particular the interaction of biological and environmental influences (Birchwood, Hallett and Preston, 1988). The potential to provide such a conceptual integration is essential in dealing with such a complex phenomena as schizophrenia. Nor should the potential of vulnerability conceptualisations to drive a holistic approach to assessment, treatment and service-delivery be underestimated.

The analogy of the relationship of vulnerability models to the holistic treatment of schizophrenia and the relationship between learning theory and behaviour therapy in the treatment of emotional disorders made by

Innovations in the Psychological Management of Schizophrenia.
Edited by Max Birchwood and Nicholas Tarrier. © 1992 John Wiley & Sons Ltd

Clements and Turpin is entirely appropriate. Behaviour therapy arose out of a learning theory formulation of psychopathology, initially situational anxiety. Clinical practice was generated from theory and rapidly expanded to address more and more disorders and problems found in various child and adult populations. Eventually therapy outgrew theory and the learning formulations were found to be lacking as an explanation of the extent and success of clinical practice. Vulnerability models of schizophrenia may well in the future prove to be inadequate but they have the potential to drive clinical formulations and interventions that operate on a number of dimensions. For the psychologist, vulnerability models may be the key to bringing to bear their knowledge and skills in conceptualising and addressing the problems encountered in schizophrenia.

Is the concept of schizophrenia of any value? Certainly, there are immense problems of validity and many workers find it intellectually unsatisfactory (e.g. Bentall, Jackson and Pilgrim, 1988); we must not lose sight of the fact, however, that the concept of schizophrenia does enter into lawful relationships and may be discriminated in certain respects from other disorders in terms of aetiology, phenomenology, therapeutic specificity and outcome (Birchwood, Hallett and Preston, 1988). The continuum models of psychosis (e.g. Bentall, Claridge and Slade, 1989; Crow, 1990) suggest a continuum within the psychoses or between psychoses and normality, but in our view any such demonstration does not invalidate the utility of categories; for example, the continua of intelligence and height do not invalidate concepts such as giftedness or dwarfism. Thus we feel in the absence of a satisfactory practical alternative, the concept of schizophrenia allows a better method of addressing multiple needs than does the fragmentation into the study of individual clinical phenomena or of blurring any differences between psychopathological and normal groups. This is not to say that the study of individual clinical phenomena is not in itself useful, but it is not excluded by retaining the overall concept of schizophrenia. In fact, the adoption of broad-based models of schizophrenia, such as vulnerability, enhances the study of individual clinical phenomena such as hallucinations, delusions, avolition, skill deficits, etc. by entering psychological, environmental and psychosocial factors into the arena previously occupied by purely biomedical formulations.

INTEGRATING PSYCHOSOCIAL INTERVENTIONS

The family of psychosocial interventions outlined in this book are the outcome of a period of intense research and service-based evaluation ongoing throughout the 1980s. As we have seen, a great deal of optimism and excitement surrounds these interventions and justifiably so since hitherto the treatment outcomes have been uniformly positive. As we have indicated throughout this book, it is important that the studies supporting the efficacy of the interventions are seen as "first generation" and that the coming 10 years sees a second generation dedicated in part to replication, to exploring their internal validity and to examine to what population, under what constraints and with what outcomes they may be generalised (Birchwood, 1992).

We need in other words to keep our feet firmly on the ground: these interventions are in their infancy, each has made a significant advance yet for the most part they have been evaluated in isolation and over a limited period of one to two years, which is a short time in what can be a lifelong and very disabling disorder. Thus in addition to a second generation of studies on individual interventions, the prospect of bringing these interventions together within a service context and making them available over an extended period of time is more likely to have a deeper and durable impact on the course of the illness and on the accumulation of social disability and handicap. This echoes strongly of the point made by Matt Muijen in Chapter 11 that the time has come for a convergence between the community-care programmes and the individual psychosocial interventions.

The potential for such an integration and the form it might take is glimpsed in studies of the long-term course of schizophrenic disorders within and between cultures. The lessons from these studies are salutary when considering how best to integrate psychosocial interventions.

Lessons from longitudinal and cross-cultural studies

It is important first to underscore what is now increasingly understood, that the unfolding of schizophrenia is not a homogeneous affair as early psychiatric doctrine suggested (Kraepelin, 1902). The long-term follow-up studies all show a wide heterogeneity of outcome: in some the first episode is followed by a permanent recovery and in others, signs of long-term decline are already apparent (Macmillan et al., 1986) and very long-term follow-up studies (e.g. Harding et al., 1987) reveal that 50% recover or experience mild periodic symptoms or impairments with severe outcomes in up to one-third. Psychosocial variables are good predictors and trackers of this varying course and outcome and led McGlashen (1988) recently to conclude: "The North American long-term follow-up studies suggest that schizophrenia may be quite malleable to prolonged environmental/psychosocial perturbations. These have negative potential if applied too intensively or ambitiously, but positive potential if applied steadily in a supportive rehabilitative mode in a context of stable and supportive continuity of care" (p. 538). Cross-cultural comparisons of the developing course of schizophrenia point to a similar conclusion.

There is now overwhelming evidence that the outcome for people with schizophrenia in Western industrialised countries is markedly inferior to those in the Third World (Lin and Kleinman, 1988).

Murphy and Rahman (1971) were among the first to make this observation in their study of African and Indian schizophrenic patients living in Mauritius. They found that after 12 years follow-up involving 98% of their original sample, 64% reported no further episodes contrasting with 49% in a comparable British sample followed up after 5 years (Brown et al., 1966). This apparent resistance to relapse has been documented in less industrialised countries by Verghese et al. (1989) in India and Waxler (1979) and Mendis (1986) in Sri-Lanka. A recent investigation (Leff et al., 1987) compared first-episode samples in London and Chandigargh (a predominantly urban area of Northern India). They found a 9-month relapse rate of between 14% and 18% in Chandigargh compared with 29% in London, a difference which did not appear to rest on the use of maintenance neuroleptic drugs (Leff et al., 1990).

The problems of achieving true comparability of sampling, measurement, outcome and other criteria across cultures has been addressed in the transcultural schizophrenia research programme of the World Health Organisation (WHO, 1979; Sartorius et al., 1986).

In the first of these, a cross-sectional sample covering eight countries was followed up over 2 years. On all measures, a greater proportion of patients in Agra (India), Cali (Columbia), and Ibadan (Nigeria) had more favourable, less disabling outcomes than in Aarhus (Denmark), London, Prague and Washington. A further epidemiological study covering ten countries of first episode patients (Sartorius et al., 1986) found a uniform annual incidence rate (1 per 10 000) but variable 2-year outcome between countries, once again favouring less industrialised nations. Forty per cent of patients in industrialised countries showed a "severe" pattern (more than one episode and incomplete remission) compared with 24% in developing ones.

Several hypotheses have been offered to account for this finding. The opportunity to engage in socially valued and productive roles may be enhanced in non-industrial societies where there is a more flexible use of labour. The WHO field workers in India for example, had difficulty interviewing ex-patients as they were so busy—the men in the fields and the women in domestic work. It is interesting to note that the pattern of recovery in Moscow paralleled that of less industrialised countries; perhaps a reflection on the emphasis on full employment and vocational rehabilitation in the USSR (Warner, 1983).

Another hypothesis argues that the extended family structure, which is more common in the Third World, may help to diffuse burden and increase tolerance (Waxler, 1979). El-Islam (1979) reports a better outcome for patients in extended versus nuclear families in Qatar on the Persian Gulf. A study of expressed emotion (EE) among the extended families of patients in Chandigargh (Leff et al., 1987, 1990) found a much lower prevalence of high EE (23%) compared to London (47%) which was associated with a lower short-term rate of relapse. The extended family structure of Mexican–American families was shown to be associated with a lower prevalence of high EE compared to British and American samples (Karno et al., 1987).

Social isolation and social support was identified by the Determinants of Outcome Study (Sartorius et al., 1986; Leff et al. 1987) as one of the few strong predictors of outcome where many more patients lived alone in several of the industrialised society centres. Thus weak or absent social supports may contribute to poor outcome. Greater social support and increased opportunity to engage in valid social roles may contribute to a superiority in social functioning for patients in less industrialised countries (WHO, 1979) and social functioning has been identified as an independent variable within cultures (Hogarty et al., 1979).

Several authors have argued that the stigma of mental illness is much more pronounced in industrialised countries where the view is widespread that insanity is an incurable life-long affliction, where the notion of individuality and illness are conjoined in the collective mind (e.g. Warner, 1985). The loss of self-esteem and despair this creates may be pernicious and self-fulfilling. It seems unlikely that these cross-cultural differences in outcome are the result of a single factor such as family structure but represent a more complex clustering of culturally related variables such as attitudes to mental illness, opportunities for social re-integration, social isolation, engagement in valued social roles, continuity of stable care and so on.

Taken at face value, these longitudinal studies suggest that, psychosocial interventions could halve the rate of "severe" social disability and increase the survival time between episodes by up to 50%. Engaging individuals in valued social roles and stable social networks, maximising independence and purposeful activity, within the constraints of the illness, promoting psychological adjustment to long-term illness and widening the burden of care beyond close family members in the context of a community which is stable and familiar would be among the key features of a model package of care.

The timing of interventions

Timing here has a dual meaning: for how long should the interventions be applied and at what point in the history of the disorder should they ideally begin? One could of course simply argue that they should be applied throughout a lifetime but this is neither practically feasible nor desirable for services to maintain such an intensity of contact or input with each individual. What is the evidence then for the notion of "critical periods" for the application of these interventions? The chapters on family intervention (Chapters 4 and 10), early intervention (Chapter 6) and community-care programmes (Chapter 11) describe interventions lasting for between 6 months and in some cases 2 years whose impact can still be observed 2 years on, although the passage of time sees this steadily diminish. This declining impact may arise because the needs, problems and social situations of patients may change over time requiring a flexible response from services; there may also be changes in the vulnerabilities and impairments which are intrinsic to the illness and of course interventions may themselves prove frail unless applied beyond a minimum period of time. Whatever the reasons, these individual studies suggest that, at the very least, a minimum period of two years sustained intervention would be required. The longitudinal studies may offer further guidance here.

It is now widely understood that deterioration of function does characterise the illness in its early stages, apparent within 2 years following the illness onset (Macmillan et al., 1986). Longer term follow-up studies reveal that deterioration "plateaus" between 5 and 10 years after the onset with some recovery and greater responsiveness to rehabilitation (Harding et al., 1987). The Washington centre of the WHO study followed up their sample for 11 years and found little or no change in functioning from 5 to 11 years across the range of disability (Carpenter et al., 1987).

Thus containing and stabilising any deterioration in functioning within the *first 5 years* post onset may have a disproportionate impact on long-term outcome. McGlashan (1988) argues that after 10 to 15 years, a relenting of the illness is apparent and a sustained response to rehabilitation can then be made.

Thus the first 5 years post-onset might therefore be regarded as a critical period: a multimodal psychosocial intervention operating during this period may set a ceiling on long-term deterioration in functioning and provide a better platform for future rehabilitative efforts. Whether environments (both psychological and social) are more malleable in the early years is not clear, although there is some suggestion that families of recently ill patients respond better to education (Birchwood, Smith and Cochrane, 1992) and that family characteristics such as emotional over-involvement are relatively rare among first-episode patients (Macmillan et al., 1986). Suicide risk is also concentrated in these early years and is firmly linked to despair about the future (Caldwell and Gottesman, 1990) which sustained intervention should help to offset.

Interventions and their support structures

From the mid-1980s, the needs of people with serious mental illness have returned to the top of the mental-health agenda in the UK and the USA. The tendency of community services to "drift upmarket" to client groups that respond for example to psychotherapy, is slowly being reversed (Shepherd, 1990). The availability of new therapeutic strategies has raised the status of work with this client group, a change which is to be welcomed. Case management has proved to be the "big idea" of the 1980s that has provided an intellectual basis and a structure around which community services have and can develop (Muijen, Chapter 11). The approach emphasises explicit prioritisation and the configuration of services to fit clients needs; as Kate Woof points out in Chapter 12 this contrasts with traditional approaches to planning where clients are fitted into existing services (e.g. the day-hospital) which explicitly follows other priorities or is driven by needs other than clients'.

Geoff Shepherd (1990) recently suggested that we are in danger of becoming intoxicated by the concept and argues that it can only be as good as the service infrastructure will allow: "it must be acknowledged at the outset that case management represents the latest in a long line of 'magic' solutions to hit community psychiatry. Like many good ideas, it risks being 'oversold' and then rejected as people become disillusioned and it has failed to live up to expectations ... it is not a panacea ... not a substitute for an adequate range of community provisions" (p. 59). We would wholeheartedly concur with this view. Not only is case management not a replacement for service infrastructure but, it is also not a replacement for clinical interventions either. As Matt Muijen indicates, evaluations of community care programmes driven by case-management ideas or their precursors have been paradoxically anachronistic in their excessive reliance on the basics of drugs, housing and finance aid which is partly because they are delivered by a narrow skill mix of doctors and nurses. The framework of case management is widely accepted. There needs now to be a much greater emphasis on the function of case management as a means of enabling the delivery of proven (or promising) interventions such as those outlined in this book. Without this we run the risk of innovation without change, of transferring services to the community without introducing anything positive to the lives of people with schizophrenia that will bring about significant long-term change. The marriage of psychosocial interventions within a case-management framework using resources of an appropriate service infrastructure is, we believe, the next step and the challenge for the 1990s. In Figure 13.1 we outline what we believe to be essential components of a service attempting to implement and integrate psychosocial interventions into routine practice. We have deliberately

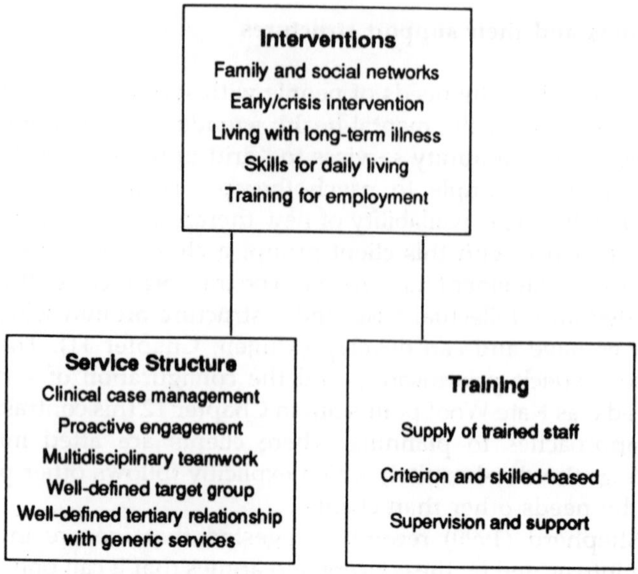

Figure 13.1 Interventions and their support structures.

placed "service structure" and "training" as subordinates to the interventions: they are needed to enable the delivery of care, not an end in itself.

Five core interventions are suggested, some of which are included in this book others are just developing. *Family interventions* and *training in skills for daily living* are now reasonably well developed, notwithstanding the observations made at the beginning of this chapter. They remain the most well-researched and will take a central role. Increasing opportunities to engage in wider *social networks* is a relatively neglected area, yet longitudinal studies repeatedly demonstrate the vulnerabilities associated with social isolation (McGlashen, 1988). Realistic efforts to develop with patients a social network which includes genuine friendships, confidantes as well as one which responds promptly and supportively in crisis, may well prove rewarding and requires further research attention (Thornicroft and Breakey, 1991). Of all the interventions, this is one which cannot be provided solely through training, education or therapy; it requires a service to explore community resources and to create where necessary, its own community infrastructure: drop-in centres, "cafe clubs" and the like.

Early and crisis intervention strategies are discussed in Chapters 3 and 6. Chapter 6 describes how, in order to assist the detection of early relapse, a close and trusting relationship between clients and services is needed, in which learning lessons from recent studies of intermittent pharmacotherapy, the responsibility for detecting early relapse is a joint one.

Without this, medication non-compliance, denial of loss of well-being may well occur and early intervention is likely to prove difficult. The management of relapse is exclusively pharmocological; this is so even in the most progressive community maintenance programmes. Chapter 3 by Valerie Drury discussed the possibilities for accelerating recovery from episodes of disorder through psychosocial interventions involving direct dialogue with the individual about his disturbed mental world. To be taken seriously in this way may well be valued by the patient and also provide a framework for productive interactions between patients and professionals during periods of relapse, in both hospital and community settings. The outcome studies of this approach are eagerly waited.

Living with long-term illness is a set of interventions which recognise the reality of the disorder and its long-term implications and involves a form of psychotherapy empowering individuals with understanding of their disorder and practical strategies for control; and to assist them in adjusting to a future in which their expectations may be blunted (Warner et al., 1989; Birchwood and Preston, 1991; Birchwood et al., 1992). Teaching and enhancing early intervention strategies and methods for controlling hallucinations and delusional thinking would be appropriate here. Services are, however, notoriously poor at empowering individuals in this way yet these are issues of real concern for clients and often the origins of suicide (Caldwell and Gottesman, 1990). Achieving the proper balance between the risk of neglect in the name of liberty and the delivery of adequate care without over controlling paternalism, will require professionals to articulate ideas of empowerment and partnership in services to clients (Robertson, 1991). The seeds of real empowerment are contained in some of these interventions but require the promotion of this framework within services to realise its full potential.

Serious attempts to guide clients into the employment market are lamentably lacking, presumably because of the cognitive constraints on performance and the competitive nature of the employment market. There are notable exceptions. The "Speedwell Project" in London (Lipsedge and Butterfield, 1991) has developed a "niche" approach to employment; they have targeted the acquisition of computer skills as a means of facilitating patients' passage into the employment market. They boast a high success rate of placing patients into open employment. Targeting "niche" areas of the labour market clearly requires an inter-agency approach and should form part of the service infrastructure required to support interventions.

Turning to service structures, we have already identified continuity of care as a critical component of care and the importance of case management in this respect has been emphasised. The fragmentation of services which is increasing with the closure of hospitals and the distinction between "health" and "social" care envisaged in British social policy, make this an absolutely essential framework. Engagement and maintenance of patients and their carers in treatment requires a clear psychological formulation of the determinants of engagement and maintenance and how they can be successfully manipulated (Tarrier, 1991). The problem of maintaining patients' adherence to psychosocial interventions (Smith and Birchwood, 1990) requires the use of proactive engagement both in terms of initial and ongoing contact. This combination of assertive follow-up and clinical case management has been shown to be the more favourable option (Olfson, 1990).

Matt Muijan writing from personal experience in the London Daily Living Project highlights the intense pressures and diverse skill requirements placed on case managers and argues strongly for an appropriate skill mix of professional staff rather than the more usual dominance of psychiatrists and nurses. Indeed the interventions outlined in this book are highly skilled activities requiring the skills, expertise and background of psychologists, occupational therapists and social workers. Multidisciplinary teamwork can only operate effectively in the context of realistic staff:client ratios in the region of 1:10 to 1:15.

The evaluations of community-care programmes and psychosocial interventions described in this book have been conducted under research conditions, often with external funding, and largely without service pressure bearing upon them. Integrating these into normal service practice requires considerable thought. As Kate Woof argues in her chapter, explicit statements about target populations and the priority they are assigned in the service as a whole, need to be made and agreed at the outset. If these interventions form part of a sectorised generic service team, then problems of "upmarket drift" in client groups and "dilution" of interventions that come from service pressure and a generic caseload, will prejudice these priorities. Thus for reasons of continuity of care, the maintenance of a consistent quality of intervention and the need for a genuine skill mix, these interventions can only be provided through a specialist multidisciplinary team acting as a tertiary resource to "front line" generic services, with the capacity to control service pressure through proactive (versus referral-based) engagement.

Training is the second support structure outlined in Figure 13.1. If the psychosocial interventions were like a new drug treatment, it would be relatively straightforward to incorporate them into clinical practice. However, as Jo Smith points out in relation to family interventions in service settings (Chapter 10), they are skilled activities demanding of human resources with a difficult and often refractory client group. Thus it follows that an ongoing system of training, support and supervision are essential.

As in all training situations, a decision needs to be reached about the numbers of staff required to implement interventions. This cannot be a "one-off", but a system needs to be put in place to ensure continuity. Many of the interventions in this book are new and the research centres involved have somewhat different approaches (e.g. to family interventions). Greater clarity about the content of interventions is required since there are many non-specific clinical skills involved in many of them (e.g. listening, empathy with the psychotic experience, conducting a family session, target-setting, etc.) which will not be evident from manuals written by leaders in the field (e.g. Falloon, 1984; Barrowclough and Tarrier, 1992). The standardisation and operationalisation of all the component skills of the interventions has yet to be developed; but in respect of family interventions a start has been made (Lam, 1991). In Birmingham, UK, a diploma in psychosocial intervention is under development as a joint scheme between the health and higher education authorities, to meet this need. In Manchester, UK a training programme in family management for CPNs has been run on a project basis from 1989 to 1992 and involved the evaluation of such training and its clinical effect. Initial results suggest that this programme has a positive outcome for patients and their carers (Brooker et al., in press).

Ongoing supervision and support are crucial when working with this client group, and has been noted by others: "... schizophrenic patients are generally seen as unattractive to work with; they are often difficult to motivate, they can be uncooperative, unwilling or unable to try new experience and services ... they are seldom top of the popularity ratings among ... professionals who see their role as treating people and making them better ... good support and supervision from experienced and high status practitioners is essential" (Shepherd, 1990). This aspect of supervision, the provision of leadership and emotional support needs to be complemented by a quality control function to ensure that interventions are being appropriately and flexibly applied.

WHAT NEXT?

It always behoves authors at this point to speculate about emerging trends and what the future holds for their subject both clinically and in research. To generate idly lists of possible future directions is not of great use here but there are some trends which we as professionals should work hard to realise. The last decade has seen the rise of consumerism in mental health as well as across society generally. Aspects of consumerism which result in the enablement of the sufferers of mental illness and the shedding of the reductionism which leads to the treatment of the person as a diagnostic category must continue. We feel that the approaches advocated in this text *will* go some way to normalising the abnormal. That is the recognition that although some processes are abnormal and functioning is disrupted, many are normal and our knowledge of normal processes can assist in therapeutic endeavours as well as to maintain the dignity of those who suffer this most debilitating disorder. We also feel that a move towards multifaceted therapeutic approaches will improve the quality of mental health services and increase their acceptability with those who are their users. In relation to this, the interaction between pharmacological and psychosocial interventions needs to be further investigated and developed so as to maximise the effect of medication by minimising its use. Lastly, the developments of assessment and treatment need to be assimilated into clinical practice and service delivery so as to provide a wide range of service options that will be continually updated and reviewed. In this book we have hoped to review some of these developments so that they can become more readily accessible and available as options to the clinical practitioner.

REFERENCES

Barrowclough, L. and Tarrier, N. (1992) *Cognitive–Behavioural Intervention with Families of Schizophrenia Patients: a Practitioners Guide*, Chapman and Hall, London.

Bentall, R.P., Jackson, H.F. and Pilgrim, D. (1988) Abandoning the concept of schizophrenia: some implications of validity arguments of psychological research into psychotic phenomena. *British Journal of Clinical Psychology*, **27**, 303–24.

Bentall, R.P., Claridge. G.S. and Slade, P. (1989) The multi-dimensional nature of schizotype traits: a factor analytic study with normal subjects. *British Journal of Clinical Psychology*, **28**, 363–75.

Birchwood, M. (1992). Family interventions. *British Journal of Psychiatry*, **160**, 272–5.

Birchwood, M., Hallet, S. and Preston, M. (1988) *Schizophrenia: an Integrated Approach to Research and Treatment*, Longman, Harlow, Essex.

Birchwood, M.J. and Preston, M.C. (1991). Schizophrenia. In: W. Dryden and C. Rentoul (eds), *Adult Problems: a Cognitive–Behavioural Approach*, pp. 171–202, Routledge, London.

Birchwood, M.J., Smith, J. and Cochrane, R. (1992) Specific and non-specific effects of educational intervention with families living with a schizophrenic relative: a comparison of three methods. *British Journal of Psychiatry* (in press).

Birchwood, M., Mason, R., Macmillan, J. and Healy, J. (1992) Depression, demoralisation and control over psychotic illness: A comparison of schizophrenic and manic-depressive patients. *Social Psychiatry and Psychiatric Epidemiology*.

Brooker C., Tarrier, N., Barrowclough, C., Butterworth, C. and Goldberg, D. (in press) Training community psychiatric nurses for psychosocial intervention: report of a pilot study. *British Journal of Psychiatry*.

Brown, G.W., Bone, M., Dalison, B. and Wing, J.K., (1966) *Schizophrenia and Social Care*. Maudsley monograph No. 17, Oxford University Press, London.

Caldwell, C.B. and Gottesman, I.I. (1990), Schizophrenics kill themselves too. *Schizophrenia Bulletin*, **16**, 571–90.

Carpenter, W.T., Strauss, J.S., Pulver, A.C. and Wolyniec, P.S. (1987) The prediction of outcome in schizophrenia: Eleven year follow-up of the Washington IPSS cohort. Quoted in McGlashen (1988).
Crow, T.J. (1990) The continuum of psychosis and its genetic origins. *British Journal of Psychiatry*, **156**, 788–97.
El-Islam, M.F. (1979) A better outlook for schizophrenics living in extended families. *British Journal of Psychiatry*, **135**, 343–7.
Falloon, I.R.H. (1984) *Family Management of Mental Illness: a Study of Clinical and Social Benefits*, Johns Hopkins University Press, Baltimore.
Harding, C.M., Brooks. G.W., Ashikeya T., Strauss, J.S. and Brier, A. (1987). The Vermont longitudinal study of persons with severe mental illness II: long-term outcome of subjects who retrospectively met DSM-III criteria for schizophrenia. *American Journal of Psychiatry*, **144**, 727–35.
Hogarty, G.E., Schooler, N.R. and Ulrich, R. (1979) Fluphenazine and social therapy in the aftercare of schizophrenic patients. *Archives of General Psychiatry*, **36**, 1283–94.
Karno, M., Jenkins, J.H., De La Selva, A., Santana, F., Telles, C., Lopez, S. ana Mintz, J. (1987) Expressed emotion and schizophrenic outcome among Mexican–American families. *Journal of Nervous and Mental Disease*, **175**, 143–51.
Kraepelin, E. (1902) *Clinical Psychiatry: a Textbook for Students and Physicians*. Translated by A.R. Defendorf, 6th edn of *Lehrbuch Der Psychiatrie*, Macmillan, New York.
Lam, D. (1991) Psychosocial family interventions in schizophrenia: review of empirical studies. *Psychological Medicine*, **21**, 423–41.
Leff, J., Wig, N., Bedi, H., Menon, D.K., Kuipers, L., Korten, A., Ernberg, G., Day, R., Sartorius, N. and Jablensky, A. (1990) Relatives' expressed emotion and the course of schizophrenia in Chandigargh. *British Journal of Psychiatry*, **156**, 351–6.
Leff, J., Wig, N., Ghosh, A., Bedi, H., Menon, D.K., Kuipers, L., Korten, A., Ernberg, G., Day, R., Sartorius, N. and Jablensky, A. (1987) Influence of relatives' expressed emotion on the course of schizoprenia in Chandigargh. *British Journal of Psychiatry*, **151**, 166–73.
Lin, K. and Kleinman, A. M. (1988) Psychopathology and clinical course of schizophrenia: a cross cultural perspective. *Schizophrenia Bulletin*, **14**, 555–68.
Lipsedge, M. and Butterfield, A. (1990) Hospitals that offer a rare screenbreak. *Guardian*, 11 October.
McGlashen, T.H. (1988). A selective review of recent North American follow-up studies of schizophrenia. *Schizophrenia Bulletin*, **14**, 567–81.
Macmillan, J.F., Crow, T.J., Johnson, A.L. and Johnstone, E.C. (1986) The Northwick Park first episodes of schizophrenia study. *British Journal of Psychiatry*, **148**, 128–33.
Mendis, N. (1986) The outcome of schizophrenia in Sri Lanka: a ten year follow-up study. *Ceylon Medical Journal*, **31**, 119–34.
Murphy, H.B.M. and Rahman, A.C. (1971) The chronicity of schizophrenia in indigenous tropical peoples. *British Journal of Psychiatry*, **118**, 489–97.
Olfson, M. (1990) Assertive community treatment: an evaluation of the experimental evidence. *Hospital and Community Psychiatry*, **41**, 634–41.
Robertson, J.A. (1991) Case management. *British Journal of Psychiatry*, **159**, 142–8.
Sartorius, N., Jablensky, S., Korten, A., Ernberg, G., Anker, M., Cooper, G.E. and Day, R. (1986) Early manifestations and first-contact incidence of schizophrenia in different cultures: A preliminary report of the initial evaluation phase of the

WHO study of determinants of outcome of severe mental disorder. *Psychological Medicine*, **16**, 909–28.
Shepherd, G. (1990) Case management. *Health Trends*, **22**, 59–63.
Smith, J. and Birchwood, M. (1990) Relatives and patients as partners in the management of schizophrenia. *British Journal of Psychiatry*, **156**, 654–60.
Tarrier, N. (1991) Some aspects of family interventions in schizophrenia I: Adherence to intervention programmes. *British Journal of Psychiatry*, **159**, 475–80.
Thornicroft, G. and Breackey, W.R. (1991) The COSTAR programme 1.: Improving social networks of the long-term mentally ill. *British Journal of Psychiatry*, **159**, 245–9.
Verghese, A., John, J.K., Raikumar, S., Richard, J., Sethi, B.B. and Trivedi, J.K. (1989) Factors associated with the course and outcome of schizophrenia in India. *British Journal of Psychiatry*, **154**, 499–503.
Warner, R. (1983). Recovery from schizophrenia in the Third World. *Psychiatry*, **46**, 197–212.
Warner, R. (1985) *Recovery from Schizophrenia: Psychiatric and Political Economy*, Routledge and Kegan Paul, London.
Warner, R., Taylor, D., Powers, M. and Hyman, J. (1989) Acceptance of the mental illness label by psychotic patients: effects on functioning. *American Journal of Orthopsychiatry*, **59**, 398–409.
Waxler, N.E. (1979) Is outcome for schizophrenia better in non-industrial societies?: the case of Sri Lanka. *Journal of Nervous and Mental Disease*, **167**, 144–58.
World Health Organisation (1979) *Schizophrenia: an International Follow-Up Study*, John Wiley, New York.
Zubin, J., Magaziner, J. and Steinhaur, R. (1983) The metamorphosis of schizophrenia: from vulnerbility to chronicity. *Psychological Medicine*, **13**, 551–71.
Zubin, J. and Spring, B. (1977) Vulnerability: a new view of schizophrenia. *Journal of Abnormal Psychology*, **86**, 260–6.

Index

Accommodation scale, 9
ACORN information package, 280
activation–inhibition, 52
aetiology
  approaches, 22
  relatives' knowledge, 92
aggression, 174 177–8
  prodromal, 120
anger
  cognitive interpretation, 195–6
  Spielberger Inventory, 180
"antipsychiatry", 209
antipsychotic drugs, effects of (*see also* medication; neuroleptic drugs), 111–12
antisocial behaviour 174
anxiety, prodromal, 120, 122, 126–8
apathy, 173
applied relaxation training (ART), 154
Approved Social Workers, 211
Archer Centre (Birmingham), 247
assault, 175
assessment
  contextual factors in, 182–3
  functional, 112, 113
  methods, 6–16
  for problem management, 175–84
  practical applications, 14–16
  scales, *see individual scales*
  of symptoms, *see* symptoms, assessment of
"asylum community", 224
attention
  impairment, 173
  performance, 36
Audit Commission report (1986), 255
auditory hallucinations, 11, 15, 16, 149
Auditory Hallucinations Record Form, 16
auditory input, control of, 149

baseline recording, 181
Beck Depression Inventory, 180
behaviour
  assessment, 3–17
  bizarre, *see* bizarre behaviour
  violent, *see* violent behaviour
behavioural approaches, (*see also* cognitive–behavioural approaches), 189–91
belief modification, 150
beliefs, delusional, *see* delusional beliefs
Beliefs and Convictions Scale, 62–61 68–70
Better Services for the Mentally Ill (White Paper, 1975), 212, 255
biofeedback, 149–50
bizarre behaviour, 174
  assessment of, 12–14
Brief Psychiatric Rating Scale (BPRS), 6–7, 122
Buckingham Project, 116, 245

Camberwell Family Interview, 87
care
  balance of, 253–71
  clinical issues, 265–70
  community, *see* community care
  continuing, *see* continuing care
  day-, *see* day-care
  evaluation of models, 267
  funding, 255
  home, *see* home care
  methodological issues, 265–8
  model programmes, validity of, 265–8
  outcome criteria, 267
  priorities, 291
  target groups, 265–6
  UK developments, 254–6
  US developments, 256–7
Caring for People (White Paper, 1989), 226–7, 255, 278
case-loads, 294
case management, 220, 311

case management (*cont.*)
  role of, 229–3
  Salford, 299
  services, 215–16
challenging behaviour, 174–5
  assessment, 181, 184
  baseline recording, 181
  case example, 198–200
  cognitive–behavioural approaches, 195–6
  goal setting, 184–5
  group behavioural regimes, 187–9
  individual behavioural approaches, 192–3
  interviewing carers, 179
  interviewing patients, 176, 177–9
  maintaining factors, 181–3
  management, 171–200
  rating scales, 179–81
  reinforcement, 193
  therapeutic interventions, 185–6
  therapeutic milieu approaches, 187
Characteristics of Delusions Rating Scale, 9, 14
chromosome 5 linkage, 31
chronicity, 297–8
cognitive–behavioural approaches, 194–6
  challenging behaviour, 195–6
  impairments long-term, 194–5
cognitive impairments, 111, 113
cognitive markers, 35–7
cognitive modification, 150
cognitive processes, modification of, 150–1
"collaborative ethos", 49
communication skills, (*see also* social skills), 105–6
community care, (*see also* continuing care), 171–2
  co-ordination of, 215–16
  costs, 264–5
  history of, 207–10
  policy developments, 216–17
  prisons and, 213–14
  problems with, 211–13
Community Care: An Agenda for Action (Griffiths), 255
community mental-health centres (CMHCs), 277–8
Community Mental Health Centres Act (USA), 256
community psychiatric nursing (CPN), 209, 277–8
Community Support Programmes (UK), 261
Community Support Programs (USA), 256
competencies, inter-professional agreements, 287–9
Comprehensive Psychopathological Rating Scale (CPRS), 7
Computerised Axial Tomography (CAT) abnormalities, 32
consumer satisfaction, family intervention studies, 84
contingency management, 148
continuing care (*see also* community care)
  case managers, 220
  central authority, 218
  client advocacy, 221
  components of, 217–26
  crises, 225–6
  future directions, 226–7
  information systems, 219
  models of, 207–27
  multi-disciplinary team, 219–22
  residential services, 223–5
  service planning, 218
  structured day activities, 222–3
Continuous Performance Test (CPT), 36
contradiction hypothetical, 64–5
convalescence, favourable environment (*see also* recovery), 60
conviction (in delusion beliefs)
  fluctuations during recovery, 65
  level of, 6–4
coping responses, 94–6
coping skills training, 103–13
coping strategies, 151–2
  classification, 159
  effectiveness, 158–9
  treatment method, 152–65
Coping Strategy Enhancement (CSE), 153
  assessment, 156
  case example, 162–4
  clinical procedure, 156–62

clinical report, 153
education, 160–1
evaluations 153–6
implementation difficulties, 164–5
interview, 156
problem solving and, 153, 155
procedure, 161–2
rapport building, 160–1
symptoms and emotional reactions, 156–7
CPN services, 288–9
crisis counselling, 139
crisis intervention, 312
cross-cultural studies, 308–9
"custody and containment", 283

day-care, 212, 223, 255, 257–61
as alternative to hospital care, 258–9
as alternative to out-patient care, 259–60
drop-out rate, 258
efficacy of, 258
long-term mentally ill, 260–1
day-hospitals, 254, 257–8
decompensation, 51
psychotic, 124
delusional beliefs (*see also* hallucinations)
compensatory, 51
conviction,
degree of, 63–4, 65
fluctuation in, 72
dimensions of, 8
disintegration during recovery, 54–6
eliciting, 69
evidence for, 69
hypothetical contradiction, 69–70
interference degree of, 64
measures of, 8–10
multi-dimensional view, 55
preoccupation
degree of, 64, 65
fluctuation in, 72
primary, 55
prodromal, 122
secondary, 55, 56
depression
cognitive–behavioural approach, 194
prodromal, 118, 120, 122, 126–8
Deviant Behaviour sub-scale, 13

diagnosis
interviews, 6
relatives' knowledge, 92
dimensional model, 4, 5, 71
discharge, timing, 73
disease model, 4
disinhibition, prodromal, 126–8
double awareness, 54, 55
drug dependence, 113
drugs, neuroleptic, *see* neuroleptic drugs
dysphoria, 52–3

early intervention (*see also* prodromes), 115–42, 312
clinical applications, 139–42
education, 135–7
engagement, 135–7
monitoring methodology, 140–1
neuroleptic drug studies, 131–4
procedures, 135–9
selection of suitable subjects, 135
service response, 141–2
time window for, 137
early signs approach (*see also* symptoms, prodromal), 41
Early Signs Questionnaire (ESQ), 123, 125
prodromes detected, 126–8
Early Signs Research Group, recovery monitoring procedures, 61–7
Early Signs Scale (ESS), 62, 70
in recovery, 57, 66–7, 71
education, family, 91–3
electrodermal non-responding, 33–4
electroencephalogram, P300 amplitude, 35
emotion
expressed, *see* expressed emotion
restricted expression of, 173
employment, "niche" approach, 313
epidemiology, 219
episode markers, 27, 41
euphoria, prodromal, 118
Event Related Potentials, 35
expressed emotion (EE), 85–6, 235
arousal levels and, 83
dimensions of, 83
family intervention and, 80–6, 239–40

expressed emotion (EE) (*cont.*)
  low EE families, 85, 239, 240
  recovery and, 60
  relapse and, 80–3
eye movement abnormalities, 34–5

family burden, 84, 215
Family Centre for Advice Resources and Education (Birmingham), 246–7
family intervention, 312
  adherence to, 237–8
  components of, 90–8
  consumer satisfaction, 84
  continuity of, 241
  coping responses, 94–6
  economic factors, 84–5
  education, 91–3
  engaging families, 237–9
  expressed emotion and, 80–6, 239–40
  goal-defined, 242–3
  goal setting, 96–8
  initial assessments, 86–90
  integration with community sources, 243
  long-term, 241
  needs-led, 242–3
  practical guidelines, 85–6
  relapse rates, 236
  relatives, 84, 86–9
  services
    delivery issues, 241–2
    implications, 235–49
    models in practice, 244–8
    provision implications, 243–4
  social functioning, 84, 90
  strengths/needs assessment, 97–8
  stress management, 94
  studies, 79–98
    early, 79–80
    multiple outcome measures, 83–5
    patient assessment, 90
    patient strengths, 90
Family Questionnaire (FQ), 88, 89
family services, development of, 237–43
family therapy, 242, 262
"Fountain House" philosophy, 222
functional assessment, 112, 113

General Health Questionnaire (GHQ), 88, 89
General Household Survey, 280
genetic counselling, 39
genetic markers, 27, 28, 30–1
goal setting, family intervention studies, 96–8
Good Practices in Mental Health group, 281
group behavioural regimes, 187–9

hallucinations (*see also* delusional beliefs)
  auditory, 11, 15, 16, 149
  dimensions, 11
  prodromal, 122
  reality characteristics, 10
  scales, 10–11
hierarchical model, 4, 5
home care, 261–5, 269–70
  costs, 264–5
  evaluation of, 262–4
homelessness, 214–15
Hopelessness Scale, 180
hospital admissions, 277
"Hospital Hostels", 224
Hospital Plan for England and Wales (1962), 255
hypothetical contradiction, reaction to, 64–5

impairments, long-term, 173–4
  assessment, 176–7, 181, 183–4
  baseline recording, 181
  case example, 197
  cognitive–behavioural approaches, 194–5
  goal setting, 184–5
  group behavioural regimes, 187–9
  individual behavioural approaches, 189–91
  interviewing carers, 179
  interviewing patients, 176
  maintaining factors, 181–3
  management, 171–200
  rating scales, 179–81
  therapeutic interventions, 185–6
  therapeutic milieu approaches, 186–7

under-stimulation, 186
impulsivity, prodromal, 118
Industrial Therapy, 222
information systems, 219
Inpatient Scale of Minimal Functioning, 13
insight
dimensions of, 57–8
during recovery, 66, 72
as epiphenomenon, 56
"pseudo", 58
recovery and, 56–9
Integrated Psychological Therapy (IPT), 195
inter-professional agreements on competencies, 287–9
"intermediate states", 40
intervention (*see also* early intervention; family intervention)
support structures, 311–15
timing, 309–10
interviews
carers, 179
challenging behaviour, 177–9
in problem management, 176
irritability, prodromal, 120

Knowledge about Schizophrenia Interview (KASI), 91–2

Launey–Slade Hallucination Scale, 12
legislation, changes in, 211
linkage markers, 30
London Daily Living Project, 314
long-term impairments, *see* impairments, long-term
longitudinal perspective, 27
longitudinal studies, 307–9

Magical Ideation Scale, 11
maintaining factors assessment, 181–3
management
relatives' knowledge, 92
responsibility, 286–92
Manchester Scale, 7, 180
Medicaid (USA), 256
Medicare (USA), 256
medication (*see also* antipsychotic drugs; neuroleptic drugs)
relatives' knowledge, 92
timing of reduction, 73
Mental Aftercare Association, 208
Mental Health Act 1959, 254
Mental Health Act 1983, 211
modelling skills, 190
models
care, 266
dimensional, 4, 5, 71
disease, 4
hierarchical, 4, 5
recovery, 53
stress-vulnerability, 4, 25, 104
vulnerability, 21–42, 305–6
monoamine oxidase (MAO) activity, 30–1

National Mental Health Act (USA, 1946), 256
National Schizophrenia Fellowship (NSF), 211, 281
needs
assessment, 292
availiable statistics, 280
importance of basics, 282
size and nature of, 279–82
neuroleptic drugs (*see also* antipsychotic drugs; medication), 116, 147
early intervention, 131–4
low-dose strategies, 134
targeted dose, 139, 141
neurotic restitution, 52, 53
night shelters, 214
normalisation principles, 209–10

objectives, strategies and, 289
operant principles, 149
orienting, electrodermal, 33
out-patient care, 259–60
Overt Aggression Scale, 13

PAS ratings, changes during recovery, 63
patients, assessment, 90
Perceptual Aberration Scale, 11

Personal Ideation Inventory, 8
planning
  model, 278
  services, 278–95
Positive and Negative Syndrome Scale for Schizophrenia (PANSS), 7
preoccupation (with delusions), 64, 65
pre-psychotic thinking, 118, 119
Present State Examination (PSE), 6, 68, 156
prisons, community care and, 213–14
problem management, 171–200
  assessments, 175–84
  interviews, 176
problem solving, 194–5
  coping strategy enhancement and, 153, 155
processing skills, 106
prodromes (*see also* early intervention), 117–31
  between-subject variability, 130
  clinical studies, 117–19
  crisis counselling, 139
  frequency of emergent symptoms, 125
  interviews, 138
  monitoring for, 137–9
  non-psychotic symptoms, 123–4
  prospective studies, 121–9
  relapse, identifying, 137
  retrospective studies, 119–21
  sensitivity, 121
  specificity, 121
  timing of onset, 121
prognosis, relatives' knowledge, 92
prompts, 96, 98
"pseudo" insight, 58
Psychiatric Assessment Scale (PAS), 62, 90, 154
  in monitoring recovery, 68
"psycho-education", 242
psychological treatment, 105–11 148–52
psychophysiological markers, 33–5
psychosis, incipient, 126–8
psychosocial interventions, 40
  integration of, 306–15
psychosocial triggering factors, 40
psychotic disorganisation, 52, 53
"psychotic equilibrium", 51
psychotic restitution, 52

QUARTZ system, 221

rating scales
  care programmes, 267
  challenging behaviour, 179–81
  long-term impairments, 179–81
Reaction to Hypothetical Conviction (RTHC), scale, 9, 15
"rebuilding", 60
receiving skills, 106
recovery (*see also* convalescence)
  acceleration, timing of efforts, 73–4
  dimensions of, 52
  disintegration of delusional beliefs, 54–6
  duration of, 50
  Early Signs Scale, 57, 66–7, 71
  ethnicity and, 50
  expressed emotion and, 60
  insight and, 56–9, 66, 72
  modal patterns, 70–2
  monitoring, 49–74
    applications and implications, 73–4
    procedure, 61–7
  non-psychotic symptoms, 56
  psychiatric assessment scale, 63, 68
  psycho-social influences on, 59–61
  remission and, 49
  stage and dimensional models, 53
  stages in, 51, 52
  timing of discharge, 73
  ward atmosphere and, 59–60
referral systems, "open", 288
registers of "people in need", 219
regression, post-psychotic, 51
rehabilitation
  "Fountain House" philosophy, 222
  family intervention and, 243
Rehabilitation Evaluation Hall and Baker (REHAB) scale, 180
reinforcement, 191
  challenging behaviour, 193
  social, 148–9
    versus tangible, 191
  token economy, 187–9
reintegration
  phases of, 51
  process, 50–9

relapse
  assessment and prediction, 21–42
  crisis counselling, 139
  expressed emotion and, 80–3, 235, 239–40
  identification of prodrome, 137
  medication, 241
  prediction of, 116–17
  prevention of, 115–16
    social skills training, 103
  rates, 236
  reduction, effective interventions for, 82
  resistance to, 40
  signature, 130, 137, 139–40
relatives (*see also* family intervention)
  burden, 84
  groups, 242
  interview content areas, 87
  needs, 89
  problems, 89
remission, recovery and, 49
residential services, 223–5
resource management, 291–2
"respite house", 226
role play, 109

Salford experience, 297–302
  chronicity, 297–8
  service aims, 298–9
  strategies, 299–302
Scale for the Assessment of Aggressive and Agitated Behaviours, 13
Scale for the Assessment of Negative Symptoms (SANS), 7, 180
Scale for the Assessment of Positive Symptoms (SAPS), 7
Scale for the Assessment of Thought, Language and Communication (TLC), 7
scales, assessment, *see individual scales*
Scales for Rating Psychotic and Psychotic-like Experiences as Continua, 11
Schedule for Affective Disorders and Schizophrenia (SADS), 6, 11
schizophrenia
  concept of, 5, 22, 306
  doubts about existence as disease entity, 4–5
  life-time risk, 28, 29
  Type I and Type II, 32
Schizophrenia Therapeutic Education Project (STEP), 247
SCL-90, 123
self-esteem, timing of efforts to increase, 74
self-instructional training (SIT), 150 195
self-management, 151
sending skills, 106
services
  budgets, 290
  case-loads, 294
  contract development, 286–7
  delivery styles, 285
  functions of components, 289–91
  implementation, 295–6
  inter-professional agreements on competencies, 287–9
  management
    arrangements, 286–92
    control, 293–5
  managing resources, 291–2
  monitoring, 293–5
  needs, size and nature of, 279–82
  organisation
    and planning, 277–302
    principles of, 283–4
  priorities, 284, 291
  strategies, 286–92
  structures, 313–14
skills
  generalisation, 191
  modelling, 190
sleep problems, prodromal, 120
smooth-pursuit eye movement (SPEM) abnormalities, 34–5
Social Assessment Scale (SAS), 90
Social Behaviour Schedule, 13
social deprivation, ill-health and, 280
social functioning family intervention studies, 84
social networks, 312
social reinforcement, 148–9
Social Situations Questionnaire, 180
social skills training, 103–13, 242
  learning activities, 108
  modular approach, 107–11, 112

social skills training (*cont.*)
problem solving method, 109
research findings, 107
role play, 109
successful living approach, 110–11
Span of Apprehension Test (SAT), 36
speech impairment, 173
Speedwell Project, 313
Spielberger Anger Inventory, 180
Staff Observation Aggression Scale, 13
stage theory, 71
stimulus control, 149
strategies, objectives and, 289
stress management, 94
stress-vulnerability models (*see also* vulnerability models), 4, 25, 104
stressors, 25
structural markers, 31–2
successful living approach, 110–11
symptomatology, relatives' knowledge, 92
symptoms
assessment of, 3–17, 148
specific symptoms, 8–11
borderline, 119
emotional reactions to, 156–7
management methods, 148–52
negative, 6, 32, 93, 103, 104
timing of efforts to decrease, 74
non-psychotic
and recovery, 56
prodromal, 123–4
relapse, 122–3
positive, 6, 32
residual, management and modification, 147–66
predisposition measures, 11–12
prodromal, 117–19, 119–21, 123–4
timing of onset, 121
rating scales, 6–7
residual, 129

therapeutic alliance, 104
therapeutic community movement, 208
Three Hospitals Study, 222
time-out, 192–3
'token economy" (TE), 187–9
training, 314–15
"transinstitutionalisation", 213

under-stimulation, 186
untreated illness duration of, 115–16
USA, care developments in, 256–7

violent behaviour, 12
rating scales, 13
vocational rehabilitation technology, 113
vulnerability markers, 27–37
vulnerability models (*see also* stress-vulnerability models), 4, 21–42, 104, 305–6
clinical utility, 40–1
general characteristics, 23–5
implications for assessment and intervention, 38–41
intervention targets, 39
and multimodal approaches, 38
status of, 37–8
testing, 28
vulnerability research, 25–9

ward atmosphere, 59–60
"ward restrictiveness", 187
work schemes, sheltered, 222
Working for Patients (1989), 278
"worried well", 268
Wykes hostel–hospital practice profile, 187

Index compiled by A. C. Purton